Demographics

A RAND Book

Demographics

A Casebook for Business and Government

EDITED BY

Hallie J. Kintner, Thomas W. Merrick, Peter A. Morrison, and Paul R. Voss

Westview Press

BOULDER • SAN FRANCISCO • OXFORD

A RAND Book

To receive a list of RAND books, write or call Distribution Services, RAND, 1700 Main Street, P.O. Box 2138, Santa Monica, CA 90407-2138, (310) 393-0411, extension 6686.

Published in 1994 in the United States of America by Westview Press, Inc., 5500 Central Avenue, Boulder, Colorado 80301-2877, and in the United Kingdom by Westview Press, 36 Lonsdale Road, Summertown, Oxford OX2 7EW

Library of Congress Cataloging-in-Publication Data
Demographics : a casebook for business and government / Hallie J.
    Kintner ... [et al.].
        p.   cm.
    Includes bibliographical references.
    ISBN 0-8133-1918-8—ISBN 0-8133-1919-6 (if published as a paperback)
    1. Demography—United States—Case studies.   2. United States—
Population—Case studies.   3. Marketing research—United States—
Case studies.   I. Kintner, Hallie J.
HB871.D435   1994
304.6'0973—dc20   94-16015
                                                                                              CIP

Printed and bound in the United States of America

The paper used in this publication meets the requirements
of the American National Standard for Permanence of Paper
for Printed Library Materials Z39.48-1984.

10   9   8   7   6   5   4   3   2   1

Contents

Preface

This book grew out of a shared interest in how the science of demography is being applied to real-world problems in the private and public sectors. The contributors to this casebook represent a broad spectrum of practitioners in both domains; we thank each author for the substantial effort to present each case in a clear and instructive format.

Some of the cases herein have been tested informally in university classroom settings. We are grateful to the instructors for their feedback, and especially to the students for their critical comments and suggestions for improvements. The coeditors continue to welcome user comments and suggestions, which will help reshape future editions of this book.

This undertaking would have been difficult in the absence of two Population Association of America committees ("Business Demography" and "State and Local Demography") that continually foster informal networks of applied demographers. The activities of both committees connected us with prospective authors and ideas for case studies. We appreciate efforts by the Population Association of America to provide forums where applied demographers can share their work and broaden exposure of academic demographers and students to it.

We appreciate the support of RAND in its funding of editorial and secretarial services for the preparation of this casebook. Special thanks are due to Jerold Kellman of Gabriel House, who edited the entire text; to Cynthia Kumagawa of RAND's book program, who encouraged our efforts and facilitated development and production of the book; to Kimberly Crews of the Population Reference Bureau, who prepared the questions for classroom discussion; and to Rose-Marie Vigil, who managed the preparation of the manuscript.

Hallie J. Kintner
Thomas W. Merrick
Peter A. Morrison
Paul R. Voss

PART ONE

Introduction

1

Introduction

Hallie J. Kintner, Thomas W. Merrick,
Peter A. Morrison, and Paul R. Voss

In 1980, applied demography was little more than a collection of activities on the periphery of academic research. Since then, these activities have coalesced into a recognizable field of endeavor, with analysts applying the specialized knowledge and technical tools of demographic analysis to an ever-widening arena of concerns in both private and public sectors.

What does applied demography now encompass, how has it evolved, and where is it headed? In this chapter, we offer an overview of how demographic analysis is being put to use in government and the business world: the scope of applications today and their historical origins.

Current Scope of Applied Demography

Applied demographers practice their profession in a variety of settings. Many work for state and regional governmental agencies; some are employed within the commercial data industry; a small but increasing number operate as entrepreneurs. Most are occasional practitioners who respond to various commercial, legislative, and judicial concerns when those concerns demand the use of demographic information.

The range of problems that command the attention of demographers (and others who make use of demographic methods) continues to widen, thereby broadening the scope of this expanding field. The following profiles of representative applications illustrate the problems that applied demographers address.

State and Local Government Applications

The concerns of state and local governments define one continuing area in applied demography. The long interval between decennial U.S. censuses generates a continuing need for "official" estimates of each local jurisdiction's current population. These estimates are exceedingly important because they constitute one basis on which jurisdictions compete for various types of resources from higher levels of government. For example, funding formulas for state contributions to maintain county health services are tied to population. The "fair share" of government subsidized housing that localities are obliged to accept also may be tied to official estimates of local population.

Local governments and authorities need current population data and forecasts for many other purposes: to delineate or reconfigure local election districts, to calculate vital rates and various indicators of service delivery, public health, accessibility to hospitals and other health facilities; to forecast future demands (e.g., school enrollments); and to certify compliance with particular legal mandates (e.g., for demographically representative trial juries).

Certain structures have evolved over the years to address these needs. Usually, a state agency prepares the "official" set of estimates and forecasts for localities, using methods approved by and coordinated through the Census Bureau's Federal-State Cooperative Program. Typically, these estimates and projections extend down to the county level, and sometimes to individual cities. Below the county level, the task of preparing estimates and forecasts usually gravitates to regional planning authorities and county health departments. These agencies prepare postcensal estimates (and sometimes forecasts) for traffic analysis areas, health planning areas, census tracts, and other neighborhood level geographic units. Whatever the agency, someone within it typically fills the "applied demographer" role—either someone trained in applied demography or someone who has learned the necessary skills on the job.

Complementing these established activities in the public sector are the varied commercial enterprises, conducted by for-profit and nonprofit organizations. Some organizations concentrate on regional economic forecasting (using proprietary econometric models) and the future populations such forecasts imply for multicounty regions. Below the county level (and especially for census tracts), the commercial data industry is virtually alone in forecasting demographic variables. Typically, such firms rely on an in-house applied demographer to devise forecasting methodology, audit the input data, and develop innovative ways to package small-area data to meet various client needs.

Business Applications

Business applications of demography lack the kinds of structures that have evolved with state and local government applications. The types of business concerns that call upon the services of applied demographers are exceedingly varied. Marketing and retailing businesses (probably the dominant type) constantly strive to link products and services to consumers who have particular wants and needs. These wants and needs, of course, have diversified as households and lifestyles have diversified.

Corporate human resource concerns define another area of business applications. Corporate leaders increasingly rely on demographic information to deal with the changing structure and makeup of the workforce as well as emerging "family-workplace" issues. Framing strategic business decisions with reference to future demographic contexts constitutes a third developing area of application.

Finally, applied demographers periodically are drawn into the business arena as outside advisors—typically for brief interludes. The purpose may be to inform or advise, to broaden business leaders' perspectives, or even to be a catalyst for organizational change. In all these business applications, applied demographers make themselves useful in various ways that, more often than not, stretch beyond the boundaries of demographic analysis per se.

Marketing and Retailing. Demographic information and analysis have become essential to identifying, locating, and understanding the diverse consumer groups that form markets for goods and services. The commercial data industry furnishes the information (and the technology for accessing it) that some marketers need, but they often do not provide the analytic depth that these marketers may require. Analysts who know how to use demographic data to link products and services to consumer needs are, therefore, in demand.

Part of the appeal of applied demographers to marketers and retailers is their technical familiarity with census data and definitions. Demographers know where to access the data and what the numbers mean. Indeed, any data-oriented individual (regardless of training background) who possesses a solid command of census data can find a useful niche as an applied demographer.

The analytically more sophisticated applied demographers not only track population shifts, they also provide marketers with insights into how those shifts may shape consumer choices. For example, with the growing number of dual-income couples, marketers know they must distinguish segments that are primarily "time-sensitive" from the traditionally "price-sensitive" segments. As demographic shifts orient more people toward convenience, consumers seek to purchase what they need quickly, at hours of their own choosing, and preferably all in one store. Growth in one-stop shopping, direct marketing, and home-delivered food reflects the demographic shift taking place.

Human Resource Planning. Corporate leaders increasingly recognize that the demographics of their workforces have important long-term implications for benefits, productivity, and business profitability. This recognition has spurred greater interest in how demographic changes affect the workplace.

One perennial concern involves the effects of contracting or expanding the number of workers at different age ranges. At the entry level in some industries, spot shortages may appear when the size of entering cohorts shrinks. In addition, companies that once curtailed new hiring may find they have a disproportionate number of employees entering the middle and later stages of their careers. With career ladders becoming congested as too many employees compete for too few mid-level positions, corporations are being challenged to find ways to retain the best of their more experienced workers.

Another perennial concern involves family-workplace issues. The influx of mothers into the workforce along with changes in family structure and composition have transformed dependent-care needs. These changes demand employer flexibility in daily work schedules and other forms of responsiveness. Increasingly, corporate leaders need more detailed information on their own workforce: the number of employees who face family obligations that conflict with workplace requirements, the nature of those obligations, and the ways in which those obligations can be met without disrupting the workplace. The existence of these family-workplace issues has created a strong need for demographic analysis, advice, and forecasts in regard to human resource planning.

Strategic Business Issues. Whether to enter or avoid a particular market, where to site a shopping mall, and how to accommodate the gradual aging of a corporation's workforce are all strategic decisions that focus the attention of business leaders on the long term. Applied demographers can play several potential roles in addressing these issues.

First, the applied demographer can act as a catalyst, opening up thought processes within an organization and sparking new insights and ideas. Demographers excel at calling attention to long-range shifts, and they introduce a useful frame of reference for comprehending such shifts. Describing trends with reference to cohort changes—e.g., in women's labor force participation, in older workers' propensity to retire or to work part-time, in the comparative health and vigor of the aged—provokes thought and generates discussion between a corporation's own analysts and its senior managers.

Second, the applied demographer can give specific empirical meaning to various facets of an overall business strategy. For a business manager seeking to target certain types of markets, demographers can identify which census measures to use.

Third, the applied demographer can provide an analytic framework for making decisions by systematizing the various factors that must be weighed and quantifying each factor.

Serving as "Outside Advisor." Applied demographers inevitably get drawn into other roles that go beyond their technical competence. Businesses retain demographers for a variety of reasons: to furnish new perspectives and frames of reference; to focus attention on long-term issues; to serve as a catalyst for opening up thought processes within an organization; to lend legitimacy to proposed actions under consideration; and to communicate information, ideas, and viewpoints to top management from subordinates who want to get their leaders' attention. As an outside advisor, the demographer is in a unique position to enlighten and broaden management horizons or to advance internal change.

The Field's Origins

Applied demography is not a theory-directed body of knowledge. It is driven by problems and has been so from the start. In fact, what we today call applied demography has been practiced for decades (even centuries) as scientists—or simply observers of the human condition—attempted to make some numerical assessment of the extent or likely growth of human populations.

Many of the technical foundations of applied demography were established prior to 1970, primarily in academic settings and in the Federal Census Bureau. By the end of this period, a third important venue for the application and expansion of demographic methodology emerged: executive agencies of state governments.

The 1970 Census of Population and Housing, which afforded public access to computerized census data for hundreds of thousands of small geographic areas across the country, sparked a new era in applied demography. This first "electronic census" also spawned a new set of players in the burgeoning information industry: data firms that repackage and update census data for commercial use. Existing organizational networks of applied demographers grew stronger and new networks emerged, affording practitioners in the field a sense of common identity and shared purpose.

As much as the decade following the 1970 Census represented a watershed, it is the period since the 1980 Census that has witnessed the most noteworthy developments for the users of this casebook. The information industry matured, firms consolidated and merged, and powerful new alliances came into existence. Practitioners of demographic science in state and local agencies—building on the proliferation of databases and utilizing advances in demographic methodologies and other standard tools of the trade—began generating population estimates and forecasts.

The Future of Applied Demography

Where is applied demography headed? The best we can do is speculate, but certain trends appear likely to shape the field and enlarge its scope.

Greater Public Awareness of the Field

The public is increasingly aware of how useful applied demography can be. Accordingly, we anticipate a gradual widening of public familiarity with the perspectives, data, and tools of demography. This development will result from personal experience, media exposure, and increased governmental and business attention to the "demographics" of a program or market. Nondemographers frequently become aware of applied demography when it contributes to a decision-making process that concerns them. For instance, state political parties retain applied demographers to assist in redrawing political district boundaries after a census.

Applications of demography receive increasingly widespread media coverage. Local newspapers analyze what the census data show about their city or town. National magazines publish stories (written by demographers) about changing life styles and attractive places to live.

Growing Demand Will Lead to Specialization

Applied demographers collectively address a wide array of issues, but further specialization is likely in particular areas of business and government. More users will be knowledgeable in both demography and fields like finance, strategic planning, and human resource management. As demographers are called on to provide insights into increasingly complex problems, they will need to acquire greater depth of knowledge. Many of the authors of case studies in this book exemplify such specialization.

Changes in Data Products Will Pose Challenges

The information applied demographers use changes and evolves continually. The U.S. Census Bureau, for instance, develops data products that link demographic information to geography in new, more flexible ways. Businesses continue to devise new applications for existing data. For instance, companies that monitor credit card transactions transform such data into profiles of who buys what, or who moves where. Other companies draw on their administrative databases to gain strategic insights into improving their workforce and work processes. These different data products pose challenges to usual demographic techniques and may lead to methodological innovations.

Broader Societal and Economic Forces Will Widen the Scope of Applications

Applied demography will continue to be drawn into an ever wider array of applications because the societal institutions to which it is tied are themselves evolving. Policymakers need scientists to harness knowledge from basic research and apply it to solving problems and creating new technologies. Applied demographers can make contributions in both these ways.

Like governments, many U.S. businesses also feel increased competitive pressure. They are striving to become more responsive to customers while simultaneously restructuring their operations to produce more from less. Applied demographers will help companies to understand their customers' requirements and to allocate resources more effectively.

These four trends will gradually heighten the prominence of applied demography. One possible change will be more full-time employment rather than project-based assignments. Occasional practitioners will find employment with client firms and with large management consulting businesses. Another change will be an increase in the number of applied demographers, including those with little formal training in demography. A third change will be training in fields complementary to demography (e.g., computer science, geography) that will take advantage of new data products.

Conclusion

Businesses and governmental agencies retain demographers for diverse reasons. These reasons have political as well as analytical and technical facets. As an applied demographer, you may inform or advise, broaden perspectives on the future, or even act as a catalyst for organizational change. Your effectiveness in these roles will hinge, in part, on your own ability to discern the form of help needed and how best to provide it. Some situations will call upon you to introduce perspectives that will elevate people's thinking from an operational to a more strategic level. Other situations will involve effecting change in an organization's culture—change that is aimed, for example, at managing diversity in the work place. Whatever your role, it will demand both intellectual flexibility and political instincts attuned to the concerns that prompted the call for demographic advice and analysis.

In mastering applied demography, you will find that no textbook can substitute for concrete experience. As in learning to ride a bicycle, your progress may be rapid but it is likely to be punctuated by sudden unexpected lessons. In the chapters that follow, authors describe their own varied experiences and reflect on the lessons they learned.

2

Orientation to Case Studies

Hallie J. Kintner and Thomas W. Merrick

A key development in the field of demography during the 1980s was the expansion of work in applied demography. Applied demography puts to work the theory, data, analytic techniques, and findings of demographic research to inform both public- and private-sector decision making. The field's recent expansion has created a demand for analysts possessing the methodological skills and substantive knowledge to tackle a wide variety of applications.

In response to the upsurge in demand, an increasing number of colleges and universities have initiated courses and degree programs in applied demography. Several textbooks now exist, but an information gap persists that can best be filled by material that provides concrete illustrations of how applied demographers do their work.

It is a well-recognized pedagogical principle that learning requires more than exposure to textbooks and lecture notes. In most academic fields, students acquire this broader exposure through readings and discussion of articles in professional journals; graduate students become involved in their mentors' research and in professional activities. The problem in our field is that many academic demographers have only limited experience in applied work, while demographers who are involved in such work on a full-time basis outside academia have neither the time nor the incentive to publish accounts of their experiences. Also, many applied demographers perform proprietary work that cannot be widely disseminated.

This casebook was designed to fill the information gap about applied demography for both instructors and students. The objective was to illustrate how—given practical problems—an analyst can utilize demographic concepts, data, and techniques to assist decision makers in finding answers to those problems. To achieve this objective, case-study authors were asked to provide:

- An explanation in nontechnical terms of the generic problem that each case presents—e.g., how to identify a site for a new store or hotel, how to redraw the boundaries of legislative districts, or how to plan for the expansion of a university system.

- A description of the case's institutional context—who the client was, the context in which the decision was made, who the decision makers were, what criteria they used in making the decision, and who was affected by their decision. For example, the decision maker in a redistricting case was the administrative law judge, who based his/her decision on the arguments by attorneys representing the parties whose political representation was to be affected.

- An explanation of the demographic perspective in the case and how that perspective shaped the way in which various parties perceived the problem and its solution. Few cases are exclusively demographic, and the nondemographic considerations may carry more weight than the demographic ones. The applied demographer has to demonstrate how demographics affect both the problem and its solution—from the client's perspective, of course. For example, in a case involving a bank's decision to finance a motel project, the demographer—in order to establish the rate of return on the investment—had to identify a segment of the overnight-visitor population that would use a motel in the price range being considered.

- A summary of the demographic work done for the client: what data, methods, analytical techniques, and assumptions were required in order to get the job done. How did the availability or choice of data affect the outcome? For example, a key demographic issue in a Los Angeles County redistricting case had to do with whether intercensal population estimates were adequate for redistricting decisions.

- A synopsis of the results of the analysis, how the client actually used the results, and how they shaped the decision or problem-solving process in question. The case-study authors also describe the practical lessons they learned from the applied demography work in question, and they explain how their analytical approaches and data might be applied in similar settings.

Our casebook was designed to complement, not replace, textbooks in population studies and demographic analysis. Instructors will find the case studies useful in introducing concepts to students having no prior background in the field. The case studies can also be used to change the cadence of the course and to promote classroom discussion. Class discussion often can bring to life very dry demographic concepts or measures. For instance, discussion of the case study about the hospital birthing center can improve understanding of the strengths and weaknesses of different types of birth rates as analytical tools.

In planning this book, the editors wanted more than summaries of reports submitted to clients. In several instances, the authors reworked their case studies several times in order to make them more responsive to the requirements outlined above. Many of the studies have been tested in the classroom with very positive results. Classroom testing has shown that the case studies are particularly helpful to students doing term projects or papers because the cases provide examples of research topics, discussions of the pros and cons of various data sources, insights about the advantages and disadvantages of different analytical techniques, and formats for presenting results. Study questions outline the general issues involved and alert readers to some of the specific approaches and lessons to be learned from each case.

The cases represent a broad range of demographic techniques and applications. The 18 cases were selected from nearly 50 proposals because they illustrate interesting issues posed by actual clients and addressed by quality demographic research.

For Students

The best thing about the case approach to demographics is that you "learn by doing"—wrestling with an array of the problems and dilemmas that applied demographers routinely face. By analyzing the cases, you gain expertise in applying demographic perspective, data, and techniques to a variety of situations that most students acquire only through on-the-job experience. The challenge of analyzing one situation after another yields two benefits: (1) It sharpens your analytical skills, and (2) it enables you to see how demographers attack practical problems to provide advice to decision makers.

Case analysis benefits you in four ways:

1. You gain skill in conducting demographic analysis in a variety of settings and circumstances.
2. You get valuable practice in diagnosing issues from a demographic perspective, evaluating alternative data sources and methodological procedures, and presenting advice based on demographic analysis to decision makers.
3. You become adept at using your judgment when there is no obvious "right" course of action.
4. You repeatedly face real-life conditions and problems that require a variety of different applications for solutions.

Case analysis is not a search for "correct" answers. You may be frustrated at first when a discussion of a case does not culminate in a concrete solution. Good case discussions usually produce good arguments for more than one course of action. The goal of this casebook is to help you learn to reason well within the framework of demographics.

Preparing a Case for Class Discussion

You may have to change your study habits if this is your first experience with the case method. Case analysis requires considerable preparation before class. To prepare a case for class discussion, we suggest the following:

- *Read the case through quickly to familiarize yourself with it.* Acquire a general grasp of the generic problem, the institutional context, the demographic perspective and analysis, and the results. Read the study questions for the case carefully.
- *Read the case a second time, focusing on details and facts.* Begin to develop tentative answers to the study questions. Now is the time to analyze the situation. Pay particular attention to tables, figures, and maps; they often tell the real story.
- *Identify where the clients' issues lie.* Until you do so, you will not know what to analyze, what information and tools to call upon, and how to proceed.
- *Determine the demographic considerations.* Apply a demographic perspective to both the issues and the possible solutions. Is the case exclusively demographic or should you consider nondemographic factors as well?
- *Use any tools and techniques of demographic analysis that you deem applicable.* Demographic analysis does not rest on doctrine or a collection of opinions. Rather, it consists of applying powerful tools and techniques that dive below what is often a deceptively simple surface to yield valuable insights.
- *Evaluate the demographic work done for the client.* Case analyses often produce unfounded or contradictory views and opinions, forcing you to evaluate the data, methods, and assumptions utilized. This evaluation process helps you develop your powers of inference and judgment. Applied demographers are accustomed to having to defend how they obtained their results. Support your evaluation with reasons and evidence; be prepared to answer the question "Why?"
- *Develop a set of recommendations for the client.* Use the findings from the demographic analysis to develop an "action agenda" for clients. This agenda must include specific recommendations about what to do. Be prepared to argue convincingly why your recommendations are better than other courses of action.
- *Examine how the demographer communicated results to the client.* The applied demographer's work does not end with a summary of the results of the demographic analysis. The demographer must communicate the results to the client in terms the client can use to advantage.
- *Ask yourself whether you would have done the analysis differently.* If you would have, describe your perspective, the data you would have needed, and the analysis you would have performed. How does your approach address the client's issues better than the approach presented in the case study?

Participating in Class Discussion

In classroom discussions of cases, students do most of the talking. The instructor serves as a moderator, soliciting student participation and guiding the discussion.

This kind of discussion demands your involvement in sizing up and analyzing the issues and in describing what actions should be taken and why. Don't be surprised if your classmates have insights that never occurred to you. Expect to hear different views and analyses, and always respect the differences. The class as a group will perform a more penetrating job of case analysis than will any one person working alone. The goal is for students to integrate all of their ideas.

You can expect the following in a classroom case-study discussion:

- Students will do most of the talking.
- The instructor will listen and ask questions rather than lecture.
- The instructor and your classmates will challenge you to provide evidence to back up your statements.
- Everyone's views will be challenged. All students must be willing to volunteer their opinions without fear of disapproval.
- Everyone may not reach agreement. The goal is integration, not consensus.

Here are some activities that you can do to better prepare yourself for class discussions:

- Discuss the case with other students outside of class to refine your thinking.
- Prepare to make a contribution to the discussion, not just to talk.
- Assume everyone has already read the case study.
- Give evidence for your views to avoid being asked "Why?"
- Make notes about the case study and refer to them when you speak.

Now you're ready to go.

Since casebooks in demography are relatively new, the authors and editors encourage you—after reading through these case studies—to contact them with suggestions for improving the format and/or the study questions.

PART TWO

Politics and the Law

3

Empowered or Disadvantaged?
Applications of Demographic Analysis
to Political Redistricting

Peter A. Morrison

Local jurisdictions periodically draw on demographic analysis and expertise when it is time to establish or adjust political boundaries. The boundary-drawing process is subject to exacting legal standards which, if not met, may invite legal challenge under Section 2 of the Voting Rights Act. Increasingly, legal scrutiny and challenge focus on measurement and other technical demographic issues. This case examines several representative applications of demographic analysis in political redistricting and in the legal challenges to local election systems that sometimes ensue. The first section describes the institutional setting and rules that apply when redistricting is done. The second section focuses on the legal standards embodying those rules and illustrates how those standards can be quantified in local situations. The third section distinguishes several roles that applied demographers can take on throughout the redistricting process. The fourth and final section presents emerging developments in this area.

As the redistricting done in the early 1990s undergoes legal scrutiny, applied demographers are apt to become even more involved in the issues and questions posed and in litigation. They will be needed to refine the measurement of populations at small-area scales and to assist in the efforts of jurisdictions to comply with legal mandates. At later stages, they may perform technical analyses of redesigned districts and give expert testimony in court, either on behalf of plaintiffs seeking to identify and redress injustices or on behalf of jurisdictions defending themselves against legal challenges.

The Actors

Redistricting is a politically sensitive, sometimes contentious, process that follows each decennial census. Local officials in counties, cities, school districts, and other jurisdictions that elect representatives are required to redraw election district lines based on the new census data. Here are several typical situations:

- The boundaries of five supervisorial districts must be redrawn in a county whose population is about one-fifth Hispanic, one-fifth black, and one-fifth Asian. Each group insists that it should compose the majority of voters in one of the five districts; that being so, each opposes any boundary change that would dilute its potential voting strength. Local officials cannot ignore their fervor. Legally, each group is entitled to challenge the redistricting process and its end result if the group's legitimate demands are not met.

- A public districting commission is charged with transforming a 35-member city council, on which serve six black and three Hispanic members, into a 51-member body in which the city's various minority residents would be better assured of fair and effective representation.

- A plaintiff challenges a city's election system, claiming that it abridges the people's right to vote based on race or national origin. To bring suit under Section 2 of the Voting Rights Act, the plaintiff must demonstrate that a voting district can be formed in which the majority of its voting-age citizens belong to a particular racial group. Before deciding how to proceed, the defendant jurisdiction wants to determine whether or not that precondition can be met.

- A community college trustee board must adjust its trustee election district boundaries. The existing officeholders seek to avoid any appearance of gerrymandering—creating districts to protect their incumbency at the expense of minority voting power.

Because boundaries that divide up the political landscape typically bestow an advantage on one group at the expense of another, constructing such boundaries or changing them generally foments controversy and acrimony. The actors in the process (unlike applied demographers) cannot view redistricting neutrally. In boundary-drawing, each has an agenda; when litigation ensues, each will face adversaries.

Sooner or later, the applied demographer is caught up in dealings with the court and with certain actors. These actors may include the attorney who represents a city council or school board; the elected members themselves (often having different racial, ethnic, and partisan identities); one or more advocacy groups striving to empower one or more of the minority groups; and any interested citizens.

During the 1990s, the process of redistricting became more open than it had been. The public became more involved and informed through hearings and other kinds of local participation as technology brought boundary-drawing within easy reach of any lay person with access to a personal computer. As a consequence, anyone who cares about the process can actively participate in it, devising and formally proposing a redistricting plan of one's own.

Rules on Redistricting

Boundaries can scatter or concentrate like-minded persons in ways that may either disadvantage or empower them as voters. Laws that safeguard the right to vote are intended to prevent minority voters from being disadvantaged or to empower them where they have been disadvantaged.

One way whereby boundaries can disadvantage people is by engendering unequal legislative representation, as illustrated in Table 3.1. In 1990, Salinas, California had "outgrown" its existing city council district boundaries, which had been established after the 1980 Census.[1] Under the old plan, District 5 (with 24,291 inhabitants) had become 34 percent overpopulated relative to the ideal one-sixth of population (18,130) that a district should contain. In contrast, District 3 (with only 13,848 inhabitants) was 23.6 percent underpopulated. The sum of these two extreme deviations—57.6 percent—expresses a legally-relevant measure known as the "total deviation from ideal." Such disparities produce unequal legislative representation: The council member in District 5 represents almost twice as many people as does the council member in District 3. Political boundaries that make the ratio of persons to legislators unequal produce representational imbalances among districts. Such imbalances disadvantage the residents of overpopulous districts.

Another way boundaries can disadvantage people is by failing to confer on each eligible voter in every district a vote that carries equal weight. That disadvantage may persist even after representational imbalances have been corrected. Again, Table 3.1 provides an example. The proposed "New Plan" for Salinas allocated to each new council district very close to the required one-sixth of the population. With respect to voting-age population, though, District 1 contained just 10,786 (or 14.6 percent) of the city's 73,895 persons 18 and older, whereas District 3 contained 13,922 (18.8 percent). As a result, electoral power would be shared among 10,786 eligible voters in District 1 and among 13,922 in District 3—i.e., a vote in District 1 would carry more weight than a vote in District 3.

In other words, demographic structure produced electoral imbalance, and that imbalance was not ethnically neutral. Hispanics happened to constitute 81 percent of the voting-age population in District 1 but only 31 percent in District 3. Accordingly, votes cast by the mostly Hispanic electorate of District 1 carried more weight than votes cast by the mostly non-Hispanic electorate of District 3. It is not uncommon to find that an electoral imbalance favors or disadvantages one group over another.

Lastly, yet another way in which boundaries can disadvantage people occurs in areas where people form a politically cohesive group. In such areas boundaries can disadvantage them by including either too few or too many of the group's eligible voters in a given district (see Figure 3.1). Where boundaries spread the group too evenly across voting districts, they dilute the group's voting strength through "cracking" (center panel). This hypothetical city has five election dis-

Table 3.1 Population Balance: Old and Proposed New Salinas City Council
Districts

Council District	Total Population				Voting-Age Population			
	Old Plan	% Dev.	New Plan	% Dev.	Old Plan	% Dev.	New Plan	% Dev.
1	21,700	19.69	18,287	0.87	12,874	4.53	10,786	−12.42
2	17,605	−2.90	17,923	−1.14	10,950	−11.09	11,061	−10.19
3	13,848	−23.62	18,707	3.18	10,628	−13.71	13,922	13.04
4	13,989	−22.84	17,699	−2.38	10,105	−17.95	12,702	3.13
5	24,291	33.98	17,510	−3.42	17,413	41.39	12,588	2.21
6	17,344	−4.34	18,651	2.87	11,925	−3.17	12,836	4.22
Totals	108,777	—	108,777	—	73,895	—	73,895	—
Ideal	18,130	—	18,130	—	12,316	—	12,316	—
Total Dev.	—	57.60	—	6.60	—	59.34	—	25.46

Source: Census of Population and Housing, 1990: PL 94-171 data.
NOTES: "% Dev." is each district's relative deviation from ideal. "Total Dev." is the sum of
the largest negative and largest positive % deviation, regardless of sign.

tricts and an electorate that is 40 percent Hispanic. In no district, however, are
Hispanics the majority voters because their voting strength has been dissipated
through boundary drawing. Alternatively, boundaries may excessively concentrate a politically cohesive group, thereby "wasting" its voting strength. If Hispanics make up 80 percent of the voters in one of the city's election districts but
only 30 percent in each of the other four, then Hispanics may have been disadvantaged through "packing" (top panel). Of course, an underlying presumption in
cracking and packing is that people vote exclusively along ethnic or racial lines.

Boundaries also can be drawn to enhance voting strength, as shown in the bottom panel of Figure 3.1. In this example, Hispanics would constitute a majority of
the voters in two of the five districts.

Figure 3.2 shows the simultaneous occurrence of both cracking and packing in
a proposed council districting plan for New York City. Those challenging the plan
claimed that it would discriminate against Hispanic voters because (1) two districts (15 and 17) were packed with more voting-age Hispanics than would be
needed for a majority; and (2) natural concentrations of Hispanic voters nearby
were split up to give two other districts (14 and 18) large Hispanic minorities instead of majorities.[2]

The evolving body of case law that governs voting rights is too extensive and

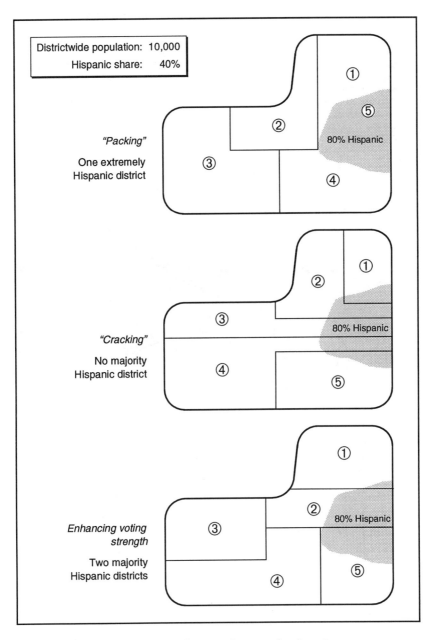

Districtwide population: 10,000
Hispanic share: 40%

"Packing"

One extremely
Hispanic district

80% Hispanic

"Cracking"

No majority
Hispanic district

80% Hispanic

*Enhancing voting
strength*

Two majority
Hispanic districts

80% Hispanic

Figure 3.1—Packing, cracking, and enhancing

According to the voting rights advocates who are challenging the plan, the new city council district map adopted by the city discriminates against Hispanic voters in two ways: A few districts are packed with far more Hispanic voters than would be needed for a majority, while nearby, natural concentrations of Hispanic voters are split up to give several districts large Hispanic minorities instead of majorities. When the number of registered voters in each district is considered instead of the overall population, the number of Hispanic-majority districts drops even further.

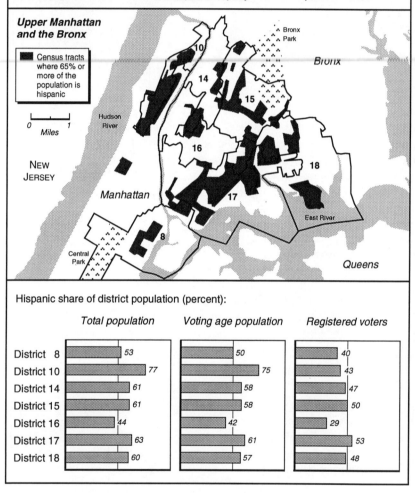

SOURCE: *The New York Times*, Thursday, July 18, 1991, p. B-8.

Figure 3.2—Illustration of boundaries claimed to dilute Hispanic voting strength in New York City

complex to summarize here. For our purposes, three noteworthy legal requirements pertain to political boundary drawing. First, principles of representative government accord representational equality. That is, each legislator should represent roughly the same number of persons as every other legislator (thus lowering the "total deviation from ideal" in Table 3.1 almost to zero for the total population). Second, the constitutional "equal protection" clause embodies the principle of electoral equality. That is, each citizen's vote is supposed to carry equal weight ("one person one vote"). In practice, this means that the jurisdiction's entire population should be so distributed among the districts being formed that a citizen's vote in one district carries the same weight as that of a citizen in every other district (the other problem illustrated in Table 3.1). And third, Section 2 of the 1965 Voting Rights Act prohibits abridging the right to vote by diluting the voting strength of a protected group (the problems illustrated in Figures 3.1 and 3.2). Section 2 requirements pose questions about whether districts that might be formed under existing demographic circumstances are in fact created. Simply put, if a minority's voting strength would be bolstered in a district whose boundaries concentrated that group's voters, then the law may require such a district to be formed.[3]

Resources Demographers Use

Legal challenges brought under Section 2 of the Voting Rights Act generally arise when minority groups claim that their voting strength has been diluted. The concept of "dilution" focuses attention on counting those members of the population who are entitled to vote and delineating this voter-eligible population geographically with reference to voting districts. The resources demographers use in such instances are census data for small geographic units (e.g., census tracts, block groups, and individual blocks) showing age and citizenship composition separately for each relevant minority group. Much of this information is readily available in tabular form from the latest decennial census; some information, however, may necessitate special tabulations from a census Public Use Microdata Sample (PUMS). Since categories are not always neatly delineated, however, measurement can be tricky. For example:

- "Black" and "Hispanic" are not mutually exclusive categories.
- Many Hispanics in the Southwest are noncitizens.
- The terms "Asian" and "Hispanic" can blur the discreteness of separate nationalities, obscuring what may be genuine political differences within each grouping.

The demographic discipline trains one to respect the fine print about data and definitions and to recognize the limitations inherent in the data one uses. It also enables one to apply demographic principles to problems of estimating or at least to set bounds on the variables of interest. The important quantitative issues that arise in redistricting, then, draw heavily on the applied demographer's technical familiarity with census and other data sources and on his/her competence in using data to reach conclusions.

Quantifying Legal Standards in Voting Rights Claims

Strength in numbers is no strength unless those numbers are politically empowered. That was the thrust of the 1965 Voting Rights Act, which gave full effect to the Fifteenth Amendment's promise that no citizen's right to vote would be abridged by reason of race, color, or previous condition of servitude. In time, at-large election systems, reapportionment plans, and other local government practices fell under attack as violating a citizen's right to vote. Courts eventually identified two characteristics of a violative practice: (1) previous official discriminatory intent, and (2) the actual discriminatory effect of the practice itself. In 1982, Congress amended the Voting Rights Act to provide that abridgment of citizens' right to vote could be established by proof of discriminatory effect alone.

The first Supreme Court interpretation of the 1982 amendment came in 1986 with *Thornburg* v. *Gingles,* which provided some further direction to lower courts considering Section 2 claims. Among other things, this decision cautioned that only those plaintiffs who prove they can form an "effective voting majority" within the jurisdiction are entitled to judicial relief. That interpretation has focused the efforts of both plaintiffs and defendants on demonstrating—or disproving—the existence of an "effective voting majority" in a place. These concerns, in turn, have introduced demographic data and analysis into the process of quantifying three preconditions that courts require in order to entertain a Section 2 claim:

1. Geographic compactness: The plaintiffs must show that they can form a system of voting districts that will enable the protected minority group to constitute over half the eligible voters (citizens aged 18 and older) in at least one district.
2. Political cohesiveness: The plaintiff must show that members of the minority group vote together as a group.
3. Majority bloc voting: The issue here is whether the majority group usually votes as a bloc to defeat the minority group's candidate of choice.

In the following sections, I draw on examples from several Section 2 claims to show how the issues arise, consider the importance they can assume, and illustrate practical ways to address them.

Geographic Compactness

With the "compactness test," demography is at the heart of a key issue: Can the plaintiff group (e.g., Hispanics) demonstrate that a district could be formed so that the protected minority would constitute at least half the eligible voters there? This precondition involves several issues of demographic measurement.

First, precisely how is the minority population defined? The law designates a "protected minority" by name (e.g., blacks, Hispanics). Membership within a legally defined "protected" group ultimately translates into some precise quantification of that membership based on census-defined categories of people. In some instances, the issue of whom the court means to designate as members of a "protected" group requires clarification. In such instances, the applied demographer can inform judicial review on this issue and help put into practice the intent of the law.

Suburban Hempstead, New York, for example, needed to determine whether a "protected minority" district could be delineated in which Hispanics would be concentrated sufficiently to form a majority among the eligible voters in one of the town's eight election districts. According to data from the 1990 Census, Hempstead's 725,639 inhabitants included 48,149 Hispanics (4,376 of them black) and 83,268 non-Hispanic blacks. On the face of it, one might define "Hispanic" to include all 48,149 persons of Spanish origin. Given local political rivalries, though, one faction might insist on lumping together all 87,644 blacks (irrespective of ethnicity) in a district the faction might term majority-black; another faction conceivably might assert that only non-Hispanic blacks should count toward an effective voting majority in that district.

Where the local population is highly diverse, membership within a legally defined "protected" group may be ambiguous (or at least controversial). Demographic realities have already rendered the term "minority" obsolete in some places. California's cities, for example, are populated by a dazzling array of nationalities and ethnic groups, including Filipinos, Koreans, Vietnamese, Cambodians, Hmong, Armenians, Thais, and Japanese as well as Latinos and blacks. But enumerating Chinese, Japanese, Koreans, and Filipinos as "Asian" does not make them a single cohesive minority. Thus, the social, economic, and cultural diversity of national and ethnic groups cloud (and even nullify) the logic of lumping them together under umbrella categories such as "Hispanic" or "Asian."

A second issue involves differences in age composition and citizenship, both of which determine the population eligible to vote. For example, 35 percent of Hispanics nationwide are younger than 18 while only 25 percent of non-Hispanics are. In certain California jurisdictions, moreover, close to half of all voting-age Hispanics are noncitizens.

In a Section 2 claim against National City, California, the "geographic compactness" question before the court was: Could Hispanics constitute a majority in any conceivable single-member district in a four-district plan? The then-current (1980) census showed that 38.4 percent of National City's 48,772 inhabitants were Hispanic. We can estimate the hypothetical upper limit of Hispanic compactness by combining the city's most heavily Hispanic contiguous census block groups into an area containing one-fourth of National City's total population. This packing exercise shows that Hispanics could constitute up to 59 percent of the total population in such a hypothetical district of 12,193. Only 48.5 percent of the voting-age citizens, however, would be Hispanic in this predominantly Hispanic district.

Political Cohesiveness

Applied demographers are also involved in quantifying political cohesiveness, another Section 2 precondition. Simply put, the question before the court is: Does the minority group vote cohesively as a group? Although "cohesiveness" is a political science concept, its measurement calls for applied demographic analysis. The consistency of a minority group's political cohesiveness can vary across elections. For example, one would expect black voters to favor heavily the black candidate in a single black-white contest. But only if that pattern recurred in most such contests would one regard such behavior as political cohesiveness.

In 1980, the city of Marianna, Arkansas had 6,220 persons of voting age, 55 percent of them black. One of the city's four wards was heavily (94 percent) black and encompassed roughly three-fifths of all voting-age blacks citywide. In the November 1986 general election, there were two contests with opposing black and white candidates. In one (for county judge), voters in the heavily black ward favored the black candidate (Perry) over the white one (Hunter) by a two-to-one margin. In the other (for state senator), these voters favored the black candidate (Lewellen) over the white one (Benham) by better than a three-to-one margin.

Such voting behavior in a small Southern city invites the conclusions that blacks vote cohesively and that voting is racially polarized. This apparent "cohesiveness"—based on a single election—was not consistent, however. In the preceding general election (November 1984), there were also two black-on-white contests, one involving the same two opponents (Perry and Hunter). In the contest for county judge, however, three-fifths of the vote from the heavily black ward went to the white candidate (Hunter) over the black one (Perry). Simultaneously, three-fourths of these same voters supported the black candidate for municipal judge over the white incumbent.

In short, the voters in Marianna's black ward voted in opposite ways for the same two contestants in successive elections. Moreover, these same voters simultaneously supported candidates of both races (each running in separate contests) on the same election day. This pattern of choice and the shifting loyalties among black voters are inconsistent with racially polarized voting. They underscore the importance of drawing conclusions about cohesiveness from a sufficient sample of contests.

Majority Bloc Voting

Conclusions about majority bloc voting may depend on how one has defined the "majority." A Section 2 case illustrates the central role of demographic measurement.

An analyst distinguished two segments of the population in Stockton, California—Hispanics and non-Hispanics—whose voting behavior was at issue. Since "non-Hispanics" included many of the whites in the city and virtually all of the blacks, what was being contrasted was the voting pattern of the Hispanic minority versus that of a combined white-black "majority." The analyst next distinguished "black" and "nonblack" segments of the population in order to contrast black minority voting with nonblack "majority" (Anglo and Hispanic) voting.

Such artificial "majorities" are not necessarily politically cohesive. Consider a hypothetical election in which the Hispanic minority (30 percent of all voters) supports the Hispanic candidate, and the other 70 percent supports the non-Hispanic candidate. If this non-Hispanic "majority" happens to be 25 percent black, 15 percent Asian, and 30 percent Anglo, can one properly characterize its vote as a racial bloc? In multiple-minority settings, the potential pairings invite such artificial "majorities" as Hispanics and blacks ("non-Anglos"); blacks and Asians ("nonwhites"); Asians and Hispanics (also "non-Anglos"); Hispanics and Anglos ("nonblacks"); or Anglos and blacks ("non-Hispanics"). Small wonder that harried officials sent out a call for demographers.

Emerging Developments

Redistricting in the 1990s will undergo more stringent legal scrutiny than it did in the 1980s. Legislative bodies elected in single-member districts will pay close attention to how the boundaries drawn create or obstruct minority electoral opportunities. This application of legal standards to demographically diverse or complex settings will expand the potential applications of demographic analysis. Below we consider two developments likely to come into more widespread use: public access and surname analysis.

Public Access

Increasingly, jurisdictions will seek to formalize the openness of the redistricting process and document their intent to recognize each protected group. Doing so from the outset may insulate the jurisdiction against charges that officeholders created districts solely to protect their incumbency, even though doing so diminished minority voting strength.

At least two large jurisdictions (New York City and Los Angeles County) have sought to formalize the openness of their redistricting process by establishing a database and set of analytic procedures to compute minority representativeness and compactness. Each jurisdiction retained an applied demographer to help design a "plan-drawing database" that would contain all the data elements directly pertinent to boundary-drawing. This database would be open to the public.

The New York City Districting Commission (responsible for forming 51 new council districts) developed a database containing the official census counts; 1990 voter registration data geocoded (through surname analysis) by race and ethnicity; results of recent elections; and basic geographic and cartographic data. The commission's public access program included a public access terminal loaded with this database and staffed by a commission analyst. Members of the public could have plans developed according to their own instructions and submitted to the commission for formal consideration. Los Angeles County, following a similar procedure to facilitate public involvement, developed a "redistricting kit" and made it available to any individual or group wanting to develop and submit a plan for consideration. Both of these data access programs were more extensive than any past effort, and both are appropriate to the task of redistricting in jurisdictions as diverse as New York and Los Angeles.

Surname Analysis

On occasion, a jurisdiction must verify that the voting strength of a particular minority in a proposed election district exceeds a specified level. Although census data precisely measure the size and composition of a district's voter-eligible population, the electorate consists of the registered voters (or, more correctly, those who actually turn out) within that population. A particular group's electoral strength, then, is partly a function of how its demographic presence translates into a presence among the district's voters.

Surname analysis is one technique that demographers have at their disposal for gauging the potential voting strength of particular racial, ethnic, and language communities in a proposed district. This technique can show the makeup of local electorates and establish how a particular group's demographic presence translates into an electoral presence. Ordinarily, voters' surnames are publicly available in machine-readable form. Insofar as the surnames of voters belong uniquely to one racial or ethnic group, it is possible to identify their probable membership in such groups from well-formulated surname lists.[4] While identifying the probable racial or ethnic background of voters from surnames alone is not a substitute for a census enumeration, it can confirm that a given level of minority electoral strength (e.g., 51 percent) exists among registered voters.

For example, it was necessary to gauge the potential voting strength of Hispanics in two of the newly rebalanced Salinas City Council districts shown in Table 3.1. Districts 1 and 2 were intentionally designed to concentrate Hispanic voting strength, and each had a predominantly Hispanic adult population: Hispanics made up 81 percent of District 1 and 73 percent of District 2 (Table 3.2). The unanswered question was whether a district's majority-Hispanic population translated into an actual majority of Hispanic voters, given that many voting-age Hispanics were noncitizens and therefore ineligible to vote.

The County Registrar of Voters furnished a publicly available, machine-read-

Table 3.2   Indices of Hispanic Voting Strength in Proposed New City Council
               Districts: Salinas, 1990

Council District	Percentage of Population Hispanic		Percentage of Registrants Spanish Surnamed
	All Ages	18+	
1	84.9	81.2	60.4
2	77.9	73.0	53.7
3	36.1	31.0	15.1
4	33.1	29.1	17.7
5	28.6	25.1	17.1
6	42.8	37.8	27.0
Totals	50.6	44.4	26.0

Sources: Census of Population and Housing, 1990: PL 94-171 data; official voter registration tapes as of June 1991.

able file of the names of all registered voters by precinct. Surname analysis of
these voters (aggregated up to districts) demonstrated that Hispanics were indeed
a majority of present-day electors in each district: Spanish-surnamed persons constituted 60 percent and 54 percent, respectively, of all registrants as of 1991.
Clearly, Hispanics constituted a majority of each district's voting-age citizens.

Potential Roles of Applied Demographers

Because controversy is inevitable in redistricting, the applied demographer can
expect to play a role in it. One's technical analyses may well advantage or disadvantage particular actors (or be perceived as doing so). Yet, the demographer cannot lose sight of the fact that his or her analyses are supposed to inform the court.
As a consequence, the demographer must be an honest broker of whatever truth
can be teased or tortured out of the data. The foremost obligation is the professional one—i.e., to do an honest job and respect the limitations of what can be
known from the data.

That obligation, though, ought not to confine one's role to purely technical
matters. ("The numbers speak for themselves. My role has no connection with the
interests of any stakeholders.") In a setting where adversaries need to find common ground and negotiate their competing interests and differences, demographers who take too narrow a view of their role can inhibit their effectiveness. A
demographer's technical analysis can narrow the scope of controversy, thereby
fostering political compromise. By making the numbers speak for themselves, ap-

plied demographic analysis clarifies what lies beyond dispute, leaving what remains controversial for political resolution.

The applied demographer's role, then, consists of exploring what is demographically feasible and delineating demographic constraints, allowing political adversaries to negotiate conflicting aims or a court to resolve a dispute. This view of the applied demographer's role emphasizes skills that extend beyond the technical training demographers receive.

Applied demographers can play several distinct roles in voting rights analysis. Following the decennial census, jurisdictions need both technical advice and actual boundary-drawing to put themselves in accordance with legal requirements. Initially, the demographer may refine measurement and adjust boundaries or redesign districts.

The actual crafting of redistricting plans exploits demographers' analytic and spatial skills and their technical familiarity with census data. Such skills can ensure that redistricting meets the legal requirements, untainted by technical measurement problems (e.g., data suppression, split census tracts, or citizenship misreporting). The presence of special populations (e.g., military residents registered to vote elsewhere, or felons ineligible to vote) may call for special adjustments.

A jurisdiction that anticipates a challenge to its election system may retain a demographer as a confidential advisor. A plaintiff intending to challenge a jurisdiction may do likewise, seeking to devise a hypothetical new districting plan and then pressure for its adoption. The role of confidential advisor affords useful experience in exploring the outer limits of what a determined plaintiff could prove with respect to the Section 2 preconditions, given the data at hand.

A jurisdiction, for example, might want to ascertain whether a potential plaintiff could possibly construct an election district where minority group X would compose 50 percent or more of all voting-age citizens, or whether a pattern of racially polarized voting could be discerned. If the answer were "definitely not," then the jurisdiction might opt to defend against any challenge rather than settle. If the answer were "probably yes," however, the demographic facts might persuade the elected officials that it would be in their interest to alter district boundaries or even to change the election system to avoid a challenge. Either way, the unvarnished truth—favorable or not—would have the effect of sharpening the problem definition (if one exists) and inducing change where the law would require it.

At a later stage, applied demographers might perform technical analyses on behalf of either plaintiffs seeking to identify and redress injustices or defendant jurisdictions. The most challenging role for demographers involves giving expert testimony. Giving testimony (especially during cross-examination) is a demanding, high-pressure role far different from that of confidential advisor.

Legal challenges necessarily focus on the demographic composition and spatial distribution of local electorates. Questions must be resolved through demographic measurement and analysis: What is the racial and ethnic composition of the population eligible to vote? Does the apportionment base weight votes equally? Do people who have been put together as a group necessarily vote together? The applied demographer provides the reviewing judge with information on technical points, enabling the court to reach a decision.

The applied demographer, therefore, can play a crucial role in voting rights analysis. To be effective, the applied demographer needs technical demographic skills, detailed knowledge of demographic data and technical definitions, familiarity with patterns of minority spatial distribution at and below the census tract level, and familiarity with the key legal principles that apply to redistricting and voting rights.

Discussion Questions

1. Outline the three legal requirements pertaining to boundary drawing. Give examples of demographic changes that could make redistricting necessary.

2. Weigh the advantages and disadvantages of having a representational imbalance versus an electoral imbalance.

3. Do you think the proposed New York City Council Districts are satisfactory? Why?

4. Are there any geographic (spatial) rules that govern the drawing of political boundaries?

5. Section 2 of the 1965 Voting Rights Act prohibits abridging the right to vote by diluting the strength of a protected group. What are some interpretations that would challenge this provision? What is a protected group?

6. What are the limitations to using census data for redistricting?

7. What are some ways to measure political cohesiveness?

8. The illustration for Stockton, California, highlights certain problems with the given definition of "majority" (in "effective voting majority"). From a demographic perspective, how should majority be defined?

9. What are some disadvantages to using surname analysis?

10. Consider other methods of analysis that might be employed in redistricting cases.

11. What are the possible roles of a demographer in redistricting cases? List the vital aspects of each of these roles.

Notes

Views expressed in this chapter are those of the author, not those of RAND or sponsors of its research. Portions of this chapter draw on collaborative research reported in Morrison and Clark 1992; and Clark and Morrison 1991.

1. In 1980, Salinas was a city of 80,000, 38 percent of whom were Hispanic. By 1990, the city had grown 35 percent to 109,000, 51 percent of whom were Hispanic. Politically, Salinas is divided into six city council districts, each of which is supposed to contain one-sixth of the population (18,130 persons following the 1990 Census).

2. *The New York Times,* July 18, 1991, p. B8.

3. We remind the reader that legal interpretations of these requirements evolve and change as case law develops. Accordingly, one should not assume that standards discussed here are necessarily the ones currently in effect.

4. The Census Bureau has developed a list for identifying persons of probable Hispanic origin. This list has been used to gauge the makeup of electorates in California, and its detection characteristics are well documented. No comparably established surname list exists for the Asian population, although the Census Bureau has conducted exploratory work to develop such a list.

References

Clark, W.A.V., and Peter A. Morrison. "Demographic Paradoxes in the Los Angeles Voting Rights Case." *Evaluation Review,* Vol. 15, No. 6. December 1991: 712–728.

_____. "Gauging Hispanic voting strength: Paradoxes and pitfalls." *Population Research and Policy Review.* Vol. 11, 1992: 145–156.

Gobalet, Jeanne G., and Shelley Lapkoff. "Changing from At-Large to District Election of Trustees in two California Community College Districts." Presented at the 1991 Population Association of America meetings (dated October 1990).

Leoni, Marguerite Mary. "1990s Redistricting Under Section 2 of the Voting Rights Act: Beyond *Thornburg* v. *Gingles.*" *Public Law News* (published by the Public Law Section of the State Bar of California). Vol. 14, No. 4. Fall 1990: 10–13.

Morrison, Peter A. "Quantifying Legal Standards in Voting Rights Cases." Presented at the 1989 Population Association of America meetings.

Morrison, Peter A., and William A.V. Clark. "Local Redistricting: The Demographic Context of Boundary Drawing." *National Civic Review.* Winter/Spring 1992: 57–63.

Wattson, Peter S. "Maps That Will Stand Up In Court." *State Legislatures.* September 1990: 15–19.

4

The Use of Intercensal Population Estimates in Political Redistricting

*William J. Serow, E. Walter Terrie,
Bob Weller, and Richard W. Wichmann*

In the fall of 1988 the electorate of Palm Beach County, Florida, approved an amendment to the county's charter that revised the structure of the county commission. Instead of five members elected at large, the commission would now consist of seven members, each of whom would be elected from a single district.

Although the 1990 census results for blocks would not be available for the entire county until early in 1991 (and all counties in Florida must, by law, redistrict in 1992), the language of the referendum required that the redistricting be accomplished in time for the 1990 general election. In order to give the supervisor of elections enough time to prepare a new set of voting precincts, the redistricting had to be completed by the fall of 1989. The Board of County Commissioners chose the Center for the Study of Population at the Florida State University to serve as consultants to this project.

The project had two parts. The first part entailed preparing current population estimates for 827 "Traffic Analysis Zones" (TAZ) within the county. The second part involved formulating the redistricting plan. This plan had to create seven districts of approximately equal population, and it had to be acceptable to both the sitting commissioners and the many interest groups that are inevitably present in a large (830,000 persons in 1988), extremely diverse political jurisdiction.

This paper deals with both parts of the project, with particular emphasis on the first of them. Florida has an active and highly respected population estimates and projection program located at the University of Florida's Bureau of Economic and Business Research. We used the program's county and municipal level estimates as controls for our very small area level estimates.

The Setting

Palm Beach is a large and heterogeneous county in southeastern Florida, located at the northern end of what the tourist and economic development literature calls

33

Florida's "Gold Coast." At almost 2,000 square miles, it is larger than any county east of the Mississippi River; Palm Beach County is, in fact, 64 percent larger than the entire state of Rhode Island.

According to census data, the county had 576,758 residents in 1980, an increase of 65 percent from the final (revised) count of 348,993 in 1970. Its intercensal rate of increase exceeded that for the entire state by a factor of 50 percent (U.S. Bureau of the Census, 1982). During the 1980s, when the population of Florida was growing faster than that of any other large state, the population of Palm Beach County was growing at an even greater pace. Current estimates for 1988 show the total population at 831,146, an increase of 44 percent over the 1980 census enumeration. Since Florida's 1988 population is estimated at 12,417,606, an increase of 27 percent over 1980 (University of Florida 1989), Palm Beach County has not only maintained but slightly widened its growth differential in relation to the rest of the state during the decade just completed. While the population of Florida has been growing at an annual rate of about three times the national average since 1970, the population of Palm Beach County has been growing at a rate of more than four and one half times the national average (Figure 4.1).

Net migration accounted for most of the population growth in Palm Beach County during the 1980s. From January 1, 1980, to December 31, 1987, there were 72,161 births and 65,659 deaths registered among county residents. These figures produced a level of reproductive change equal to 6,502 (Florida Department of Health and Rehabilitative Services, various years). By contrast, during the almost entirely coincident period from April 1, 1980, to March 31, 1988, total population growth in Palm Beach County was 254,283. Net migration, therefore, accounted for some 97 percent of the county's population growth after 1980.

In addition to being very large and growing very rapidly, Palm Beach County is very heterogeneous. While it contains one of the wealthiest communities in the United States—the town of Palm Beach—it also contains large expanses of land used for commercial agriculture, especially the production of sugar cane. Persons living in the western portion of the county (generically called "the Glades" by local residents) are largely dependent upon agriculture for their livelihood. Disproportionately black or Hispanic, the residents of the Glades see themselves as geographically separated from the eastern portion of the county, and they feel looked down upon culturally and discriminated against both politically and economically by the remainder of the county.

At the time that redistricting was mandated, the representative for the most western district in Palm Beach County lived in the southern portion of the county, very near Boca Raton. Not surprisingly, therefore, inhabitants of the Glades strongly favored changing the at-large electoral system. They wanted a district made up only of persons living in the western portion of the county or at least a district in which they would be demographically and politically predominant.

Many prominent members of the business community were also quite vocal in supporting the single-member district concept. They believed that having each

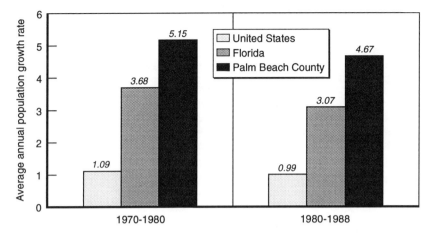

SOURCES: University of Florida, 1989, U.S. Bureau of the Census, 1989.

Figure 4.1—Average annual population growth rate: Palm Beach County, Florida, and the United States (1970–1980 and 1980–1988)

commissioner elected from a single district rather than countywide, along with the increase from five to seven commissioners, would raise the number of seats held by members of the Republican party—or at least by persons who would be more sympathetic to development interests.

Florida traditionally has been a Democratic state. In recent years, however, many prominent political figures have shifted to the Republican party. Among those who have switched from the Democrats to the Republicans are the present governor, the present secretary of state, and several members of the state legislature and U.S. House of Representatives. In addition, recent migrants to Florida have been somewhat more likely to register as Republicans than have the state's longer term residents (Sly et al. 1989). As a result, the Republican party has become increasingly influential on a local basis in some areas; Palm Beach County is one of those areas. When the redistricting project began in May 1989, two of the five county commissioners were Republicans.

In 1980 about 86 percent of the county's population was white, and that proportion remained about constant through the decade. Nearly all (96 percent) of the nonwhite population in 1980 was black, and this too has remained stable since then. The black population has been heavily concentrated in (1) a narrow band running through much of the eastern portion of the county, and (2) the three small municipalities (Belle Glade, South Bay, and Pahokee) located along the shores of Lake Okeechobee in the extreme western section of the county. In 1980 the proportion of blacks ranged from zero in several of the county's smaller municipalities to as much as two-thirds in Riviera Beach, with majorities in South Bay and Pahokee (Table 4.1).

Table 4.1   Population by Race and Ethnicity: Municipalities of Palm Beach
County, Florida: 1980

Municipality	Total	White	Black	Other Races	Hispanic Origin
Atlantis	1,325	1,309	1	15	29
Belle Glade	16,535	6,633	8,751	1,151	3,075
Boca Raton	49,505	47,974	960	571	2,203
Boynton Beach	35,624	28,767	6,274	583	1,433
Briny Breezes	387	387	0	0	1
Cloud Lake	160	157	2	1	2
Delray Beach	34,325	25,724	8,222	379	1,158
Glen Ridge	235	234	0	1	1
Golf	110	110	0	0	0
Golfview	210	210	0	0	2
Greenacres City	8,843	8,623	12	208	485
Gulf Stream	475	464	11	0	2
Haverhill	1,249	1,242	1	6	35
Highland Beach	2,030	2,026	0	4	28
Hypoluxo	573	567	2	4	4
Juno Beach	1,142	1,139	0	3	12
Jupiter	9,868	9,742	44	82	133
Jupiter Inlet Colony	378	377	1	0	0
Lake Clark Shores	3,174	3,139	1	34	185
Lake Park	6,909	6,221	624	64	121
Lake Worth	27,048	25,261	1,365	422	1,261
Lantana	8,048	7,811	161	76	195
Manalapan	329	324	5	0	2
Mangonia Park	1,419	999	416	4	71
North Palm Beach	11,344	11,258	2	84	161
Ocean Ridge	1,355	1,349	0	6	15
Pahokee	6,346	3,235	2,881	230	907
Palm Beach	9,729	9,602	73	54	239
Palm Beach Gardens	14,407	14,210	38	159	267
Palm Beach Shores	1,232	1,221	3	8	5
Palm Springs	8,166	8,026	54	86	418
Riviera Beach	26,489	8,575	17,675	239	537
Royal Palm Beach	3,423	3,292	60	71	139
South Bay	3,886	1,044	2,637	205	488
South Palm Beach	1,304	1,300	0	4	4
Tequesta	3,685	3,663	2	20	36
West Palm Beach	63,305	44,416	17,671	1,218	5,430
Total Incorporated	364,572	290,631	67,949	5,992	19,084
Unincorporated	212,291	196,867	9,627	5,797	9,421
County Total	576,863	487,498	77,576	11,789	28,505

Table 4.1   (continued)

Municipality	Total	White	Black	Other Races	Hispanic Origin
Atlantis	0.23	0.27	0.00	0.13	0.10
Belle Glade	2.87	1.36	11.28	9.76	10.79
Boca Raton	8.58	9.84	1.24	4.84	7.73
Boynton Beach	6.18	5.90	8.09	4.95	5.03
Briny Breezes	0.07	0.08	0.00	0.00	0.00
Cloud Lake	0.03	0.03	0.00	0.01	0.01
Delray Beach	5.95	5.28	10.60	3.21	4.06
Glen Ridge	0.04	0.05	0.00	0.01	0.00
Golf	0.02	0.02	0.00	0.00	0.00
Golfview	0.04	0.04	0.00	0.00	0.01
Greenacres City	1.53	1.77	0.02	1.76	1.70
Gulf Stream	0.08	0.10	0.01	0.00	0.01
Haverhill	0.22	0.25	0.00	0.05	0.12
Highland Beach	0.35	0.42	0.00	0.03	0.10
Hypoluxo	0.10	0.12	0.00	0.03	0.01
Juno Beach	0.20	0.23	0.00	0.03	0.04
Jupiter	1.71	2.00	0.06	0.70	0.47
Jupiter Inlet Colony	0.07	0.08	0.00	0.00	0.00
Lake Clark Shores	0.55	0.64	0.00	0.29	0.65
Lake Park	1.20	1.28	0.80	0.54	0.42
Lake Worth	4.69	5.18	1.76	3.58	4.42
Lantana	1.40	1.60	0.21	0.64	0.68
Manalapan	0.06	0.07	0.01	0.00	0.01
Mangonia Park	0.25	0.20	0.54	0.03	0.25
North Palm Beach	1.97	2.31	0.00	0.71	0.56
Ocean Ridge	0.23	0.28	0.00	0.05	0.05
Pahokee	1.10	0.66	3.71	1.95	3.18
Palm Beach	1.69	1.97	0.09	0.46	0.84
Palm Beach Gardens	2.50	2.91	0.05	1.35	0.94
Palm Beach Shores	0.21	0.25	0.00	0.07	0.02
Palm Springs	1.42	1.65	0.07	0.73	1.47
Riviera Beach	4.59	1.76	22.78	2.03	1.88
Royal Palm Beach	0.59	0.68	0.08	0.60	0.49
South Bay	0.67	0.21	3.40	1.74	1.71
South Palm Beach	0.23	0.27	0.00	0.03	0.01
Tequesta	0.64	0.75	0.00	0.17	0.13
West Palm Beach	10.97	9.11	22.78	10.33	19.05
Total Incorporated	63.20	59.62	87.59	50.83	66.95
Unincorporated	36.80	40.38	12.41	49.17	33.05
County Total	100.00	100.00	100.00	100.00	100.00

Table header: Percentage of county total (spanning Total, White, Black, Other Races, Hispanic Origin)

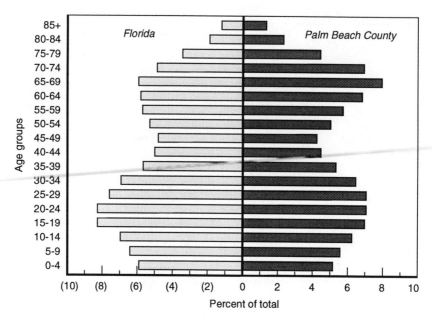

SOURCES: 1980 Census of Population

**Figure 4.2—Age distribution (percent) for Palm Beach County
and Florida: 1980**

Despite the sizable number of blacks, however, there has never been a black commissioner in Palm Beach County. Based on their perceived lack of influence on the county commission under the existing electoral system, therefore, political leaders of the county's black community could, in general, be characterized as favoring the change to single-member districts. Members of the black community also expressed the hope that redistricting would yield a district containing a black majority or at least one in which there were enough black voters to compel one or more commissioners to respond to black interests and concerns.

About 5 percent of the 1980 population (28,505 persons) were of Hispanic origin. More recent estimates for 1985 (Word 1989) suggest an increase to 37,800, but this still represents only a very slight rise (from 4.9 to 5.2 percent) in the proportion of Hispanics in the county's total population (estimated at 713.3 thousand in 1985). Although somewhat less geographically concentrated than blacks in 1980, Hispanics nonetheless accounted for more than 10 percent of the population in each of the three western cities (Belle Glade, South Bay, and Pahokee).

County Hispanics are divided into two basic groups. Those in the western communities are primarily agricultural workers who tend to align themselves politically with the black community. A significant portion of the Hispanics in the eastern part of Palm Beach County, however, are Cuban Americans with close ties to the business community. Regarding the shift from at-large to single-member districts, both groups of Hispanics were thus aligned with portions of the county population that tended to favor changing the electoral system.

As is true of many other areas in southern and central Florida, Palm Beach County contains a large number of retired persons who moved there from another part of the country. Nearly one-fourth (23.3 percent) of the county's population in 1980 was at least 65 years of age, and the median age was 39.7 years. For Florida as a whole in 1980, 17.3 percent were at least 65 years of age, and the median age was 34.7 years (Figure 4.2). In 1988 the county's proportion of older residents remained at its 1980 level, while that of Florida increased slightly to 17.8 percent. Actually, the county's population with the highest rate of growth (65 percent) since 1980 has been the group from 25 to 44 years old. The county's population under age 15 has increased by 46 percent, while those over age 65 have increased by 45 percent (Smith and Bayya 1989). These data are summarized in Table 4.2.

The county's older residents constitute an active force in politics, accentuated by their high rates of voter registration and participation. Many of these residents live in retirement-oriented communities scattered throughout the eastern (Atlantic Coast) portion of the county, especially in the southern portion of the county immediately west of Boca Raton, Delray Beach, and Boynton Beach (Figures 4.3a and 4.3b). As a general statement, the political leaders of these retirement communities could be characterized as opposing the change to single-member districts. They feared a dilution of their influence on the county commission and wanted to retain the existing system of countywide elections.

The Center for the Study of Population at Florida State University was selected to prepare Palm Beach County's political redistricting estimates and plans for several reasons. In addition to its demographic expertise and distinguished faculty, the Center had experience in other county commission redistrictings brought about by a switch from at-large to single-member elections. Moreover, the various population groups in Palm Beach County regarded the Center as objective and not having any vested interest in how the district boundaries were actually drawn. Even those groups that opposed redistricting did not object to the Center's involvement. Their attitude seemed to be: We don't agree with the voters' decision to change our system for electing county commissioners. We think the at-large system is better. Given that the system has to be changed, however, we'd rather have an outside party do it than some local group that would manipulate the situation to their advantage.

Data and Methodology

Two types of data were available for preparing estimates at the TAZ level: (1) a current count of housing units by structural type (i.e., single- versus multiple-unit) for each TAZ, and (2) a time series of registered voters by election precinct for

Table 4.2   Population by Age, Gender and Race: Palm Beach County and
               Florida, 1980 and 1988

	Palm Beach County			Florida		
	Male	Female	Total	Male	Female	Total
1980						
White:						
0–14	37,536	35,614	73,150	740,342	704,098	1,444,440
15–24	32,998	32,371	65,369	670,818	650,453	1,321,271
25–44	57,708	56,453	114,161	1,027,817	1,048,618	2,076,435
45–64	50,727	63,751	114,478	875,757	1,019,621	1,895,378
65+	56,887	71,670	128,557	684,318	897,606	1,581,924
Total	235,856	259,859	495,715	3,999,052	4,320,396	8,319,448
Black:						
0–14	12,278	12,218	24,496	207,863	204,205	412,068
15–24	7,636	8,118	15,754	137,738	149,402	287,140
25–44	9,803	10,568	20,371	159,469	184,706	344,175
45–64	5,452	6,270	11,722	91,971	110,314	202,285
65+	2,382	3,258	5,640	42,186	58,947	101,133
Total	37,551	40,432	77,983	639,227	707,574	1,346,801
All Races:						
0–14	50,146	48,182	98,328	958,454	918,320	1,876,774
15–24	40,880	40,708	81,588	815,703	807,064	1,622,767
25–44	68,225	67,649	135,874	1,200,503	1,249,686	2,450,189
45–64	56,373	70,248	126,621	972,606	1,136,415	2,109,021
65+	59,367	75,085	134,452	728,360	959,213	1,687,573
Total	274,991	301,872	576,863	4,675,626	5,070,698	9,746,324

every year from 1980. In our professional judgment, estimates based on two independent data sources would prove more reliable and more robust than would estimates based solely on one set of data.

We employed two alternative estimation methodologies. The first utilized recent refinements in the housing unit method (Smith and Lewis 1980, 1983) to prepare estimates of the household population for each TAZ. The second used a variant of ratio-correlation to estimate this same population at the precinct level.
Because precinct boundaries only rarely coincided with those of TAZs, we initially aggregated the TAZs so they would conform to precinct boundaries, averaged the two sets of estimates, and redistributed the estimates back to the TAZ
level based on the TAZ-level housing unit estimates. Finally, we estimated the
group quarters population by contacting large institutions within the county (nurs-

Table 4.2   *(continued)*

	Palm Beach County			Florida		
	Male	Female	Total	Male	Female	Total
1988						
White:						
0–14	56,998	52,310	109,308	920,434	883,176	1,803,610
15–24	37,644	36,117	73,761	699,345	662,009	1,361,354
25–44	97,867	93,966	191,833	1,503,545	1,492,147	2,995,692
45–64	72,098	87,879	159,977	1,076,647	1,236,722	2,313,369
65+	80,967	105,311	186,278	890,002	1,183,127	2,073,129
Total	345,574	375,583	721,157	5,089,973	5,457,181	10,547,154
Black:						
0–14	16,602	16,648	33,250	268,436	259,453	527,889
15–24	8,510	9,134	17,644	156,003	159,886	315,889
25–44	14,857	15,509	30,366	250,765	280,225	530,990
45–64	7,514	8,774	16,288	114,833	139,647	254,480
65+	3,300	4,691	7,991	53,372	78,407	131,779
Total	50,783	54,756	105,539	843,409	917,618	1,761,027
All Races:						
0–14	74,048	69,443	143,491	1,202,156	1,155,342	2,357,498
15–24	46,433	45,500	91,933	863,652	829,820	1,693,472
25–44	113,817	110,398	224,215	1,775,125	1,797,686	3,572,811
45–64	79,882	96,972	176,854	1,197,744	1,384,808	2,582,552
65+	84,419	110,234	194,653	945,993	1,265,279	2,211,272
Total	398,599	432,547	831,146	5,984,670	6,432,935	12,417,605

Sources: 1980 Census of Population; Smith and Bayya 1989.

ing homes, college dormitories, correctional institutions) to obtain their exact geographic location and their precise number of residents in mid-1988. We allocated the remaining (small) group quarters population to the TAZ level in accordance with the distribution of this "residual" group quarters population at the tract level in 1980, and estimated TAZ shares of their corresponding tracts in 1988.

Because the Metropolitan Planning Organization of Palm Beach County intentionally constructed the TAZs to be consistent with 1980 census tracts, we were able to determine—simply by assuming that the tract level parameters would apply to each TAZ within that tract—both the average number of persons per household and the vacancy rate for each TAZ by type of dwelling unit. We then reduced the 1980 figure for persons per household by TAZ and type of unit by the esti-

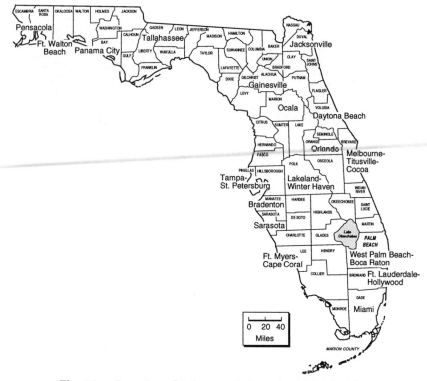

Fig. 4.3a—Location of Palm Beach County within Florida

mated change in average household size for the entire state of Florida during the period 1980 to 1988, or by some 3.5 percent (U.S. Bureau of the Census 1989). Due to the separate treatment of single- versus multi-unit structures, we would argue that this process would not introduce, a priori, any systematic bias into the population estimates.

In the absence of any more current information, we assumed that vacancy rates by TAZ and type of unit had not changed from their 1980 levels. This assumption introduced an upward bias favoring those portions of the county that had experienced substantial increases in new residential construction because new units typically have higher vacancy rates than older units, at least in the period immediately following their completion. Without a census enumeration, however, we had no basis for estimating the magnitude of this potential bias.

The office of the supervisor of elections supplied us with data on the number of registered voters by precinct. While there had been a substantial increase in the number of voting precincts in the county during the 1980s, most of the changes took the form of "splitting" existing precincts rather than reconstructing precinct boundaries. Because precinct boundaries were not consistent with those of census

43

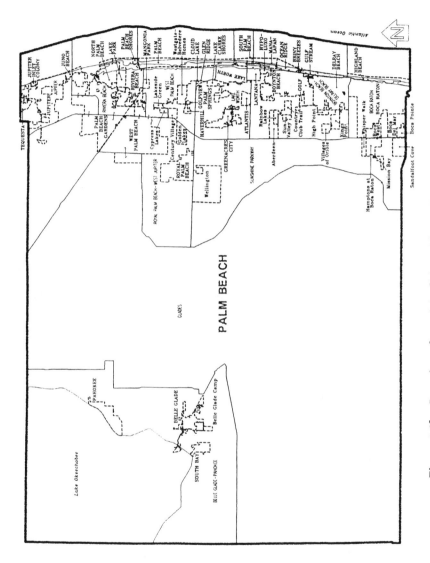

Figure 4.3b—Location of municipalities within Palm Beach County

tracts, we had to aggregate precincts into clusters that would be geographically consistent with clusters of tracts. This process, developed from 141 census tracts and more than 200 precincts, produced a total of 51 clusters incorporating contiguous sets of both voting precincts and census tracts.

We utilized 1980 data for both registered voters and total household population in a regression equation that predicted cluster level shares of the latter as a function of cluster level shares of the former. This equation was estimated as follows:

$$PCTHHPOP = .362 + .586 \ PCTVOTERS$$

$$(t = 4.1), \ r^2 = .681, \ F = 14.3$$

We then "solved" this equation for 1988 by entering appropriate cluster level shares of registered voters and controlled it so that the sum of the predicted values of PCTHHPOP was equal to unity. This equation is not the standard ratio-correlation format. That approach would require registered voters by precinct and household population by tract for 1970 as well as 1980. In the case of Palm Beach County, precinct boundaries had changed so much between 1970 and 1980 that it was impossible for us to consider utilizing 1970 data and consequently to develop the conventional double-ratio equation.

As one would expect, there was wide variation in the actual 1980 and implicit 1988 ratios of adult population to voters across clusters, with much of the variation depending upon the age and racial structure of the cluster. Observed ratios ranged from near unity in the few instances where there was a perfect correspondence between precincts and tracts (a small number of retirement communities) to levels of nearly three in some of the predominately black and Hispanic areas. The latter areas could be characterized as having not only a disproportionately large share of children in the population but also relatively low voter registration rates.

As a result of our utilizing both sets of estimating procedures, we obtained two independently derived sets of population estimates covering the entire county. While our final estimates were based on an average of these two sets, we were of course interested in the accuracy of each set of estimates and the degree of confidence we could place in either of them. In the absence of a current census enumeration for Palm Beach County, our only basis of comparison was that between our TAZ- and precinct-level estimates aggregated to the municipal level (before the imposition of control totals) and the current estimates prepared by the University of Florida (1989). In some cases, we were able to produce an estimate for a locality using one or the other of the methods.

In all but four of the municipalities we were able to aggregate precinct level estimates to correspond precisely to municipal boundaries. In the other cases we had no basis for using voter registration data to estimate the population of the municipalities because each of the municipalities did not include an entire voting precinct. Additionally, the TAZ-level housing data were not compiled for the western portion of the county; accordingly, we were unable to prepare estimates based on housing units for those jurisdictions. In sum, we prepared estimates derived from both housing and voter registration data for 30 of the county's 37 municipalities. For three municipalities our estimates were based solely on voter registrations, and our estimates for the remaining four were prepared solely from housing counts.

The summary of these estimates in Table 4.3 shows a mean weighted (by population size) error of 7.5 to 8.0 percent for each of the estimates as well as the expected positive association between accuracy and population size. While each method displayed some degree of directional bias, the direction of this bias was different for each set of estimates, affording some higher level of confidence in the final, averaged, set of estimates. This set of estimates was approximately equally divided between positive and negative errors and showed a mean weighted error more than one percentage point lower than that resulting from the estimates based upon a single set of data.

These results can be compared with some (Table 4.4) prepared for all Florida municipalities in 1980 (Smith 1986, 294). Although the Smith estimates were prepared using the housing unit and administrative records techniques, only the former is shown here.

Our estimates appear to compare favorably with those for the entire state in terms of overall accuracy (mean error), directional bias (distribution of over- and underestimates), and the presence of extreme outliers (here taken to be estimates more than 10 percent different from the point of comparison). The mean weighted (by population size) error of the final estimates for the 37 municipalities in Palm Beach County is 6.6 percent, compared with 5.6 percent for all Florida municipalities and 7.5 percent for all municipalities in the state when those with more than 100,000 residents are excluded (the largest city in Palm Beach County had an estimated 1988 population of about 75,000). Similarly, 54 percent of the county estimates were higher than the University of Florida estimates; this was the same share of underestimates that Smith reported for all municipalities (53 percent for those under 100,000). Finally, slightly more than half of the estimates for Palm Beach County municipalities (19 of 37, or 51 percent) were within 10 percent of the University of Florida estimates. This figure is somewhat lower than the level Smith reported for all municipalities (58 percent) or for those with fewer than 100,000 residents (56 percent).

Similar comparisons can be drawn for the different groupings of cities according to their population size. Our final estimates for places with fewer than 5,000 persons show higher mean error, greater (negative) directional bias, and about the same share of outliers. Our mean error for places with 5,000 to 10,000 residents is about the same as Smith reported, although Palm Beach County included only three such places. For places with 10,000 or more residents, mean error was the same or lower than Smith's findings for places of this size with fewer than 100,000 inhabitants; there was, moreover, a similar amount and degree of both di-

Table 4.3a Estimates of the Population of Municipalities in Palm Beach County Based on Housing Units and Registered Voters: 1988

Municipality	Estimates from			U of F Estimate	Percent Difference from University of Florida		
	Housing Units	Registered Voters	Average		Housing Units	Registered Voters	Average
Atlantis	2,075	2,921	2,498	1,649	25.8	77.1	51.5
Belle Glade	NA	18,206	18,206	17,009	NA	7.0	7.0
Boca Raton	56,133	59,921	58,027	59,585	−5.8	0.6	−2.6
Boynton Beach	41,017	41,061	41,039	46,310	−11.4	−11.3	−11.4
Briny Breezes	606	NA	606	371	63.3	NA	63.3
Cloud Lake	171	184	178	153	11.8	20.3	16.0
Delray Beach	42,463	44,336	43,400	45,441	−6.6	−2.4	−4.5
Glen Ridge	185	NA	185	226	−18.1	NA	−18.1
Golf	225	201	213	131	71.8	53.4	62.6
Golfview	172	NA	172	208	−17.3	NA	−17.3
Greenacres City	17,547	27,948	22,748	27,295	−35.7	2.4	−16.7
Gulf Stream	566	679	623	537	5.4	26.4	15.9
Haverhill	947	1,483	1,215	1,262	−25.0	17.5	−3.7
Highland Beach	2,823	3,149	2,986	3,208	−12.0	−1.8	−6.9
Hypoluxo	866	1,271	1,069	760	13.9	67.2	40.6
Juno Beach	2,435	3,042	2,739	2,037	19.5	49.3	34.4
Jupiter	26,604	23,772	25,188	26,258	1.3	−9.5	−4.1
Jupiter Inlet Colony	382	NA	382	394	−3.0	NA	−3.0
Lake Clark Shores	3,508	3,998	3,753	3,317	5.8	20.5	13.1
Lake Park	6,359	6,327	6,343	6,756	−5.9	−6.3	−6.1
Lake Worth	26,886	28,132	27,509	27,471	−2.1	2.4	0.1

Table 4.3a   (continued)

Municipality	Estimates from			U of F Estimate	Percent Difference from University of Florida		
	Housing Units	Registered Voters	Average		Housing Units	Registered Voters	Average
Lantana	8,288	8,221	8,255	8,507	-2.6	-3.4	-3.0
Manalapan	377	455	416	376	0.3	21.0	10.6
Mangonia Park	1,174	1,402	1,288	1,278	-8.1	9.7	0.8
North Palm Beach	10,854	15,489	13,172	12,742	-14.8	21.6	3.4
Ocean Ridge	1,249	NA	1,249	1,542	-19.0	NA	-19.0
Pahokee	NA	7,733	7,733	6,610	NA	17.0	17.0
Palm Beach	11,827	10,646	11,237	10,859	8.9	-2.0	3.5
Palm Beach Gardens	22,984	22,198	22,591	24,130	-4.7	-8.0	-6.4
Palm Beach Shores	1,358	1,219	1,289	1,263	7.5	-3.5	2.0
Palm Springs	9,534	11,023	10,279	10,284	-7.3	7.2	-0.1
Riviera Beach	27,776	23,790	25,783	29,191	-4.8	-18.5	-11.7
Royal Palm Beach	10,581	13,661	12,121	11,538	-8.3	18.4	5.1
South Bay	NA	5,060	5,060	3,736	NA	35.4	35.4
South Palm Beach	1,512	1,456	1,484	1,473	2.6	-1.2	0.7
Tequesta	4,507	6,159	5,333	4,448	1.3	38.5	19.9
West Palm Beach	72,288	72,521	72,405	73,830	-2.1	-1.8	-1.9
Total Incorporated			458,768	472,185			-2.8
Unincorporated			372,378	358,961			3.7
County Total			831,146	831,146			

Table 4.3b   Analysis of Differences

Differences between Housing Unit and University of Florida Estimates

Size of Place	N	Number		Mean Error		Number of estimates with error less than:		
		negative	positive	absolute	weighted	5%	10%	20%
< 5,000	15	3	12	29.5	28.4	3	4	6
5 to 9999	3	2	1	9.4	8.9	1	2	3
> 10,000	14	7	7	8.1	6.2	6	10	13
> 25,000	8	5	3	6.1	5.1	5	6	8
Total	32	12	20	18.3	7.7	10	16	22

Differences between Registered Voter and
University of Florida Estimates

Size of Place	N	Number		Mean Error		Number of estimates with error less than:		
		negative	positive	absolute	weighted	5%	10%	20%
< 5,000	19	7	12	17.5	11.7	4	8	15
5 to 9999	2	2	0	4.2	4.0	1	2	2
> 10,000	13	11	2	8.8	7.7	5	10	12
> 25,000	8	7	1	8.7	7.6	4	6	7
Total	34	20	14	13.4	7.9	10	20	29

Differences between Final Florida State University
and University of Florida Estimates

Size of Place	N	Number		Mean Error		Number of estimates with error less than:		
		negative	positive	absolute	weighted	5%	10%	20%
< 5,000	20	6	14	21.8	20.0	5	6	14
5 to 9999	3	2	1	8.7	8.2	1	2	3
> 10,000	14	9	5	5.6	5.6	8	11	14
> 25,000	8	7	1	6.6	5.8	5	5	8
Total	37	17	20	14.6	6.6	14	19	31

Table 4.4   Accuracy of Housing Unit Population Estimates for Florida
Municipalities: 1980

Size of Place	N	Number Positive	Mean Error absolute	Mean Error weighted (%)	Number of errors <10%
<100	13	6	74.4	76.5	0
100–499	46	23	32.4	29.5	11
500–999	49	24	18.0	18.1	21
1,000–2,499	75	34	15.7	15.7	37
2,500–4,999	56	32	8.9	8.6	33
[<5,000]	239	119	21.0	12.6	102
5,000–9,999	70	38	7.9	8.0	52
10,000–24,999	64	25	8.3	8.1	40
25,000–49,999	43	18	6.7	6.7	35
50,000–99,999	20	8	6.7	6.5	15
[10,000–99,999]	127	51	7.5	7.0	90
[25,000–99,999]	63	26	6.7	6.6	50
100,000+	21	5	3.8	3.8	19
Total	460	213	14.4	5.6	266
Total, excluding 100,000+	439	208	14.9	7.5	247

Source: Smith [1966]

rectional bias (35 to 40 percent overestimates) and presence of outliers (20 to 30 percent).

In brief, based on the limited means of comparison available, we believe the estimates of population for the municipalities of Palm Beach County—and, by extension, the unincorporated areas—to be both credible and consistent with existing demographic standards. These estimates exhibit a pattern of error with respect to size of place that conforms precisely to what would be predicted by past experience. As a result, we would argue that the TAZ-level estimates (from which those at the municipal level are aggregated) should provide a reasonable and equitable basis for the development of redistricting plans that would meet the demographic criterion of approximate equality of population size for each district.

The Development of Commission District Boundaries

The final stage of the project called for the actual formation of seven commission districts that would both satisfy the criteria approved by the Board of County Commissioners and prove politically acceptable to the various constituencies and interest groups in the county's electorate. The Commission's criteria were—in priority order—as follows:

1. Each district will include the same number of persons, based on the population estimates for 1988.
2. The geographic composition of each district will be as compact and contiguous as possible.
3. The integrity of existing communities of interest (such as the western portion of the county, major residential subdivisions, and minority populations) will be maintained.
4. The integrity of municipal boundaries will be maintained.
5. The boundaries of newly formed districts will follow major manmade and natural boundaries.
6. The integrity of existing voting precincts will be maintained.

Using these criteria and working in close cooperation with county officials, we developed five alternative proposals for consideration by the Board and for presentation to interested parties during a series of "public forums" conducted throughout the county. With a total of more than 800 TAZ-level population estimates, we theoretically could have developed a wide range of plans, each emphasizing one or another of the Commission's criteria. For example, one plan (which did not gain wide acceptance) included nearly all of the eastern portion of the county's black population in a single district. This district ran nearly the entire length of the county but was only a few blocks wide in some places.

After several rounds of discussion with the Board and other interested parties, we found a consensus emerging in favor of one of the five plans. With slight modification, this plan (shown in Figure 4.4) was eventually approved by the Board of County Commissioners in October 1989. While no plan could have perfectly satisfied all of the criteria, this particular configuration met the main criterion of minimal variance among districts in terms of population size. According to this plan, the largest district contained just 0.9 percent more people (119,818) and the smallest district just 0.8 percent fewer people (117,722) than a theoretical division into completely equal districts (118,735).

The approved plan placed the western portion of the county, which had felt alienated from the political process, in a separate district. It was not possible, however, to create a district having a black majority (even in the "gerrymandered" district mentioned above) simply because the number of blacks in the county was not sufficiently large. Two districts (6 and 7 in Figure 4.4) were more than one-third black, and two others (3 and 5) had about the same proportion of blacks as did the county as a whole.

While it was impossible to maintain the complete integrity of municipal boundaries in this or any other plan, just seven of the county's 37 cities were placed into more than one district in the adopted plan. In most cases, these municipalities were so large in terms of population and were in such a physical location that no alternative was possible. In addition, some municipal officials voiced the

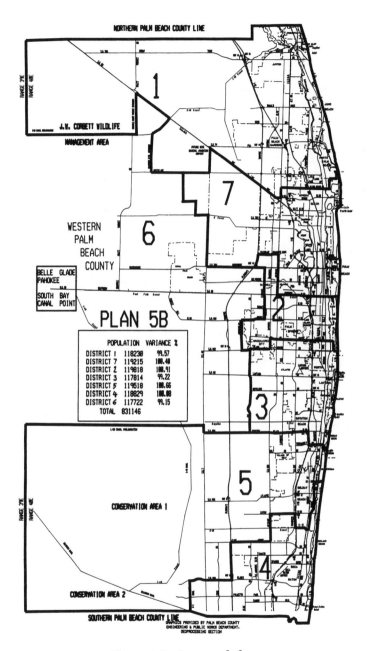

Figure 4.4—Approved plan

opinion that the interests of their cities might be better served by having more than one commissioner accountable to their respective electorates.

Finally, it must be noted that the adopted plan adhered to an unspoken—but quite real—concern of the sitting commissioners: namely, that the redistricting process not place more than one of them within the boundaries of a single district. Fortunately for these commissioners, the county is sufficiently large that (except in one instance) it would have been difficult to construct boundaries that placed more than one incumbent commissioner within the same district.

Conclusion

This paper has recounted how a team of professional demographers (1) utilized an existing data base maintained by a county government, (2) applied proven demographic techniques to these data in order to produce a set of subcensus tract-level postcensal population estimates that could stand up to professional scrutiny, and (3) worked with county officials to prepare a set of viable redistricting alternatives that would satisfy demographic, legal, and political criteria. While it would be both naive and inaccurate to assert that all parties were satisfied with the outcome, those who were dissatisfied were less concerned about demographics than about the larger question of changing from at-large to single-member districts and about the legality of the charter amendment, which mandated both changing from at-large to single-member districts and increasing the size of the board from five to seven members. Insofar as the demographic side of the matter—i.e., the accuracy and unbiased nature of the underlying population estimates—was concerned, we were satisfied that our estimates were as accurate and reliable as possible. We look forward to the availability of the 1990 census, which will afford us the opportunity to evaluate the accuracy of our estimates in light of census results.

The primary function of demographers in a case such as the one in Palm Beach County is consultative. The elected county commissioners set forth the ground rules in preparing redistricting options when they adopted and placed in priority the set of six principles we were to follow, and they made the ultimate decisions regarding district boundaries. Our function was primarily to inform the commissioners whether a given set of proposed boundaries was consistent with their principles.

Often the first of the ground rules—create districts of equal size—ruled out some other potentially desirable objectives. For instance, the three small communities in the Glades area in western Palm Beach County lacked a sufficient number of persons to exist as a separate district. The numbers weren't even close. Similarly, it was impossible to adhere to the equal-size mandate and create a district that was predominantly black. We were unable to meet requests to create such a district because our first priority was to create districts of equal size. A different set of ground rules, or a different priority sequence, would have produced different district boundaries.

Although limited to working within the confines (and sometimes protection) of an established set of ground rules, we were nonetheless able to recommend a western district that the Glades community should be able to dominate politically. In addition, we created at least one district in which no one will likely be elected without the active support of blacks. Most importantly, we were able to meet the criteria of the Board of County Commissioners without sacrificing our image of neutrality or compromising our impartiality in the face of entreaties from special interest groups.

Discussion Questions

1. When redistricting must be completed just prior to the new census, what data limitations arise?

2. After reviewing the information provided in the "the setting," describe any special challenges caused by the demographic and political setting of Palm Beach County.

3. Evaluate the data sources utilized to prepare estimates at the Traffic Analysis Zone (TAZ) level. Could the team have considered any other data sources?

4. Why are TAZs used as the level of estimation? Why did the team use precinct level data for their alternative estimation methodology? Evaluate the use of these two estimation bases.

5. Review the principles of population estimates. How do they apply to this case?

6. This case was written for an audience of demographers. Given 10 minutes to make your public presentation, how would you explain the procedures undertaken to produce the estimates and new districts to the County Commissioners and the press?

Notes

This paper is based on a project supported by contract R89 814D between the Board of County Commissioners, Palm Beach County, Florida, and the Florida State University.

References

Florida Department of Health and Rehabilitative Services, various years. Florida Vital Statistics. Jacksonville: Office of Vital Statistics.

Sly, D.F., W.J. Serow, and S. Calhoun. "1989. Migration and the Political Process in Florida." *Florida Public Opinion.* 4:8–11 (Winter).

Smith, S.K. 1986. "A Review and Evaluation of the Housing Unit Method of Population Estimation." *Journal of the American Statistical Association.* 81:287–296.

Smith, S.K., and R. Bayya. 1989. "Population Estimates and Projections by Age, Sex and Race for Florida and its Counties, 1988–2000." *Population Studies.* 22: numbers 3–4 (passim) [Bulletin no. 89–90].

Smith, S.K., and B.B. Lewis. 1980. "Some New Techniques for Applying the Housing Unit Method of Local Population Estimation." *Demography.* 17:323–339.

―――. 1983. "Some New Techniques for Applying the Housing Method of Local Population Estimation: Further Evidence." *Demography.* 20:407–413.

U.S. Bureau of the Census. 1982. 1980 Census of Population. Number of Inhabitants: Florida [PC80-1-A11]. Washington: U.S. Government Printing Office.

―――. 1989. "Households Continue Growing Faster than Population, Census Bureau Reports." *United States Department of Commerce.* May 5, 1989 [CB89-73].

University of Florida. 1989. *Florida Estimates of Population: April 1, 1988.* Gainesville: Bureau of Economic and Business Research.

Word, D.L. 1989. "Population Estimates by Race and Hispanic Origin for States, Metropolitan Areas, and Selected Counties: 1980 to 1985." *Current Population Reports.* Series P-25, No. 1040-RD-1.

5

The Use of Population Estimates and Projections in the Court-Mandated Reapportionment of Los Angeles County

Nancy Bolton

In June 1990, Federal Judge David Kenyon ruled that the Los Angeles County Board of Supervisors had, in the 1981 redrawing of supervisorial districts, divided the Hispanic community in a manner that diluted Hispanic voting strength. By doing so, the judge ruled, the supervisors had denied to the Hispanic community of Los Angeles equal opportunity participation in the political process. To remedy this condition the judge ruled that the supervisorial district boundaries had to be redrawn in such a way that at least one of the five districts would have a majority Hispanic electorate. The judge further ruled that the new districts could be drawn using population estimates and projections produced earlier for the County of Los Angeles Department of Health Services. This author designed and implemented the model that had produced this population data—known as the PEPS (Population Estimate and Projection System) data—and subsequently served as an expert witness in the use of that data.

While population estimates had been used in other reapportionments, this was the first time that population projections had been so used. This case also constituted the most politically potent use of population estimates and projections, and its legal ramifications were far reaching. The county appealed Judge Kenyon's decision, but on November 2, 1990, the U.S. Court of Appeals upheld his ruling; on January 7, 1991, the U.S. Supreme Court refused to review the decision. These judicial actions contributed to giving a solid legal foundation to the use of demographic analysis in redistricting.

This paper describes:

- The issues that led to this use of estimates and projections.
- The PEPS data—how and why these estimates and projections were produced.

- The dilemma faced by the court over accepting the PEPS data.
- Issues for the future.

The Issues

The Political Setting and Timing of the Data

The Los Angeles County Board of Supervisors is composed of five members, one elected from each of five districts. Despite the growth of a large Hispanic community centered in the eastern portion of the county, the Board of Supervisors has never in this century had a Hispanic member. In the fall of 1989, a suit was filed in the United States District Court in Los Angeles seeking an immediate redrawing of the supervisorial districts in order to create a district with a Hispanic voting majority (*Garza* v. *County of Los Angeles*).

The plaintiffs charged that the 1981 redistricting produced gerrymandered boundaries which served to split the Hispanic community and thereby dilute Hispanic voting strength. The county contended that at the time of the 1981 redistricting it was not possible to draw a district that contained both 20 percent of the population and a Hispanic voting majority. Even though Hispanics represented about 27 percent of the county's population in 1980 and were in a reasonably compact community geographically, they had a low rate of citizenship; roughly half of the adults were citizens, and a large proportion of the population was under 18 years of age.

When the penalty phase of the trial concluded on April 18, 1990, the 1990 Census had already been conducted. Board attorneys argued during the trial that reapportionment should await the forthcoming census data (available in 1991), but the two supervisorial districts from which a majority Hispanic district might be carved were scheduled to elect their representatives in June 1990. Once elected, those representatives would, by law, serve until 1994. The plaintiffs argued that waiting for the census data would deny the Hispanic community representation for three years past the postcensus redistricting. If the plaintiffs objected to waiting for the new census data, why not use data from the 1980 Census instead? The reason lay in the explosive and uneven growth of Los Angeles County.

The Changing Demographics of Los Angeles

In 1990, the population of Los Angeles County reached 8.86 million people, having added almost 1.4 million residents since 1980. This increase was nearly equal to the entire population of a supervisorial district in 1980. In addition, the county had experienced substantial ethnic changes since 1980. Anglos and Blacks had been leaving Los Angeles County while Hispanics and Asians had been entering. Both the exiting and entering populations involved large numbers. Based on drivers license changes and immigration data, we can calculate that perhaps one-third of 1990's Los Angeles residents arrived after the 1980 Census—and that does not include the growth component of the population due to natural increase.

As a result, the Anglo portion of the county population has declined from 53 percent in 1980 to 45 percent in 1990. At the same time, the Hispanic portion of the population has increased from 27 percent in 1980 to 34 percent in 1990. The Asian portion of the population has risen from about 7 percent in 1980 to over 10 percent in the same years. As in previous decades, there was growth at the urban fringe; but unlike other decades, Los Angeles experienced a resurgence of growth in some of the older urban areas. Nearly 40 percent of this growth was due to increased household size.

Reapportionment Data

For reapportionment purposes, courts favor the conservative approach of using decennial census data rather than estimates. In this case, however, the 1980 Census was clearly obsolete. The plaintiffs, therefore, sought current data on age and race both to argue the issues and to redraw the district boundaries. The data, moreover, had to be available at the census tract level.

The relevant data was available from the Population Estimate and Projection System—PEPS. The PEPS projection data was especially valuable because it indicated growth trends and thus current concentrations. It should be noted that the drawing of district boundaries to form a Hispanic majority district was not a trivial task. Because of the low Hispanic citizenship rates, a district would have to be carved with a highly concentrated Hispanic population in order to obtain a Hispanic voting majority.

The California Election Code that permits interdecennial redistricting provides that the boundaries may be adjusted "on the basis of population estimates prepared by the State Department of Finance or the county planning department or planning commission, pursuant to section 35000." The PEPS data, while not prepared by the planning department, were being used for planning purposes by several county departments. In addition, the PEPS estimates used input data from, among other sources, the Department of Finance (DOF) and the U.S. Census Bureau.

The inclusion of these widely used sources of population information no doubt lent legitimacy to the PEPS estimates. In fact, it was probably the source of the PEPS data (Los Angeles County government) and the apparent consistency of the data with more widely regarded estimates (DOF and the Census Bureau) that caused the plaintiffs to choose the PEPS data and the court to rule in favor of using the data in reapportionment. In addition, the data had been produced before litigation began and thus was not suspect as politically motivated.

The PEPS Data

The Original Purpose

The PEPS project began in 1984. Its goal was to create a system to estimate and project the population of LA County by age, race, and sex for small geographic areas. The data was to be used primarily by the County Department of Health Services for health facility planning. Because the department provides services that range from pediatrics to geriatrics, it needed data by age, race, and sex. Because the department must provide service at the community level, it needed the data by census tract.

The original plan was to make a new set of estimates and projections every two years. Projections were always to be made for years ending in "0" and "5" for 15 years into the future. The first set of estimates, completed in 1985 (called PEPS 85), had an estimate for 1984 and projections for the years 1985, 1990, 1995, and 2000; the one-year projection is usually referred to as an estimate, but it was in reality a projection. The second iteration, completed in 1989 (called PEPS 87), had an estimate for 1987 and projections for 1989, 1990, 1995, 2000, and 2005.

Technical Features of the Data

The PEPS system begins by constructing a county-wide estimate of population distribution by age and sex for four ethnic groups: "White Non-Hispanic," "Black," "Hispanic," and "Asian/Other" (a group which combines Asians, Pacific Islanders, and all those who do not fit into the other three categories).

It should be noted here that the definition of Hispanics in the PEPS system is different from that in the census. For Blacks and Asians, race takes precedence over Spanish origin. Thus, Blacks and Asians who indicate Spanish origin are subtracted from the count of Hispanics and are counted with their racial groups. The reason for this classification relates to the original purpose of the PEPS data, namely for use in public health service planning. Since Blacks have a much higher mortality rate than Hispanics, it was deemed more important in health care planning to classify a person who is a mix of Black and Hispanic as Black.

In the Asian/Other group, the crossover of race and Spanish origin comes up most often with Filipinos. In 1990, about six percent of Filipinos in Los Angeles—a smaller percentage than in 1980—classified themselves as Spanish origin. The Filipino population of Los Angeles is much closer in educational and economic terms to the Asian population than it is to the Hispanic population. Thus, for public health service planning it seemed most appropriate to keep all Filipinos with the Asian subgroup.

As a result, the Hispanic population is labeled the "Latino" population in the PEPS data and consists primarily of non-Black and non-Asian people whose origins were in Mexico, Central America, and South America. Since this Latino population represents roughly 97 percent of the Hispanic population of Los Angeles, the two terms were used interchangeably throughout the redistricting trial.

The PEPS age groups comprise five-year cohorts up to age 75, except for the youngest group which is divided into children less than one year of age and children ages one to four years. Researchers independently estimate the county-wide distribution of these groups from two sources—vital records and the Current Population Survey (CPS)—using two years of data from each source. Each estimate is controlled to the county population estimate from the California Department of Finance (DOF) as of January 1 of the estimate year. Researchers then average the two estimates.

The control to DOF estimates is done for at least two reasons. First, the funds for many local governments in California are tied to DOF population estimates. Second, the DOF estimates are in turn tied to Bureau of the Census estimates of California's population. By tying PEPS to DOF estimates, we therefore have at least some consistency with the other widely used estimates.

We derive tract level estimates from linear regression equations based upon vital records, drivers licenses, and housing unit counts. The tract estimates of each cohort are controlled to the county-wide estimate of that cohort. The forecasts at both the county and tract level utilize a cohort survival model. The projected levels of migration and fertility have been based on observations of trends in those parameters since 1980 and on interviews with local demographers as to how those trends might change. The Appendix to this study provides a more detailed description of the entire procedure.

The Acceptance of the PEPS Data by the Court

The Dilemma

The Los Angeles case posed a dilemma. By 1989, the data from 1980 no longer accurately described the county's demographics, but there was no other reliable source of small area data that reflected the necessary ethnic detail. To my knowledge, none of the demographers participating in the trial (and there were many) argued that the 1980 Census data was appropriate for use in redistricting. The only question in the trial was whether to use the PEPS data or to wait for the 1990 Census. The answer hinged on whether the PEPS data was reliable enough to use for redistricting. My role in court was to give all the information I had about the data that would help to answer that question.

While my goal in producing the PEPS data was to be as accurate as possible, the PEPS data was not flawless. One serious problem emerged early in the trial. The plaintiffs had begun their case using the 1985 iteration of the PEPS estimates and projections, but during the process they shifted to using the 1987 iteration. Sometime in the late summer of 1989 we discovered that birth and death records from hospitals in two cities in Los Angeles County (Long Beach and Pasadena) were no longer being sent to the County Department of Health Services. At first we believed this to be a problem only for future iterations of PEPS—that it did not affect any past work. We ultimately determined, however, that those two cities had dropped out of the system in early 1987, which meant that the 1987 iteration was missing a considerable amount of data from two rather large and geographically concentrated areas. Pasadena has a population of about 132,000, and Long Beach has a population of 429,000.

The lack of birth and death records from Pasadena and Long Beach presented more of a problem for the tract level estimates than for the county-wide estimates. The tract level estimates were, of course, critical for redistricting purposes. The PEPS system cannot be easily converted to the state vital record system (which includes all LA County residents), and the missing data from these cities is difficult to bypass. If a Long Beach resident dies in a Beverly Hills hospital, the death will be reported; but a Beverly Hills resident who dies in a Long Beach hospital will not be reported. The fact that there was this spillover effect precluded us from simply treating the two cities as missing data points.

When the problem with the 1987 data came up in court, the plaintiffs quickly made an assessment of the PEPS data compared to other estimates available at the city level. Because many cities split census tracts and the PEPS data covered whole tracts, this comparison was an approximation. Due to lack of staff, we had never done a comparison of this sort. Table 5.1 presents a summary of that analysis by the plaintiffs. In the right-hand column I have added the 1990 Census figures for those cities.

Note the marked increase in the error rate of the 1987-based data, particularly in Long Beach and Pasadena. At the time of the trial I personally felt that for reapportionment purposes it would be better to use the 1985 estimates and projections because of the uneven effects produced by the missing data in 1987. The court ruled, however, that the 1987 data and the projections based on those data were a more accurate reflection of the population distribution than the 1980 Census and therefore were appropriate to use in the redistricting.

In retrospect, as I shall discuss later, the use of either set of projections had some inherent problems. In some ways it should not have been surprising that the PEPS estimates, especially the 1985 estimates, would be close to the Census Bureau estimates. While we do not control tract summaries to any level of geography other than the county total, the county totals at the estimate year are, after all, essentially the same for both the Census Bureau and the PEPS data. Moreover, both estimates rely on much the same data.

The fact that the missing data in 1987 produced a relatively small impact seems both a strength and weakness of the model. The missing data affected just one of the two years of death records used in the 1987 work, and the 1987 birth data had not been used at all because of other problems associated with those data. The small impact of the missing data could indicate that, due to all the controls

Table 5.1 Correspondence of PEPS to Census Bureau Estimates: Los Angeles County Cities over 100,000 Population*

City	1989 Estimate**	1990 Census
Los Angeles		
Census Bureau	3,377,000	3,485,000
PEPS	3,441,000	
PEPS % Difference	+1.9	
Long Beach		
Census Bureau	420,000	429,000
PEPS	85,000	
PEPS % Difference	−8.3	
Glendale	163,000	
Census Bureau	159,000	180,000
PEPS	−2.5	
PEPS % Difference		
Pasadena	133,000	
Census Bureau	125,000	131,000
PEPS	−6.0	
PEPS % Difference		
Torrance	139,000	
Census Bureau	136,000	133,000
PEPS	−2.2	
PEPS % Difference		
Pomona	121,000	
Census Bureau	124,000	132,000
PEPS	+2.5	
PEPS % Difference		
Inglewood	104,000	
Census Bureau	104,000	109,000
PEPS	0.0%	
PEPS % Difference		

*Santa Clarita, a Los Angeles County city with a 1990 Census population of 110,000, was not included because it was only recently incorporated.

**Using the 1987 series of projections.

imposed on it, the model is relatively insensitive to rapid changes. It certainly is an issue worth further study.

Despite these problems, and considerable testimony as to the limitations of data of this type, the court accepted the PEPS data as the data base for reapportionment. The plaintiffs used the 1990 projections from PEPS 87 to draw the new districts. It was probably the source of the PEPS data (Los Angeles County government) and the apparent consistency of the data with more widely regarded estimates (DOF and the U.S. Census Bureau) that caused the court to rule in favor of using the PEPS data in reapportionment. In the final analysis, the data's weaknesses were less important than the fact that the court regarded the PEPS data as reflecting the changes that had occurred since 1980.

Limitations of the PEPS Data

During the course of the trial several experts testified as to the limitations of the PEPS data. I shall review some of their criticisms and then evaluate them in the light of the original purpose of PEPS and the most recent evidence regarding the reliability of PEPS.

One criticism was that PEPS estimates are not controlled to any lower level of geography than the county. Given that we have no way of calibrating the reliability of the model in postcensus years, the errors may be increasing in an uneven pattern. This is a legitimate criticism and is something that we will consider when we modify the model in the future. Another criticism centered on the use of the residual method to estimate migration. Because the residual method assigns estimate errors to migration, those errors are propagated in the projections. Again, this is a legitimate criticism of the method.

While the PEPS model takes into account the different migration patterns of the four ethnic groups, it is clear that in an area like Los Angeles—with high volumes of migration—errors in migration assumptions can lead to distortions in the projections. In work that I am conducting at the UCLA Business Forecast Project, we have developed a similar model for California. We have spent considerable time looking at the effects of migration on the projections. We have separated migration into components and allowed the components to operate independently. The components we are using are domestic (U.S.) migration into the state, domestic migration out of the state, and immigration. Each of these components contains ethnic and age detail.

We have found that the projections are quite sensitive to changes in the relative contribution of these components. When net migration is zero there can still be large numbers of people leaving and entering an area. The age distribution of the components of migration is quite different, however. Over a period of a few years this population replacement can make a significant impact on the age and ethnic composition of the population.

In my analysis of the results of the projections for both Los Angeles and California, I have observed that a model using net migration tends to underestimate births and to overestimate deaths. This could, of course, be due to errors in the assigned fertility and mortality rates, and there is some evidence for this explanation. I also believe, however, that through migration both Los Angeles and California are maintaining a more youthful population than the models that use net migration would predict. Migrants out of Los Angeles tend to be older than migrants into Los Angeles. Therefore, even in a situation of zero net migration, which is the current situation in Los Angeles, we are still undergoing significant demographic changes. This situation, while not unique to Los Angeles or California, is probably more pronounced in our area than in most other regions of the country.

Finally, critics noted that the further out in time from the base year one projects the lower the reliability of the PEPS estimates and projections. While this is a valid criticism, it is a problem common to all estimates and projections. It is, in a sense, inherent in the methods of demographic analysis.

Comparison to the 1990 Census

The 1990 Census count for Los Angeles County was 8,863,000 people. The PEPS 87 projection for the county's 1990 population was 8,880,000 people, a difference of only 17,000 people. While the totals are extremely close, these figures do not validate the geographic distribution of the PEPS data. Preliminary results of the 1990 Census by city show that the PEPS 1990 projections for the urban fringe areas were generally too low. Construction activity in the newer suburbs of the northern part of the county was especially feverish in 1987, 1988, and 1989. Because the 1987 iteration picked up only a small segment of that growth, the 1990 projection tended to be low. This again is a problem that is inherent in projections; if actual trends do not follow assumed trends, then the projections do not match the outcome. If PEPS 87 failed to capture the growth at the edge of the county, then PEPS 85 missed it even more. In that sense, the 1987 projections—even with the missing data—were better to use.

The county asserted in its brief to the Court of Appeals that the PEPS data severely overestimated the population of the plaintiffs' Hispanic district. The 1990 Census showed that assertion to be true, though the error was not quite as large as the county had indicated. Table 5.2 shows the PEPS estimates of population compared to the actual 1990 Census counts. The districts shown are the districts created by the plaintiffs, using PEPS data, and approved by the court.

The largest error occurred in the Hispanic district, District 1—a 13 percent deviation from the ideal. The next largest error, an 8 percent deviation, took place in District 5, which is contiguous to District 1 on its northern boundary. District 5 contains rapidly growing suburban, and predominantly Anglo, communities like Palmdale and Lancaster. The underestimate in District 5 encapsulates two of the known types of errors in the PEPS system. Pasadena, one of the known problem

Table 5.2   Comparison of 1990 Census to PEPS 1990: Supervisorial Districts of
Los Angeles County

District	Ideal Population	PEPS 1990 Projection	1990 Census	Difference: Census Minus PEPS	Percent of Ideal
1	1,772,633	1,779,835	1,549,641	−230,194	−13.0
2	1,772,633	1,775,665	1,760,271	−15,394	−0.9
3	1,772,633	1,763,985	1,825,032	+61,047	+3.4
4	1,772,633	1,776,240	1,798,048	+21,808	+1.2
5	1,772,633	1,784,383	1,930,172	+145,789	+8.2
Total	8,880,108	8,863,164	−16,944		

Table 5.3   Comparison of 1990 Census to PEPS 1990 Projection: Population by
Ethnic Group in Los Angeles County*

Ethnic Group	PEPS 1990	1990 Census	Difference: Census Minus PEPS	Percent Difference
White/Non-Hispanic	3,534,283	3,634,722	+100,439	2.8
Black	976,812	967,835	−8,977	−0.9
Asian/Other	1,118,894	1,042,597	−76,297	−7.3
Hispanic	3,250,120	3,218.010	−32,110	−1.0
Total	8,880,109	8,863,164	−16,945	−0.2

*See "Technical Features of the Data" for definitions of ethnic groups. The census data
shown in this table were recalculated to conform to the PEPS definitions.

cities, is in District 5 (the other, Long Beach, is in District 3), and District 5 also
contains the areas where residential construction began to accelerate in the late
1980s. The reason for the overcount of population by PEPS in the Hispanic district (District 1) is not clear. A possible explanation lies in an overcount of Hispanics by the PEPS model, but comparison to the census does not lend credence to
that explanation.

Table 5.3 shows a comparison by ethnic group of the PEPS estimate with the
census in the county's population. The largest absolute error was an undercount of
the white population. The largest error on a percentage basis was an overcount of
the Asian population. These errors may have contributed to the overcount in District 1, but they are probably only a part of the problem. By underestimating the
number of housing units in District 5, we caused an overcount in each of the other
districts. Why that overcount was so concentrated in District 1, however, is not yet
clear.

What is clear is that data with validity at a large scale does not uniformly translate to data with validity at a smaller scale—even in areas as large as the supervisorial districts. This again points to caution in the use of estimates and projections in such precise work as redistricting.

Summing up, we can say that PEPS was intended as planning data. We envisioned that at each estimate year we would look for changes in trends in the data and that we would use such data changes as a guide to shaping our assumptions in the next set of projections. We planned to modify and fine-tune the model as users informed us of anomalies in the data. Redistricting called for a more rigorous use of the data than we had envisioned and in some ways a more rigorous use than we were prepared for in terms of experience in using the data.

For example, the growth of the Hispanic population in the San Gabriel Valley signaled a growing need for health care facilities in that region since utilization of county health facilities is high in the Hispanic community. Any overestimate by PEPS of population in that area did not change the need for additional health services facilities in the San Gabriel Valley. In redistricting, however, the distribution of population among districts must meet court-imposed standards of one-man, one-vote, and an overestimate of the Hispanic population in the area is much more critical. This does not mean that planning data should never be used for redistricting; rather, it means that one has to be sensitive to the difference in standards when evaluating its use. One has to be even more sensitive when using projections.

Issues for the Future

The Questions Raised

It is not clear that a Hispanic-majority district could have been constructed in 1980 within the constraint of having five districts of equal population. The difficulty was related to the low citizenship rates of Hispanic adults. The plaintiffs argued, however, that even in the absence of a clear majority in 1980, the county could have created a district that would have grown to a Hispanic majority during the decade, given the population trends. They contended further that the county should have foreseen the need to do so.

The Court of Appeals questioned whether governments have to anticipate demographic shifts when drawing district boundaries. Such a requirement would create a most difficult problem for governments (and full employment for demographers!). In its opinion supporting the plaintiffs, the court ruled that the use of predictive data had been sanctioned by the U.S. Supreme Court in its 1969 ruling in *Kirkpatrick* v. *Preisler.*

In that case, the Supreme Court had stated that "(s)ituations may arise where substantial population shifts over such a period (the ten years between redistricting) can be anticipated. Where these shifts can be predicted with a high degree of accuracy, States that are redistricting may properly consider them." This would seem to leave the burden of proof on plaintiffs to show that estimates or projections meet the "high degree of accuracy" test.

Although this constraint should temper the problem for government, other questions now must be answered. How accurate is a "high degree" of accuracy? How far into the future should projections be believed? Will there be liability if the projections prove wrong? If two projections differ, which one is to be believed and on what technical grounds?

The use of projections was not the only noteworthy demographic issue in this case. The county argued that the use of total population rather than citizen population estimates would create districts in which citizens had more political power than citizens in other districts. In the new (Hispanic-majority) District 1 formed by the plaintiffs, for example, there are fewer than 400,000 registered voters. In the suburban (largely Anglo) District 5, there are over 800,000 registered voters. Thus, every vote cast by a citizen in District 1 counts for more than a vote cast by a citizen in District 5. This may violate the equal protection (one person/one vote) requirement of the Constitution. In addition, the smaller electorate would make it less expensive to run a campaign in District 1 than in District 5—or even in District 2 where the Black population is concentrated.

Previous court decisions have allowed the use of either total population or eligible voters as an apportionment base, largely because the choice of base hardly mattered. But it matters greatly in California today. A ruling that citizens are the appropriate apportionment base would greatly compound the demographic complexities of redistricting. Although lower courts have ruled that the Constitution includes noncitizens in its reference to equal protection of "persons," the issue has not yet been resolved at the Supreme Court level.

The Expanding Role of Demographers in Court

The increased responsiveness of courts to ethnic considerations seems to be stimulating an expanding role for demographers. In California and other areas with rapidly changing ethnic patterns, this greater demand for demographic expertise in courts will no doubt continue during the current decade and beyond.

In jurisdictions with relatively stable populations, decennial redistricting with the 1990 Census will, most likely, still be the preferred redistricting method. The Los Angeles case is atypical in its combination of rapid change, timing of scheduled elections, and size of the community represented by the plaintiffs. In California, however, this situation may become a good deal more typical as a result of the growth and ethnic shifts expected throughout the decade. The same may be true in other places—notably the Southwest and East where large immigrant populations are concentrated. The Los Angeles case could well be a foreshadowing of what lies ahead, especially the growing need for technical demographic analysis to inform both courts and governmental agencies.

Conclusion

This case undoubtedly will lead to the increased use of estimates and projections for redistricting purposes. As professional demographers, we are all aware of the many limitations inherent in these data, but we will still need to provide the data to courts—and to make the courts aware of the data's limitations.

Demographers called on to use estimates and projections in litigation need a set of standards to guide the production and evaluation of these data. The creation of such standards is a formidable problem. In the case of the PEPS data, we relied heavily on vital records—especially death records—for making estimates. We chose such data as input for the model because the coverage was nearly universal and reasonably consistent. We did not use other available data—such as voter registration—because of the large fluctuations in registration that may accompany heated local elections.

Even vital records, however, are not without problems. For example, how will the AIDS epidemic affect the estimates in the PEPS model? Some demographers have eliminated AIDS-related deaths from their data base. Yet one has to consider that those patients who acquired AIDS through drug use would have been in a high mortality risk group even without AIDS. Therefore, we have not made any correction in our model for those deaths. We will have to address the AIDS issue in the near future, and we will have to change the model.

Record keeping and data sources change. The problem of cities missing in the vital records, discussed earlier, has not been resolved. It appears that we may have to modify the model to accommodate this problem as well. All this means that we cannot depend on having the same model over an extended period of time, and this in turn hinders tests of reliability. These kinds of issues will necessarily accompany the use of demographic estimates into court and represent an important area to be addressed by demographers in the future.

Discussion Questions

1. Explain the rules governing redistricting that are relevant to the decisions made in this case?

2. How would the composition of the Hispanic population make the case of dilution of voting strength difficult to prove?

3. Would you recommend the use of PEPS for boundary drawing?

4. In general, do you think that it is appropriate to use projections for redistricting? List the advantages and disadvantages. What are the legal implications? What are the demographic implications?

5. The issue of using eligible voters vs. total population as a base for apportionment raises important concerns in California. Are such concerns likely to intensify in other states as well? Why?

Appendix: An Outline of the PEPS Model

After estimates are made from the CPS and vitals data, the two distributions are merged to produce the final estimate. Prior to the merger, however, several adjustments are made to the individual estimates. In the case of the CPS, adjustments are made to the distribution prior to controlling it to the DOF estimate. Because the sample size is small (about 2200 households in each year) and we are dividing it into many groups, the number observed in the youngest group (less than one year) is erratic from year to year. The youngest groups (less than five years of age) are therefore weighted heavily toward the vitals estimate. Also, the oldest group (over 75 years of age) appears to be underestimated by the CPS. I suspect this is because the CPS does not cover the population in group quarters, thereby excluding those elderly persons in retirement homes. Again, the older cohorts are heavily weighted toward the vital records estimate.

Once a county-wide estimate is made the county-wide projections begin. The projection model is based on cohort survival that carries the population to January 1 of the next year in each cycle. Fertility rates are estimated in the base year (1980) and at the estimate year. Based on the observed trends, fertility rates are forecast for the projection period. In general, from 1980 to 1987, we observed declining rates for Hispanics and Asians, stable rates for white Non-Hispanics, and slightly increasing rates for Blacks. We currently believe, however, that fertility rates have changed direction since about 1986–1987, trending up in all ethnic groups.

Migration rates are calculated using the residual method—i.e., the 1980 population was aged to the estimate date using the mortality and fertility rates for 1980. That aged population was then compared to the estimated population. The differences in each cohort are assumed to reflect net migration. Based on that observation of net migration, migration rates are forecast for the projection period.

In the case of both fertility and migration rates, the observed trends serve as a guide to the forecasted rates but are not the only input. Interviews with local demographers and immigration officials also influence the forecasts. No employment or congestion constraints are applied in the model.

In both the 1985 and 1987 forecasts, the assumption was for a continuing decline in the fertility rates of Hispanics and Asians and a basically stable rate for Blacks and whites. Net migration was assumed to trend toward zero, with a decline of the in-migration of Hispanics, relative stability in the in-migration of Asians, and a gradual cessation of the out-migration of Blacks and whites.

The next step in the process is to make tract level estimates. The tract estimates employ 45 regression equations. The tract level estimates are made using only five age categories by sex and race. A separate estimate is made for each racial group as a whole and for the total population of the tract. The five large age cohorts are later apportioned into the smaller age cohorts based on county-wide distributions.

The tract level estimates use vital records, drivers license data, and housing unit counts. The equations estimate not the number of people but the proportion of the county population in that cohort residing in the tract. The equations are also designed to contain no negative terms (other than the intercept term). This means that we never predict a negative population.

After each cohort is estimated, the distributions are checked to make sure the male/female ratio is close to that observed in the census; tracts with large inmate populations may have sex ratios quite different than 1.0. The age distributions are checked for outliers. This checking is particularly extensive when the ethnic group is small. Due to the small size of the Asian population in most tracts in 1980, the regression equations with the lowest reliability (as measured by R^2) in the 1985 and 1987 estimates were for the Asian/Other group. In 1990, this will not necessarily be true since Asian population in Los Angeles now outnumbers the Black population. The sum of age cohorts of the Asian group are checked against the estimate of the total population for that group, and the difference is used to scale the cohorts toward that total.

Finally, the sum of all cohorts are compared to the estimate of total population in the tract, and the difference is again used to scale the cohorts toward the total population estimate. Once these checks are completed, each cohort is controlled to the previously estimated county total for that group.

Projections at the tract level are also done with a cohort survival model that projects the population to January 1 of the next year. Migration into or out of each tract is estimated for each ethnic group as a whole. Each estimate is calculated from the increase or decline in that group from the base period to the estimate period. The age distribution of migrants is assumed to reflect the age distribution of that ethnic group in the county. This assumption is based on the premise that most migrants within the county are residents of Los Angeles County.

County Department of Regional Planning projections of the future housing stock in 14 regions of the county are used to increase the housing stock over time in areas projected for increased development. Areas projected to gain new housing are allocated additional population to fill those units. At the end of each five years, cohorts are controlled to the county-wide projection for each cohort. That adjusted population is output and then serves as the starting point for the next five years, continuing until the end of the projection period has been reached.

6

Evaluating Boundary Changes for Discriminatory Effect

W.A.V. Clark

Boundary changes lie at the heart of litigation over political redistricting and school district desegregation. Although legally distinct, both political boundaries and school boundaries involve the interaction of demography and geography, and both create winners and losers. This chapter describes several cases in which demographic and geographic concepts were applied to changing electoral district and school attendance area boundaries. These cases illustrate the complexity of the issues involved and the nature of the techniques that demographers can use to evaluate the impact of boundary changes.

Why does boundary analysis matter? It matters, of course, in the same sense that careful analysis matters in all legal and political decision making. Demographers have an important role to play in advising the judiciary as courts undertake the process of adjusting and modifying boundaries. That courts have been able to choose between competing views on the importance of boundary changes is at least partly due to a lack of *spatial demographic* research. This lack of basic spatial demographic research has allowed the courts to rely on anecdotal evidence and has left them free to act as policy-making bodies rather than courts of adjudication.

Although the two common boundary issues now subject to litigation involve voting and school districts, any changes in boundaries and districts that produce unequal effects may, in the future, be the focus of legal proceedings. Future boundary and districting issues may involve access to health care, access to police and fire services, or the pattern of insurance ratings. Thus, the technical and conceptual tools discussed in this chapter can be generalized to a host of spatial contexts.

Electoral districts and school attendance zones get changed in cities that are changing. The change may involve the growth or decline in numbers of people, or it may involve a major alteration of the city's racial/ethnic composition. The focus of interest and concern is the impact of the boundary changes. Often, one side in a dispute will assert that a proposed boundary change will disadvantage some minority group (voters or students). The frequent assertion that boundary changes increase the proportion of minorities or dilute their numbers lies at the heart of boundary change disputes. The implication of such an assertion is that other political districts or school attendance plans could have been developed that would have produced much different results—e.g., results which would have been desegregative or would have fostered the ability of minorities to elect candidates of their own choice.

Rarely, though, is the issue that clear-cut. Boundary changes are made against a backdrop of changing demography and must be evaluated in the larger context of demographic change.[1] In the future, applied demographers will be called on to evaluate boundary changes for potentially discriminatory effect. Therefore, this paper examines a range of boundary changes and the extent to which each can be evaluated as discriminatory in order to provide a context and methodology for evaluating boundary changes. The specific cases to be considered include historical school attendance boundary changes in Charleston, South Carolina; student assignments in Belmar, New Jersey; attendance area changes in Topeka, Kansas; and the impact of changing supervisorial district boundaries in Los Angeles County, California.

Readers will readily see that the problem cutting across all these cases is a generic one: How do we divide up territory and show who gets affected? We shall see how quantitative analysis can help replace anecdotal evidence with more informed judgments about the supposed discriminatory effects of boundary changes and how adjusting boundaries in response to changing demographic circumstances often involves considerable complexity and subtle problems.

The Legal and Political Background

Political redistricting raises two legal questions: (1) whether the actual boundary drawing violates the equal protection clause of the Constitution (that districts should be approximately equal in voting power), and (2) whether there has been either dilution ("cracking") or overconcentration ("packing") of minority voters.[2] Analogously, changing school attendance areas raises questions about whether the changes are racially discriminatory in the organization of the "schooling space." In the case of political redistricting, it is the division of geographic space to create individual districts that empowers groups.[3] The division of the schooling space emphasizes the existing pattern of urban housing—i.e., the wealthy and poor areas of the city. In each instance several legal cases have established the standards and concepts to be used in redistricting and school attendance area adjustments.[4]

The following four cases involved the assertion that city and county representatives and defendant school boards adjusted voting district boundaries and school attendance boundaries to exclude the participation of minority voters and to concentrate minority children. All four illustrate the range of allegations and assertions that applied demographers will encounter in these disputes. This paper deals with how demographic analysis was used to evaluate the divergent positions in these cases.

In Charleston, South Carolina, one claimant stated that a previous combination of school districts was such that minority school attendance areas would emerge over time and that the combination was discriminatory in both intent and effect (*U.S.* v. *Charleston County School District and the State of South Carolina,* Civil Action, 1988, No. 81-50-8).

The Belmar School District in Belmar, New Jersey, sought termination of a sending-receiving relationship (i.e., changing the boundaries) with the nearby Asbury Park district. Plaintiffs responded that the termination would constitute de jure segregation in violation of the federal and state constitutions (*Belmar Board of Education* v. *Asbury Park Board of Education,* Office of the Administrative Law Judge, State of New Jersey Agency, 1987, H51-3/87).

In a further court hearing on *Brown* v. *Board of Education* (1954) in Topeka, Kansas, attorneys and experts for the minority plaintiffs claimed that "the primary effect of attendance boundary changes from 1967 to 1988 was the achievement of the goal suggested in 1975, i.e., fine tuning a system of racially separate provision of education services at the elementary level" (Lamson 1985).

In *Garza et al.* v. *County of Los Angeles Board of Supervisors* the plaintiffs claimed that "the 1981 County of Los Angeles supervisorial redistricting plan and predecessor plans were adopted and maintained for the purpose of diluting, minimizing, and canceling out Hispanic voting strength in violation of the rights of Hispanics as guaranteed by the Fourteenth and Fifteenth Amendments" (*Garza et al.* v. *County of Los Angeles Board of Supervisors,* CV88-05143KN, 1988, Plaintiff's statements of contested facts).

Boundary Changes and District Consolidation

In cases involving school district consolidation, plaintiffs generally assert that the actions of either the school board or some other group of officials generated patterns of racial imbalance across schools in a school district. The courts then must disentangle the direct intervention by state and local officials from the impact of demography to assess the uneven distribution of black and white students within a school district. Some observers are quick to assume (based on the history of de jure segregation in the South) that the decision to combine school districts and the particular combination that resulted were motivated by the desire to keep blacks and whites apart. Others deny such intent.[5] Thus, there often is a dispute, and the demographer is called on to determine the "truth."

Determining whether segregative effects or other racial impacts have been produced as a result of combining districts is far from straightforward. One approach is to calculate "before" and "after" measures of racial separation. What levels of racial separation prevailed before consolidation? What levels existed after consolidation? If the levels are similar (or if they have declined), the effect of the boundary changes would not appear to have been segregative.

Applied demographers can use two indices to evaluate such changes: the Dissimilarity Index and the Exposure Index. Both indices range between 0 and 1 (or 0 and 100 in percentage terms). An index value of 1 would indicate complete separation; conversely, a value of 0 would indicate that the distribution is even.

The Dissimilarity Index indicates the minimum proportion of blacks or whites who would have to change their area of residence (in this case the districts) to obtain even distribution of that race across all districts. The Exposure Index is a measure of how actual racial composition is seen from the perspective of an individual resident. Under complete separation blacks would meet (be exposed to) only other blacks, and under complete exposure they would encounter members of the other race at a rate equal to the city-wide proportion of that group.

Both indices provide useful measures of levels of separation, and both have been used widely in the social science literature (Massey 1989; Clark 1987). For our purposes their importance lies in their ability to detect change following the boundary changes in a district consolidation. If the consolidation placed all blacks together and all whites together, then the indices would increase. Conversely, a nonsegregated grouping would potentially decrease the indices.

The Charleston case provides a useful illustration. In 1986, the Charleston County School Board was sued to require further school integration. Earlier consolidation of several small districts, it was asserted, had been undertaken with the purpose of segregating children in Charleston County. In the complaint (and at the trial), plaintiffs asserted that the consolidation had been racially motivated. Defendants counterclaimed that the consolidation merely sought to group together small and inefficient districts.

Prior to 1951, Charleston County comprised 18 school districts. After consolidation it comprised eight districts (Figure 6.1). In the consolidation old districts 1, 7, and 8 were combined into a new district 1; 2 and 5 were combined into a new district 2; 11, 12, and 21 were joined into a new district 9; and 13, 15, 17, 18, and 19 were brought together to make up the new district 23. The larger districts of 3, 4, 10, and 20 were unchanged.

The court had to determine whether the districts were combined in such a way that racial separation increased. The applied geographer/demographer can make this determination by computing pre- and post-consolidation indices of dissimilarity and exposure as shown in Table 6.1[6] The results of such computations refute the assertion that combining the several small school districts increased the level of racial separation. In fact, the figures in Table 6.1 show that the consolidation decreased levels of separation (albeit slightly) and that alternative combinations or districts would not have achieved lower levels of separation.[7]

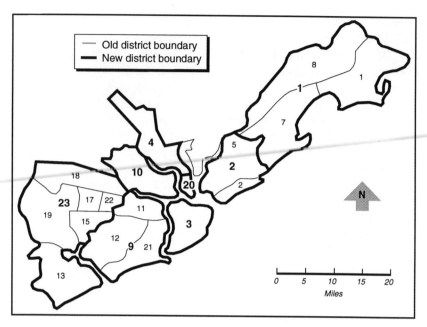

**Figure 6.1—School district boundaries in Charleston County before
and after the 1951 consolidation**

Student Assignments and Attendance Boundaries

A different type of school boundary issue arises when school districts are linked. The state of New Jersey has numerous small school districts. Those with only elementary schools usually have "feeding" relationships with one or more nearby local high schools to which their graduates go. The New Jersey school district of Belmar has such a relationship with two contiguous high schools, Asbury Park to the north and Manasquan to the south.

During the 1970s and 1980s, Asbury Park became a predominantly minority high school system; Manasquan, by contrast, remained approximately 95 percent white. The percentage of white students at Asbury Park declined from just over 30 in 1983/84 to 17 in 1987/88 (Table 6.2). During this same period (1983–1988), the percentage of whites from Asbury Park who attended the local high school declined from 27.1 to 15.2. The percentage of white students from Belmar at Asbury Park declined from 3.4 to 2.2.

In 1987, the Belmar School Board petitioned to sever the relationship with Asbury Park and send students only to Manasquan. The Asbury Park School Board petitioned the administrative law judge (who handles such disputes in New Jersey) to deny the request on the basis that severing the sending relationship would have a segregative effect. The disputing parties here were the school superinten-

Table 6.1 Charleston County School District Effects of 1951 Consolidations

Status	Dissimilarity Index	Exposure Index
1. Situation Prior to 1951 Consolidation Actions (18 separate districts)	.31	.14
2. Situation After 1951 Consolidation Actions (8 separate districts)	.29	.11
3. Alternative Plan A (Combine 3 and 20; combine 10 and 18)	.29	.10
4. Alternative Plan B (Combine 3 and 9; combine 10 and 18)	.29	.10
5. Alternative Plan C (Combine 3 and 20)	.29	.11
6. Alternative Plan D (Combine 3 and 9)	.29	.10
7. Alternative Plan E (Combine 3 and 10)	.29	.10

dents and school boards of Belmar and Asbury Park. The hearing—with expert witnesses including demographers, geographers, and psychologists—was held in 1987 to determine which side was correct.

The increase in minority enrollment at Asbury Park from 83.0 to 84.8 percent did not appear to be segregative; the school was already a predominantly minority school. But it was the changing composition of student transfers which suggested that the end of the sending relationship had produced little effect (Figure 6.2). Because more minority than white students were being allocated from Belmar to Asbury Park, by definition the relationship could not be desegregative.

Why were more minorities than whites from Belmar attending Asbury Park? The explanation has to do with the differential response rates by white and minority students assigned to the Asbury Park School System. While neither white nor minority students preferred to attend Asbury Park, a higher proportion of white students from Belmar assigned to Asbury Park failed to "show up" at the high school to begin ninth grade. In the last two years of the study, 80 to 87 percent of the white students from Belmar either moved or attended private school rather than enroll at Asbury Park. Fifty to 71 percent of Belmar's minority students did likewise (Table 6.3). These figures—higher than national "no show" rates (Rossell 1988)—reflect individual responses to imposed boundaries.

Although Asbury Park was already a predominantly minority high school and

Table 6.2 Enrollment Change in Asbury Park

Year	Enrollment in Asbury Park with Belmar Students		Enrollment in Asbury Park without Belmar Students	
	% Minority	% White	% Minority	% White
1983–84	69.5	30.5	72.9	27.1
1984–85	71.8	28.2	75.8	24.3
1985–86	77.0	23.0	79.9	20.1
1986–87	79.0	21.0	81.5	18.5
1987–88	83.0	17.0	84.8	15.2

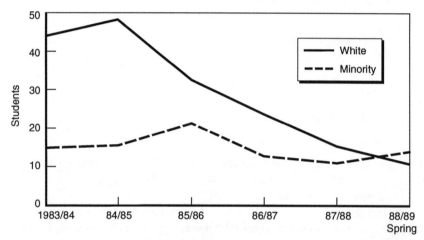

Figure 6.2—Belmar School District students assigned to and attending the Asbury Park High School

Table 6.3 Percent of Belmar Students Assigned to Asbury Park Who Did Not Enroll in Asbury Park

Year	White	Minority
1983–84	84	25
1984–85	81	50
1985–86	81	60
1986–87	87	71
1987–88	80	50

allowing the Belmar students to withdraw would have produced statistically insignificant impacts, the administrative law judge found for the plaintiffs, noting that despite small statistical effects the severing of the sending-receiving relationship would result in psychological harm to Asbury Park.

School Closing and Changing Attendance Areas

The issue of how school boards change attendance areas has always been at the center of debates over school board liability for segregated schools. School boards may be accused of gerrymandering boundaries to keep some schools "black" and others "white." Court findings at district and appellate levels contain numerous references to the effect of school boundary changes and optional attendance zones on the levels of separation in the schools (Wolf 1981). Of course, some schools lose pupils and others gain them as populations change within the metropolitan area. Over time, attendance areas must change, and some schools must close and others open. As always, the crucial question is: How can one determine whether the school closings and boundary changes are race neutral?

The following case study illustrates the geographer/demographer's role in assessing attendance area boundary changes. The Topeka School Board was accused of closing schools and making attendance area boundary changes that were segregative on the school system as a whole (see Clark 1987). The Topeka School Board denied that the changes were undertaken with the intent of racial discrimination.

To determine the merit of the case against the Topeka School Board, we need to measure the impacts of attendance area changes. Simply calculating the percentage of blacks or minorities in a school before and after a boundary change, though, is not satisfactory. An increase in the black population may reflect changing distributions of blacks or other minorities as well as the effect of the boundary change. Disentangling the two is critical to evaluating the impact of the boundary change.

Similarly, closing a school may increase the proportion of black or other minority students in other schools, but without an analysis of the sending and receiving relationships it is impossible to evaluate the overall impact of the school closing. The following illustrative analysis evaluated the impact of closing two schools and making changes in attendance areas of 12 schools in the Topeka School District from 1963–1964 to 1985–1986 (Clark 1987).

Both Monroe and Parkdale, two predominantly black schools, were closed between 1974–1975 and 1979–1980 due to declining enrollments. Monroe and Parkdale students switched to the nearest elementary schools, all of which experienced increases in the percentage of minority students (Figure 6.3). As the analysis will demonstrate, however, the overall impact both within the subset of schools and in the Topeka district was desegregative.

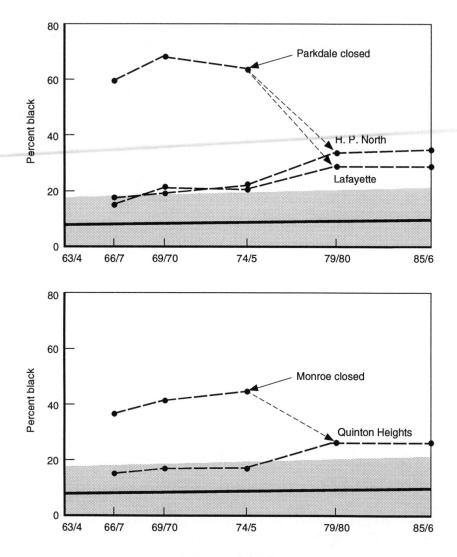

NOTE: The solid line and the shaded area represent the plus and minus 10 percent variation of the black proportion (10 percent) in the Topeka school system. It is a visual representation of the degree to which individual schools are disproportionately black.

Figure 6.3—Measuring the impact of school closing

The indices of dissimilarity and exposure can help us in capturing the overall impact of the many boundary changes and the two school closings. To reiterate, the indices—used to measure the extent to which the distribution of the black population is similar to or different from that of the white population—vary from 1.0 (for total separation of the races) to 0 (for a perfectly mixed racial distribution). The Dissimilarity Index measures racial balance while the Exposure Index is an attempt to measure the amount of contacts between racial groups.

Calculating the indices for the set of attendance areas over the period for which there are data both for the residential structure of the attendance areas and the schools provides an important way of compressing a large number of details into one table. The results are striking (Table 6.4). Both indices decline over time. Student populations and school attendance area populations examined in this study are moving toward greater racial balance and more interracial exposure. Not only do the 12 schools examined here show increasing levels of integration, but also the whole elementary school system is less segregated today than it was 20 years ago (Figure 6.4). The evidence does not support arguments of attendance boundaries gerrymandered for racial discrimination purposes. The indices do not show evidence of segregative boundary changes, and that was the finding of the district court (*Brown v. Board of Education of Topeka, Kansas* 1987: 49).

Drawing Boundaries and Minority Dilution

Boundaries are a critical element of the spatial organization of cities and the entities within them. Evidence of discriminatory boundary changes can be evaluated only with detailed statistical and demographic analysis.

Occasionally, demographics and politics run headlong into each other. The Los Angeles voting rights case is just such a case study. In this case the Mexican American Legal Defense Fund (MALDEF) and the U.S. Department of Justice brought suit to compel the County Board of Supervisors to create an Hispanic "seat." With the failure of an attempt to delay the redistricting until the release of 1990 census data, the case moved forward to a consideration of two main issues. First, could a 50 percent Hispanic district have been created in 1981 at the time of the last redistricting? And second, at that time and at earlier redistricting did the Board of Supervisors create boundaries intended to fragment the growing Hispanic population?

Most voting rights cases that involve a dispute over boundaries focus on whether the boundaries were drawn to (1) pack minorities into a single district in order to limit their power to influence the total electoral body, or (2) divide a concentrated minority community among several districts in order to dilute the power of the minority group. This issue of dilution was at the heart of the Los Angeles voting rights case. The district court judge and the appeals court concurred that the boundaries had split the concentrated Hispanic district in such a way as to re-

Table 6.4   Indices of Separation (Dissimilarity) for School and Residential
                    Populations for a Subset of Schools with Attendance Area Boundary
                    Changes in Topeka, Kansas

	School Enrollment by Attendance Area	Residential Population in the Attendance Area
1969–70	.39	.38
1974–75	.31	.32
1979–80	.25	.23
1985–86	.15	.22

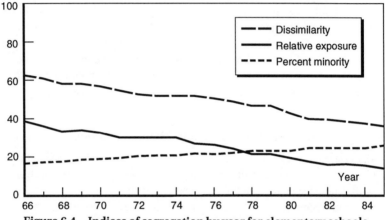

**Figure 6.4—Indices of segregation by year for elementary schools
in the Topeka School District**

duce the possibility that Hispanic voters could elect an Hispanic candidate (Clark
and Morrison 1991a; Clark and Morrison 1991b).

A plaintiff's report to the court contained anecdotal evidence supporting the
charge of discriminatory boundary changes. The report stated that "the repeated
rejection of cities in greater East Los Angeles (with significant Hispanic populations) by Third District (most Hispanic district) Supervisor Ernest E. Debs constitutes a racially discriminatory pattern … of largely successful attempts to minimize the Hispanic percentage of the population in the most Hispanic county
supervisorial district" (Kousser 1990, p. 1a).

What do the statistical measures reveal about the extent of dilution as a result
of the 1981 redistricting? Was the boundary between the First and Third districts,
which in 1981 split the Hispanic community, evidence of discrimination? M
oreover, how did previous boundary changes—and especially those in 1966 and

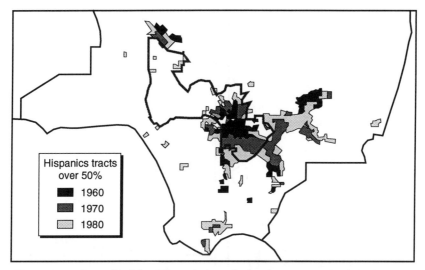

Figure 6.5—Growth of the Hispanic population in Los Angeles in reference to 1971 District 3 boundaries

1971—affect the proportions of Hispanics in the most Hispanic districts? And finally, did the redistricting of the Third District away from the growing core of the Hispanic population represent evidence of a racially discriminatory intent in reapportionment?

The answers to these questions are embedded in the demographic changes occurring in Los Angeles County. In 1960 the Hispanic population was 9.6 percent of the total county population; by 1970 it rose to about 18.3 percent. During the 1960s the "core" Hispanic area was within supervisorial District Three (Figure 6.5), but throughout that decade and the following one there was a significant demographic redistribution of the Hispanic population. By 1980 Hispanics constituted 27.6 percent of the county's total population.

It would not be unreasonable to expect that Hispanics would form a majority of the population in one of the five Los Angeles supervisorial districts. Yet, while Hispanics make up more than a quarter of the county's total population, they constitute less than 15 percent of the citizens of voting age within the county. This latter fact tends to undermine the plaintiffs' contention that district boundaries were designed to fragment the Hispanic core and the accompanying implication that without this fragmentation Hispanics would have been able to elect an Hispanic representative.[8]

How did the spatial expansion of the Hispanic population interact with the boundary changes? There were boundary changes between 1963 and 1966, 1966 and 1971, and 1971 and 1981 (Figure 6.6). The proportion of Hispanics inside District Three increased steadily (Table 6.5). The 1963–1966 boundary change

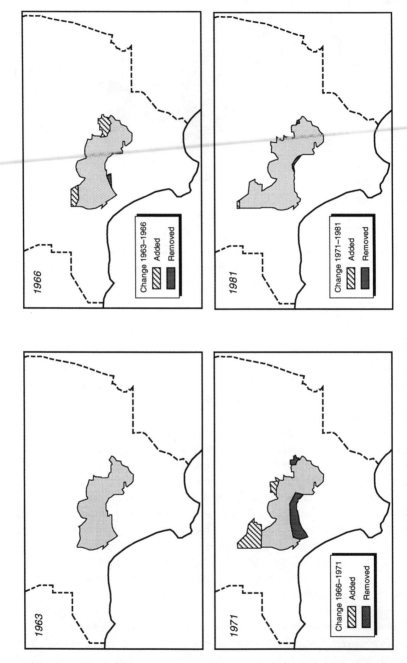

Figure 6.6— The changing boundaries of the third supervisorial district

was minor, but there was a significant increase in Hispanics in District Three—a clear result of demographic shifts. The number of Hispanics also increased in the 1966–1971 redistricting (a much larger spatial change than 1963–1966). By 1981 the percentage increase was almost ten points, but if the boundaries had remained unchanged (as they were in 1971) it would have been fractionally higher. That is, alternative boundaries could have been drawn to increase the Hispanic proportion.

Only the 1966–1971 boundary change was spatially extensive (Figure 6.6). In this instance a group of tracts in northwestern San Fernando Valley were added, and tracts adjacent to the black district were moved from District Three to District Two. What was the effect? Was there dilution? The impact of the spatial change was to increase the percentages of whites and Hispanics and to decrease the percentage of blacks (Table 6.6).[9] The percentage and absolute increase of Hispanics in District Three certainly provide no evidence of dilution.

But recall that if the 1971 boundaries had been maintained the Hispanic percent would have been marginally higher. The implication (and the assertion of the plaintiffs) is that alternative boundary adjustments would have increased the Hispanic proportion. The argument of discriminatory boundary changes thus turns into an issue of affirmative action rather than discriminatory action. While no doubt the boundaries could have been drawn to increase the Hispanic percentage in a modified District Three, the crucial question is whether the supervisors had an affirmative duty to do so.

The 1971 boundaries could not have been maintained because of one-person one-vote requirements. Two very different (from the existing) plans were developed that produced a district composed of nearly 50 percent Hispanics.[10] The decision to reject these plans and instead marginally alter the boundary to the north rather than to the east (where there were more Hispanics) presented a classic confrontation between politics and demography.[11]

Does the political structure have an affirmative duty to change the boundaries to take into account the changing spatial demography of ethnic groups? In this case the board tried to create a more Hispanic district in 1981, but it could not do so due to partisan political tradeoffs (*County of Los Angeles* v. *Garza,* Petition for Certiorari, p. 15). Each of the Republican and Democratic supervisors tried to gain a political advantage. While the Republicans tried to make District Three—with a sitting non-Hispanic Democratic supervisor—more Hispanic (and hence more Democratic), Democrats tried to make Republican districts more Hispanic and hence less Republican. With no agreement among the supervisors, the boundary (unchanged) which had not split the Hispanic concentrations in 1960 did so by 1981.

It can be argued that the extension of the Third District to the north showed discriminatory intent. It can also be argued that the boundary was evidence of a political stalemate. There is no clear evidence of statistical dilution, but there is evi-

Table 6.5   Hispanic Proportions in District Three Between 1963 and 1981

	1963 (1960 data)	1966 (1966 data) interpolated	1971 (1970 data)	1971 (1980 data)	1981 (1980 data)
Total	1,155,692	1,310,160	1,372,055	1,491,803	1,596,387
White	857,962	865,074	844,327	658,356	678,909
Hispanic	223,096	353,432	439,294	622,515	676,695
% Hispanic	19.30	26.98	32.02	41.73	42.49

Table 6.6   Impacts of 1966 – 1971 Redistricting on District Three*

	Total Population	White (percent)	Black (percent)	Hispanic (percent)
New Tracts included in District Three	202,107	168,516 (83.4)	735 (0.4)	28,843 (14.3)
Old Tracts excluded from District Three	114,697	82,219 (71.7)	17,762 (15.5)	9,362 (8.2)
Net Change	+87,410	+86,297	–17,027	+19,481

* The changes were principally between District 2 (the majority black district) and District Three.

dence of a lack of affirmative action. Apart from the issue of whether such affirmative action might be a racial gerrymander (Montague 1988), this case illustrates perfectly the boundary drawing dilemma.

Conclusion

These case studies show how in some cases statistical/spatial analysis is straightforward and can clarify our understanding of the impacts of boundary changes. But they also show that in other cases—even where the quantitative analysis casts doubt on simple anecdotal assertions of dilution—the confrontations of politics and demography cloud any simple solution. The evidence from the voting rights case in Los Angeles certainly highlights the care with which political bodies must examine the claims of minority groups.

Boundary changes are not invariably discriminatory, although some stakeholders consistently discern such effects. All four cases reviewed here emphasize the need for careful, nonanecdotal analysis of claims of discriminatory boundary changes. In general, we must insist on more intensive quantitative demo-geographic analysis of boundary changes. Perceptions of the law and legal process could alter dramatically as *spatial analysis* (my emphasis) exposes gaps in the legal system (Blacksell et al. 1980, p. 387). When adversarial proceedings are set in motion, the judiciary becomes involved in the oversight of managerial actions (Johnston 1981, 1983); as interpreters and arbiters, the judiciary play a crucial role in altering spatial arrangements. Thus, it is critical for demographers and geographers to provide a full range of analysis for the arbitration process.

Discussion Questions

1. Compare and contrast political redistricting and boundary changes involving school districts.

2. What are the inherent limitations of the Dissimilarity and Exposure indices? Which limitations are important for each situation featured in this essay?

3. What kind of data are needed to construct these indices?

4. How much can you evaluate the results of the court decisions, given the information provided for each case?

5. Are there other methods that you would use to analyze these cases?

6. What demographic changes in Charleston County may have contributed to the complaint that the consolidation of districts was racially motivated?

7. Compare the legal question in each case. How do these compare to the legal questions raised in the redistricting cases?

8. Suppose plaintiffs retained you to help them seek to reverse each of these court decisions. How would you go about constructing evidence, and how would you present it?

Notes

1. This issue is not new. Sheldon and Glazer (1965) in a study of attendance areas in New York concluded that even constant changes in attendance lines are unlikely to promote large-scale ethnic balance. With increasing proportions of minority children attending the city public schools and increasing geographic extensiveness of ethnic ghettos, no amount of boundary changes will integrate schools.

2. In a new significant number of cases the redistricting or lack of redistricting has led to extensive litigation (Thernstrom 1987). Central to past cases of litigation have been plaintiff assertions that boundaries have been drawn in order to dilute the voting power of minorities.

3. In their study of Mobile, O'Loughlin and Taylor (1982) emphasized the importance of the way in which the superimposition of district boundaries on the "spatial mosaic" of voting blocks (social classes, ethnic and racial groups, etc.) determined the success and failure of these groups. The boundaries are what determine who is in and who is out and so become critical in the districting process. (O'Loughlin and Taylor 1982, p. 324)

4. In the political arena, *White* v. *Regester* (1973) specifically addressed gerrymandering (boundary drawing) that discriminated against a racial minority. *Gingles* v. *Edmisten*

(1984) and *Thornburg* v. *Gingles* (1986) did likewise and also addressed the issues of multi-member districts and polarized voting. These cases and the Voting Rights Act of 1982 have set out the criteria to be used in redistricting. These criteria include such geographic phenomena as the integrity of political units, the desirability of "spatial" compactness, and the recognition of communities of interest. In school desegregation a similar structure of cases outlines the issues of changing attendance areas and school siting. In particular, *Keyes* v. *School District No. 1* (Denver) identified the role of attendance zone manipulation as a force in creating school segregation. *Brinkman* v. *Gilligan* (1976) identified school closing and site selection as school practices that allegedly maintained and expanded the segregated school system. *Penick* v. *Columbus Board of Education* (1978) identified findings of the potential discriminatory effects arising from attendance line drawing and optional attendance zones.

5. Indeed, in the Charleston case noted above, the plaintiff's brief stated: "The effect of the 1951 school consolidation was to create black and white districts within Charleston County." Similarly, plaintiffs in Topeka (in additional litigation over *Brown* v. *Board of Education*) alleged boundary gerrymandering in the creation of black and white attendance areas (Clark 1987).

6. The indices can be computed as shown in the Appendix to this paper.

7. When units are combined it is possible that the index will decrease as a result of aggregation. The point here, however, is that separation as measured by these "administrative"—not statistical—units did not increase.

8. Two points should be emphasized, one demographic and one political. First, it was impossible to create a district in 1980 (and it still is today) that had a majority of Hispanic citizens of voting age. Second, the Hispanic coalition in 1981 refused a concentrated Hispanic district (*Garza et al.* v. *Los Angeles County Board of Supervisors,* R.R. 1-3-90. pp. 67–73).

9. The shift of the black population maintained the proportion black in District Two.

10. The Hoffenblum Plan had 50.2 percent Hispanic (31.0 percent Hispanic citizens of voting age), and the *Californios Plan* had 40.4 percent Hispanic (30.4 percent Hispanic citizens of voting age).

11. The changes were principally between District Two (the majority black district) and District Three.

References

Backstrom, C.H. 1982a. "Problems of Implementing Redistricting." In *Representation and Redistricting Issues*. B. Groffman, A. Lijphart, R. McKay and H. Scarrow, eds. 45–53. Lexington, MA: Lexington Books.

——. 1982b. "The Practice and Effect of Redistricting." *Political Geography Quarterly.* 1:351–359.

Blacksell, M., C. Watkins, and K. Economides. 1986. "Human Geography and Law: A Case of Separate Development in Social Science." *Progress in Human Geography.* 10:371–396.

Clark, W.A.V. 1982. "The Social Scientist as Expert Witness." *Environment and Planning A.* 14:1468–1470.

——. 1987. "Demographic Change, Attendance Area Adjustment and School System Impacts." *Population Research and Policy Review.* 6:199–227.

Clark, W.A.V., and P.A. Morrison. 1991a. "Demographic Paradoxes in the Los Angeles Voting Rights Case." *Evaluation Review.* 15:712–726.

_____. 1991b. "Postcript: Should the Court Rely on Postcensal Estimates for Redistricting." *Evaluation Review.* 15:727–728.

Johnston, R.J. 1976. "Spatial Structure, Plurality Systems, and Electoral Bias." *Canadian Geographer.* 310–328.

_____. 1981. "The Management and Autonomy of the Local State: The Role of the Judiciary in the U.S." *Environment and Planning A.* 13:1305–1315.

_____. 1983. "Texts, Actors and Higher Managers: Judges, Bureaucrats and the Political Organization of Space." *Political Geography Quarterly.* 2:3–19.

Kousser, J.M. 1990. *Report for the Garza Case.* Los Angeles, unpublished.

Lamson, W. 1985. "Race and Schools in Topeka, Kansas." Unpublished report to the court.

Massey, D., and N. Denton. 1989. "Hyper Segregation in the U.S. Metropolitan Areas: Black and Hispanic Segregation along Five Dimensions." *Demography.* 26:373–391.

Montague, B. 1988. "The Voting Rights Act Today." *American Bar Association.* August: 52–57.

O'Loughlin, J., and A.M. Taylor. 1982. "Choices in Redistricting and Electoral Outcomes: The Case of Mobile, Alabama." *Political Geography Quarterly.* 1:317–339.

Rossell, C. 1988. "Is it the Bussing or the Blacks?" *Urban Affairs Quarterly.* 26.

Sheldon, E., and R. Glazer. 1965. *Pupils and Schools in New York City.* New York: Russell Sage Foundation.

Thernstrom, A. 1987. *Whose Votes Count?* Cambridge: Harvard University Press.

Wolf, E. 1981. *Trial and Error.* Detroit: Wayne State University Press.

Appendix

Two indices of separation are commonly used to assess levels of integration. Both indices, the Dissimilarity Index and the Exposure Index, range between 0 and 1. An index value of 1 would indicate complete separation, and, conversely, a value of 0 would indicate complete balance in the distribution. The Dissimilarity Index (D) is used to compute the difference between the numbers of blacks and whites in some unit—for example, a census tract or a school in a metropolitan area. The index indicates the minimum proportion of blacks or whites who would have to change their area of residence or school in order to obtain an even distribution of that race across all subareas. It can be expressed as

$$D = \frac{1}{2} \sum_{i=1}^{n} \left| \left(\frac{b_i - w_i}{B - W} \right) \right|$$

where

b_i is the number of black students in a school (or tract)

w_i is the number of white students in a school (or tract)

W   is the total number of whites in the schools (tracts) in the system—in this case, region

B   is the total number of blacks in the school (tracts) in a region

The second index, the Exposure Index, is a measure of how actual racial composition is seen from the perspective of a typical white or black person. The exposure measure (E) is a description of one group's isolation from or potential for interaction with another group. Under complete separation, blacks or nonblacks would meet only other blacks; under complete exposure, they would encounter members of the other race at a rate equal to the city-wide proportion of that group. The Exposure Index, usually calculated in its relative form, is, in effect, taking into account the total number of the minority race whereas the Dissimilarity Index does not. It is this difference that accounts for the reversals in the trends as measured by the two indices.

The exposure index can be expressed as

$$E = 1 - \frac{B_w}{W/T}$$

where

$$B_w = \frac{1}{B} \sum_{i=1}^{n} \left(b_i \frac{w_i}{T_i} \right)$$

and where, in addition to the previously defined terms, T is the total population and T_i is the total population in a school or tract.

Discussion Questions
for Part Two

1. Explain how the redistricting cases followed the rules of redistricting. Outline and compare the major policy issues in each case.

2. Did the resources used for population estimates vary by the type of legal challenge or redistricting purpose?

3. Examine cases in which the 1965 Voting Rights Act applied. Were the preconditions of the Act met in each case?

4. Compare the legal questions raised in political redistricting and school boundary changes.

5. How does the role of the demographer in chapter 4 differ from that in chapters 3 and 5?

PART THREE

Markets

7

Improving Cellular Market Area Valuation with Demographic Data

George H. Billings and Louis G. Pol

Recent reports concerning the widely publicized buyout of LIN Broadcasting Corporation by McCaw Cellular Communications Inc., were laden with figures regarding the value of the markets being purchased (e.g., Hof 1989). For approximately $6.3 billion, McCaw acquired about 18 million potential customers to add to the 50 million it already had. By one estimate, McCaw paid about $350 per potential customer (POP) and took on $1.8 billion in long-term debt to do so.[1] The $350 per POP was about $100 higher than any previous purchase price.[2] As some analysts have noted, in order for the investment to pay off, the industry must experience significant growth. While less than 2 percent of Americans use cellular telephones today, the model McCaw used to justify the LIN purchase price reportedly assumes 15 percent usage by the turn of the century.

Other markets have sold for and are valued at considerably less money per POP. Centel's $796 million acquisition of United Telespectrum in 1988 worked out to be $85 per POP. A 1989 Donaldson, Lufkin, and Jenrette report valued existing MSA markets from a high of $230 (e.g., Los Angeles and New York) to a low of $100 (e.g., Athens, Georgia and Glenn Falls, New York) per POP (Gross 1989). A more recent Bear Stearns report predicts that the range for Rural Service Area (RSA) valuations in the near future will stretch from less than $40 up to $250 (Leon 1989). Moreover, it has been reported that most cellular stocks are selling for $110 to $125 per POP (Leon 1990).

This wide range in market valuations clearly indicates that not all markets are valued the same even when population size differentials are accounted for. It is surprising, therefore, that for many analysts the industry standard in valuing a market simply involves multiplying the population size by some per capita dollar value. One earlier industry study attempted to compare two demographically different (size and growth) markets in order to improve the evaluation of markets; that study's methods, however, have not been adopted by the industry (Sanders 1987).

The industry standard of POP obscures such individual factors of target customers as age, occupation, industry classification, or income level. On the aggregate side, industry structure, the number of households, and the number of automobiles should be—among many other factors—indicators of a market's worth. Determining the dollar value depends upon a host of factors, including the costs of procuring and maintaining the network equipment needed to provide cellular service and the costs of subscriber acquisition.

Another critical part of arriving at an appropriate dollar value involves estimating how many persons in the population reasonably can be expected to become cellular customers. Making this kind of an estimate is a much more difficult task than assessing current subscribership because, given some analysts' projections that penetration will expand more than 13 points during the next ten years, penetration must occur among groups that are not presently using cellular. Some data on the characteristics of current cellular customers do exist, however, and these figures indicate that not all POPs are created equal. That is, usage rates are highest among several very narrowly specified demographic groups. The following case presents some procedures for improving/refining POP by looking beyond population size to the characteristics of the population being studied.

The need for such information should be apparent to all. Whether one considers an existing cellular service provider growing through acquisition (e.g., McCaw buying LIN or GTE agreeing to pay $710 million, more than $189 per POP, for the Providence Journal cellular properties) or a new RSA that is weighing development against sale of its FCC license, the stakes are high. What we need are improved methods for determining the differential value of a POP within a given market area.

For example, two urban or rural areas both containing one million persons with approximately the same population density and topography might be valued equally. A per POP figure of $200 would yield a $200 million valuation. If, however, one market were considerably different from the other in that it contained a very high proportion of persons who were not likely to purchase cellular services, then that market should be valued lower.

It is our contention that the difference in valuation is quantifiable. Furthermore, we hold that when these markets are valued, data regarding projected demographic change should be included. Consider the previous example. While the two markets might be the same size in current POPs, population projections for the year 2000 may show that one area's population count will be stable while the other will add 50,000 persons. If all other factors were to remain the same, the market with the growing population would be worth substantially more.

The current and future dollar value of any business, of course, are largely a function of projected cash flow, discounted at a rate that reflects the degree of risk in the business. In cellular, future cash flows are most highly correlated with subscribership—that is, with market penetration. Subscribership can be expected to vary substantially according to the demographic characteristics of the markets.

A 35-year-old investment banker is a more likely subscriber than is an infant or a pensioner; the POP convention obscures such quantification of the real target market.

Projected penetration rates and demographics would appear, therefore, to have a major impact on several significant decisions in the cellular industry. Consider investors' decisions affecting the billions of dollars in public and private cellular equity values or the lending decisions of bankers. The cash flow projections of both investors and bankers must reflect reasonable penetration rates—not so much of the total population but rather of market segments that reasonably can be expected to buy cellular in the future.

Consider, as well, a major automobile manufacturer weighing an investment in either a factory or a dealer cellular program. Presumably, the manufacturer would find value in thoughtful aggregate penetration projections that would affect order quantities and program profitability. In other words, the manufacturer would want to know what the absolute cellular market penetration is likely to be during the forecast period. From a demographic and program management point of view, the manufacturer would probably find the relative penetration by market segments even more critical.

Most likely, the manufacturer has a refined profile of the buyers of each of its product lines. Comparing the buyer profiles with the demographic profiles of prime cellular target customers would allow more enlightened program management regarding, for example, the setting of priorities for timing (i.e., roll-out) and for investment of scarce resources (e.g., promotional dollars) among the manufacturer's different automobile models.

The Industry

After years of deliberating about and experimenting with cellular markets, the Federal Communications Commission (FCC) began allocating radio frequencies and associated operating licenses to cellular carriers in 1983. Not having enough frequencies to grant licenses to all interested parties and not wanting to create a single license monopoly structure, the FCC decided to award licenses to two competing carriers in each of 305 Metropolitan Statistical Areas (MSAs) and 428 Rural Service Areas (RSAs) throughout the United States.

Typically, the local telephone company operating in the market (the "wireline carrier") owned one licensee; the other duopolist initially was an independent nontelephone company (the "nonwireline carrier"). Today, many nonwireline cellular carriers are owned by major wireline telephone companies as a result of the major carriers acquiring companies operating outside their home regions. In Washington, for example, Southwestern Bell competes as the nonwireline Cellular One against the Bell Atlantic wireline cellular company.

The eagerness of many regional Bell telephone operating companies, of GTE, and of independent cellular operators like McCaw to grow through acquisition has been fueled, in part, by the spectacular growth of the cellular industry. Part of that growth is a product of the FCC's allocation of licenses to new geographic areas and the subsequent introduction of cellular services to new prospects as systems begin operations, or "go on line." While just two markets were operating in 1983, nearly all MSAs offered cellular by the end of 1989. Virtually all 428 RSAs are expected to have service by mid-year 1992. Figure 7.1 traces the growth of the industry.

Consumers have exhibited a tremendous appetite for cellular service. Figure 7.2 depicts that growth. From 92,000 subscribers at year-end 1984, the industry grew to 5,283,000 subscribers at year-end 1990, a compound annual growth rate of 125 percent!

Figure 7.3 presents revenue data. Service revenues grew from $178 million in 1984 to more than $1.9 billion in 1989, a compound annual growth rate of 61 percent! Figure 7.4 charts capital investment in cellular. Cumulative cellular capital investment approached $4.5 billion by mid-year 1989, and the industry continues to show exceptional growth by any standard.

Many observers question how long the industry can sustain its spectacular growth. Naturally, the future rate of growth will depend in large measure on consumers' perceived need for the service, their ability to pay, the utility they derive from cellular service, and related factors. If adequate data are available, thoughtful demographic analysis should be able to illuminate reasonable penetration rates over time.

The Client

The client—a group of investors considering the purchase of two neighboring cellular properties—faced four options: buy one market, buy the other market, buy both properties, or pass on the opportunity entirely. Each property was priced at $200 per POP. Underlying the price quote were two key assumptions. First, it was assumed that market penetration would reach 9 percent of the total population within five years; that is, penetration would be 9 percent of POPs. Second, it was assumed that average revenue per customer would continue at the 1989 level of approximately $82 per month.

Taken together, these two assumptions implied that subscriber growth would continue among presumably more price-sensitive segments without any corresponding decline in average revenue per subscriber—i.e., that demand was not price elastic. Otherwise, these assumptions implied that relatively price-insensitive subscriber prospects would exist in sufficient numbers to support the 9 percent penetration projection without any reduction in average revenue per customer.

Data and Methods

To estimate the value of a cellular market, one needs a wide assortment of data. While some of these data are a part of estimation methods currently in use, many

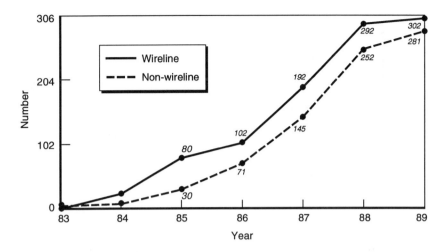

Figure 7.1—MSA's on-line per year (wireline and non-wireline carriers)

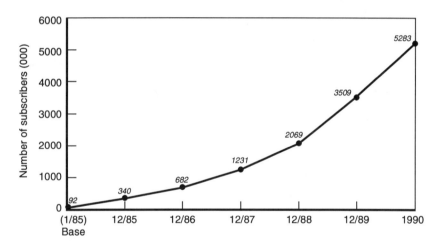

Figure 7.2—United States cellular telephone subscribers

are not. As Figure 7.5 shows, the information needed can be grouped into three categories—though these aggregations are highly interdependent. Under "Customer," we have aggregated type of use (business or personal) with the demographic characteristics of present and future user groups and the extent of use (calls per day and minutes of use per call).

"Industry" contribution includes the technological factors and the regulatory environment that drive the availability of services. Also relevant are market factors such as product substitution (e.g., beepers) and product penetration. Elements of the "Market Environment" include competitors (competitor aggressiveness

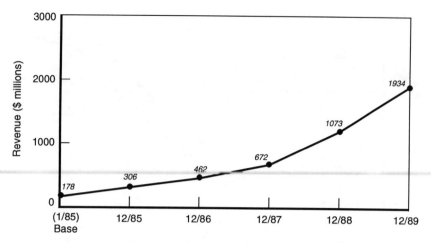

**Figure 7.3—United States cellular telephone service revenues
($ millions)**

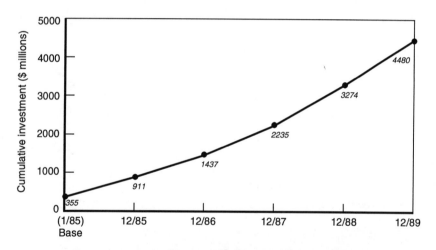

**Figure 7.4—United States cellular telephone cumulative
capital investment ($ millions)**

and penetration), topography (which determines to some extent the equipment required), and the cost of equipment and maintenance needed to deliver services.

In addition to the foregoing data, one needs information regarding churn and roaming. Churn refers to the fact that many subscribers choose to discontinue service. Unlike telephone services—where the current residential market consists essentially of last year's customers minus deaths and out-migrants plus new households—this year's cellular market does not contain virtually all of last year's customers.

Customer	Industry	Market environment
Type of user demographics	Technological advancement	Competitors
Demographic change	Regulatory environment	Topography
Usage propensity		Cost of equipment/ maintenance
	Churn	
Increase in usage		
	Product substitution	
Characteristics of potential customers	Product penetration	

Figure 7.5—Information required for sufficient market valuation

Historically, churn data have not been available for the industry as a whole, but information on disconnects is now available from Cellular Telecommunications Industry Association (CTIA) surveys. In December 1988, there were about 2.1 million cellular subscribers in the United States. During 1988, there were 263,000 disconnects—or about 13 percent of the subscriber figure (Leibowitz, Buck, and Gross 1989). Some industry experts argue that churn is decreasing as a response to lower equipment and service costs, though such a decline has not been documented.

Roaming traffic refers to persons who utilize the service of another cellular provider as they drive into another area from out of their home service area. CTIA estimates show that roamer traffic now accounts for 18 percent of all revenue nationwide (Roscoe and Wallace 1989). Furthermore, roamer revenue is increasing faster than total revenue (Hill 1989).

Ideally, all of these data would be both available to and utilized by analysts who make market valuations. Unfortunately, many points of information are either incomplete or nonexistent. Furthermore, some existing data are not used at all. The process of creating and utilizing these types of data in the valuation of a market is, as a consequence, in the early stages of development.

While we can get relatively good and current data regarding the number of cellular customers, these data have serious shortcomings. Aggregate customer counts are difficult to maintain because of the high level of churn that is occurring. As a result, while growth in a particular market area could be 5 to 10 percent over a relatively short period of time, the number of continuous customers would be smaller. Analysts must consider churn seriously when estimating market value. If a large proportion of those included in the decision to purchase cellular services are just curious and do not become sustaining customers, then actual growth rates will be substantially lower.

What is known about the characteristics of people who subscribe is yet another factor affecting data quality. Typically, customer account data include industry affiliation (i.e., SIC code) and the information required for credit and billing purposes. Some carriers capture data on subscribers' titles, company sizes, and makes of cars, for example; but data sets often are incomplete within a single company's records. Confident comparisons among carriers are, therefore, virtually impossible.

More detailed demographic and use data for both individual and corporate subscribers must be obtained via surveys. Again, however, survey methods are complicated by the high level of churn (along with the typical problems encountered in these types of research activities). While many of the larger cellular providers have conducted surveys of current customers, all of these efforts have produced lower-than-desirable response rates.

Typical surveys gather information about customer demographics, cellular use and ownership, customer service, media usage, and level of satisfaction with service. Demographic inquiries include those for occupation, industry worked in, gender, age, income, and education. Additional data may also be gathered regarding company worked for, sales, size (number of employees), and number of company cellular phones.

The data we used came from separate surveys conducted by three of the largest cellular service providers in the country. Although the companies represent a substantial degree of geographic diversity, we would not argue that they are "representative" of the nation as a whole. The surveys, moreover, were dissimilar in methodology and each contained different inquiries. We selected the items that were best suited to the analysis at hand. The remaining data came from demographic sources—e.g., population size and compositional data from the 1980 Census of Population and Housing, statistical abstracts, and other sources identified in the analysis section.

Analyses

Our analysis begins simplistically, using POP as the measure of comparison. For illustrative purposes, we selected two counties in Florida—Orange (Orlando) and Sarasota (Sarasota)—treating each as a distinct market. We designed each component of the analysis to assess the "reasonableness" of the 9 percent penetration assumption, though some components also focus on intermarket comparisons.

Population Size

In 1986, Orange County's population was 575,200, Sarasota's 247,600—a ratio of about 2.32. Assuming a figure of $200 per POP, the Orange County market was worth about $115 million and the Sarasota County market nearly $50 million. The simple product of population (POP) and dollars per POP provides the initial parameter of a market's value. The differences in population go beyond 1986 size, however.

Utilizing population projections (the U.S. Census Bureau's middle series) for the year 2000, we projected Orange County's population to be 807,300 in that year as compared to 328,600 for Sarasota—a ratio of 2.46. This 6 percent increase over the earlier 2.32 ratio is an indication that the initial POP analysis masked some of the differential in potential growth and, therefore, value between the two market areas. Based on projected POPs in the year 2000, and assuming a value of $200 per POP (1986 dollars), the Orange County market would be valued at $161 million as opposed to $66 million for Sarasota.

Assuming $200 per POP for both markets, however, raises two issues. First, the assumption implies that the POPs in each market will be roughly equivalent, exhibiting equal propensity to buy cellular services. Second, assuming a per POP value perpetuates the basic problem with the POP convention: "Dollars per POP" should be the result of dividing the discounted cash flow valuation of the given carrier's business by the market population; it is not an input that drives the valuation.

Composition

Table 7.1 contains data (collected by a leading cellular carrier) on the demographic characteristics for a sample of cellular subscribers. The table shows how the distribution of subscribers varies markedly by income, age, gender, and occupation. In terms of age, nearly 70 percent of the subscribers are between 25 and 44, and nearly 90 percent are between 25 and 54. Returning to our 9 percent total penetration assumption, we can ask: "Given the age structure of both markets, is it reasonable to expect such penetration?"

Table 7.2 provides data on the age structures for the two markets in question. Assuming that the highest number of subscribers will come from the age groups identified in Table 7.1 (now and in the future) and that the age structure of customers will not change markedly, we can argue that there are some age structures which foster more subscribers than others. The data in Table 7.2 show that while 39.3 percent of Orange County's population falls in the key age category 25 to 54, only 30.2 percent of the Sarasota County population is in that age group. Furthermore, the smallest usage figure in Table 7.1 (2 percent) is for the population 65 and over. In Orange County, 10.8 percent of the population is 65 or over, while 30.3 percent of the Sarasota County population falls in this category.

If we ignore the two age groups "under 25" and "55 and over," (only 10 percent of current cellular subscribers come from these age groups), the penetration rate of the target population must be much higher in order to equal a 9 percent penetration of the total population. For Orange County, a 9 percent penetration rate results in 51,768 customers (575,200 × .09); for Sarasota, the corresponding figure is 22,284. Using the population age category of 25 to 54 as the denominator

Table 7.1   Demographic Differences for Cellular Subscribers: 1989

Household Income	Percent	Age	Percent
<$25,000	6	<25	3
$25,000–$35,000	11	25–34	29
$35,001–$50,000	22	35–44	39
$50,001–$75,000	23	45–54	20
$75,000 and over	38	55–64	7
Total	100	65 and over	2
		Total	100

Gender	Percent	Occupation	Percent
Male	81	Company/Business Owner	54
Female	19	Sales Representatives	15
Total	100	Professional/Technical/ Managerial	13
		President/Vice President	12
		Other	6
		Total	100

Source: Cellular Subscriber Surveys

Table 7.2   Age Structure for Orange and Sarasota Counties: 1986

Age	Orange (Orlando)		Sarasota (Sarasota)	
	Population	Percent	Population	Percent
Under 5	40,839	7.1	9,656	3.9
5–14	78,802	13.7	22,036	8.9
15–24	109,864	19.1	25,750	10.4
25–34	97,209	16.9	27,731	11.2
35–44	70,750	12.3	24,512	9.9
45–54	58,095	10.1	22,532	9.1
55–64	57,520	10.0	40,359	16.3
65–74	37,963	6.6	44,074	17.8
75 and over	24,158	4.2	30,950	12.5
Total	575,200	100	247,600	100

Source: U.S. Bureau of the Census, 1988; City and County Data Book, 1988; Washington, D.C.: U.S. Government Printing Office, Table B.

for the new penetration rates results in a figure of 22.9 percent for Orange County and 29.8 percent for Sarasota County. In other words, more than 20 percent and nearly 30 percent of the relevant target customers for the Orange and Sarasota markets, respectively, would have to become subscribers in order to achieve a total penetration rate of 9 percent. We could have reached a decision regarding the asking price of the properties based upon these data, but a few additional calculations proved quite valuable.

Table 7.3 presents age-specific penetration rates required of each market given four alternative total penetration figures. Given the large differences in age-specific usage rates (Table 7.1) and the substantial intermarket age differences (Table 7.2), we can see diverse sets of penetration rates emerge. In the Orange County market, more than 30 percent of the "most likely to subscribe" category (age 35 to 44) would have to become customers under the 10 percent scenario. In Sarasota County, nearly 40 percent of the same group would be required.

We can combine the data in Tables 7.1 and 7.2 to create indices of market attractiveness (by age). Table 7.4 presents the calculations required for such an index, which applies the use by age data (column 2) from Table 7.1 as the weights and allows the age distribution (columns 4 and 6) for both markets to vary. In this instance, the index values could vary between 200 (100 percent of the population is age 65 or over) and 3,900 (100 percent of the population is between the ages 35 and 44).

Our interest here, however, is in the intermarket comparison. We derive index components by multiplying the weight (usage) by the percent of county specific population in that category. Summing over all components yields a final index score. As we would expect given our observations from Table 7.2, the index score for Orange County is significantly higher than that for Sarasota County. The ratio of the two is 1.23, indicating that the age structure for cellular is more favorable in Orange County. Therefore, our initial POP ratio of 2.32 understates the differential in market values. Utilizing 1986 age data alone, we can conclude that if the Orange County POP value is $200, the Sarasota County value should be $163 (100/123 ×$200), all other factors being equal.

Income

Table 7.5 presents an estimate of the 1986 household income structure for the Orange and Sarasota markets. We derived the table by adjusting the 1980 Census of Population and Housing income structure for 1980 to 1986 increases in income occurring in each market area. The table becomes most useful when we compare it to the subscriber characteristics data in Table 7.1 and when we consider differences in household size. Again, the important question is: "How reasonable is a 9 percent total penetration assumption?"

Demographic estimates in 1985 showed Sarasota County with 2.20 persons per household. The corresponding figure for Orange County was 2.59. By adjusting the 9 percent total penetration figure for the number of persons per household, we find that 19.8 and 23.3 percent, respectively, of the households in Sarasota and Orange counties would have to contain a subscriber in order to achieve 9 percent total penetration. The data in Table 7.5, however, indicate that we must consider at least one other factor: Nearly half of all the households in each market fall outside

Table 7.3 Age-Specific Penetration Rates Required for 2, 5, 10, and 15 Percent Total Penetration

Age	Orange				Sarasota			
	2%	5%	10%	15%	2%	5%	10%	15%
<25	.2	.4	.8	1.1	.2	.6	1.2	1.8
25–34	3.4	8.6	17.3	25.7	5.2	12.9	26.0	39.0
35–44	6.3	15.8	31.7	47.6	7.9	19.7	39.4	59.1
45–54	4.0	9.9	19.8	29.7	4.4	11.0	22.0	33.0
55–64	1.4	3.5	7.0	10.5	.8	2.1	4.2	6.3
65 +	.4	.9	1.8	2.8	.1	.3	.6	.9

Table 7.4 Age-Based Index Values for Orange and Sarasota Counties

Age	Usage	Orange	Index	Sarasota	Index
<24	3%	39.9	119.7	23.2	69.6
25–34	29	16.9	490.1	11.2	324.8
35–44	39	12.3	479.7	9.9	386.1
45–54	20	10.1	202.0	9.1	182.0
55–64	7	10.0	70.0	16.3	114.1
65>	2	11.8	23.6	30.3	60.6
Total	100		1,403.1		1,137.2

POP Index (from Table 7.2) = 2.32
Age Index (from calculation above) = 1.23
Source: Tables 7.1 and 7.2.

Table 7.5 Estimated Income Structure for Orange and Sarasota Counties: 1986

Income	Orange		Sarasota	
	Households[a]	Percent	Households[a]	Percent
Less than $25,000	83,829	49.7	44,249	49.7
$25,001–$35,000	26,341	15.4	13,875	15.6
$35,001–$50,000	43,140	25.2	21,037	23.7
$50,000 and over	17,810	10.4	9,753	11.0
Total	171,120	100.0	88,914	100.0

[a] 1980 household counts
Sources: U. S. Bureau of the Census, 1988; City and County Data Book, 1988; Washington, D.C.: U.S. Government Printing Office, Table B; U. S. Bureau of the Census, 1983; 1980 Census of Population, Census Tracts (Sarasota and Orlando Metropolitan Statistical Areas); Washington, D.C.: Government Printing Office, Tables P1 and P10.

the requisite income figures if we use the data in Table 7.1 as a guide. Since only 6 percent of households with incomes of $25,000 or less become subscribers, about 39 and 45 percent, respectively, of the Sarasota and Orange markets in the household income category $25,000 and above would have to contain a subscriber if the 9 percent total penetration rate is to be achieved. If we use a more conservative figure of $35,000 and over, we get required penetration rates of 57 percent for Sarasota County and 65 percent for Orange County!

Discussion

Once the clients reviewed our analysis and understood both the data and calculations, they judged the asking price for both markets to be exceedingly high. We substituted a more reasonable penetration rate and calculated an adjusted market value, but the seller judged the resulting price to be too low and temporarily stopped negotiating. Faced with objective demographic analysis, however, the seller later returned to the negotiating table at a lower price.

Several issues arose as our research progressed, though we did not address all of them for various reasons. Our analyses were narrow in scope due to (1) the limited amount of information gathered by cellular service providers, (2) the inability to match much of the data collected to identifiable demographic categories for which market area data were available, and (3) the lack of multiple variable cross tabulation for both cellular user data and demographic groupings.

Regarding limited information, planners of cellular user surveys should consider additional inquiries, especially those focusing on car usage. For example, while some surveys ask questions about commuting activities, they fail to acquire enough detail. Table 7.6 presents data from the 1980 Census of Population and Housing (latest data available) on commuting patterns for Orange and Sarasota counties. Recall that the POPs ratio was 2.32. Utilizing Orange to Sarasota county ratios for some of these variables, we found that the worker ratio was 3.09, the private vehicle ratio 3.00, the drive alone ratio 2.88, and the carpool ratio 1.15. We suggest that each of these factors is important in determining usage and therefore market value—the higher the ratio the better the Orange County market—though we have no data to support this suggestion. The soon-to-be-available data in the 1990 Census will aid in this effort.

The second shortcoming—the inability to match data—is also demonstrated by the data-gathering efforts of service providers. Some accounting data are gathered via surveys, but these data cannot be readily linked to the existing market area characteristic data for comparison. For example, some cellular providers gather data for a narrow set of occupational groupings. While those groupings may be useful to an individual cellular company, they do not lend themselves to comparisons with available market area characteristic data because they create nontraditional and nonduplicatable data categories.

Table 7.6　　Worker and Commuting Data for Orange and Sarasota Counties: 1980

	Orange	Percent	Sarasota	Percent
Workers 16 and over who did not work at home	220,355		71,546	
Private vehicle	195,317	89	65,142	91
Drive alone	151,238	67	52,579	73
Carpool	44,079	20	12,563	18
Public transportation	4,752	2	597	1
Other	20,186	9	5,429	8
Travel time to work				
Less than 10 minutes		15	13,693	19
10–19 minutes	34,271	35	29,964	42
20–29 minutes	77,100	25	15,094	21
30–44 minutes	54,385	18	9,056	13
45 or more minutes	40,566	7	3,694	5
Mean	15,823		17.7	

Sources: U.S. Bureau of the Census, 1983; 1980 Census of Population, Volume 1, Characteristics of the Population, Chapter C, General Social and Economic Characteristics, Part II Florida, Table 174.

The lack of multiple variable characteristic cross tabulations is a product of the first two shortcomings, though some similar types of presentations are possible with existing data. Our analysis here was limited because we looked at one factor at a time and examined its effect on the POP measure. Ideally, we would examine a host of factors jointly as they determine the value of a market. Because the 1990 Census presents new data and permits current multiple cross tabulations for large and small market areas, the competitors in the cellular industry would be wise to reconsider data-gathering activities and analyses. Standardization and purging analytic techniques would fit well here.

At a more general level, the data analyses indicate that a different type of modeling technique must be incorporated for valuing cellular properties. At present, many industry observers use a top down approach—i.e., first estimating a dollars per POP value, followed by gross cash flow, penetration rates, and finally demographic factors associated with penetration. Reversing the order of these steps is required for best results. The first step in a successful valuation process is to generate penetration rates (now and projected) at the same time demographic correlates of usage are ascertained. A more firmly based cash flow analysis is then possible, taking into account demographic change, shifts in penetration rates, and the cost of equipment and marketing. Only after generating data-based cash flow scenarios can one assign reasonable market values.

Our analyses focused on the relative comparison of market values. With a model such as the one described, it would have been possible to assign absolute values and actually generate the financials needed to determine value. With the demographics and use of cross classifications described above, generating these financials would have been possible.

In summary, our elementary review of data on Orange and Sarasota counties revealed substantial differences in current and future demographics and, therefore, in probable cellular subscriber penetration in the two areas. Virtually all cellular observers understand that not all markets or POPs are created equal. Demographic distinctions (among other factors) undoubtedly played a role in McCaw's decision to buy Lin for $350 per POP while selling selected McCaw properties to Contel for about $210 per POP.

The discounted cash flow analysis of a cellular property's forecasted performance and, therefore, its value, are highly correlated with the number of subscribers captured over time—i.e., the carrier's forecasted cellular penetration of the market multiplied by the projected population of the market. In today's environment, this linkage between market demographics and projected penetration is more casual than scientific, often driven by judgments as to what penetration rates "feel comfortable" given relative demographic attractiveness (e.g., "Sarasota's penetration rate will be lower than Orange County's.").

The critical question, of course, is how much lower? Given what we know about cellular demographics today and population measures for the future, what are reasonable absolute penetration forecasts for the two markets, for any other market area, or for the industry as a whole? Demographic methods and analyses can help address this question by tightening the linkage between consumer demographics and subscriber forecasts.

The issues here are not trivial. The stakes are high, whether one considers equipment vendors' factory and inventory investments to meet uncertain future demand, individual carriers' network investment decisions, or investors' absolute and relative valuations of cellular equities. In a single illustrative RSA, a decrease of two percentage points in projected market penetration (from 5 to 3 percent) reduces the market valuation by $8 million. The shareholders in that small market certainly are not indifferent to such a reduction, nor are individuals and companies whose economic futures will vary substantially depending upon whether cellular penetration reaches 5 percent, 7 percent, 9 percent, or some higher figure.

The success of the cellular industry has been built, in large measure, on the value subscribers find in timely information, conveniently delivered. If better information can provide more accurate valuations and a competitive advantage, intelligent cellular players will turn to comprehensive demographic analysis to improve decisions and bottom-line performance.

Discussion Questions

1. In the ideal world, which variables would you use to evaluate the cellular market?

2. Restate the client's problem, as if you were making sure he/she understood that you knew the key points that needed to be addressed.

3. Given your limited understanding of cellular markets, whose advice would you seek if you were the demographer in this case? What questions would you ask?

4. What factors might affect the projections of "penetration?" Evaluate the author's assumptions about penetration trends.

5. Prepare a modelling technique for valuing cellular properties.

6. Evaluate the method of analysis in this case. Could a different method yield distinctly different results?

7. How would you present the results of your analysis to your client? Prepare portions of your report.

8. How would you use the 1990 census to examine data relevant to this project?

Notes

This case study demonstrates the value of demographic analysis in the context of an investment decision. The decision concerned the purchase of two cellular telephone markets. A group of venture capitalists, wishing to know whether the price being asked for each market was reasonable, approached the senior author. The identity of the two properties, and therefore the client's identity, must be kept confidential.

1. Cellular industry convention and jargon equate "potential customers" with the resident population (POPs) in a given market area.

2. The $350 per POP figure should be viewed with some caution given the fact that McCaw simply purchased LIN stock.

References

Gross, Joel D. *Telecommunications Services.* Donaldson, Lufkin, and Jenrette Report. May 9, 1989.

Hill, Eric. "Saying Goodbye to Roamer Invoices." *Cellular Business.* November 6, 1989: 12–16.

Hof, Robert D. 1989. "Will McCaw Be Ensnared by the Net of His Dreams?" *Business Week.* December 18, 1989: 43–44.

Leibowitz, Dennis, Eric Buck, and Joel Gross. *The Cellular Communications Industry.* Donaldson, Lufkin, and Jenrette Report. May 1989: Table 1.

Leon, Kenneth M. *Cellular Mobile Industry: Investor Worries.* Bear Sterns Report. March 6, 1990: 25.

———. *Cellular Mobile Industry Part III: Rural Licenses.* Bear Sterns Report. June 16, 1989: 55.

Roscoe, Andrew D., and Gordon Wallace. "Roamings Growth." *Communications.* April 1989: 48–58.

Sanders, John. 1987. "A Tale of Two RSAs." *Cellular Business.* December 4, 1987: 14–20.

8

Targeting Wealthy Ex-Wisconsinites in Florida: A Case Study in Applied Demography

Paul R. Voss

This brief illustration of the use of decennial census data as one aspect of a major business decision fits neatly into that broad category of demographic marketing applications called location or site analysis. In the following sections we describe the dilemma facing a Milwaukee financial institution, and we focus on the analytical approach we took to resolving the dilemma. In a final section we summarize subsequent steps leading to a resolution of the dilemma and how the final decision was reached.

The work was prompted by an inquiry brought to the Applied Population Laboratory (a small research and outreach unit on the Madison campus of the University of Wisconsin) by one of Wisconsin's larger financial institutions. Could we, by using data from the 1980 Census, assist this institution in screening several potential sites for the location of a distant branch office? Specifically, could we help in pinpointing the principal destinations of Wisconsin outmigrants who retire and settle in Florida?

For quite some time the trust division of this financial institution had been experiencing a troubling predicament. Long established clients (often with very substantial assets held in trust) would retire, move to Florida, and, after a period of settling in, seek to have the management of their trust portfolios located closer to home—their new home. In a desire to hold onto these valued clients and to continue serving them in their new residential locations, the trust company decided to explore the possibility of establishing an office in Florida.

The company's marketing staff needed to have answers to several questions: Do migrants from northern states settle in those Florida communities having relatively high proportions of residents from their former states, or do they tend to settle somewhat randomly among Florida's retirement communities? If the former, then which communities seem particularly attractive to Wisconsin retirees, and

what kinds of information are available to help identify the Wisconsin people in
them? And, even more to the point, is there a data set that in addition to pinpointing Wisconsin retirees in Florida can help to separate the locations of those elderly outmigrants with sizable assets from the locations of outmigrants with more
modest estates?

The Analytical Approach

When it comes to Sunbelt retirement for Wisconsin workers, Florida clearly is the
state of choice (Table 8.1). The 1980 Census found that persons over the age of 64
who had moved away from Wisconsin sometime during the previous five years
were twice as likely to choose Florida for their destination as they were to choose
Arizona, the second most popular state. Indeed, one out of every four older persons who left Wisconsin between 1975 and 1980 took up residence in the Sun-
shine State.

In an early planning meeting, the demographic research team and a marketing
officer from the trust company quickly reached the conclusion that the 1980 Census ought to be useful in addressing the relevant questions. They discussed two
potential data files, each having its own particular advantages.

The County to County Migration Flows File

The Applied Population Laboratory had acquired this massive and incredibly rich
data resource not long before the trust company made its inquiry. Might this be an
early opportunity, we wondered, to test the file's utility in a rather straightforward
demographic application?

The file has some significant advantages. First, it is based on the largest possible migrant sample from the 1980 Census. Since sampling error is a very real concern when dealing with relatively small streams, this file is a useful resource because it contains migration stream frequencies based on a sample of
approximately 10 percent of the 1980 population.

Second, its geographic detail is impressive. Since the file identifies all U.S.
counties, it allowed us to identify both the flows of Wisconsin residents to each
Florida county and the Florida-bound outmigrants from each Wisconsin county.

Third, the County to County Migration Flows File provides access to migration stream frequencies by age, sex, and income. Even though the file is formatted
like a census "summary tape file"—i.e., the records consist of preformatted tables, the structure of which the user has no control over—it is remarkably detailed
in the kinds of data it presents. If we were to focus, say, primarily on the table
cells that reveal the number of Wisconsin migrants to each Florida county who
were age 65 and over and had incomes in excess of $50,000, this file could carry
us a long way toward satisfying the trust company's inquiry.

Fourth and finally, this data file contains tables for nonmovers and for

Table 8.1   Destination of Wisconsin Outmigrants Between 1975 and 1980 (Age 65 and Over in 1980)

State	No. of Migrants	Percent
Florida	5,009	25.2
Arizona	2,363	11.9
California	1,849	9.3
Texas	886	4.5
Other States	9,766	49.1
Total Wisconsin Outmigrants Age 65+	19,873	100.0

Source: 1980 Census of Population and Housing, County to County Migration Flows file, Table M-1.

intracounty movers that parallel the tables for in- and outmigrants. As a consequence, this single file held all the information we needed to construct migration rates as well as to determine migration stream frequencies.

But the County to County Migration Flows File also had some serious disadvantages for our proposed application. First, its summary tape format meant that we could have only limited control over specific age categories. Since withdrawal from the work force occurs before age 65 for a significant proportion of workers, we thought we should try to identify the migration of at least some individuals to Florida who were younger than age 65 in 1980. Unfortunately, the income table in the Flows File combines persons ages 45 to 64 into a single age group. It would not make much sense, we felt, to bring migrants as young as age 45 into our analysis.

Second, the Flows File's emphasis on counties means that, outside of New England, no subcounty information is available. This is true even for highly populated metropolitan counties. For our purposes, it would have been very helpful to have Wisconsin outmigration streams to specific Florida cities.

Third, the income data in the Flows File represents income from all sources in one single summary number. Such data does not provide the information we needed regarding the assets of ex-Wisconsinites. For example, $15,000 in wage or salary income is hardly a clue to significant wealth. The same income derived as a return on investments, however, does point to a fairly substantial asset base. Therefore, the inability to identify income by source in the Flows File represented a significant impediment to satisfying the trust company's objective.

The Public Use Microdata Sample (PUMS) File

This popular file from the 1980 Census provides access to individual census records. It quickly became apparent that we could use the advantages of this file to overcome many of the shortcomings of the Flows File.

First, the PUMS File makes it possible to determine age and income category breaks with considerable flexibility. Second, it provides access to substantial numbers of subcounty areas in Florida. This is not the case in every state, but because many Florida counties far exceed the Census Bureau's population threshold for identifying specific geographic areas (and because Florida made the effort in 1980 to help the bureau identify appropriate community clusters for the Florida PUMS File), data for several counties of interest to the trust company provided considerable subcounty information (Figures 8.1a and 8.1b).

Third, the PUMS File identifies income by source. This meant that older Florida-bound migrants from Wisconsin could be stratified according to level of investment-derived income. Moreover, the PUMS data permitted us to combine the investment income for husbands and wives in married couple households in order to obtain a better assessment of joint assets. In short, the flexibility of the PUMS File made it an attractive potential data set for addressing the trust company's inquiry.

Yet, we had to consider the price we would have to pay for this flexibility. Most critically, the largest PUMS sample (5 percent) is found in individual state PUMS-A files. Because the Census Bureau coded the migration questions for only half of the 1980 "long form" questionnaires, the effective sample size when analyzing migration data is 2.5 percent. That is one-fourth the sample size of the Flows File, and the smaller sample size translates into larger relative sampling errors for the numbers we would derive in the analysis. An additional disadvantage of the PUMS data is that it does not identify all counties. For portions of Florida where the counties have small populations, the smallest geographic area it identifies consists of aggregates of two or more counties (Figure 8.1a).

After weighing the various advantages and disadvantages, we decided to base most of our analysis on the Florida Public Use Microdata Sample File.

Procedure

We then proceeded to identify two groups of former Wisconsin residents. "Recent migrants" are persons who, though enumerated as residents of Florida in 1980, reported that Wisconsin had been their usual place of residence five years earlier on April 1, 1975. The PUMS data identified 617 such persons who, when appropriately weighted, represented an estimate of the recent migration stream of 24,680 individuals. We identified "lifetime migrants" as persons born in Wisconsin but residing in Florida in 1980. The PUMS data included 3,949 individual sample cases. When appropriately weighted, these sample cases represented a lifetime migration stream of 78,980 individuals. It is important to note that the two groups of migrants thus identified are not mutually exclusive. Some "recent migrants" are also "lifetime migrants" and vice versa.

We then further stratified these two groups by age, income, and place of resi-

**Figure 8.1a—County groups identified for Florida in the 1980 census
public use microdata sample (File A). See Figure 8.1b for county
group numbers for shaded counties.**

dence to identify those areas in Florida having significant concentrations of older,
wealthy ex-Wisconsinites.

Age

We split the migrants into three age groups: younger than 50, 50–64, and 65 and
over. Our analysis focused largely on the two older groups.

Income

The 1980 Census provides considerable detail regarding income received in 1979.
For our analysis, we studied 1979 income from several sources for both the recent
migrant and lifetime migrant groups. With just two exceptions, we retained only
unearned income derived from interest, dividends, royalties, net rent, private pensions, annuities, and payments from estates and trust funds as a proxy for an individual migrant's level of wealth and for the likelihood of having assets held trust.

Broward County
036 Fort Lauderdale City
037 Hollywood City
038 Deerfield Beach City
    Hillsboro Beach Town
    Lauderdale-by-the-Sea Town
    Lighthouse Point City
    Pompano Beach City
    Sea Ranch Lakes Village
039 Coconut Creek City
    Tamarac City
    Coral Springs City
    Margate City
    North Lauderdale City
    Parkland City
040 Dania City
    Davie Town
    Hacienda Village City
    Plantation City
    Sunrise City
041 Cooper City
    Hallandale City
    Miramar City
    Pembroke Park Town
    Pembroke Pine City
042 Balance of county

Dade County
043 Miami City
044 Bay Harbor Islands Town

Dade County (Con't.)
044 Surfside Town
(Con't.) Bal Harbour Village
    Indian Creek Village
    Miami Beach City
    North Bay Village City
045 North Miami Beach City
    North Miami City
    Opa-Locka City
    Biscayne Park Village
    El Portal Village
    Miami Shores Village
046 Carol City (CDP)
    Miami Lakes (CDP)
    Aventura (CDP)
    Norland (CDP)
    Ojus (CDP)
    Opa-Locka North (CDP)
    Scott Lake (CDP)
    Sunny Isles (CDP)
    Golden Beach Town
    Ives Estates (CDP)
    Lake Lucerne (CDP)
047 Hialeah City
048 Gladeview (CDP)
    Westview (CDP)
    Brownsville (CDP)
    Golden Glades (CDP)
    Pinewood (CDP)
    West Little River (CDP)

Dade County (Con't.)
049 South Miami City
    West Miami City
    Westchester (CDP)
    Coral Gables City
    Coral Terrace (CDP)
    Glenvar Heights (CDP)
050 Olympia Heights (CDP)
    Westwood Lakes (CDP)
    Kendale Lakes (CDP)
    Sunset (CDP)
    Sweetwater City
    Tamiami (CDP)
051 Richmond Heights(CDP)
    Kendall (CDP)
    Lindgren Acres (CDP)
    Palmetto Estates (CDP)
052 Goulds (CDP)
    Homestead City
    Leisure City (CDP)
    Naranja-Princeton (CDP)
    Perrine (CDP)
    South Miami Heights (CDP)
    Cutler (CDP)
    Cutler Ridge (CDP)
    Florida City City
053* Balance of county

Hillsborough County
022 Tampa City
023 Balance of county

Orange County
017 Orlando City
018 Balance of county

Palm Beach County
C33 Lake Worth City
    Riviera Beach City
    West Palm Beach City
034 Delray Beach City
    Boca Raton City
    Boynton Beach City
035 Balance of county

Pinellas County
024 St. Petersburg City
025 Largo City
    Clearwater City
    Dunedin City
026 Balance of county

Volusia County
014 Daytona Beach City
    Daytona Beach Shores City
    Holly Hill City
    Ormond Beach City
    Ormond-by-the-Sea (CDP)
    Port Orange City
    South Daytona City
015 Balance of county

Figure 8.1b—County group numbers of counties having multiple groups identified

Generally, the returns on income- and dividend-generating assets in 1979 were below 10 percent. As a consequence, we assumed that a person who reported 1979 interest and dividend income of $10,000 very likely had investments in excess of $100,000 that income.

The exceptions to relying solely on unearned income as an indicator of wealth entered into the final stage of the income analysis. Our attention focused primarily on households containing at least one member over the age of 50 who reported unearned income in excess of $5,000. At this point, however, we brought into the analysis two additional kinds of migrants, migrants who reported unearned income of less that $5,000: business proprietors and farmers reporting substantial earnings. We did this under the assumption that proprietors—farm and nonfarm alike—often invest their disposable income back into their establishments rather than into portfolios of growth and income instruments. An older migrant reporting substantial proprietorship income likely owns a business or farm, the eventual sale of which may generate significant investable assets. We set the lower income thresholds at $30,000 for nonfarm proprietors, at $10,000 for farm proprietors. Even at these fairly low earnings thresholds, however, we added only one recent migrant household and six lifetime migrant households to the household analysis.

Residence

We studied the detailed census geographic information concerning 1980 residence to isolate specific cities or clusters of cities in Florida where elderly Wisconsin migrants tend to settle. In the numbers displayed in most of the tables and maps presented to the trust company, however, we showed aggregates of larger geographic units. We did this in order to reduce the level of sampling error.

Sampling Error

Although the Public Use Microdata Sample (PUMS) File permits the analysis of individual household and person records from the census, all personal identifying information has been stripped from the records in order to preserve confidentiality. As part of the Census Bureau's requirement for preserving confidentiality, the bureau codes place of residence only for county groups, counties, individual cities, or other municipal aggregates having a minimum population of 100,000. PUMS files are constructed from a sample of the so-called "long form" census questionnaires, which in 1980 were completed by approximately one out of every six households in larger urban areas and by every other household in more rural communities.

Due to the nature of the sample—and by virtue of the fact that the Census Bureau chose to code the place of residence in 1975 for only half of the sample questionnaires—each recent migrant in the sample represented 40 other persons; each lifetime migrant represented 20 others. Since this analysis focused on a rare subgroup of Florida's population (i.e., older, wealthy former residents of Wisconsin), the sample numbers are relatively small.[1] When a situation like this arises, the ability of small sample numbers to truly "represent" the total group diminishes and relative "sampling error" increases.

To minimize sampling error, we combined the data in this analysis in ways that increased the size of the samples from which we drew conclusions. For example, we sacrificed the original census geographic detail and used larger geographic areas (Figure 8.2). In addition, we combined individual migrants into just a few age groups and lowered the minimum income threshold for identifying "wealthy" migrants. We made these compromises to strike a balance between our desire for rich detail in the data and our need for statistical precision. At each step we compromised only after ensuring that the objective of the trust company's site analysis would not be distorted by the higher level of aggregation.

Summary of Findings

We report here only the findings based on recent migrants. The numbers supporting these findings appear mainly in Tables 8.2 through 8.5. Figure 8. 3 shows the location of several Florida cities mentioned in the discussion, and Figures 8.4a through 8.4c reveal several "density" numbers. We calculated these densities to "control" for the fact that areas with larger populations also tend to be those that show higher numbers of Wisconsin migrants. The data on lifetime migrants that we reported to the trust company revealed patterns that largely paralleled those of migrants during the 1975–1980 PERIOD.

The 1980 Census enumerated almost 25,000 persons in Florida who had been Wisconsin residents just five years earlier.[2] These ex-Wisconsinites represented 7 percent of the total outmigration from Wisconsin (336,000) during the five-year interval 1975 to 1980.[3]

Approximately 14,500 (59 percent) of these Florida-bound migrants were under the age of 50. Another 5,300 (22 percent) were between the ages of 50 and 65, and 4,800 (19 percent) were 65 years of age or older. In relation to outmigrants bound for other states, this Wisconsin-to-Florida migration stream had a disproportionately high share of elderly migrants. Overall, less than 6 percent of all outmigrants from Wisconsin between 1975 and 1980 were 65 or older.

Of the nearly 25,000 migrants who moved from Wisconsin to Florida, almost 3,000 individuals reported 1979 unearned income (derived from investments or pensions) exceeding $5,000. Just under half of these persons (1,300, or 5 percent of all the migrants) reported income of $10,000 or more.[4] Approximately 25 percent of the total migrant stream reported unearned income under $5,000, and 63 percent reported no unearned income.

A reasonably high correlation exists between age and level of income. More than half of those migrants reporting unearned income in excess of $10,000 were over age 64, and more than three-fourths of those reporting no unearned income were under the age of 50.

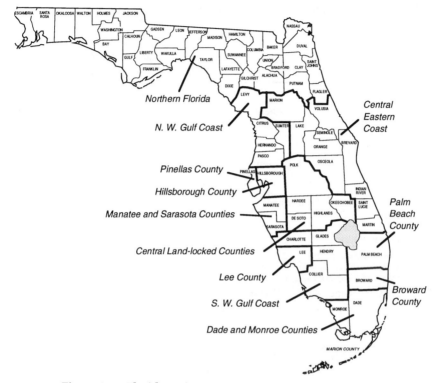

**Figure 8.2—Florida regions consisting of groupings of
PUMS county groups**

It is important to note, however, that it was predominantly men—especially among the older migrants—who reported significant levels of unearned income. Among those households in which an older man (age 50+) reported income of $5,000 or more, half of them included a spouse reporting no unearned income, and another 16 percent included a spouse with unearned income less than $5,000. The remaining 34 percent of households in which an older man reported significant unearned income included a spouse who also reported unearned income exceeding $5,000. Only seven sample cases among the recent migrants (representing a weighted estimate of 280 migrants) involved older women living alone who reported unearned income in excess of $5,000.

Older migrants from Wisconsin to Florida reveal a preference for settling on the state's Gulf Coast. Among migrant households consisting of at least one person over age 50 who reported 1979 unearned income in excess of $5,000, just under half reside along the Gulf Coast from a little north of Tampa Bay to Naples. The largest single concentration of this group lives outside St. Petersburg in Pinellas County. A smaller concentration resides in Lee County.

Table 8.2   Recent Migrants All Ages by Florida Residence and Income

	Income*			
	None	Under $5,000	$5,000 or more	Total
Northern Florida 34 panhandle and other northern counties	1,960	720	200	2,880
N.W. Gulf Coast 5 coastal counties north of Tampa	1,440	1,000	200	2,640
Pinellas County St. Petersburg-Clearwater and environs	1,800	760	560	3,120
Hillsborough County Tampa and environs	1,000	320	0	1,320
Manatee and Sarasota Counties 2 coastal counties south of Tampa	1,160	720	240	2,120
Lee County Fort Myers-Cape Coral and environs	1,120	280	160	1,560
S.W. Gulf Coast 4 counties S.W. of Lake Okeechobee	480	440	120	1,040
Central Eastern Coast 10 counties including Orlando and Daytona Beach	2,240	840	480	3,560
Central Landlocked Counties 5 counties N.W. of Lake Okeechobee	720	200	200	1,120
Palm Beach County West Palm Beach and environs	1,080	360	200	1,640
Broward County Ft. Lauderdale and environs	1,000	280	480	1,760
Dade and Monroe Counties Miami-Miami Beach and environs	1,560	280	80	1,920

*Includes only "unearned income," less public assistance and Social Security. Earned income (derived from wages, salaries, or proprietorships) is excluded. The principal types of income included are interest, dividends, royalties, net rent, private pensions, annuities, and payments from estates and trust funds.

Table 8.3   Recent Migrants Under Age 50 by Florida Residence and Income

	Income*			
	None	Under $5,000	$5,000 or more	Total
Northern Florida 34 panhandle and other northern counties	1,800	520	40	2,360
N.W. Gulf Coast 5 coastal counties north of Tampa	880	160	0	1,040
Pinellas County St. Petersburg-Clearwater and environs	1,320	160	40	1,520
Hillsborough County Tampa and environs	760	240	0	1,000
Manatee and Sarasota Counties 2 coastal counties south of Tampa	680	160	80	920
Lee County Fort Myers-Cape Coral and environs	800	200	0	1,000
S.W. Gulf Coast 4 counties S.W. of Lake Okeechobee	320	120	40	480
Central Eastern Coast 10 counties including Orlando and Daytona Beach	1,960	400	0	2,360
Central Landlocked Counties 5 counties N.W. of Lake Okeechobee	400	40	0	440
Palm Beach County West Palm Beach and environs	680	160	0	840
Broward County Ft. Lauderdale and environs	800	80	120	1,000
Dade and Monroe Counties Miami-Miami Beach and environs	1,400	160	40	1,600

*Includes only "unearned income," less public assistance and Social Security. Earned income (derived from wages, salaries, or proprietorships) is excluded. The principal types of income included are interest, dividends, royalties, net rent, private pensions, annuities, and payments from estates and trust funds.

Table 8.4   Recent Migrants Age 50–60 by Florida Residence and Income

	Income*			
	None	Under $5,000	$5,000 or more	Total
Northern Florida 34 panhandle and other northern counties	160	160	160	480
N.W. Gulf Coast 5 coastal counties north of Tampa	200	520	120	840
Pinellas County St. Petersburg-Clearwater and environs	240	360	200	800
Hillsborough County Tampa and environs	120	40	0	160
Manatee and Sarasota Counties 2 coastal counties south of Tampa	480	320	80	880
Lee County Fort Myers-Cape Coral and environs	280	80	40	400
S.W. Gulf Coast 4 counties S.W. of Lake Okeechobee	120	120	0	240
Central Eastern Coast 10 counties including Orlando and Daytona Beach	160	160	160	480
Central Landlocked Counties 5 counties N.W. of Lake Okeechobee	200	0	120	320
Palm Beach County West Palm Beach and environs	320	120	80	520
Broward County Ft. Lauderdale and environs	40	0	40	80
Dade and Monroe Counties Miami-Miami Beach and environs	120	0	0	120

*Includes only "unearned income," less public assistance and Social Security. Earned income (derived from wages, salaries, or proprietorships) is excluded. The principal types of income included are interest, dividends, royalties, net rent, private pensions, annuities, and payments from estates and trust funds.

Table 8.5   Recent Migrants Age 65 or Over by Florida Residence and Income

	Income*			
	None	Under $5,000	$5,000 or more	Total
Northern Florida 34 panhandle and other northern counties	0	40	0	40
N.W. Gulf Coast 5 coastal counties north of Tampa	360	320	80	760
Pinellas County St. Petersburg-Clearwater and environs	240	240	320	800
Hillsborough County Tampa and environs	120	40	0	160
Manatee and Sarasota Counties 2 coastal counties south of Tampa	0	240	80	320
Lee County Fort Myers-Cape Coral and environs	40	0	120	160
S.W. Gulf Coast 4 counties S.W. of Lake Okeechobee	40	200	80	320
Central Eastern Coast 10 counties including Orlando and Daytona Beach	120	280	320	720
Central Landlocked Counties 5 counties N.W. of Lake Okeechobee	120	160	80	360
Palm Beach County West Palm Beach and environs	80	80	120	280
Broward County Ft. Lauderdale and environs	160	200	320	680
Dade and Monroe Counties Miami-Miami Beach and environs	40	120	40	200

*Includes only "unearned income," less public assistance and Social Security. Earned income (derived from wages, salaries, or proprietorships) is excluded. The principal types of income included are interest, dividends, royalties, net rent, private pensions, annuities, and payments from estates and trust funds.

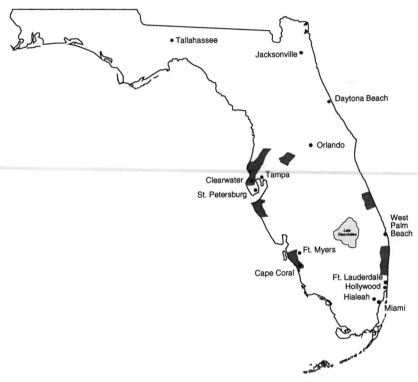

**Figure 8.3—Principal concentrations of wealthy older recent
migrants from Wisconsin**

On Florida's Southeast Coast, the heaviest concentration of older and wealthier former Wisconsin residents is found outside Fort Lauderdale in Broward County, predominantly along the northern coastal portions of the county from Pompano Beach to Deerfield Beach. These households represent a considerably smaller concentration than the migrant households in Pinellas County. A small concentration also lives in Palm Beach County, south of the city of West Palm Beach, along the coast from Boynton Beach to Boca Raton.

Additional small concentrations of older, wealthier recent migrants are located just north of Sarasota near Bradenton, in the greater Lakeland area, and along the coast near Fort Pierce.

Outcome

We presented our report to the marketing department of the trust company in August 1985, approximately four weeks after the company's initial inquiry. Six weeks later the marketing team responded, asking the Applied Population Labo-

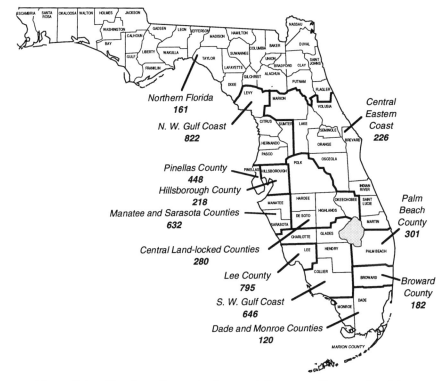

Northern Florida
161

N. W. Gulf Coast
822

Central
Eastern
Coast
226

Pinellas County
448
Hillsborough County
218
Manatee and Sarasota Counties
632

Palm
Beach
County
301

Central Land-locked Counties
280

Lee County
795

Broward
County
182

S. W. Gulf Coast
646

Dade and Monroe Counties
120

**Figure 8.4a—Number of recent migrants (all ages and income levels)
per 100,000 Florida residents**

ratory to prepare population profiles for 22 specific areas in Florida. The company had chosen these areas as branch potential sites on the basis of our migration analysis.

In its examination of our analysis, the trust company noticed that many of the communities of elderly, wealthy ex-Wisconsinites in Florida were quite small. As a consequence, the company asked us to include in our profiles the Florida-bound migration streams from other midwestern states on the assumption that migrants from states neighboring Wisconsin might feel kindly toward a trust company with strong midwestern roots. Figures 8.5a and 8.5b show sample profile sheets.

Following our delivery of the profile sheets in December, the trust company hired a consultant to carry out the final stages of the site analysis. The consultant evaluated a handful of potential locations—selected on the basis of the profiles and other relevant information—on site. After examining the competition, scouting potential properties, and studying the variety of considerations that enter into a business decision, the trust company announced its plan to open a Florida office in West Palm Beach.

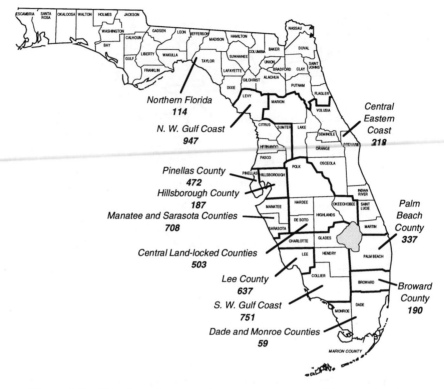

Figure 8.4b—Number of recent migrants over age 50 (all income levels) per 100,000 Florida residents over age 50

On the basis of the migration analysis alone, West Palm Beach was not the most likely location. The preliminary demographic work, however, played the role it was intended to play. It narrowed the decision field for the trust company. Our analysis permitted the company to eliminate sizable portions of the state, and it allowed the marketing team to focus its attention on 22 specific areas. In the second stage of the project, we profiled these 22 areas, and these profiles further narrowed the field. Once this was accomplished, the trust company based its final decision largely on nondemographic site considerations.

Discussion Questions

1. Do you agree with the demographer's decision to use the PUMS file? Explain.

2. Evaluate the appropriateness of the two groups used as sample cases (recent migrants and lifetime migrants). Consider the original needs of the client.

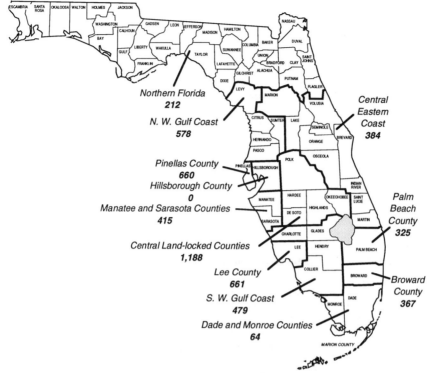

Figure 8.4c—Number of households having at least one recent Wisconsin migrant over age 50 who reported 1979 unearned income over $5,000 per 100,000 Florida households having household heads with similar age and income characteristics

3. Can you think of other income anomalies that would have added additional households to the household analysis?

4. Did the analysts adequately address the issue of sampling error?

Notes

This paper was presented at the Annual Meeting of the Population Association of America, Baltimore, MD, March 31, 1989.

1. Elderly migrants (65 and over) from Wisconsin constituted only 1.7 percent of the total 286,734 elderly migrants who moved to Florida from another state between 1975 and 1980.

2. Numbers used in this analysis frequently are rounded to the nearest hundred or thousand to convey the important point that all of the data examined here are based on samples and contain a certain level of imprecision (or "sampling error"). The tables accompanying this case study contain figures that represent the weighted sample frequencies. As such,

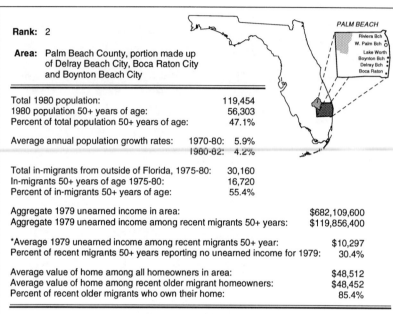

Rank: 2

Area: Palm Beach County, portion made up
of Delray Beach City, Boca Raton City
and Boynton Beach City

Total 1980 population:	119,454
1980 population 50+ years of age:	56,303
Percent of total population 50+ years of age:	47.1%

Average annual population growth rates:	1970-80:	5.9%
	1980-82:	4.2%

Total in-migrants from outside of Florida, 1975-80:	30,160
In-migrants 50+ years of age 1975-80:	16,720
Percent of in-migrants 50+ years of age:	55.4%

Aggregate 1979 unearned income in area:	$682,109,600
Aggregate 1979 unearned income among recent migrants 50+ years:	$119,856,400

*Average 1979 unearned income among recent migrants 50+ year:	$10,297
Percent of recent migrants 50+ years reporting no unearned income for 1979:	30.4%

Average value of home among all homeowners in area:	$48,512
Average value of home among recent older migrant homeowners:	$48,452
Percent of recent older migrants who own their home:	85.4%

Origins of Recent Migrants

Rank	State	Number of migrants 1975-80 from this state to area	Number of migrants 50+ with unearned income $5,000+ from this state to area	Percent (column 4 ÷ column 3)
1	NY	9,040	2,560	28.3 %
2	NJ	3,160	1,040	32.9
3	PA	2,720	520	19.1
4	MA	2,000	200	10.0
5	IL	1,640	400	24.4
	•••	•••	•••	•••
	MI	1,520	440	28.9
	OH	1,280	360	28.1
	IN	840	120	14.3
	MN	600	120	20.0
	WI	480	80	16.7
	MO	120	0	0.0
	KS	40	0	0.0
	NE	40	0	0.0
	IA	0	0	—
	SD	0	0	—
	ND	0	0	—

*Rank determined using this indicator

SOURCE (except growth rates): 1980 Census of Population, published reports and Public Use Microdata Samples. Growth rates determined from 1970 and 1980 Censuses and estimates published in Current Population Reports, P-26.

Figure 8.5a—Sample profile sheet: Palm Beach County

Rank: 11

Area: Lee County

LEE

Fort Myers •
○ Cape Coral

Total 1980 population:	205,266
1980 population 50+ years of age:	87,330
Percent of total population 50+ years of age:	42.5%

Average annual population growth rates:	1970-80:	6.7%
	1980-84:	4.9%

Total in-migrants from outside of Florida, 1975-80:	59,720
In-migrants 50+ years of age 1975-80:	28,040
Percent of in-migrants 50+ years of age:	47.0%

Aggregate 1979 unearned income in area:	$672,369,410
Aggregate 1979 unearned income among recent migrants 50+ years:	$112, 673,600

*Average 1979 unearned income among recent migrants 50+ years:	$6,921
Percent of recent migrants 50+ years reporting no unearned income for 1979:	41.9%

Average value of home among all homeowners in area:	$50,550
Average value of home among recent older migrant homeowners:	$46,760
Percent of recent older migrants who own their home:	82.9%

Origins of Recent Migrants

Rank	State	Number of migrants 1975-80 from this state to area	Number of migrants 50+ with unearned income $5,000+ from this state to area	Percent (column 4 + column 3)
1	NY	10,400	1,320	12.7 %
2	OH	7,520	880	11.7
3	IL	5,760	760	13.2
4	IN	4,320	400	9.2
5	PA	4,200	640	15.2
•••		•••	•••	•••
	MI	4,040	560	13.9
	WI	1,560	160	10.3
	MO	1,120	40	3.6
	MN	640	160	25.0
	KS	280	120	42.9
	IA	80	40	50.0
	SD	80	0	0.0
	NE	0	0	—
	ND	0	0	—

*Rank determined using this indicator

SOURCE (except growth rates): 1980 Census of Population, published reports and Public Use Microdata Samples. Growth rates determined from 1970 and 1980 Censuses and estimates published in Current Population Reports, P-26.

Figure 8.5b —Sample profile sheet: Lee County

they are approximations of the actual migrant numbers—and only that, approximations. The smaller the numbers, the larger the likely extent of imprecision. The figure of 25,000 given here refers to persons five years of age or more in 1980. Migration status is determined by comparing "usual place of residence" as of April 1, 1980, with residence on April 1, 1975. Children under the age of five in 1980 were born after the migration reference date.

3. For the record (but not discussed further in this analysis), almost 9,000 persons migrated from Florida to Wisconsin during this same five-year period, yielding a net loss of about 16,000 Wisconsinites to Florida.

4. Unless otherwise indicated, the word "income" (used interchangeably with "unearned income") in this report refers only to unearned income, less public assistance and Social Security. Earned income (derived from wages, salaries, and proprietorships) is excluded, except for the discussion of migrant households in which a small number of business proprietors are included (See the discussion of income in the Procedure section). The principal types of unearned income are interest, dividends, royalties, net rent, private pensions, annuities, and payments from estates and trust funds.

9

Selecting Markets
for Corporate Expansion:
A Case Study in Applied Demography

Kenneth M. Johnson

Applied demographers are often called upon to aid senior corporate managers in planning for expansion. Demographic insights and information are valuable to this planning process in a variety of contexts, ranging from strategic planning to site selection. In this case, the task was to identify promising market areas for corporate expansion.

Selecting markets is a complex problem requiring the simultaneous consideration of many demographic, economic, social, and business factors. Further complicating the selection process is the need to examine a large pool of possible markets in order to identify those with the greatest potential. This case illustrates how demographic variables can be combined with other data and used in conjunction with statistical modeling to identify promising markets. It also considers a number of practical problems that demographers working in applied settings are likely to confront.

Background and Statement of Problem

An established firm in the travel and lodging industry operated a mix of corporate-owned and franchised units. The demographic task was to examine a large pool of possible markets and select from among them a limited number having the potential to support corporate expansion. The market development staff of the corporation would then examine each promising market (defined here as a county or city encompassing multiple counties) in detail and decide whether to build a new unit in it.

The selection of an appropriate site within the market was not at issue here. Although such site selection is usefully informed by demographic analysis, it is also acutely sensitive to factors such as real estate costs, traffic flow and street layout, proximate competitors, and the general commercial climate in the area. The corporation had ample expertise to handle site selection once it had identified the promising markets. What it lacked was demographic expertise—someone who knew how to use census data and do statistical modeling—to help identify the most promising markets for expansion.

As an outside consultant, I provided such expertise. I developed and executed the study, and I interacted with relevant components of the corporation both to obtain needed information and to report the study results. My primary institutional contact was the vice president of corporate development and her staff, but the project required extensive interaction with other elements of the firm as well.

The institutional context for applied research of this type is largely defined by the nature of the work product and the employment relationship between the demographer and the organization. In this case, I was an outside consultant with primary responsibility for the research. The firm in question wished to expand, and it recognized the importance of incorporating demographic, economic, and social information into the selection process—but it did not know how to do so. Thus, I was charged with formulating a strategy to accomplish the firm's goals.

Under such circumstances, I found it necessary to engage in extensive interaction with relevant corporate staff in order to (1) define the problem, (2) obtain pertinent corporate data, and (3) identify factors that the corporate staff thought might be important to market selection. As the project progressed, I found that I also needed to educate members of the corporate staff about the modeling strategy so that they would use it intelligently.

The interplay of employment status and work product in structuring the institutional context is evident when this case is compared with two other common settings for applied work. A demographer employed by a corporation has a number of advantages, including a greater familiarity with the problem, a better grasp of what internal data and resources are available, and an ongoing presence to ensure that results from the models are used properly. In contrast, a demographer retained to deliver a well-defined product (i.e., population projections) need interact only minimally with the corporate staff. In each of these instances, the work product and the demographer's employment status interact to set the institutional context. The demands placed on applied demographers, the resources available to them, and the course of action they pursue are all constrained by the institutional context within which they operate. This case study serves to illustrate several of these points.

Selecting Markets for Welcome Motels

Consider the problem facing the vice president of corporate development for the Welcome Motel chain.[1] Senior management was planning a major corporate expansion, and she had been asked to identify sites with high potential to support new Welcome units. Already well established in the major metropolitan markets, the firm now wanted to increase its presence in middle markets—defined as having populations between 50,000 and 250,000. Such markets were either Metropolitan Statistical Areas (MSAs) or, in nonmetropolitan areas, a county of at least 50,000 containing a city of 25,000. Welcome already operated units in 100 such middle markets. Some of these units were doing quite well, others not so well. The task of the vice president of corporate development was to decide which of the numerous middle markets not yet served offered the greatest potential.

Using Models to Select Markets

After extensive conversations with the vice president, her staff, and other relevant Welcome managers, I recommended the use of general linear models to identify those middle markets having the most potential. General linear models are particularly appropriate to problems like Welcome's because they offer researchers several important pieces of information. First, they produce a specific revenue prediction for each market of interest. These revenue predictions can then be used to rank the markets. Second, such models generally provide more accurate revenue estimates than simple models can offer because general linear models simultaneously consider the impact of numerous factors on revenue. Third, with a general linear model one can estimate the contribution of each predictor variable to revenue. As a result, the model may be made more efficient by excluding variables that do not improve the prediction of revenue, thereby reducing the expense and time required for data collection. Fourth and finally, the statistical technique provides an explicit measure of the quality of the overall prediction model, thereby giving managers a means for assessing the model's accuracy.

General linear models use information about a firm's existing units to generate predictions of the likely activity levels in similar potential markets. Thus, the procedure discussed here is highly appropriate for established regional or national firms—like Welcome—that are seeking to expand. It is not appropriate for new firms or those with only a few locations, however, because such firms lack information about enough existing locations to provide a database for modeling. For such firms the checklist or analog approach may be more appropriate (Craig et al. 1984). Although not discussed here, general linear models also have been used for site selection (Lord and Lynds 1981; Olsen and Lord 1979).

Having accepted my recommendation to use general linear models, the staff assembled data on the performance of the 100 Welcome units already operating in middle markets. When such information was combined with appropriate demographic, economic, and business information for these markets, the resulting database could be examined using general linear modeling. If the resulting model could provide accurate estimates of performance in the existing locations, it could then be used to predict performance in the potential markets.

Phase I: Modeling Existing Locations

A project like Welcome's should be executed in two phases because a phased approach gives senior corporate staff an opportunity to monitor the progress of the project and terminate it if the model proves to be unsatisfactory. I will discuss a number of steps within each phase, but it is important not to lose sight of the overall goal—to generate revenue estimates for potential markets in order to identify those with the greatest promise. In the first phase of the project, I used data about existing markets to develop a statistical model which I could then use to estimate revenue for potential locations.

The dependent variable to be predicted by the model was the annual revenue that a Welcome Hotel would produce in each market. Phase I of the project examined the feasibility of making accurate revenue predictions for existing Welcome units. The accuracy of such predictions depended on the extent to which the statistical model could capture and represent the factors that stimulate hotel spending. In the process of evaluating the model with the client, I also began to educate the managers about the applications and limitations of statistical modeling. Such client education is an important component of the consultant's work.

The first step in Phase I was to select a group of current locations similar to the potential markets. For Welcome, the 100 existing middle market locations were the most likely candidates. Major markets (those with populations greater than 250,000) were not included in the modeling process because the dynamics in such markets are quite different from those in middle markets, particularly in the accommodations industry.

I screened these existing locations to exclude unusual markets that were influenced by extraordinary factors not present in most markets. An example of such unusual markets would be gambling markets, which generate lodging revenues far in excess of those generated in other markets of similar size. Including such unusual markets would so distort the prediction model that it could not predict well for the majority of markets. Although unusual markets must be excluded from the model, one must include both locations that are doing well and those that are doing poorly. It would be a serious error to exclude underperformers because the model must be sensitive to what exerts a negative impact on revenue as well as to what exerts a positive influence. The next step was to identify potential predictor variables. This is a critical step because if important predictor variables are excluded, the model will not make accurate revenue estimates, thereby jeopardizing the entire project. The variables that I identified reflected major factors believed to influence the revenue potential of a Welcome location (Figure 9.1). The first of these major factors is the character of the local population and economy. Welcome staff know that much of their business comes from the local community through accommodations for visitors weddings, business meetings, and so forth.

A second major factor is the size of transient population. A substantial proportion of motel revenue comes from individuals who are in an area temporarily for business, vacations, special events, and so forth. The third major factor consists of the extent and quality of competition from other motels and hotels. Welcome locations without extensive competition may do better than similarly situated Welcome units having significant competition. The fourth and final major factor is the

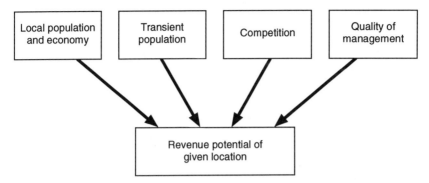

Figure 9.1—Factors expected to influence revenue potential

quality of the management at the Welcome location. A well-managed Welcome unit may do much better than a unit that is in a similar market but has lackluster management.

In all, I identified 61 predictor variables that together measured the four factors. Relatively few of these variables remained in the final model, but it was best to start with a large pool of variables and eliminate the ones that did not prove useful based on statistical analysis. At this point, my greatest concern was not to exclude a potentially useful variable.

As soon as the database on Welcome's 100 existing middle market locations was assembled, I began my statistical analysis. I focused on identifying a subset of the 61 predictor variables that estimate, with reasonable accuracy, the revenue for the existing locations. Although statistically complex, the modeling procedure was conceptually simple. What I needed was a statistical abstraction of the local market that responded to differences in the factors influencing revenue. The modeling procedure provided such an abstraction by using a weighted combination of predictor variables to account for revenue differences among the existing markets.

In this case, eight of the original 61 variables were particularly important in predicting revenue for existing Welcome locations. Among the eight, population and number of firms employing 100+ workers reflected the character of the local area (Table 9.1). Hotel sales also partially reflected the character of the local market, but they were primarily a measure of the transient population. The size of the transient population was reflected in the number of daily nonstop commercial flights, number of vehicles entering the county, and the number of major annual events (i.e., festivals, conventions). The impact of competition was reflected in the number of major competitors that the Welcome unit faced in each market.

Finally, I needed to assess the quality of management at the Welcome unit in each market in order to make accurate revenue predictions. Measuring the quality of management is not an easy task. Welcome maintains an elaborate set of finan-

Table 9.1   Example of Prediction Model, Welcome Hotels, Eau Claire, Wisconsin

Variable	Regression Value	Weight	Contribution
Population 1987	137500	4.1	$563,750
Lodging Sales (000s)	12424	30.8	382,659
No. Firms Employing 100+	55	5147.0	283,085
No. Major Events	8	11457.0	91,656
No. of Nonstop Flights	3	140300.0	420,900
No. Vehicles Entering Area	37640	2.7	101,628
No. Major Competitors	4	-97843.0	-391,372
Quality of Management	3 (good)	43354.0	130,062
Constant	1	101543.0	101,543
Total			$1,683,911

Standard Error of Estimates = 328,000
Squared Multiple Regression Coefficient = .86
Sample Size = 100

Where:

Population 1987 = Area population in 1987 (Federal State Cooperative Series)

Lodging Sales = Total Hotel and Motel Revenue in 000s (1987 Census of Service Industries)

Firms Employing 100+ = No. of firms employing more than 100 workers (County Business Patterns)

Major Events = No. of festivals, conventions, and other tourist events (Chamber of Commerce)

Nonstop Flights = No. of daily nonstop flights by commercial carriers (Official Airline Guide)

Vehicles Entering County = No. of vehicles entering area daily (State Department of Transportation)

Major Competitors = No. of motels with 100+ rooms and toll free reservations (Tourist Industry Sources)

Quality of Management = Rating of local Welcome management from 0 (poor) to 4 (excellent) (Welcome Operations Staff)

Constant = Coefficient derived from statistical modeling and set to 1 for each location

Data are for the Eau Claire, MSA, including Eau Claire and Chippewa counties.

cial indicators of management quality (e.g., staff costs/revenue night, electrical consumption/revenue night), but such indicators were not useful for modeling. Instead, the quality of management at existing units was rated on a simple subjective scale by the operations staff and regional vice president.

My decision to use these eight variables to estimate revenue represented a tradeoff between accuracy and efficiency. While including additional variables marginally improved the predictive power of the model, it made the model less efficient and more sensitive to factors unique to one or a few markets which may not be relevant to the potential sites. What I needed were the general factors likely to influence the revenue potential of a Welcome unit in any city.

The weight assigned to each of the eight variables for predicting revenue was determined by the statistical model. In principle, each weight reflected the difference in revenue expected between two locations that differed by one unit on the specific predictor variable if the two locations were in the same position on all other predictors. For example, if two existing Welcome locations were the same on all the predictors except that city A had one more daily nonstop flight than city B, then the Welcome location in city A would be expected to generate $140,300 more revenue annually.

Examination of the weights has some heuristic value as well because it helps clients see a factor's impact in a straight-forward way and emphasizes the interrelationship among the factors. This formal interpretation of regression weights is of limited utility in applied settings, however, because if cities differ on one important predictor, they typically differ on others as well. Although this complicates the analytical task of deriving the appropriate statistical model, it does not influence the actual prediction of revenue for each market.

Evaluating the Quality of the Model

For any given Welcome location there was likely to be a difference between the actual revenue generated and the revenue predicted for that location by the model. Such variation was to be expected given the multiplicity of variables that influence how well a specific location does. The modeling procedures were designed to minimize the differences between the predicted and actual revenue for all locations.

Once the best model for predicting revenues for existing markets had been selected, the quality of the predictions derived from it had to be evaluated. The key point was whether revenue predictions derived from the model were accurate enough to aid the firm in planning its expansion. While there would be differences between the predicted and actual revenue for the existing locations that had been used to derive the model, the managers and research team had to determine whether the model predicted revenue for existing locations accurately enough to justify its use in selecting new markets.

One can assess the quality of the predictions generated by the model with a number of formal statistical measures. The most common of these measures is the squared multiple correlation coefficient (R-square). R-square varies from zero to one, with values closer to one suggesting more accurate solutions. In this case, it reported the proportion of all the variation in revenue among the locations accounted for by the prediction model. The R-square of .86 for Welcome suggested that the model was providing quite accurate predictions of revenue for the existing locations.

The abstractness of statistical measures such as R-square limits their utility in evaluating the quality of models in applied settings. Therefore, a number of other techniques may be more appropriate. One can, for example, calculate the percentage difference between the actual and predicted revenue for each market and then average that difference over all markets. In the case of Welcome, the average deviation of the predicted from the actual was 20 percent. Thus, a location with a predicted revenue of $1,000,000 per year could reasonably be expected to have sales between $800,000 and $1,200,000.

An even more useful technique was available in Welcome's case because the market development staff could specify revenue thresholds for what constituted locations that were unsuccessful (revenue less than $1,000,000), moderately successful (revenue of $1,000,000 to $2,000,000), and highly successful (revenue in excess of $2,000,000). Using such information, one could construct a cross tabulation that compared the predicted and actual revenue of the 100 existing locations (Table 9.2).

This cross tabulation clearly illustrated the ability of the model to discriminate between unsuccessful and successful locations. For example, in 80 percent of the cases where the model predicted inadequate revenues, the actual revenues generated were, in fact, inadequate. In contrast, nearly 80 percent of the locations identified as highly successful by the model were, in fact, highly successful; only 3 percent were unsuccessful. To managers who are evaluating the quality of a model, a presentation emphasizing such applied criteria is often more meaningful than is one focused on the more abstract statistical measures.

At Welcome, Table 9.2 was critical to the evaluation process and an important heuristic device. Table 9.2 appealed to managers because it helped them understand the risks and benefits involved in using the modeling process. For example, they could see that the odds were 4 to 1 that a unit in a market predicted to generate substantial revenue would actually do so, whereas the chances were only 1 in 32 that a unit placed in such a market would fail. The table also helped illustrate for the managers the limitations of modeling. They were quite attentive to the model's limited ability to predict accurately for markets with moderate revenues. Although I provided Welcome managers with other measures of the model's quality, it was Table 9.2 and the following case-by-case review that they relied upon most heavily.

At the aggregate level, evaluation of the model should be supplemented by a case-by-case comparison of the predicted and actual revenues. In applied settings decisions are invariably made case by case, not statistically. Although the applied demographer provides statistical predictions and rankings to aid decision makers, managers must make each choice case by case. Thus, a case-by-case review of the results of the prediction model is a critical part of the project.

Such review serves the dual purpose of identifying extreme outliers (cases for which the predicted and actual revenue are quite different) and giving managers a better feel for the results of the modeling procedure. Often the outliers are well known to the managers and the fact that they appear as outliers may actually increase management's confidence in the model.

In Welcome's case, several existing locations performed much better than the model predicted while a few locations did much worse than predicted. Concerned

Table 9.2 Comparison of Predicted and Actual Revenues for Current Welcome Locations in Middle Markets

		Predicted 1987 Revenue		
		Inadequate Revenue	Moderate Revenue	High Revenue
	Inadequate Revenue	80.0%	32.7%	3.0%
Actual 1987 Revenue	Moderate Revenue	20.0	53.0	18.2
	High Revenue	0.0	14.3	78.8
		100.0 (20)	100.0 (37)	100.0% (43)

Where:
Inadequate Revenue = Less than $1,000,000
Moderate Revenue = $1,000,000 to $2,000,000
High Revenue = Greater than $2,000,000

that these outliers might reflect a flaw in the model, I reviewed them with Welcome staff. Each outlier was well known to the managers and had a logical explanation (e.g., strong competitor, poor site, excellent operator, historically strong market). The fact that the model was sensitive enough to identify such markets impressed the Welcome staff. Occasionally such a review will uncover a new factor that accounts for such outliers, in which case the new information can be incorporated into the model thereby improving the quality of the solution. In any event, a case-by-case review of the locations provide an excellent way of educating the managers about the strengths and limitations of the modeling procedure because it exposes them to the differences (whether minimal or substantial) between the predicted and actual revenue for existing locations.

Phase II: Predicting Revenues for Potential Locations

After management reviews the model's results for existing locations, a decision must be made as to whether to continue the project. In Welcome's case, management was satisfied that the model produced reasonable predictions of revenue and that such predictions would be useful in selecting new locations.

Phase II began with the identification of a pool of markets that could be examined as potential locations. This identification had to be done carefully because those selected had to have characteristics reasonably close to the existing markets used for modeling. Because the existing Welcome locations used to develop the model were all middle-size markets (50,000–250,000), it was important that those included in the pool of potential locations should be of roughly the same size. After reviewing the available demographic data, I identified 150 markets of the proper size to be examined as possible Welcome markets.

Having selected the pool of possible markets, I collected data for each. Since it was necessary to collect data only for the variables to be included in the modeling procedure, the time and cost of collecting data was dramatically reduced. In the Welcome case, I needed to collect information only on the eight predictor variables used in the model. One problem that nearly always arises in data collection is missing data—i.e., data on one or more of the predictor variables in some markets will not be available either because some agencies did not report the data required or because the Census Bureau suppressed the data to avoid violation of confidentiality. Often the demographer can make a reasonable estimate of such missing values and thereby allow the case to be included. Only if data are missing on several variables should a market be eliminated from the pool.

Once the demographer constructs the database for the potential locations, he or she can use the model developed for existing markets to generate revenue estimates for each of the potential markets. Consider the example of the Eau Claire metropolitan area in Wisconsin. It was identified as a potential Welcome site because it was an MSA of less than 250,000. Having collected data on each of the relevant variables, I inserted the appropriate values into the model and produced a revenue prediction for the potential market (Table 9.1). I multiplied the value for each predictor by the weight assigned to it in order to determine what contribution it would make to the model. For example, I multiplied the population of 137,500 by the weight of 4.1 to provide an estimated contribution to revenue of $563,750.

In reviewing the relative contribution of each variable, one might note the particularly strong influence of airline flights. Other things remaining equal, each additional flight could be expected to contribute $140,300 dollars to annual revenue. The model's sensitivity to airline flights undoubtedly reflected the strong relationship between air travel and the number of transients coming to the area.

Note also that the model included an estimate of management quality even though no location yet existed in Eau Claire. This predictor allowed Welcome executives to better understand the impact of management quality on revenue. The demographer can increase the heuristic value of the model by "walking" managers through the calculation process because it provides an opportunity to illustrate the impact of measurement errors and because it lets them consider the impact of change in local conditions. For example, the impact of measurement errors becomes clearly evident when one asks the managers to consider how a misreporting of the number of flights would impact on revenue predictions for a city. Similarly, by asking the sort of "what if" questions common in strategic planning, the demographer encourages managers to consider the implications of changes in local conditions. For example, asking what impact the opening of a new unit by a competitor will have on Welcome revenue shows managers how easy it is to answer such a question with reference to the model: It would reduce the Welcome unit's revenues by $97,843.

I calculated the predicted revenue for each of the other 149 potential markets in a manner similar to that for Eau Claire. I then ranked the markets based on predicted revenue and selected the most promising among them for further detailed review by the market development staff. Ranking is valuable in that it tends to mitigate the error likely contained in the specific revenue estimate for each potential market. While it is unlikely that a given potential market will generate exactly the amount of revenue predicted by the model, it is likely that a market predicted to have high potential revenue will generally perform significantly better than those with low revenue predictions.

After I generated predictions and ranked the potential markets, both senior managers (responsible for market development) and field staff (charged with making the detailed investigations of the most promising markets) reviewed the results. In the course of our meetings, those with firsthand knowledge of the markets reviewed the predictions and, in some cases, revised the rankings. The field staff, in particular, was often sensitive to nuances of the local markets not evident in the statistical abstractions of the modeling process.

Outcomes

Of the 150 potential markets, the model indicated 40 that had predicted revenues high enough to warrant further investigation. The vice president assigned these 40 markets to her field staff for detailed review, and out of this review came a decision to purchase sites and construct motels in 33 markets. If the units perform at the level predicted by the model, they will generate over $80 million in additional revenue each year for the corporation.

The success of the model in predicting revenue for existing middle market locations encouraged Welcome managers to use the same techniques to evaluate the performance of existing locations. They discovered that they could also use the model to identify underperforming markets, allowing them to take corrective action sooner than otherwise would have been the case. In a similar fashion, they could examine markets performing above expectations to determine what caused these sites to be successful, thereby allowing them to apply the successful techniques system wide. As a result, management plans to utilize such model-based evaluation procedures among both its middle and major market locations.

Lessons for Applied Demographers

The Welcome case highlights a number of important lessons pertinent to applied demographers serving as outside consultants to firms or agencies. Some of these lessons relate directly to the application of statistical models to market selection; others are more generally applicable.

The Importance of Client Involvement

It is absolutely essential that the demographer involve the client in the development of the research project. Such client involvement is critical at several points.
First, the client must be fully involved in the original statement of the problem.
When a project begins, the client often has only a general idea of what he or she
wants to accomplish. The demographer must convert this general idea into a well-
defined project that will provide the client with needed information for planning
or decision-making. Failure to ascertain fully what the client wants at this stage
will lead to serious problems later. Only through extensive and ongoing communications can a consulting demographer hope to understand fully what the client
wants from the project.

Client involvement is also needed to identify appropriate variables for study.
Often the consulting demographer is unfamiliar with the factors likely to influence a client's business. The consulting demographer needs to listen carefully to
the client's discussion of factors regarded as important to success in a given market, and then the demographer must translate this discussion into variables. It is
also imperative to talk to the field staff, not just the senior managers. Often the
field staff is more sensitive than are the senior managers to important factors affecting the success or failure of a unit in a given market.

By the same token, clients are generally unaware of the wealth of information
to which the consulting demographer has access. For example, most people know
of the decennial census, but few are familiar with the Census of Business, County
Business Patterns, Current Population Surveys, or the Federal-State Cooperative
small area population and income estimates. Yet each of these sources may prove
extremely useful for a modeling project such as the one outlined here.

It is incumbent upon the applied demographer to educate the client as to the
strengths and limitations of the model used. I outlined several techniques to further this process of client education in the Welcome example. Such education is
critical if the client is to use the model results intelligently. If the consulting demographer presents the model as essentially a black box, making no effort to educate the client as to its limitations, there is a very real possibility that the client
will misinterpret the results or use them inappropriately. Such misuse of the
model can produce potentially disastrous results for the client and significant legal complications for the consultant. Experienced attorneys suggest that a consultant who fails to inform a client fully of the limitations of such statistical models faces a significant risk of legal liability should the client choose to sue after
sustaining economic losses as a consequence of acting upon model results.

The Limits of Statistical Modeling

Statistical models of the type discussed in this case can be powerful aids to a corporation intent on expanding into new markets, but they are not without limita-

tions. First, the models are only as good as the decisions made in constructing them. If the demographer fails to include important predictor variables, the model may be inaccurate. A more subtle problem involves the dissimilarity between the existing markets used to construct the model and the potential markets for which predictions will be made. If there are significant differences between these two groups, the model may not predict revenues properly for the potential markets.

Second, the construction of the statistical model is itself an extremely complex task. I have purposely avoided discussion here of the technical issues related to model construction, assuming that the reader either is well enough versed in these techniques to immediately see their application or will seek the help of those who are. The statistical subroutines for general linear models are readily available in most mainframe statistical packages (SPSS, SAS) and in the newest generation of packages for micros (SPSS-PC, SYSTAT).

There is, however, more to model construction than simply running the data through the program. Many of the decisions that the demographer must make when developing models such as those considered here require a great deal of judgment complemented by a detailed knowledge of statistics and the data available. An inexperienced researcher uncritically running the data through the default options of a stepwise regression procedure could well produce a flawed model that will eventually cost the client dearly.

Third, predictions derived from the model must be interpreted with caution. Even when the overall performance of the model is quite good, the actual revenues that a location generates will vary from what the model has predicted. Generally the difference between predicted and actual revenues will be modest, but in a few markets the differences may well be substantial. The point here is that it would be inappropriate for the demographer to put heavy emphasis on the actual dollar revenue predicted for a potential market. Of much greater importance is the position of the market relative to other potential markets.

The fourth and final limitation of statistical models is that they do not negate the need for careful work by managers and field staff. The modeling procedures provide a means for estimating the revenue potential of a large number of markets and identifying the most promising among them. The final decisions about which markets to enter, however, must rest on the managers' assessments in consultation with the field staff.

Beyond Demographic Data

Keep in mind that just because you are a demographer, all your variables need not be demographic. Demographers have long been critical of economists for failing to give adequate attention to demographic processes in econometric models. Demographers in applied settings also need to avoid such tunnel vision. In this case, demographic and census data played an important, though limited, role in the model. And while many additional demographic variables were included in the initial pool of variables, they did not prove particularly useful in the statistical model.[2]

For example, the measurement of transient populations is not directly addressed in Census or related databases. Yet, the transient population is a very important component of the revenue base in the travel and lodging industry. It was imperative, therefore, that I make an estimate of the size of the transient population so that I could incorporate it into the model. To make such an estimate, I had to look beyond the traditional demographic sources for data.

A similar problem arose with regard to the measurement of competition. The Welcome staff believed that competition had a significant impact on a unit's success. The problem was that detailed data on competition was not easy to obtain. Although the Census of Business provided information on the total number of lodging establishments in an area, the data was not detailed enough. The Welcome model required specific information on directly competitive chains. I eventually obtained such data from private sources at significant expense.

These examples illustrate the point that applied demographers must be prepared both to include nondemographic variables in their models and to seek such data from unconventional sources.

Conclusion

The case outlined here highlights some of the issues and problems that applied demographers are likely to encounter when called upon to aid organizations and corporations planning for expansion. Applied demographers can contribute to this process through both their knowledge of demographic data and processes and their expertise in the analysis and synthesis of large bodies of information. Managers in such settings are often overwhelmed with data and need to abstract from it the information critical for making decisions. Demographers called in to assist in such situations should give serious consideration to some variant of the modeling process outlined here as a possible solution to the problem.

This case illustrates how applied demographers can facilitate corporate expansion by showing firms how they can use information about their existing markets to identify promising new markets. Using multiple predictor variables, the demographer can create models able to approximate the complexity of the actual market environment, thereby allowing for more accurate predictions. Such models provide managers with the means to examine large numbers of potential markets efficiently and to identify those with the greatest promise. Managers are then able to concentrate their limited staff and resources on a detailed examination of the most promising of the potential markets. Used intelligently in combination with the expertise of the field staff and the judgment of senior corporate managers, such models provide a firm with the information it needs to expand into new markets successfully.

Discussion Questions

1. Was the recommendation to use general linear models a sound one? Explain.
2. Analyze the independent variables selected for estimating revenue.
3. Was the weighting scheme appropriate?
4. What other methods of analysis might have been used?
5. How important was the presentation of information and explanation to the managers in Phase I?
6. This model used variables beyond traditional demographic sources. What problems does this raise?
7. Describe how this model might be used for predicting success in other markets. Give a specific example and outline some of the predictor variables and data sources that might be used.

Notes

Peter Morrison reviewed an earlier draft of this manuscript and suggested several improvements that I have incorporated here. Some of the material presented here appeared previously in *American Demographics* and *The Journal of Applied Business Research.*

1. Welcome Motels is fictitious, but this case is based on consulting work I did for a Fortune 500 company in the travel and lodging industry. I have changed some of the variables and coefficients to protect the identity of the firm and the proprietary model I developed for them.

2. Such demographic variables did prove much more useful in a model developed to account for change in revenues among Welcome units.

References

Craig, C.S., A. Ghosh, and S. McLafferty. 1984. "Models of the Retail Location Process: A Review." *Journal of Retailing.* 60(1):5–36.

Johnson, K.M. 1985. "Modeling to Find Markets." *American Demographics.* 7(11):40–43, 54–55.

_____. 1986. "Using Statistical Models for Market Selection." *Journal of Applied Business Research.* 2(Winter): 110–120.

Lord, J., and C. Lynds. 1981. "The Use of Regression Models in Store Location Research. A Review and Case Study." *Akron Business and Economic Review.* 10:13–19.

Olsen, L., and J. Lord. 1979. "Market Area Characteristics and Branch Bank Performance." *Journal of Bank Research.* 10:102–110.

10

Motel 48: Evaluating
the Profitability
of a Proposed Business

David M. Ambrose and Louis G. Pol

This case in applied demography is different from most of others in four distinct ways. First, the analyses and judgments related to the decision-making process are directly linked to financial projections. That is, the end result of the data collection and analyses is a near-term financial forecast for the motel, a forecast showing that construction and operation should not begin.

Second, while it involves site selection, this case illustrates how analysis may culminate in the rejection of one favored site rather than in the choosing of one "best" site from among several alternatives. In our case, the investors/managers of the project already had acquired a site; the decision they faced was whether to proceed with constructing a motel there as planned. Our analysis provided the unwelcome news that a motel on that site was destined to be unprofitable.

Third, the case concerns the competition between facts and illusions. An initial set of financial projections, generated prior to the analyses reported here, indicated that the motel would be profitable. The perceived need for an additional analysis grew out of some skepticism on the part of the investors/managers.

Fourth, this case makes use of data that are, at first glance, not traditionally demographic. What they describe, though, is an anticipated population of prospective overnight visitors, defined by particular demographic characteristics of the potential market. Thus, this case utilizes data on traffic flow, economic activity, and competitor motel characteristics, all of which may seem far afield from standard demographic measures but which actually gauge the locational and socioeconomic dimensions that generate demand for motel usage. Data on traffic flow at the local level (measuring both commuting and business activity) and economic activity and competitor data (measuring actual and potential economic exchange) play a major role in this analysis. Applied demographers often need to merge traditional and less traditional data in order to address adequately the business issues they confront.

Setting

In 1985, several investors met to decide whether to go forward on a project involving the construction and management of a new 120-bed motel (Motel 48) in a medium-size metropolitan area. The motel would be operated as a franchise, and the franchisor had been involved in the data collection that was the basis for a financial analysis. The data for the financial analysis included an estimated occupancy rate, revenue totals, and business operation figures (including dollars to be spent on repairs, interest on the debt to be assumed, and advertising).

Moreover, the franchisor relied on a general "model" based on intuition, previous experience, and population size to ascertain the profitability of the motel. As we (the persons hired as consultants to reassess the initial decision to build the motel) soon discovered, the model was more a product of intuition than data. The only real datum utilized in the model was a total population figure for the entire Metropolitan Statistical Area (MSA). As the project progressed, it became apparent that an entirely new set of data would have to be collected.

According to the franchisor, this midwestern metropolitan area surpassed the minimum size necessary for success.[1] After the initial time needed for travelers to become aware that the motel was in business, the enterprise was expected to be profitable. The revenue and cost estimates derived from a preliminary data analysis are shown in Table 10.1. Based on an occupancy rate of about 78 percent and an average room rate of $48, the net profit before taxes was estimated to exceed $100,000.

The investors found this figure more than satisfactory, though some discussion ensued with regard to how reliable (and valid) these figures were.[2] After all, the franchisor had a role in producing the estimates, and he clearly had much to gain by the motel being built. The investors concluded that a more objective analysis was required. This analysis would include a reevaluation of the assumptions underlying the financial estimates as well as a more careful viewing of the data used to arrive at the figures. The investors hired outside consultants to perform the needed work.

Reanalysis

The first thing the consultants did was to examine the financial projections generated earlier. The net profit figure in Table 10.1 had been based upon assumed levels of sales revenues, costs associated with generating these revenues, and general administrative costs. The consultants treated the general administrative costs as fixed. That is, regardless of the level of occupancy—unless, of course, there are very few occupants—the management must be paid, repairs made, and advertising conducted. While it might be argued that a low occupancy level would result in somewhat lower costs for repairs and utilities, some damage would still occur, and the rooms would still have to be heated and cooled. An alternative model (not

Table 10.1   Initial Revenue and Cost Estimates for Motel 48

120 Rooms	
$48 Average Room Rate	
Occupancy Rate (in percent)	78.2%
Sales Revenue	$1,644,077
Cost of Operations	856,564
Gross Profit	787,513
General Administrative Costs	
Officers/Management	214,420
Repairs	8,520
Bad Debt	1,420
Interest	61,060
Depreciation	83,780
Advertising	38,340
Utilities	139,160
Other Expenses	133,480
Total G & A	680,180
Net Profit (Loss) Before Taxes	107,333

shown) which allowed some of these costs to vary had virtually no effect on either the financial forecasts or project conclusions.

Costs associated with generating revenue do vary. Hourly wages for assistants and housekeepers must be paid and laundry must be done. These costs are dependent upon the occupancy rate and therefore increase or decrease depending upon the number of rented rooms.

Given that administrative costs are fixed and that sales revenue and operating costs are a product of the number of rooms rented, the model is driven primarily by the occupancy rate. The maximum amount of annual revenue that the Motel 48 could generate would be $2,102,410—$48 (average room charge) × 120 (number of rooms) × 365, assuming that a room can be occupied only once in any given day. As the occupancy rate declines, the number of rented rooms in the formula is reduced, thus decreasing the revenue generated. Overall, the analysis hinges on the ability to estimate the occupancy rate accurately.

Because the financial projections were a product of occupancy, the consultants began the new analysis by determining a break-even point. In general, a break-even analysis involves identifying at what point (occupancy in this instance) revenues equal costs. At this point, net profit before taxes equals zero. The break-even figures appear in Table 10.2. Again, the consultants regarded all administrative costs as fixed. The required occupancy rate of 67.5 percent is more than 10 percent lower than the rate in Table 10.1, which includes the original forecasted estimate.

Table 10.2   Break-even for Motel 48

120 Rooms	
$48 Average Room Rate	
Occupancy Rate (in percent)	67.5%
Sales Revenue	$1,420,000
Cost of Operations	739,820
Gross Profit	680,180
General Administrative Costs	
Officers/Management	214,420
Repairs	8,520
Bad Debt	1,420
Interest	61,060
Depreciation	83,780
Advertising	38,340
Utilities	139,160
Other Expenses	133,480
Total G & A	680,180
Net Profit (Loss) Before Taxes	0

The next steps in the analysis involved a critical evaluation of the assumptions and data underlying the figures in Table 10.1 and the establishment of a revised occupancy rate using additional measures. Upon further examination, it became clear that there were no assumptions to evaluate. That is, a 78.2 percent occupancy rate was justified by intuition and experience, and not based upon testable data and assumptions. Therefore, the analysis had to focus on indicators that would provide insight into whether an average, higher than average, or lower than average occupancy rate could be expected. Several data sources were examined.[3]

Traffic Counts

The proposal called for Motel 48 to be built within a mid-sized metropolitan area on a major east-west segment of the interstate highway system. The motel was to be largely dependent on the traveler searching for overnight accommodations along this highway. The level of traffic on the interstate, therefore, was one indicator of the motel's future occupancy rate.

The traffic figures were impressive. Data from the state highway department showed that between 75,000 and 80,000 vehicles passed the site of the proposed motel each day. The motel had to capture fewer than two vehicles of every 1,000 to assure a full occupancy.

The concern with the data was that these counts were inflated by a large number of area commuters who quite obviously would not be prospective overnight guests. By examining traffic count data collected at other interval points west of the metropolitan area (and therefore not confounded by commuters), the consultants determined that only 11,000 to 12,000 of the vehicles were driven by distance travelers who might require accommodations. As a result of this calculation, the motel would need about 14 out of every 1,000 vehicles rather than just two.

The state highway department collects traffic data annually, and therefore the consultants were able to determine the rate of change of traffic volumes over the preceding 10 years. Surprisingly, there had been no growth. The long-distance traveler volume was the same as it had been 10 years earlier. Using these data, the consultants determined that the motel could expect, at best, only a nominal increase in prospective guests/travelers for the next five years.

Industry Conditions

We soon discovered that lodging is an industry for which there is an abundance of readily available data. Our conclusion after analyzing a great deal of these data was that lodging rooms throughout the nation had been overbuilt in the early 1980s. A slowly growing volume of guests was being spread over a rapidly growing number of rooms. The data (taken from the *U.S. Industry Outlook*) showed that the current national occupancy rate was about 64 percent, a decrease from percentages in previous years. The lodging industry had been in a steady decline for the prior six years; the forecast indicated a leveling off; and no dramatic improvement was likely in the foreseeable future.

While these data were impressive on their own, the discussion in the reports where the data were obtained caused even greater concern. Industry analysts held that some marginal lodging properties already had become victims of deteriorating occupancy and that additional lodging properties would close as this situation persisted.

Local Daily Lodging Rates

One contention in the construction proposal was that the motel would fit a very special price niche between the budget-priced accommodations and high-priced luxury rooms, giving the motel a competitive advantage. Implicit in this proposal was that no alternatives existed between these extremes. Fortunately, room charge/prices for lodging properties in the area had already been compiled and were easy to obtain. One telephone call to the local tourist bureau brought the consultants a complete listing.

The properties were listed in descending order according to room rates. The top room rate was $86.00 per day, but there were alternatives going all the way down to $15.00 per night in price intervals of about $3.00. The listing of room rates, in other words, provided no support for a price niche opportunity. The proposed motel would have to compete directly with established lodging properties.

Local Occupancy Levels

Local occupancy levels provided significant insight into the prospects for the proposed motel. These data, however, were somewhat more difficult to secure than those concerning lodging rates. No motel/hotel manager would disclose occupancy levels even though they knew what such levels were.

The state revenue office proved to be an excellent source of information in this regard. The revenue office had collected room tax revenue on a monthly basis and had data available for several years. We began by adjusting these data for general room rate increases that had occurred over the years. The resulting data allowed us not only to estimate an occupancy rate across these competing lodging properties but also to identify seasonal patterns in the occupancy levels.

While this method was not perfect, our findings did conform to commonly held beliefs within the lodging industry. The overall occupancy level followed very closely the deteriorating national trends, and seasonal patterns in the local area matched the seasonal patterns throughout the region.

Major Attraction

The local lodging industry had prospered from the operation of a major horse racing track. This track's racing season spanned about four and one-half months. Local hotels and motels always enjoyed higher occupancies starting the day the track opened each year and terminating on the track's closing date.

Obtaining attendance data for the track was easy. Because the length of the season had changed over the years, however, we had to divide each year's attendance data by the number of days in the racing season.

Historically, the track had faced no nearby pari-mutuel competition. Only the year before, though, a dog track had commenced operation about 15 miles from the horse track. The dog track was served by a different set of motels in part because it is in a different state. Already gate attendance at the horse track was down by more than 10 percent, raising the question: How much of an effect would the dog track have on the future of horse racing attendance? The conservative estimate was a further reduction of 15 percent. The more aggressive track supporters believed that the decline would be something less than five percent. Most knowledgeable observers, however, believed that another 10 percent would be added to the 10 percent reduction to date.

Using this additional 10 percent track reduction, we adjusted downward our estimates of the impact the track would have on occupancy levels. The high occupancy levels that lodging property owners enjoyed during the track season would not be matched in future years; the aggregated annual occupancy rate likewise would be reduced.

Economic Forecast

Another major portion of the guests in the lodging properties was composed of people who had come to the area to transact business. An expanding local economy would increase the number of business guests while a depressed local economy would have the opposite effect.

The local Chamber of Commerce supplied us with economic profiles and forecasts for the region. Although we found some evidence that the economy would expand, potential growth was very limited. The forecasts showed economic growth to be between two and four percent annually over the next five years, below the anticipated rate of national economic expansion.

While any growth would be a positive factor, it had a limited impact. First, commercial guests accounted for only a portion—not more than 30 percent—of guests. And second, certain business trends were not encouraging. Increasingly, sales executives and even corporate executives were transacting business by telephone, thereby avoiding the costs of overnight accommodations.

Convention Visitors and Guests

The original proposal for the Motel 48 had included conventions as a significant source of guests. While convention guests do constitute a major portion of the lodging industry's clientele throughout the country, the original proposal did not include an assessment of conventions in the local area.

The metropolitan convention bureau offered us a wealth of information. The professional staff at the convention bureau informed us that local conventions were held either at a major convention center near the site of the proposed motel or in the central city. The bureau had collected data to compare the performance of these two convention areas, and the data led to conclusions that were not encouraging.

The number of conventions and the total number of visitors attending conventions near the proposed site had been in a slight decline over the past several years. Even more worrisome, there was no significant growth forecast for that area, there were five major lodging alternatives already surrounding the convention center, and the proposed motel would be an inferior alternative as it was not within walking distance of the convention center.

The bureau staff also told us that the proposed motel could anticipate few if any guests from conventions in the central city. The distance and attractive lodging alternatives made it unlikely that many of these convention guests would choose to stay at the Motel 48.

Overall Growth in the Surrounding Area

We examined U.S. Bureau of the Census population data for the area surrounding the motel (approximately one mile radius) and the larger metropolitan area for 1960, 1970, and 1980. We also secured post-1980 population estimates and projections for the metropolitan area from the state Bureau of Business Research.

The figures showed that, overall, the metropolitan area had experienced very low percentage population increases over the past 25 years and that this pattern was likely to continue. The neighborhoods and commercial property in the area adjacent to the proposed site were virtually all built-out and had been for 20 years. There was no physical space in close proximity for the development of commercial projects that might attract people with lodging needs. The prospects for growth in the immediate area that might impact positively upon motel occupancy were, therefore, quite dim.

Our examination of establishment data from the U.S. Census Bureau's County Business Patterns data and employment data available from the state Bureau of Business Research for 1975 through 1983 substantiated the population observation. While the number of establishments in the metropolitan area had grown, the total number of employed persons had increased at a much slower rate. The increase in the number of establishments came from the growth in small businesses, those less likely to attract to the area persons in need of lodging. Overall, these data gave no support to the notion that a significant increase in lodging demand would occur.

Reevaluation

The examination of a variety of data led us to several conclusions. First, the addition of 120 rooms to a market that already had 3,000 rooms would impact the total market very little. Second, Motel 48 would face competition from several other motels at the mid-price level. Third, the location would have to be considered a modal one. That is, with respect to growth, potential growth, and competition, the immediate area was about average. In sum, our evaluation led to the conclusion that Motel 48 could expect an occupancy rate approximately equal to the percentage being experienced by all motels in the metropolitan area. The "expected" occupancy rate was 63 percent, a full four and one-half percent below the motel's break-even point.

The analysis could have stopped here because the recommendation not to go forward was already obvious. We believed, however, that it was important to complete the financial projection. We deemed it necessary to make one more adjustment to the occupancy rate. Contrary to the modal category assumption above, a more conservative occupancy rate seemed probable. Motel 48, and those near it, could probably expect a less-than-average occupancy rate when compared with other motels in the metropolitan area due to their heavy dependence upon race track patrons. Over time, the negative impact would be even greater as the reduction in track attendance continued. The expected occupancy rate at Motel 48 was set at 59 percent after adjusting downward for the loss of race track guests.

Table 10.3 presents the revenue and cost data based upon this lower occupancy rate. Note that revenue is about $165,000 below that needed to reach the break-even point. After adjusting for lower variable costs, we concluded that the annual loss in income would be nearly $79,000.

Table 10.3   New Analysis Revenue and Cost Estimates for Motel 48

120 Rooms	
$48 Average Room Rate	
Occupancy Rate (in percent)	59.7%
Sales Revenue	$1,255,133
Cost of Operations	653,924
Gross Profit	601,209
General Administrative Costs	
Officers/Management	214,420
Repairs	8,520
Bad Debt	1,420
Interest	61,060
Depreciation	83,780
Advertising	38,340
Utilities	139,160
Other Expenses	133,480
Total G & A	680,180
Net Profit (Loss) Before Taxes	(78,971)

Recommendation

The net loss figure in Table 10.3 supported but one recommendation: We advised the investors against moving forward. Other options (e.g., an increase in room rate and additional cost reduction measures) were judged to be unacceptable and unrealistic by the client. While clients do not always accept advice from consultants, the investors did reluctantly face the sobering reality that our facts conflicted with their intuition. Optimism had masked reality.

Nonetheless, our advice was not well received. The clients/investors were angry. They had invested considerable time in planning and developing the project. They made their anger and disappointment evident by not paying the consultants for nearly a year and then only after considerable difficulty.

Several years later, however, the clients conceded that our advice had been correct. By then they recognized that motels in the area had performed poorly and that their Motel 48 would have failed. A less-detailed analysis of the market two years after our work was completed showed that motel competition was substantial and that occupancy rates were still relatively low. In fact, several lodging properties in the immediate area had experienced serious occupancy problems and were attempting to readjust their competitive position in order to secure a better share of the no-growth market. Tourism never grew as originally expected, and attendance at the horse track continued to slide precipitously. An assessment of all the factors that drive motel occupancy clearly led to the conclusion that the local lodging industry was in the doldrums and that a prudent investor would have found entry unwise.

While a forecast of demand is never precise, the data relating to the estimated occupancy of the Motel 48 were rather indicative. There were no demographic or other signals at the time of our analysis to encourage development and a great many to argue against going forward with the project.

Observations

The research process described in this case typifies what the business demographer sometimes encounters. A client begins with an idea, bases financial projections on optimistic assumptions rather than on hard facts, then hopes for a commercial success. Data gathering and analysis may either confirm those assumptions or call them into question. When the latter occurs, the research process may prevent an unwise decision. Bad news, however, is not always welcome news. Analyses that fail to support the initial level of optimism are often discounted or discredited, and clients go forward with projects despite the facts.

In such situations, consultants face a special challenge in striving to be effective. They must read the situation accurately (e.g., the client's optimism versus tolerance for hard facts), and they must ask a lot of questions and gain the client's trust (or at least reduce the level of distrust). Finally, consultants must have the courage of their convictions to present results that question the viability of a project in which clients have already made an emotional—and perhaps financial—investment.

With respect to data sources and analyses, two general factors must be considered. First, in many cases demographic data drive the analyses in these types of studies. The data used, however, must be viewed more broadly and liberally because some valuable sources may not be of the sort traditionally utilized in demographic analyses. Second, demographic and nondemographic data must be merged in order to address adequately the issues that consultants are called upon to evaluate. Experience and creativity play major roles here. In our enthusiasm to bring an innovative perspective to these types of issues, though, we demographers must adhere to the fundamental tenets and procedures of demographic analysis. We must follow demographic principles without compromise and incorporate them in our analyses in a rigorous manner.

Discussion Questions

1. What was the mixture of traditionally demographic and non-demographic data used in this analysis?

2. Through which sources is the alternative data collected in this case?

3. What did demographers contribute to this analysis that consultants from other disciplines may not have been able to provide?

4. The clients in this case, upset with the results of the study, retaliated by delaying payment to the consultants. What would you have done to resolve this problem?

5. Does it appear that the analysts in this case spent enough time with the client throughout the study to gather and share data as well as develop mutual trust? Explain.

Notes

1. A number of businesses in certain industries rely on these types of models. Some retailers, for example, use the general model of one store for every 250,000 or 300,000 population, all other factors being equal.

2. Satisfactory is a rather nebulous term. Many businesses will not invest in a "new" endeavor unless projected return on that investment is at a specific target percentage or higher.

3. A major reason for the consultants' concern regarding the financial data in Table 10.1 was the 78.2 percent figure—a much higher occupancy rate than national or regional averages.

Discussion Questions
for Part Three

1. Each case in this section addresses the question of purchasing a market or site for a business. What is the main issue in each case that drove the final decision? How do they differ?

2. What different approaches were used to access census data? What drove the choice of methodology?

3. Could any of the methods used in these cases be transferred to the other cases in this section (particularly the two hotel/motel site selection cases)?

4. Describe the differences in methodology in the hotel/motel cases.

5. Describe how other traditional demographic data sources were used in each case.

6. Compare the impact of client involvement in each case. What useful information did each client provide?

7. What non-traditional data sources were utilized? Could any of these sources be transferred from one case to another?

8. Describe the role each analysis played at an important stage of the client's decision-making process. Discuss the importance of the timing of demographic analysis to market selection.

PART FOUR

Locations

11

Using Demographic Analysis in Health Services Planning: A Case Study in Obstetrical Services

Richard K. Thomas

During the 1980s, the level of competition within the health care industry reached unprecedented heights. Traditional providers of care such as hospitals and clinics were challenged by a proliferation of innovative facilities, ranging from minor medical centers to freestanding surgicenters. Similarly, traditional means for financing health care were challenged by such alternative financing mechanisms as health maintenance organizations and preferred provider organizations. For the first time in modern history, established providers of care were faced with head-on competition for patients and revenue.

As a result, the traditional institutions have had to develop capabilities for strategic planning, market analysis, and feasibility studies. All of these activities depend heavily on the techniques of applied demography. The case study that follows presents a situation in which demographic data and analyses were pivotal in the decision to reject an application for establishing a new obstetrical unit at an existing hospital. The study analyzes both the argument in favor of the new service and the counter arguments in order to demonstrate the uses and misuses of demographic data and techniques in the preparation of planning and feasibility studies. It concludes with a discussion of the lessons one can learn from this case study and of its implications for the future of applied demography.

Introduction

The establishment of a hospital obstetrical unit, it would seem, should not require particularly complicated demographic analysis. One need only estimate the likely number of births in the general area, arrange for the appropriate medical staff, and start delivering babies. This simple scenario, of course, overlooks the complexity involved in planning for any type of health service—and particularly for obstetrical services. A failure to appreciate this complexity could easily lead a hospital to disaster when its obstetrical program founders as a result of miscalculating the demand for maternity services.

This case study deals with an attempt by a suburban hospital to initiate a new obstetrical program. The facility—a satellite of a large inner-city, church-affiliated hospital—was applying to offer maternity services in a suburban area northeast of the central city. The community had recently experienced rapid population growth, outpacing the increase in health services. It seemed logical, therefore, that the area was being underserved in terms of obstetrical care. The hospital submitted its application to the local health planning board, whose responsibility it was to approve the project prior to the application being referred to the state health planning office for ultimate approval. A competing hospital, which felt that the community in question was rightfully its service area, assigned me to develop a case against the establishment of the new obstetrical unit. My "con" perspective is what appears in the analysis below.

This case study provides an excellent example of the application of demography to a concrete problem in health care. Certainly the primary issue—the demand for maternity services—deals with one of the basic dynamic processes in demography, fertility. Yet this case goes well beyond that. The analyses necessary to determine the feasibility of an obstetrical unit involve virtually every aspect of demography. Not only must the analyst be conversant with the complexities of fertility indicators, but he or she must also be knowledgeable with regard to population estimates and projections, small-area analysis, census geography, cohort analysis, and migration. This particular analysis, moreover, required considerable knowledge of the local area in terms of urban growth patterns and transportation routes, the local health care industry (including existing patterns of obstetrical service delivery), and the psychographics of the population in question.

The case serves best as an illustration of the step-by-step analysis of a problem in applied demography. It ultimately incorporated most substantive areas of demography, reading somewhat like a survey textbook in the field. It addressed the issues of population size, distribution, and composition as well as the dynamic processes of fertility and migration. All in all, the project required an advanced understanding of the content, measures, and methods of demography.

This case also serves as a useful example of the problems that can result from a superficial knowledge of demography, sloppy use of demographic data, and amateur attempts at demographic analysis. More than anything, perhaps, this case highlights ways in which one should *not* conduct a demographic analysis.

Background

The setting for this case is a medium-sized city in the southeastern United States. The city is a regional distribution center serving a hinterland of approximately 100 counties. As the health center for the region, it is home to several large hospitals of 500 beds or more. The city is located in Metro County, the core county in a four-county metropolitan statistical area. Metro County is unusual in terms of the influence of the health care industry in the community.

Historically, health services had been concentrated in the "medical center" near the downtown area. During the 1970s, however, health care followed the city's population to the suburbs. Two new independent hospitals were constructed in one of the high-growth corridors, followed by the construction of four "satellite" facilities by the city's two major hospitals. This construction produced something of a hub-and-spoke pattern, with several major health facilities remaining in the medical center encircled by a number of new suburban hospitals.

By the 1980s, it was obvious that the metropolitan area was "overbedded." Two decades of hospital construction resulted in a bed capacity that exceeded demand, despite the fact that the medical center drew from a regional population of nearly three million residents. Health planning officials at the state level recognized the situation, and they began to insist upon convincing justification before approving new facilities or services.

The situation with regard to obstetrical services had become particularly competitive. The city's major hospital—Denominational Hospital—had moved its entire obstetrical program to its suburban satellite in the late 1970s in order to position itself to capitalize on the population redistribution that was occurring. By the early 1980s, it had come to dominate the maternity market, controlling some 35 percent of total deliveries and well over 50 percent of noncharity deliveries. Its primary competitor—Sectarian Hospital—had continued to base its OB program at its Medical Center unit, resulting in a low market share and an unfavorable competitive position. As Denominational was expanding its influence during the early 1980s, Sectarian's market share remained stable at around 15 percent. More importantly, Sectarian's inner-city location meant that its obstetrical patients were increasingly unable to pay for care.

In 1984, Sectarian Hospital developed a proposal for an obstetrical unit at one of its suburban facilities located in a relatively new residential community northeast of the city. The proposal argued that this area was underserved in terms of maternity care, and it called for a maternity unit with eight delivery rooms. Sectarian submitted the proposal to the local health planning committee, basing its justification for the facility and the number of beds on its own demographic analyses. Sectarian's statistics had been developed by its market research department, and the proposal was presented by a senior administrator.

As a research analyst for Denominational Hospital, I was assigned the task of developing an argument against the establishment of the new OB unit at the Sectarian satellite. While the proposed facility was not large enough to be a factor in the overall obstetrical market, its location only a few minutes from the Denominational OB unit and its proximity to the heart of the most desirable OB market spurred Denominational to formally oppose its development (Figure 11.1).

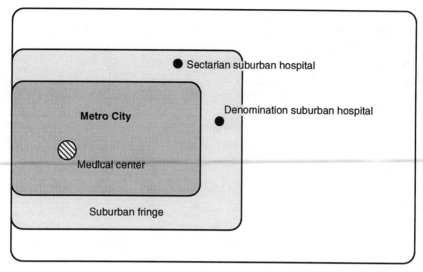

Figure 11.1—Schematic map of Metro County

The following sections outline the steps I took in developing the argument against the new OB unit. The process is presented in much the same sequence one would follow in developing the proposal. In this case, however, the objective was to discredit the proposal on as many points as possible (Staff 1987).

The Proposed Project

As submitted to the local health planning agency, the Sectarian proposal called for construction of a new wing—including eight birthing rooms—at the existing facility. The application contained details of the financing of the project and assurances, as required by statute, that the OB service could be provided economically and would result in no increase in health care costs to community residents. Although both opponents and review board members challenged the financial analysis, that issue is beyond the scope of this case study.

In addition to providing financing information, the application had to demonstrate a sufficient demand for the facility's service, show it was feasible to provide the service at this site and in the form proposed, and assure that existing patterns of medical practice would not be disrupted. Given the fact that the health planners recognized the overcapacity situation at the time of the application, the first of these contentions was obviously the most crucial. Although the feasibility and practice pattern issues were certainly important, it was the determination-of-need issue that is most relevant to this case study.

The need justification can be summarized as follows. The site of the proposed facility was in one of the county's fastest growing areas. Not only was the number of residents in this area rapidly increasing, the number of women of childbearing age was very large. The relatively high fertility rate was resulting in a large number of deliveries. The nearest obstetrical unit was ten minutes away, and Sectarian's Medical Center (for those who wanted to give birth at a Sectarian facility) was 15 to 20 minutes away. Yet, the site of the proposed service was far enough from its main competitor that it would not disrupt existing practice patterns.

When it presented its proposal, Sectarian brought in a few women from the community near the site to testify as to the need for this type of service at a convenient location. In addition, a physician on the Sectarian staff commented on the negligible impact that the new program would have on existing practice patterns. The main arguments justifying the proposed obstetrical service, however, rested squarely on the demographic analysis that had been conducted to demonstrate the need for and feasibility of the new facility.

Sectarian's Demographic Analysis

Sectarian representatives began their justification by defining the market area that the proposed facility would serve. In effect, they identified the service area as the upper third of Metro County, using the zipcode as the delineating geographic unit. The service area included several zipcodes that covered territory between this facility and its mother facility to the south, territory within two miles of the dominant Denominational OB unit to the southeast, and all of the remaining portion of the county to the north. The service area also extended into the lower portion of the adjacent county to the north.

The proponents estimated that, at the time of the application, this service area included 235,500 residents. They argued that not only was this a large population base in absolute terms, but also that the area was expected to grow substantially in the future. Parts of the service area had grown at rates in excess of 10 percent per year between 1970 and 1980, and by 1989 the service area was projected to reach 266,000 residents, producing an additional growth rate of 13 percent for the 1984–1989 period. The zipcode in which the Sectarian facility was to be located was, according to these representatives, one of the fastest growing areas of the county (Figure 11.2).

They also argued that the number of women of childbearing age in the service area had increased dramatically during the 1970s. They presented a projection from a national vendor as documentation of continued growth of the childbearing female population (i.e., females 20 to 45) between 1980 and 1989; this projection cited a 34.5 percent increase. Based on this projection, the Sectarian representatives projected that there would be 67,122 females of childbearing age in the service area in 1989.

The application described the service area population as predominantly white, upper middle class in terms of income, well-educated, and progressive in its views of health care. While these characteristics may not have held true throughout the

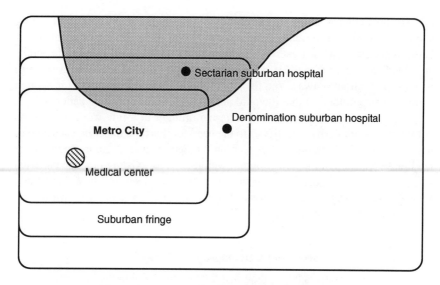

**Figure 11.2—Proposed obstetrics service area
(excluding portion of adjacent county)**

overall service area, the Sectarian's supporters argued, they were particularly true
for the primary zipcode. In fact, a focus group of individuals from the primary
zipcode not only had these characteristics but also had indicated support for such
an innovative, community-based health service.

The proponents proceeded to refine their argument by introducing the subject
of birth rates. They chose to use the crude birth rate for Metro County for a recent
year, reporting that rate to be 16 births per 1,000 residents. Utilizing this rate, they
argued that the population in the service area would yield 4,269 births annually by
1989.

The Sectarian representatives argued that a projected market share of 33 percent was reasonable. This figure, however, was based more on what they believed
was possible than on any realistic estimate based on existing practice patterns. By
their calculations this would yield 1,400 births annually for the Sectarian facility,
a number large enough to support an obstetrical unit but not so large as to disrupt
existing patterns of service delivery.

The proposal presentation offered what appeared to be a reasonable justification for a new obstetrical facility in an underserved area that wanted such care. A
clearly identifiable service area existed; the population base was adequate and
continued growth was expected; the birth rate was high and presumably would remain so; and a reasonable market share was obtainable. These points, along with
the support from the community focus group and the testimony of some women
residing in the area, appeared to justify the proposed obstetrical service. The proponents were confident that the local health planning agency would approve their
proposal.

Demographic Analysis Opposing the Proposal

When I examined the details of the proposal, however, it was obvious that a careful demographic analysis had not been conducted. At every step of the argument, I was able to identify an inappropriate demographic assumption, improper utilization of demographic data, and/or naive interpretations of the established facts. My critical analysis of each step in the determination-of-need process is presented below.

Delineating the Service Area

The proponents' first step had been to delineate the area that the program would serve. There are a number of ways in which a service area for health care can be delineated, and the method utilized often depends on the type of service being considered (Garnick et al. 1987; Massey and Blake 1987). One frequently used method is to examine the origin of existing patients and identify the geographic areas (zipcodes, census tracts, or other unit) from which a majority of the patients is drawn. This area is usually delineated so as to take in 70 to 80 percent of the facility's admissions. Another method would be to determine in which areas the hospital in question maintains the greatest market share and then to draw the service area boundaries accordingly.

Yet another method might be to determine what constitutes reasonable travel time and use this as the criterion for determining the primary service area. Although this approach has historically been more appropriate for determining the service area for ambulatory care, it has become a more viable criterion for hospital service areas now that patients are more frequently choosing a hospital on the basis of convenience. A third approach is to identify the "home" geographic unit (or units) and identify this as the primary service area. For example, the zipcode or county in which a facility is located may be considered the service area and decisions made accordingly.

Perhaps the most realistic approach is the most qualitative. Information might be combined on existing drawing areas, driving times, physician practice patterns, and existing health services utilization patterns to determine a reasonable service area.

Although not a crucial point, the proponents of the new OB unit failed to delineate convincingly a service area for obstetrical services that was appropriate to the proposed site. Since the hospital lacked a history of obstetrical services, the proponents tried to utilize its general medical/surgery service area as a proxy. Not only did they find it difficult to argue that the obstetrical service area would be comparable to the medical/surgical service area, but they also failed—for reasons discussed below—to delineate the medical/surgical service.

As noted earlier, the proponents had identified the northern third of the county and a portion of an adjacent county as the proposed service area. Available market share information indicated, however, that in only one of the included zipcodes did the hospital maintain a significant share of medical/surgical patients. In all of the other zipcodes included in the service area, at least one of the competing hospitals had a dominant share of the market. One key zipcode was controlled by Denominational Hospital which maintained a 75 percent market share there. Another zipcode—one containing a naval base—was the site of a military hospital that accounted for most of the area's births. Another included zipcode was an adjacent inner-city area that had no linkage with the distant suburban facility. The adjacent county to the north was included in the proposed service area even though Sectarian Hospital maintained only a 12 percent medical/surgical market share there.

The problem that the proponents faced was the lack of an appropriate geography on which to base service area claims. Their problem illustrates the danger of using zipcodes as the geographic unit. Zipcodes are often quite large, and it is not unusual for them to contain a heterogeneous population in terms of demographics, socioeconomic status, and lifestyles. Moreover, they are often so large in terms of land area that they become useless for planning purposes. Had the proponents been able to use census tracts as the basic geographical unit, they might have been able to make a more convincing case for the proposed service area (Chapman 1988). As it was, the proponents opened their argument by presenting an unrealistic service area for the proposed OB facility.

Determining the Service Area Population

Even assuming that the service area delineated by the proponents had been acceptable, their handling of population estimates and projections was seriously flawed. The proponents argued that the population of the identified service area was growing rapidly, and they cited growth trends for the 1970 to 1980 period, including an overall growth rate for the area of around 25 percent. More importantly, they reported a ten-year growth rate of over 100 percent for the zipcode in which the hospital was located. Thus, as evidence of an adequate population base, they submitted a 1980 population of 215,295 for the overall service area and 36,594 for the primary zipcode.

While these figures were pretty much beyond dispute (they were, after all, census figures), the need for the new unit had to be based on the future population of the service area. One could argue that the 1980 population would not yield enough births to justify a new facility. Thus, one had to examine population trends to determine whether the service area population was increasing, decreasing, or remaining stable. Obviously, a projected decline in service area population would not bode well for a new facility. The proponents of the OB unit needed to document expected population growth in order to justify their project.

One can use a variety of methodologies to make population projections (Shryock and Siegel 1976). All projections, however, model the future on the past, and that is what the proponents attempted to do in this case. The overall population of the service area had grown some 25 percent between 1970 and 1980.

The application projected it to grow by another 13 percent between 1984 and 1989. The proponents projected the primary zipcode, which had grown by an incredible 100 percent during the 1970s, to grow by another 20 percent during the five-year projection period.

A quick examination of the figures in the proposal revealed that the proponents had simply "straight-lined" the growth rate of the 1970s on through the 1980s. Once in a great while a straight-line projection based on percent increase might be appropriate, but it would be highly unusual for a rapidly developing residential area to experience comparable change for two decades in a row.

As it turned out, it was easy to identify the flaws in the proponents' method. Housing start information (available from the county planning commission) indicated that the rate of new housing development in the primary zipcode in the early 1980s was well below that of the 1970s. In fact, an analysis of these data indicated that the bulk of the population growth in the primary zipcode had occurred during the first five years of the 1970s, with development tailing off dramatically between 1975 and 1985. My own population estimates, made at the time of the proposal, indicated a level of growth significantly below that projected by the proponents. My estimates were "reality based" in that they used an enumeration of actual households (as provided by the U.S. Postal Service) to determine the current population.

The final piece of evidence against the proponents' purported growth rates was the simple fact that there was not enough developable land remaining within the zipcode to support the projected growth (O'Hare 1988).

As a result of this analysis, a five-year growth rate of 2 percent for the service area appeared to be more reasonable than the 13 percent projected by the applicant. Most of this growth was to be accounted for by the zipcode in which Denominational was dominant. In fact, according to planning commission records, virtually no new development was taking place at that time in any other part of the service area.

Assessing Changing Population Characteristics

Even granting that for the foreseeable future a substantial amount of growth would be occurring within the primary zipcode and in some other portions of the service area, one would have to conclude that the proponents failed to address a subsidiary but perhaps more important issue. Their application said nothing about the changing age distribution of the population, a subject with enormous implications for reproduction.

The demographic data purportedly purchased from vendors was misleading because it apparently miscalculated trends in the size of the childbearing population. The proposal's projection of 67,122 women of childbearing age in 1989 was much higher than both a previous Denominational projection of 59,750 and a different vendor's projection of 51,867. In fact, cohort analysis indicated that the number of women between 20 and 35 throughout most of the hospital's service area would be essentially the same or lower in 1990 than it had been in 1980, despite projected overall population growth.

The only portion of the service area for which an increase in childbearing-age women was anticipated was the zipcode in the "back yard" of Denominational Hospital. In any case, data readily available from vendors indicated that the median age of women in the service area was already 30 years. By examining broad age categories (e.g., 20–45), the proponents came to the conclusion that the prime childbearing population was increasing. More detailed cohort analysis indicated that this clearly was not the case.

The proponents' analysis also had failed to take into consideration trends in migration that were contributing to population redistribution and to the changing age structure in suburban Metro County. Of the three components of population change—births, deaths, and migration—only migration is likely to have a significant effect on the size and composition of the populations of suburbanizing areas in the short run. In fact, identifying characteristics of in-migrants and out-migrants is crucial in planning for any type of service (Shryock and Siegel 1976). What types of people, for example, are moving into the community—retirees, young marrieds, middle-aged empty nesters? Can past trends related to migrant characteristics be expected to continue into the future?

The significance here lies in what the characteristics of future in-migrants might imply for fertility levels. In this case, the proponents assumed that future in-migrants would resemble already existing residents. This was a crucial point because they believed that the area's residents were characterized by high fertility levels.

This belief turned out to be questionable. As often happens in newer suburbs, successive waves of fresh migrants were distinguishable from the original "settlers." Census data indicated that those moving into the primary zipcode between 1975 and 1980 were different in important ways from those who had moved in between 1965 and 1970 when the area was originally being developed. Fragmented data based on other sources (such as real estate transactions and school enrollment trends) supported the argument for a distinction. More recent in-migrants were older, less upwardly mobile, and more likely to have completed childbearing. These facts further diminished the proponents' argument as to the future potential of the primary zipcode.

There were still other issues that the proponents should have addressed but did not. For example, unless they regarded OB services as a "loss leader," they needed to take into consideration the economic characteristics of the future population. Would future residents have the same ability as current ones to pay for health care? Would their patterns of health care utilization be the same?

In this case, the changing demographics of the adjacent zipcode to the west of the primary zipcode was an important example. During the late 1970s, this area started undergoing a transformation from a middle-class white neighborhood to a working-class black neighborhood. As a result of its transition, this zipcode was the only one in the county to report a lower median family income (unadjusted for inflation) for 1979 than for 1969. Further, the changing occupational structure meant that a smaller proportion of the population had adequate insurance coverage. Finally, the background of this population meant that the area was still oriented, for services at least, to the inner city and not to a suburban area that was socially light years away.

A related consideration was the possible changing psychographics of the population. Would the future service area population be primarily "yuppies" interested in innovative birthing arrangements, or would they be more conservative residents interested in traditional maternity services? This distinction relates squarely to the issue of image. Unless a hospital's image is in keeping with the residents of the service area, it is unlikely that the population will identify with the facility. In any case, the characteristics of future populations would be more relevant than those of the present population.

Calculating Fertility Rates

The proponents were particularly careless in their use of fertility indicators. As noted earlier, the proponents used the county's crude birth rate of 16.2/1,000 to determine the likely number of births in the proposed service area. This yielded an estimated 670 annual births for the primary zipcode and 4,269 for the overall service area by 1989. The proponents further supported their estimates by presenting a figure for the actual number of births for the primary zipcode during a recent year.

I questioned these contentions on two methodological grounds. My most important objection related to the rate the proponents used in their calculation of births. While the crude birth rate is usually the easiest fertility indicator to calculate and the simplest to understand, it is also the most misleading in many cases. In this instance, the proponents calculated the crude birth rate at the county level and applied it to a much smaller subarea. Their underlying assumption was that the county-wide birth rate was applicable to all parts of the county.

Even the most basic understanding of demographic analysis should have made it obvious that this approach was inappropriate. The crude birth rate is simply a grossly calculated average that masks a great many subgroup differences. When the crude birth rate for Metro County was adjusted for race, for example, it became clear that much of the county's fertility was due to the county's black population. The crude birth rate for Metro County blacks was 23/1,000, compared to 9/1,000 for whites. Since the proponents had already demonstrated that the service area population (especially the primary zipcode) was overwhelmingly white, they were obligated—if they chose to utilize the crude birth rate over a better indicator—to apply the white crude birth rate to the service area. Doing so would yield 2,400 rather than 4,270 births (the figure submitted by the proponents) annually for the primary zipcode. The actual crude birth rate for the Metro County portion of the service area turned out to be 11.5/1,000—higher than the white average but 29 percent lower than the figure submitted by the proponents. In addition to relying upon a questionable indicator of fertility, the proponents failed to take into consideration that the county's crude birth rate had been steadily falling.

Since this birth rate figure is "crude" in terms of the population base utilized, it is not a very direct measure of fertility. It would be more appropriate to utilize an indicator that takes the age and sex distribution of the population into consideration. The general fertility rate or the child-woman ratio would be two examples because both are based on the relevant population rather than the total population (Shryock and Siegel 1976).

While these indicators adjust for the age-sex composition of the population, there are other factors that should be taken into consideration if possible. Obviously, different ethnic and racial groups—as well as different social classes—are characterized by distinct fertility rates. Ideally, therefore, these population attributes should be adjusted for as well. It would be best, of course, to apply each population's actual fertility rate when determining the level of births. If this is not possible, the next best thing is to apply known fertility rates for a population that has similar characteristics. In this case, the proponents should have used the general fertility rate for the service area population, which would have resulted in a more accurate figure of 2,000 projected births rather than their highly inaccurate figure of nearly 5,000.

I also questioned their estimate of actual births within the primary zipcode. Birth data were available only at the census tract level, but the proponents had argued for 700 annual births within the primary zipcode. While I could not determine how accurate their estimate was, I openly challenged their "switching" of geography. The proponents had roughly converted census tracts into zipcodes. While this may be acceptable in cases where tract boundaries neatly coincide with zipcode boundaries, it was not appropriate in this case.

The procedure involved allocation of births from split tracts to the appropriate zipcodes. As it turned out, some of the split tracts contained large numbers of births. If a census tract yielded 200 births annually and were split down the middle by a zipcode boundary, how should the births be allocated on the basis of zipcodes? In the absence of more accurate data, the proponents made several value judgments with regard to allocation, in some cases including the whole split tract in one of the zipcodes or estimating the split by visually comparing tract and zipcode boundaries. Since it was unlikely that births would be distributed evenly with a census tract, neither of these allocation methods could be considered appropriate. When I made this point about the proponent's estimate of births, the review board—while not declaring the figure inaccurate—simply considered it inadmissible due to methodological misgivings.[1]

The proponents could easily have verified their birth estimates by applying their contended rate to their own population estimates and comparing the results to actual birth data. This procedure would have yielded an annual incidence of approximately 3,500 births. Health Department records for that portion of the county, however, indicated fewer than 3,000 births for the most recent year for which data were available. In actuality, the number of births in the service area had decreased over the preceding few years.

Estimating Potential Market Share

The projected number of births would be meaningful only if the new service could capture an adequate market share. Even if all of the proponents' contentions had been correct up to this point, it was unlikely that Sectarian would be able to capture the share of the market it claimed. Here, as in most communities, several facilities were competing for obstetrical patients. Since a new facility could not expect to obtain all of the anticipated births within the service area but only its "share," a realistic estimate of that share was crucial.

While the known share of medical/surgical patients might be used as a proxy, it would be unlikely that the distribution of obstetrical patients would follow the same pattern. It should also be remembered that initially a new service must capture the bulk of its patients from existing facilities. Given the fact that the patient's obstetrician exerts the most influence in her choice of facility, a new facility cannot expect to capture a major share very rapidly.[2] In this case, the proponents not only failed to appreciate this fact, but they also overlooked another fact: 700 births in the service area took place at the naval hospital. These births, of course, were not capturable, and they had to be subtracted from the pool of births available.

Two Conflicting Conclusions

Clearly, the proponents and I reached two quite distinct conclusions with regard to the proposed obstetrical unit. The proponents, of course, argued that their data and their methods of interpretation and analysis showed adequate need for the new service. My analysis, on the other hand, generated a much lower projection of potential cases for the new obstetrical program—a projection that was well below the volume needed to justify the establishment of the new program. Instead of the proponents' estimate of 1,338 expected deliveries in 1990, my more sophisticated demographic analysis indicated a potential for just 1,081 births—or 24 percent fewer than the number that the proponents contended.

In actuality, the number of deliveries required to establish a viable obstetrics unit was much lower than the proponents' projection. If they had utilized a more realistic methodology, they could have made a convincing case without "unbelievable" numbers. The steps presented below outline how the proponents and I could reach such extremely dissimilar conclusions.

In their delineation of the service area, the proponents made assumptions concerning the new facility's ability to draw patients from that portion of the county. In opposition, I pointed to existing market shares and pointed out the overly optimistic nature of Sectarian's claims. The proponents projected a 1989 service area population of 266,158, but I was able to present a case for just 240,211. Similarly, while the proponents submitted a 1989 figure of 67,122 for women of childbearing age in the service area, I was able to argue for 59,750.

Sectarian contended that a crude birth rate of 16/1,000 was appropriate; I was able to cite an actual rate of 11.5/1,000 for the service area population. Sectarian, moreover, held that the fertility rate would remain at this high (and erroneous) rate for the foreseeable future; I pointed to historically declining birth rates in the service area and a change in the age structure and composition of the population that would render past rates irrelevant. The proponents estimated a potential market share of 50 percent of the births that their projections yielded for the service area. I was able to argue convincingly that a market share somewhere below 30 percent was more realistic. I further demonstrated that Sectarian's argument for a potential pool of births was unrealistic in that it included several hundred births that were committed to other facilities and therefore not available to the proponents' OB unit.

Although I would have calculated the obstetrical potential in a different manner, I replicate the proponents' methodology here for comparison purposes. Table 11.1 shows parallel calculations that the proponents and I presented. Using the proponents' methodology (but applying more realistic assumptions), I concluded that the proponents overstated the potential number of births that Sectarian could attract to its new program by nearly 90 percent. If I had used more stringent assumptions, the projection would have been even more off target. For example, if I had insisted upon a more precise service area, fertility rates could have been reduced rather than being held stable, and cohort analysis extended another five years to reduce further the size of the childbearing population. Had I taken other, more subjective, factors into consideration, the projection would have become even more questionable. These factors could have included the lack of support by local physicians for the birthing center concept, the conservative nature of the local population, and the perception that Denominational was the place to have babies.

Results of the Hearing

After hearing the arguments of Sectarian's proponents and my counterarguments, the planning board overwhelmingly rejected the proposal. The board was not convinced of the accuracy of the proponents' projection of the potential pool of births or of the facility's ability to capture its claimed share of the market, and it remained unconvinced that existing patterns of service delivery would not be disrupted. In short, the board concluded that the proponents had failed to justify the need for the project.

Some observers noted that the board did not decide the case solely on the numbers ultimately derived. In actuality, the proponents could have demonstrated at least a modest level of need for a facility at this site. What appeared to carry the most weight with the review board was the proponents' inappropriate and sloppy utilization of demographic data and techniques. Although only one member of the

Table 11.1   Differences in Demand Calculations Using Two Different Methods, North Metro County Service

	Proponent Demand Projection	Alternative Demand Projection
Population base	266,158	240,211
Crude birth rate	16.2	11.5
Expected 1989 births	4,269	2,762
Expected market share	33%	27%
Projected 1989 deliveries	1,408	745
Less 5 percent for complications	70	37
Anticipated deliveries	1,338	708

board actually had any background in demographics, it was obvious to all that the proponents had a very poor understanding of the demographic aspects of the project. This lack of demographic understanding threw suspicion on all other aspects of their proposal. Their mishandling of the demographic aspects of the proposal encouraged board members to scrutinize every other assertion as well.

As a footnote I should point out that one year after the hearing described above the proponents returned to the local health facilities review board with a similar proposal. The composition of the board had changed, and political considerations apparently prompted a majority to vote in favor of the proposed new service. Although the proponents had modified the financial aspects to defuse some of the previous objections, their demographic component remained essentially the same. This time, however, the board refused to allow a detailed rebuttal of the proponents' assertions.

A year and a half after receiving the board's approval, Sectarian opened its obstetrical unit. After two years of operation, the unit had fallen far short of the proponents' projections, delivering just enough births (around 500 per year) to make it marginally viable financially. At this point it cannot be considered a successful program, and its low level of utilization has necessitated the discharge of some of its original staff.

Lessons for Applied Demography

Given the state of the health care industry, there is no question that the demand for sophisticated demographic analyses is going to increase. As the industry becomes more and more market driven and consumer oriented, demographic analysis will become increasingly common in health care decision making. In such a competitive environment, those who have more than just a cursory understanding of demography will enjoy a distinct advantage.

This case study points up several lessons that should be obvious but probably are not. First, to work on a case like this one must have a thorough understanding of both demographic data and analytical techniques. This case demonstrates the dangers of having a "little knowledge." One should develop a familiarity with all potential sources of demographic data, even those from unconventional sources. In the future, those who have access to the facts will have the upper hand. One should also be familiar with as many competing methodologies as possible. In this case a cursory knowledge of population projection methodologies resulted in the inappropriate use of an indicator, and of all the flaws in the application this was probably the most fatal.

There is never just one way to arrive at an answer. In determinations such as this, where one number is likely to make or break the application, it behooves the analyst to be able to derive the crucial figure from as many different methodologies as possible. The analyst should indicate the range of possible answers and, if appropriate, specify confidence intervals.

Second, this case points to the need for the demographic analyst to be familiar with the service area in question. In several instances the numbers said one thing but reality said another. The proponents weakened their case when they failed to demonstrate an understanding of urban development patterns, changing population composition within the service area, and existing patterns of health care utilization. The analyst must not only be able to interpret the numbers but also be able to see beyond them. All one has to do to verify the truth of this assertion is to conduct a demographic analysis on a distant community and then visit the community. I have never seen a case where the numbers did not "lie" about some aspect of the community.

This brings us to the third lesson: the need for understanding the industry under study. Although there may be situations in which methodologies appropriate to analyzing one industry may be transferable to another, health care is not one of them. The health care industry in extremely complex and in many ways unique. It has a language of its own and is driven by a complicated combination of factors not found in any other segment of society. The demographer who does not know the health care industry will be ineffective and, worse, easily discredited by adversaries.

The fourth and final lesson to be learned from this case is probably the most significant. One must present demographic data and analyses in a manner understandable to a wide variety of audiences. In this case, the proponents not only failed to present their analysis in an understandable manner but, when pressed, could not explain it. They could only repeat, with added conviction, their previously voiced erroneous arguments.

Trends in Health Care and Implications
for Applied Demography

As noted earlier, the 1980s witnessed a tremendous growth in the demand for applied demography in the health care industry. In response to the changing health care environment, new functions have emerged and certain old functions have received new emphasis. These functions include health services research, strategic planning, market analysis, consumer and patient research, program evaluation, and organizational analysis.

All of these functions are alike in that at their foundation is a strong demographic base. With the major trends in health care today pointing to applied demography as at least part of the solution, demographers have never experienced greater opportunities than exist today. Demographers must come to the fore and take a major role in the incorporation of demographic analysis into health care decision making and policy setting.

This situation demands several things of demographers. It requires a better understanding among rank-and-file demographers of the potential for applied demography in health care. It requires broad-based education of future demographers who will not only be skilled technicians but will also have the ability to interpret demographic trends for nontechnical audiences. It requires guidelines for professional development that will preclude every would-be applied demographer from reinventing the wheel. Finally, this growth in demand for applied demography in health care calls for a conscious effort on the part of demographers to assert themselves. History has demonstrated that the world will not beat a path to the door of someone inventing a better population projection; demographers must take their discipline to the world. As applied demography becomes more and more a standard feature of the health care industry, it is up to demographers to see that it is they who are doing the analyses—and doing them well—rather than nondemographers.

Demographic Considerations in the Planning of an Obstetrical Unit

Planning for the development of a hospital obstetrical unit, it would seem, does not require particularly complicated demographic analysis. All one needs to do is estimate the number of births in the general area, arrange for the appropriate medical staff, and start delivering babies. This simple scenario, however, ignores the complexity involved in planning for any type of health service and, particularly, for obstetrical services. A failure to appreciate this complexity—especially a miscalculation in the number of expected births—could easily result in the failure of an obstetrical program.

The planning of an obstetrical unit serves as an illustration of the step-by-step analysis of a problem in applied demography, ultimately incorporating most substantive areas of the field. It addresses issues of population size, distribution, and composition as well as the dynamic processes of fertility and migration. Successful implementation of an obstetrics unit requires an advanced understanding of the content, measures, and methods of demography.

The following step-by-step review illustrates the various ways in which demography can be used in planning an obstetrical unit.

Step 1: Delineating the Service Area

A service area for health care may be delineated in several different ways, and the method utilized often depends on the type of service being considered. One popular method is to examine the origin of existing patients and identify the geographic areas (zipcodes, census tracts, or other units) from which the facility draws a majority of its patients. Another method involves determining those areas in which the hospital maintains the greatest market share and then drawing the service area boundaries accordingly.

Yet another method for determining the primary service area is to ascertain what constitutes reasonable travel time for patients and use that as the criterion. Although historically the travel time approach has been more appropriate for determining the service area for ambulatory care, it has become a more viable criterion for hospital service areas now that patients are more frequently choosing a hospital on the basis of convenience. A fourth approach is to identify the "home" geographic unit (or units) and identify this (or these) as the primary service area. For example, the county or other political unit in which a facility is located may be considered the service area.

Perhaps the most realistic approach involves combining the above methods with other relevant information—e.g., existing physician practice patterns and health services utilization patterns. Whatever approach one takes, the prerequisite is an understanding of the "geographies" commonly utilized by demographers. One must be able not only to delineate a realistic service area but also to do it using geographic units—counties, zipcodes, census tracts, or block groups—that are meaningful for the analysis at hand.

Step 2: Determining the Service Area Population

Once the demographer has delineated a reasonable service area, he or she must determine the size of the population therein. The demographer must examine historical trends and almost inevitably make estimates of the area's current population and projections of its future population. One examines population trends to determine if the service area population is increasing, decreasing, or remaining stable. A projected decline in service area population may not bode well for a new facility while a stable or growing population may support a new service—depending on the size of the projected population and the other factors noted below.

Obviously, the demographer can choose from a variety of methodologies when making population estimates and projections. Estimates and projections may be available from data vendors and local planning agencies, or they may be created utilizing the institution's calculations. Since all projections model the future on the past, however, the demographer must take care in choosing a projection methodology to make sure that the method fits "reality." Many standard estimation and projection techniques are unable to account for rapid increases or decreases in a local population, especially for small areas. In some cases, in fact, a "forecast" is preferable because it produces an estimated future population based not so much on past trends but on anticipated future developments. Whatever the methodology or data source one selects, he or she must develop a realistic approximation of past, present, and future service area populations.

Step 3: Assessing Changes in Population Composition

Estimates and projections of the overall population are the first demographic facts required for estimating service demand. Equally important, however, is the composition of the service area population and the changes that are occurring within it. All three components of population change—births, deaths, and migration—may affect an area's population composition. Migration, however, is likely to have the most significant effect on the size and composition of a small area's population in the short run.

Thus, identification of the characteristics of in-migrants and out-migrants is crucial in planning for any type of service. What types of people, for example, are moving into the community—retirees, young marrieds, middle-aged empty nesters? Can one expect past trends related to migrant characteristics to continue into the future?

In this regard, the implications of future in-migrants' characteristics for fertility levels constitute the most important consideration. Will future residents display the same reproductive patterns as past and current residents? What are the implications of newcomers with higher (or lower) incomes or greater (or lesser) educational levels? What will happen to fertility levels if "urban gentry" replace working-class inner-city residents or if blacks replace Puerto Ricans? Unless the future residents of the service area closely resemble those already there, it is likely that fertility patterns will undergo change and along with that change will be an alteration in the level of demand for obstetrical services.

Unless the hospital considers OB services as a loss leader, it must also pay attention to the economic characteristics of the future population in its service area. Will future residents have the same ability as present ones to pay for health care? Will patterns of health care utilization be the same? A changing occupational structure may mean that a smaller proportion of the population has adequate insurance coverage.

A related consideration is the possible changing psychographics of this population. Is the future service area population going to be primarily "yuppies" who are interested in innovative birthing arrangements, or will they be more conservative residents interested in traditional maternity services? This difference in psychographics relates directly to the issue of image. Unless the hospital's image is appropriate to the orientation of service area residents, it is unlikely that the population will identify with the facility. In any case, the demographer should be more concerned about the characteristics of future populations than those of the present population.

Step 4: Calculating Fertility Rates

Once the demographer has realistically calculated the current and future service area populations and has determined the service area's future composition, his or her next step is to calculate fertility rates. The potential number of babies is, after all, the essence of the question at hand. Again, the demographer can choose from several different methodologies for calculating fertility rates, but some are more appropriate than others. The most basic approach is to apply a crude birth rate to the projected population—a method that provides a relatively "gross" approximation of fertility levels since it does not take into consideration the composition of the population. If the demographer does not know the crude birth rate for the population in question, he or she must apply a known rate for a different (but presumably similar) area.

It would be more appropriate to utilize an indicator that takes into consideration the age and sex distribution of the population. The general fertility rate or the child-woman ratio are two examples, based as they are on the female population of childbearing age rather than on the total population. While these indicators adjust for the age-sex composition of the population, there are other factors that the demographer should take into account if possible. Different ethnic and racial groups as well as different social classes are, obviously, characterized by varying fertility rates.

It would be best, of course, to apply the population's actual fertility rate when determining birth levels. If that is not possible, the next best thing is to apply known fertility rates for a population that has similar characteristics. If actual birth figures are available for the service area during a recent time period, the demographer can verify fertility calculations against them and then make appropriate adjustments for anticipated changes in population size and composition.

Step 5: Estimating Potential Market Share

The projected number of births is meaningful only if the new OB service can capture an adequate market share within the delineated service area. If more than one facility will be competing for obstetrical patients, the new facility cannot expect to obtain all of the expected births within the service area; it can expect only its "share." Therefore, it is crucial for the demographer to make a realistic estimate of the obtainable share.

While the known share of medical/surgical patients might be used as a proxy, it is unlikely that the distribution of obstetrical patients will follow the same pattern. One should also remember that initially a new service will have to capture the bulk of its patients from existing facilities. Given the fact that the patient's obstetrician is going to be the primary influence in her choice of facility, one cannot expect such a changeover to occur very rapidly. Therefore, the demographer must project a "reasonable" market share for the service area's births.

Discussion Questions

1. Do you agree with the author's assessment of the delineation of the service area? Could a different strategy using the zip-code method yield a different result?

2. How would census tract analysis yield different results?

3. Do you think the original analyst erred? If so, can you see yourself using some of the same techniques? Why?

4. Identify areas of bias in the author's analysis.

5. Which points, in the author's analysis, would you challenge?

6. You are the Sectarian Hospital Analyst. Defend yourself.

7. What additional information would have helped you evaluate this case?

8. What does this case suggest about the responsibilities of Planning Boards or other decision-making bodies regarding the use of demographic data in planning?

Notes

1. By the end of the 1980s, the technology for geocoding addresses had become widely available. In the future, births (or any other patient-related characteristic) could be assigned a latitude and longitude and pinpointed to even the block-group level of geography.

2. In this case, the Sectarian suburban facility contained few obstetricians among its medical staff. The argument was made that the existing obstetricians could not deliver the number of babies projected for the facility. The likelihood of having obstetricians "defect" from Denominational Hospital was slim, further weakening the argument for a viable program at this site.

References

Chapman, John. 1988. "Cast a Critical Eye." In P. Wickham (ed.), *The Insider's Guide to Demographic Know-How*. Ithaca, New York: American Demographics Press.

Garnick, D.W., H.S. Luft, J.C. Robinson, and J. Tetreault. "Appropriate Measures of Hospital Market Areas." *Health Services Research*. April 1987:69–89.

Massey, Tom K., Jr., and Faye W. Blake. "Estimating Market Boundaries for Health Care Services." *Journal of Health Care Marketing*. September 1977:15–24.

O'Hare, William. 1988. "How to Evaluate Population Estimates." In P. Wickham (ed.). *The Insider's Guide to Demographic Know-How*. Ithaca, NewYork: American Demographics Press.

Staff. "Reinforcing Maternity Services: Positioning Against Newcomer Competition," *Profiles in Hospital Marketing*. (3rd Quarter) 1987:26–27.

Shryock, Henry S., and Jacob S. Siegel and Associates. 1976. *The Methods and Materials of Demography*. New York: Academic Press.

12

Population Estimates, Projections, and Expert Testimony in Adversarial Legal Proceedings: A Case Study of Automobile Dealerships

Stanley K. Smith

All states have laws restricting the entry of new firms—or the expansion of existing firms—in certain industries. Hospitals, nursing homes, banks, electric utilities, cable television companies, automobile dealerships, and many other types of business enterprise may be subject to such restrictions. Firms in restricted industries are not free to expand their facilities or establish new outlets whenever or wherever they choose. Rather, they must obtain approval from state regulatory agencies before expanding or entering a new area.

State regulatory agencies approve or deny applications to expand or establish new facilities on the basis of their estimates of "need." Need is determined by comparing the output, or potential output, of current providers ("supply") with the desired consumption levels of current or potential customers ("demand"). If a regulatory agency decides that current providers are not capable of meeting current or expected future demand, it will approve the application for a new or expanded facility. If it decides that current providers are capable of meeting current or expected future demand, however, it will deny the application.

Population size is a major determinant of the demand for goods and services. Population estimates and projections, therefore, play a crucial role in the determination of need. Regulatory agencies may even develop formulas relating need directly to population size (e.g., hospital beds per 1000 persons). In addition to size, agencies may also consider population characteristics such as age, sex, race, or ethnicity.

Clearly, demographers have a major role to play in the determination of need by state regulatory agencies. They must be able to develop accurate population estimates and projections and—just as important—must be able to defend them vigorously and articulately in adversarial legal proceedings. Agencies frequently ap-

180

prove or deny applications for new or expanded facilities on the basis of administrative or judicial hearings in which the applicants and their opponents—each
with a battery of attorneys and expert witnesses—argue the merits of the case.[1]

The following discussion deals with the demographic analysis and expert testimony developed for an application to establish a new automobile dealership in
Dade County, Florida. After giving a brief description of the automobile industry
and its regulation in Florida and the United States, I will present the data and techniques used to create population estimates and projections for this project and discuss a number of general methodological issues related to small-area demographic analysis. I will then go on to discuss the role of the expert witness and
provide some practical tips for testifying effectively in adversarial legal proceedings. My intention in this discussion is to provide some guidance on how to (1)
make small-area population estimates and projections, and (2) present such estimates and projections in adversarial legal proceedings without looking like a fool
or having a nervous breakdown.

Institutional Framework

Automobile franchising in the United States is a hybrid retailing system lying
somewhere between the extremes of manufacturer-owned retail outlets and totally independent retailers (Smith 1982). In this system, automobile manufacturers and dealers are separate and independent businesses, but they are closely tied
together through franchise agreements that specify the rights and obligations of
each party.

The success of both manufacturers and dealers depends (in part) on the performance of the other party. In spite of this symbiotic relationship, however, the economic interests of manufacturers and dealers are not identical. In fact, what one
party construes as optimal behavior is often perceived by the other to be decidedly
suboptimal. The very nature of automobile franchising thus contains the seeds for
potential conflicts between manufacturers and dealers.

State and Federal Legislation

In the early 1900s, automobile dealers operated with little outside interference
from manufacturers. The dealers made their own decisions regarding site selection, orders for vehicles and parts, promotional efforts, and investment in show-
rooms and service departments. This situation began to change in the 1920s and
1930s as mergers and business failures reduced the number of manufacturers and
as technological advances altered the automobile production process. These
changes promoted large-scale production and put pressure on manufacturers to
exert more control over the business decisions previously made by dealers
(Northwestern University School of Law 1957). Manufacturers exerted this control through the terms of the franchise agreement, which could grant dealers ex-

clusive franchise areas and favorable credit arrangements but which could also permit manufacturers to set sales quotas and make threats of franchise termination (Smith 1982; Weiss 1963).

Many automobile dealers believed that greater manufacturer control over their business decisions threatened their economic survival (Weiss 1963). They responded by mounting massive political lobbying campaigns aimed at securing assistance from state and federal governments. As a result of these efforts, a number of state legislatures in the 1930s, 1940s, and 1950s passed laws limiting manufacturers' rights to dictate sales quotas and to terminate franchise agreements. In 1956, the United States Congress passed the Automobile Dealer Franchise Act, giving dealers the right to sue a manufacturer in U.S. District Court if the manufacturer failed to comply with the terms of the franchise agreement or attempted to terminate the agreement. These state and federal laws were designed to protect dealers from coercion, intimidation, and other unfair business practices; they were not designed to limit the expansion of dealership networks or to protect dealers from competition (Weiss 1963).

In recent years, however, a number of states have passed laws that protect dealers from competition by restricting the establishment of new dealerships in the vicinity of present dealers of the same line-make.[2] Colorado passed the first such law in 1963; by 1983, thirty-six states had similar laws (Rogers 1986). These restrictions usually operate as follows: First, the law requires the manufacturer to declare its intention to establish a new dealership or to relocate an existing one. Current dealers then have an opportunity to protest this action, but only dealers of the same line-make and from the same market area may file protests. Market area is typically defined by political boundaries (e.g., counties) or by distance from the proposed new site (e.g., ten miles).

A dealer protest initiates a legal process leading up to a formal hearing. Depending on the state's regulatory legislation, the hearing may be before a state agency, a special hearing board, or a state court. Finally, the appropriate agency makes the decision to grant or deny approval for a new or relocated dealership, basing its decision on evidence presented at the hearing regarding the need for the new/expanded facility. In some states, the law also requires that the agency consider the economic impact of a new dealership on existing dealers. (See Eckard 1985 and Smith 1982 for further details on state regulations affecting automobile dealerships.)

Regulation in Florida

Florida passed its first legislation affecting automobile manufacturers in 1941. This legislation provided only for the licensing of manufacturers selling motor vehicles in the state (Haskins and Forehand 1988). In 1970, Florida greatly expanded its legislation to include the obligations of manufacturers and dealers, procedures for changing distribution systems, requirements for selling franchises, procedures for establishing new dealerships, and several other aspects of the automobile industry (Florida Legislature 1989, sections 320.60–320.70). In this discussion, we are concerned solely with the regulations affecting the establishment of new dealerships.

Florida law gives the Department of Highway Safety and Motor Vehicles (hereafter, the "Department") responsibility for regulating the automobile industry. If a manufacturer wants to establish a new dealership, it must give the Department written notice, specifying the site of the proposed dealership, the opening date, a list of principal investors, and the names of all dealers of the same line-make in the same county and all contiguous counties. The Department then publishes this information and notifies all the same line-make dealers in the area. These dealers may protest the establishment of a new dealership if they have "standing." Standing is determined by (1) the distance between their dealership and the site of the proposed dealership, and (2) the size of the county population. Dealers must file their protests within thirty days of the date that the Department publishes the notice.

If any dealer files a protest, the Department schedules an administrative hearing at which the manufacturer, the dealer for the proposed franchise, and all protesting dealers may present their arguments. An officer from the Florida Division of Administrative Hearings conducts the hearing and—after all the parties have presented their arguments—makes a recommendation to the Department. The Department then makes a decision approving or denying the application for a new dealership. Dissatisfied parties may appeal the Department's decision through a Florida District Court of Appeal.

Florida law places the burden of proof for demonstrating the need for a new dealership on the manufacturer. It states that an application will be denied unless the manufacturer can show that existing dealers " ... of the same line-make in the community or territory of the proposed dealership are not providing adequate representation" (Florida Legislature 1989, section 320.642). Although the statutes do not clearly define "community or territory," legal precedents have established that the area specified in the contract between the manufacturer and the dealer may be considered to be the relevant community or territory (*Larry Dimmitt Cadillac* v. *Seacrest Cadillac* 1990). This market area may be large (one or more counties) or small (portions of counties), depending on the population size of the area.

There is no hard-and-fast rule defining "adequate representation," but the law mentions several types of evidence that may be relevant (Florida Legislature 1989, section 320.642). Evidence regarding current and projected population size is often crucial. Economic and demographic characteristics of the population may be important as well. Thus, the evidence that demographers present in administrative hearings plays a crucial role in determining "adequate representation."

About This Case

I was contacted during the spring of 1990 by an attorney representing an automobile manufacturer I will call Colossal Automobile Manufacturers, Incorporated (CAM, Inc.). CAM wanted to establish a new dealership in Dade County, Florida, for its "Shaft" line-make of automobiles. Three Shaft dealerships already existed in Dade County, but none had been established since the early 1960s. Since that time Dade County's population had almost doubled, to 1.9 million.

One of the existing dealers had filed a protest against the proposed new dealership, which meant that an administrative hearing would be required to determine the need for a new dealership. I was retained to make population estimates and projections for the new dealership's proposed service area and to testify regarding those estimates and projections at the administrative hearing. The remainder of this discussion describes the demographic analysis that I produced and the testimony that I presented at the hearing. Although it focuses on a specific case, much of the discussion is relevant to other projects involving population estimates and projections and to testimony in other types of adversarial legal proceedings.

Making Estimates and Projections

The first step in the analysis was to determine the geographic boundaries of the service area for the proposed CAM-Shaft dealership. In some cases, the consultant[3] may be asked to define the relevant service area, using information on sales, client addresses, population, income, distance from competitors, legal requirements, and so forth. Occasionally, the specification of the service area itself becomes a controversial issue. In the CAM-Shaft case, however, a marketing consultant hired by CAM, Inc., defined the service area (Figure 12.1) as 28 census tracts in northern Dade County.

The second step was to collect background data on population and housing units in the service area. Published reports provide 1980 census data for census tracts in metropolitan areas. Data for nontracted areas (e.g., enumeration districts) and for block groups and blocks can be obtained from microfiche or computer tapes. The 1990 Census divided the entire country into blocks (approximately seven million in all), making enumeration districts obsolete. Data from the 1990 Census will be available by block, block group, census tract, block numbering area, and zip code area in printed reports and/or on computer tapes, diskettes, compact disks, microfiche, and on-line data services. In the CAM-Shaft case, I used a printed report to obtain 1980 population and housing data by census tract. These data appear in Table 12.1.

In most applied research projects, subcounty areas are defined as groups of census tracts, zip codes, block numbering areas, block groups, or individual blocks. When collecting data for more than one point in time (e.g., 1980 and 1990), a demographer must take care to ensure that the area's geographic bound-

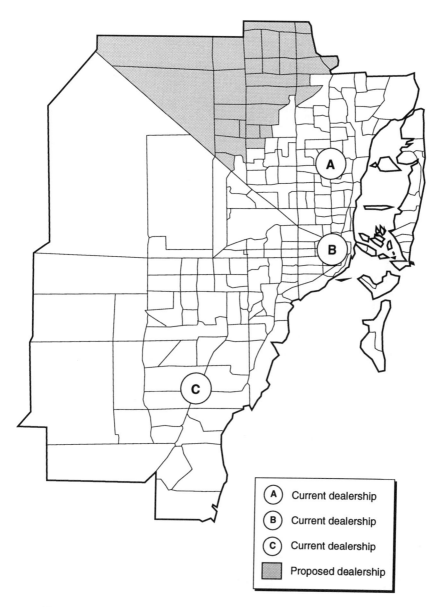

Figure 12.1—Service area for proposed dealership with reference
to Dade County census tracts

Table 12.1   1980 Population and Housing Units, Service Area

C.T.	Population	Housing Units	PPHU**
4.02	3,922	1,269	3.09
4.03	6,653	2,396	2.78
5.01	5,721	1,517	3.77
5.02	8,577	3,039	2.82
6.01	4,646	1,377	3.37
6.02	4,728	1,443	3.28
6.03	4,766	1,535	3.10
7.01	15,491	5,405	2.87
7.03	10,258	3,758	2.73
92.00	4,115	1,236	3.33
93.02	18,210	6,149	2.96
93.03	20,048	7,080	2.83
93.04	5,376	2,597	2.07
93.05	5,325	1,994	2.67
94.00	6,230	1,671	3.73
95.01	4,121	1,853	2.22
95.02	9,315	2,687	3.47
99.03	4,839	1,671	2.90
99.04	2,609	873	2.99
100.01	7,153	1,852	3.86
100.02	6,441	2,095	3.07
100.05	7,823	2,253	3.47
100.06	6,663	1,800	3.70
100.07	7,965	2,495	3.19
100.08	12,227	3,406	3.59
101.02	3,003	1,413	2.13
101.06	5,931	1,707	3.47
101.07	3,854	1,886	2.04
Total	206,010	68,457	3.009
County	1,625,781	665,382	2.443

*PPHU = persons per housing unit
  Source: U. S. Bureau of the Census. 1980 Census of Population and Housing, PHC 80-2-
241, July 1983, Tables P-1 and H-1.

aries remain constant. This can be particularly problematic when using zip code data because boundaries of zip code areas change frequently over time.

Population Estimates

As the years go by, decennial census data become increasingly outdated. Some places grow rapidly; others grow slowly; still others decline. When I performed the demographic analysis for CAM (in the spring and summer of 1990), data from the 1980 Census were ten years old and data from the 1990 Census were not yet available. A great deal of demographic change had occurred in Dade County, creating the need for updated population estimates.

A demographer can use a number of methods for making state and county population estimates, including Component II, Ratio Correlation, and Administrative Records (Murdock and Ellis 1991; National Research Council 1980). Limited data availability, however, makes these methods difficult or impossible to use for subcounty areas. More appropriate for subcounty estimates is the housing unit (HU) method, in which the demographer calculates population as the number of occupied housing units (or households) times the average number of persons per household, plus the number of persons living in group quarters facilities or other nonhousing situations (e.g., the homeless population). This method is widely applicable, flexible in terms of data sources and techniques, and capable of producing accurate population estimates for subcounty areas. (See Smith 1986, for a description and evaluation of the HU method.)

To estimate the number of households, a demographer can use any of several data sources such as building permits, certificates of occupancy, active residential electric customers, residential telephone customers, and property tax records. Building permits are by far the most commonly used because of their frequent availability for small areas and their high correlation with increases in the housing stock. To estimate the current housing inventory of an area, one merely adds the permits issued since the most recent census (net of demolitions and adjusted for estimated time lags between the issuance of permits and the completion of units) to the number of units counted in that census.

Local planning departments often compile building permit data at the census tract level. In the CAM-Shaft case, I used housing estimates produced by the Metro Dade County Planning Department. These estimates were based on data from building permit records, property tax files, building inspections, and direct contact with mobile home parks. The department's 1989 housing unit estimates by census tract are shown in Table 12.2.

The next steps in the estimating process ordinarily would consist of applying occupancy rates to the housing stock to derive estimates of occupied households, multiplying by an estimate of the average number of persons per household, and adding an estimate of the number of persons living in group quarters. In this case, however, I combined these steps into one by forming a ratio of persons per hous-

Table 12.2   1989 Housing Units, Service Area

C.T.	Housing Units
4.02	1,427
4.03	2,686
5.01	1,688
5.02	2,956
6.01	1,558
6.02	1,767
6.03	1,459
7.01	7,428
7.03	4,214
92.00	1,113
93.02	6,626
93.03	6,282
93.04	4,298
93.05	2,196
94.00	1,819
95.01	2,280
95.02	2,844
99.03	1,536
99.04	818
100.01	2,228
100.02	2,583
100.05	2,322
100.06	1,982
100.07	2,521
100.08	3,889
101.02	4,320
101.06	2,581
101.07	6,226
Total	83,647
County	765,040

Source: Metro Dade County Planning Department, unpublished printout, April 30, 1990.

ing unit (PPHU) based on 1980 census data. I simplified the process because I had no evidence that occupancy rates or the proportion of persons living in households had changed since 1980. I did, however, apply an adjustment factor to account for estimated changes in average household size since 1980. I based this adjustment factor on the official estimate of average household size in Dade County (Smith and Cody 1990), which showed a slight increase since 1980. As shown in Table 12.3, the result was a 1989 population estimate of 252,197 for the proposed dealership area.

Table 12.3   1989 Population Estimate, Service Area

83,647	Housing Units (1989)
X 3.009	PPHU (1980)
X 1.002	Adjustment Factor
252,197	Population (1989)

Source: Personal calculations

Although the clients in the CAM-Shaft case were interested only in total population data, in many cases clients also need age, sex, race, or ethnicity characteristics of the population. Demographers typically make such estimates (or projections) using cohort-component techniques. Data limitations may preclude the use of traditional cohort-component techniques in subcounty areas, but one may apply a modified version using only decennial census data (Hamilton and Perry 1962). To improve accuracy, however, demographers should generally control the estimates (or projections) derived from the Hamilton-Perry technique to estimates (or projections) of total population derived from other techniques (Smith and Shahidullah 1993).

Population Projections

The legislation regulating automobile dealerships in Florida considers not only the current population but also the projected future population of an area. Demographers can use a number of different approaches to create population projections, but most of these approaches fall into four broad categories: extrapolation, ratio, cohort-component, and economic-demographic[4] (Pittenger 1976; Irwin 1977; Ahlburg 1987).

The lack of necessary data often makes it impossible to use cohort-component and economic-demographic projection techniques for subcounty areas, leaving one with extrapolation and ratio techniques. The disadvantages of these techniques are that they provide no demographic detail, contain no causal analysis, and cannot be tied to alternative economic or demographic scenarios. The advantages are that they are simple to apply, require little base data, and provide forecasts of total population that are, on the average, at least as accurate as those produced by more complex and sophisticated cohort-component and economic-demographic techniques (Kale, Voss, Palit, and Krebs 1981; Siegel 1953; Smith and Sincich 1992).

Before demographers can make projections, they must choose the length of the forecast horizon (i.e., the number of years into the future for which population will be projected) and the length of the base period (i.e., the historical period from which data are collected to provide a base for the projection). In this case, the client set the length of the horizon by requesting projections for 1995 and 2000. I based the current projections on data from 1980 and 1989. A previous study showed that for the projection techniques used in this analysis, a base period of approximately ten years is generally sufficient to produce the most accurate set of projections (Smith and Sincich 1990). I used two extrapolation and two ratio techniques to project the population of the proposed dealership service area. The two extrapolation techniques were: (1) Linear extrapolation, in which the population is projected to change by the same annual number as the average annual change during the base period, and (2) Exponential extrapolation, in which the population is projected to change at the same annual rate as the average annual growth rate during the base period. The two ratio techniques were: (1) Share of growth, in which the service area's share of future county growth is projected to be the same as its share during the base period, and (2) Shift-share, in which the service area's share of the county population is projected to change by the same annual amount as the average annual change in its share during the base period. The latter two techniques require county population projections; I used the official county projections published by the State of Florida (Smith and Bayya 1990).

The exponential technique can produce projections that are absurdly high for areas that have been growing rapidly; and the shift-share technique can produce projections that are far too low for areas that have been growing very slowly or declining (Smith and Shahidullah 1993). Although usually not severe for short horizons (e.g., five years), this problem can become critical for longer horizons (e.g., twenty years). Consequently, for longer horizons it is inadvisable to use the exponential technique for rapidly growing areas or the shift-share technique for areas that have declined or grown very slowly during the base period.

For a final projection I calculated the average of the four individual projections. Taking an average lowers the probability of making large errors and has been found to improve overall forecasting performance (Mahmoud 1984; Voss and Kale 1985). As a final step I applied the same techniques to the county population outside the service area and controlled both sets of projections to the total county population projection. This procedure made my service area projections consistent with the rest of the county and with official county projections. Table 12.4 shows my final service area projections.

When using historical trends to make population projections for small areas, the demographer must take into account any special events or potential constraints that might cause future growth to differ considerably from past growth. Have any events occurred during the base period that are not likely to be repeated (e.g., construction of a large group-quarters facility, opening of a housing development, departure of a major employer)? Is the area near its likely maximum population—given current population densities, local government growth policies, zoning restrictions, environmental constraints, and the availability of vacant land? If so, the demographer must make adjustments to the projections. In general, the smaller the area under consideration, the greater the potential impact of special events and growth constraints. In the CAM-Shaft case, I was not aware of any special events

Table 12.4   Service Area Projections, 1990, 1995, and 2000

Technique	1990	1995	2000
Linear	257,329	282,988	308,648
Exponential	257,938	288,649	323,019
Share of growth	258,402	282,220	299,985
Shift-share	258,261	284,461	307,106
Average	257,983	284,580	309,689
Controlled	258,314	283,560	304,475

Source: Personal calculations

or potential constraints that would affect the service area population projections; consequently, I made no adjustments to the projections shown in Table 12.4.

I believe it is helpful for the consultant to visit the area being studied before completing his/her analysis. This gives the consultant a "feel" for the area and helps him/her evaluate the impact of any factors that may not be evident in the data. Spending some time in the area also adds credibility to any report that may be prepared and to the testimony given in the hearing. I rarely complete a project without some direct, firsthand experience of the area being analyzed.

It may also be helpful to develop a contact with a local resident who has intimate knowledge of the study area. This person can help the consultant become familiar with the demographic dynamics of the area, including any special events that may have occurred or may be about to occur. Knowledge of these events may alter the conclusions the consultant draws from his/her demographic analysis. Even if this additional knowledge does not affect the consultant's final conclusions, it strengthens the foundation of the analysis and makes the final report and/or testimony more authoritative.

Table 12.5 summarizes population data for 1980, estimates for 1989, and projections for 2000 for the service area. The table also includes comparative data for Dade County, the State of Florida, and the United States. Such comparisons give clients, judges, juries, and hearing officers a frame of reference from which to evaluate the service area's population characteristics.

Conclusion

I have found that the estimation and projection techniques described here work well in terms of accuracy, applicability in a wide variety of cases, and acceptability in legal proceedings. These techniques are certainly not the only ones that a demographer could use, however. Others are equally valid, and some might be preferable for certain purposes. The demographer's choice of techniques depends on the intended use of the estimates and projections, the time and other resources

Table 12.5 Population Changes 1980–1989 and 1989–2000 for Service Area, Dade County, State of Florida, and the United States

Region	1980 Population	1989 Population	Change	% Change
Service Area	206,010	252,197	46,187	22.4
Dade County	1,625,781	1,873,078	247,297	15.2
Florida	9,746,324	12,797,318	3,050,994	31.3
U.S.	227,757,000	248,777,000	21,020,000	9.2
Region	1989 Population	2000 Population	Change	% Change
Service Area	252,197	304,475	52,278	20.7
Dade County	1,873,078	2,128,900	255,822	13.7
Florida	12,797,318	15,988,000	3,190,682	24.9
U.S.	248,777,000	268,266,000	19,489,000	7.8

Sources: Bureau of Economic and Business Research, Population Studies, Bulletin No. 92, February 1990; U. S. Bureau of the Census, 1980 Census of Population, PC 80-1-All, Table 2; U. S. Bureau of Census, Current Population Reports, Series P-25, No. 1018 (January 1989) and No. 1047 (September 1989); personal calculations, Tables 3 and 4.

available for producing the estimates and projections, and the availability of relevant data. Every research project is unique in one way or another, and the demographer must rely on his/her best professional judgment when choosing data and techniques. There are no rules or guidelines that can provide a single estimation or projection methodology that will be superior to all others under all circumstances.

Testifying in Adversarial Legal Proceedings

Most demographic research projects are complete once the tables have been produced, the results analyzed, and the final report prepared. For a project involving adversarial legal proceedings, however, the fun is just beginning. The production of estimates and projections sets the stage for an administrative or judicial hearing in which the real drama (comedy or tragedy?) will be played out. Hearings can be anxiety-producing because they often involve very high stakes; in addition, they may subject the witness to attempts to discredit his/her testimony or even destroy his/her credibility as an expert. On the other hand, hearings give the consultant an opportunity to develop and present demographic analyses that have a direct, immediate impact on real-world decision-making. Testifying in adversarial legal proceedings can be an exciting and rewarding (but sometimes intimidating) experience.

The following discussion covers the role of the expert witness and offers some practical tips on how to prepare and present expert testimony. These tips are based on my discussions with attorneys and other expert witnesses and my own experience testifying in administrative and judicial hearings. They are meant to help the inexperienced expert witness maximize effectiveness and minimize emotional distress when testifying. These tips are not, of course, ironclad rules; other demographers may differ on specific ideas or emphasize points not mentioned here (Brodsky 1991; Dorram 1982).[5]

Role of Expert Witness

The term "expert witness" has a specific meaning in legal proceedings. An expert witness is a person accepted by the judge or hearing officer as being qualified to make judgments and offer conclusions in the area of his/her expertise. Areas of expertise may be defined broadly (e.g., demographic data and analysis) or narrowly (e.g., population estimates and projections). It is important that they be defined broadly enough to cover all aspects of the topic under consideration, but narrowly enough to indicate specific knowledge of that topic.

An expert witness is different from other witnesses who may give factual testimony but who are not permitted to draw conclusions or offer opinions. Criteria for qualification as an expert witness include educational background, training, current and past work experience, knowledge, and specialized skills. Acceptance by a judge or hearing officer is not automatic; opposing attorneys have the opportunity to object to a consultant being qualified as an expert witness. To the best of my knowledge, however, such objections are seldom sustained.

There are at least two perspectives regarding the role of the demographer as expert witness. Under the first, the expert's role is to produce any type of professionally competent demographic analysis that will help the client win the case. This does not mean that the expert will falsify data, apply improper techniques, intentionally misinterpret results, or provide false or misleading testimony. Rather, it means he/she will focus on evidence that supports the client's case (e.g., factors reflecting rapid growth) and will avoid evidence that weakens the case (e.g., factors reflecting slow growth). This perspective is consistent with the U.S. legal system, in which each side attempts to produce the strongest possible case for its clients (MacHovec 1987; Wolfgang 1974).

The second perspective sees the expert as an impartial observer who performs an unbiased analysis of the issue under consideration (e.g., past and expected future population growth in an area). The expert then forms various conclusions, which may or may not support the client's case. Based on the nature of the expert's findings and conclusions, the client decides whether or not to call upon the expert to testify at the hearing or trial. Under this perspective, the consultant is an "educator" rather than an "advocate" (Loftus 1986). By uncovering weaknesses that may have to be faced in the courtroom, the consultant provides a valuable service to the client even when his/her conclusions do not completely support the client's case.

Practitioners differ in their views regarding the validity of these two perspectives (Kalmuss 1981; Loftus 1986; McCloskey, Egeth, and McKenna 1986). Some believe the educator role is the only ethical role and that playing the role of an advocate inevitably compromises the professional standards of scientific research. Others believe the educator role is impossible to maintain in the highly charged atmosphere of adversarial legal proceedings; they favor the consultant accepting the realities of the adversarial system and striving to be a responsible advocate, presenting one side of an issue clearly and professionally, without distorting or misrepresenting research findings.

Prospective expert witnesses should carefully consider the implications of these two perspectives before becoming involved in the adversarial process. Each can lead to tensions in performing the role of the expert witness. Under the first perspective, the tension may arise from the requirement that a consultant focus only on factors that support the client's case. Such a requirement is inherently in conflict with the expert's scientific training, which emphasizes the importance of a complete, objective analysis covering all sides of an issue. Under the second perspective, tension may appear if the consultant's attempts to be evenhanded and objective come into conflict with the attorney's desire to include only those parts of the analysis that support the client's case.

Some consultants may find one or both types of tension to be quite discomforting. If so, they must operate only within the perspective with which they feel most comfortable or avoid involvement in the adversarial process altogether. Whichever perspective the consultant takes, it must be communicated clearly to the client. A positive experience testifying in hearings or trials will be possible only if the client fully understands and accepts the role the consultant intends to play when providing expert testimony.[6]

Preparation

The key to effective testimony is thorough preparation, which starts when the client first describes the proposed project and the consultant decides whether or not to become involved. It is essential to clarify at the very beginning exactly what the client wants, what the time frame and terms of financial compensation will be, and what resources will be available. The client must be very candid about his/her expectations, and the consultant must be equally candid about what he/she can provide. A clear understanding of each party's expectations from the very beginning helps avoid problems as the case progresses.

If the consultant senses that a lack of demographic expertise is preventing the client from being fully aware of all the possibilities, he/she may have to help the client determine exactly what needs to be done. In addition, if the consultant senses that the client has a hidden agenda, he/she may have to push a bit to bring that agenda out into the open. Perhaps most important, the consultant must determine whether the client simply expects an objective, competent analysis or expects support for a specific conclusion. If the latter, the consultant may wish to perform some preliminary analyses to decide whether he/she can support that conclusion. If the analyses do not support the desired conclusion, the consultant can at least show the client what problems must be faced.

Regardless of one's perspective on the role of the expert witness, the consultant must reject any attempts to pressure him/her into supporting an unwarranted conclusion. Failure to do so will diminish the consultant's personal integrity and professional reputation as well as corrupt the legal system and tarnish the profession as a whole. Such attempts rarely occur, but when they do the consultant is well-advised to withdraw from the case.

After determining the scope of the project, the consultant must formulate a work plan, collect data, and perform the required analyses. Whenever possible, I have found it helpful to use sources and techniques that are regarded as standard in the demographic profession. Data from the U.S. Bureau of the Census and other federal agencies, state government offices, departments of vital statistics, county planning departments, and so forth are usually accepted without challenge in legal proceedings. Data sources that can be termed "official" are typically accepted as more authoritative than "nonofficial" sources.

Similarly, analytic and statistical techniques that demographers commonly use and that have a known track record are easier to defend than are nonstandard techniques. This is not to say that unusual data sources and techniques must always be avoided. The demographer who chooses to use them, however, must be prepared to defend their validity and explain why he/she used them in preference to more common sources and techniques. My rule of thumb: If two data sources or techniques are equally valid, use the more standard one.

It is important to keep track of all the data sources and techniques one uses at every stage of the analysis. Never rely strictly on memory; in a long and detailed analysis, it is easy to forget exactly what took place at a given point. Keeping a written record of sources and techniques is important when preparing expert testimony because hearings sometimes do not take place for a year or more after the original analysis was performed. It is also helpful to make photocopies of all data sources rather than simply taking notes or copying numbers by hand. Not only are photocopies useful for verifying data, but they are often required for documenting sources at hearings.

Once the demographer completes the analysis, his/her next step is to prepare the exhibits that will be used at the hearing. Exhibits comprise the diagrams, charts, tables, reports, and other documents that are introduced as evidence. Figure 12.1 and Tables 12.1–12.5 (with a few minor changes made for expository purposes) were the exhibits I used for the demographic analysis in Dade County.

Producing exhibits is perhaps the most important part of the preparation process because exhibits provide the documentation and summary of testimony presented during the hearing. Exhibits should be presented sequentially and tell a consistent, coherent story. Whenever possible, list all sources that were used in the preparation of each exhibit. Pictorial exhibits (e.g., diagrams, charts, graphs, maps) are often more dramatic and more easily understood than columns of numbers. Needless to say, exhibits should be double- (or triple-) checked to ensure that they contain no factual errors.

In some cases the consultant will be asked to prepare a written report summarizing his/her analysis. This report should discuss the mission (i.e., what the expert was retained to do), the methodology (i.e., the data and techniques used in the analysis), and the final conclusions drawn by the consultant. It will typically include tables, diagrams, and maps constructed while preparing the analysis. The written report should describe and document all essential parts of the analysis, but should be as simple and clear as possible. The written report itself is frequently used as an exhibit at the hearing.

Preparation for a hearing often includes a deposition. During a deposition the attorneys for the opposing side are permitted to ask the consultant questions about his/her background and qualifications, data sources that have been used, analyses that have been performed, conclusions that have been drawn, and so forth. Typically, the opponent's attorneys will have access to the consultant's exhibits before the deposition is held. Depositions allow the attorneys for one side to learn more about the case the other side is preparing. Although depositions help the opponent's attorneys prepare their case, they also help the consultant by revealing parts of his/her testimony that need additional work and by providing a preview of the cross-examination that might occur at the hearing.

The consultant should answer all questions completely and truthfully during a deposition, but he/she should answer only the specific questions asked. In other words, do not volunteer additional information. The more the opponents know about your case, the better they will be able to prepare for it. It is during the hearing rather than during the deposition that any additional information relevant to the consultant's testimony should be brought out.

Testimony

Administrative and judicial hearings are typically set up so that attorneys ask questions and experts answer them—that is, the expert does not make a formal presentation. The question-and-answer format should follow a logical sequence, allowing the expert to discuss all steps in the analysis before presenting the final conclusions. The sequence of testimony should be consistent with the sequence of exhibits, and the testimony should use the exhibits to illustrate and summarize major points. The consultant should assist the client's attorneys in preparing the questions that will be asked during the hearing. All issues regarding the expert's testimony should be resolved at this time; the expert does not want any surprise questions from the client's attorney when on the witness stand, and the attorney does not want any surprise answers.

Shortly before testifying, the expert should review all exhibits and background data and go through all steps of the analysis, recalling exactly what was done and why. A thorough review refreshes the memory and facilitates a smooth, clear presentation; in contrast, an inability to remember or explain precisely what he/she did can drastically weaken a witness's credibility.

An expert witness must strive for both completeness and simplicity. Testimony must be comprehensive, providing an explanation of all the issues involved. Yet it must also be simple, with esoteric concepts and terminology explained in language comprehensible to a nondemographer. Avoid technical jargon whenever possible. Remember, the expert's objective is not only to produce the best demographic analysis possible, but also to convince the judge, hearing officer, or jury of its validity. Logical analyses and clear explanations are much more convincing than black-box models and arcane terminology.

Testifying at a hearing typically includes not only direct testimony guided by the client's attorneys, but also cross-examination by the opponent's attorneys. Cross-examination provides an opportunity for the opponent's attorneys to question any part of the expert's testimony. One purpose of cross-examination is to discredit that testimony by uncovering errors, omissions, contradictions, inconsistencies, or dubious assumptions. It is during cross-examination that the expert truly comes to appreciate the importance of thorough preparation.

It is very important, therefore, to spend some time before the hearing thinking about questions that might be asked during cross-examination. The client's attorney may be helpful in thinking of likely questions. Why were these data sources and techniques used instead of alternative ones? What theory and evidence support their use? What assumptions were made at various stages of the analysis? How dependent are the results on the choice of data sources, techniques, and assumptions? Have similar analyses been done? If so, what did they show? Thinking about questions like these can help the witness anticipate cross-examination questions and formulate potential responses. It may also be helpful for the client's attorneys to hold a mock cross-examination in order to prepare the witness for the rigors of the real thing. Emerging from cross-examination unscathed can tremendously enhance the effectiveness of the witness's direct testimony.

Expert witnesses must be wary of several temptations that can lead them astray when providing testimony. One temptation is to overstate the strength of the analysis or to claim greater accuracy, less uncertainty, or stronger conclusions than are warranted. I believe this temptation stems at least in part from the way adversarial legal proceedings are organized. A hearing is much like a team sports competition. Two teams are typically involved: the project's proponents and their opponents. Both teams have a number of players, each with a different role—e.g., attorneys, clerks, secretaries, and expert witnesses. Both teams develop their game plans (choice of experts, issues, and exhibits), practice their plays (testimony), and prepare for the big game (the hearing). They play on a level playing field with a clear set of rules (the law and legal precedents), a referee (the judge or hearing officer), and an unmistakable outcome (winning or losing). Each team attempts to score "points" while preventing the other team from scoring. There may even be spectators and reporters in attendance! It is easy for the expert to get caught up in the spirit of the competition and to overstate his/her case in order to "win one for the Gipper." One must guard against this temptation because it weakens objectivity and reduces one's credibility as an expert; in the long run, it may damage the consultant's professional reputation as well.

Another temptation that the expert witness must strive to overcome involves offering opinions on topics beyond his/her expertise. This temptation is more likely to appear during cross-examination than during direct testimony, The opponent's attorneys may ask a great many questions, some of which may stray into areas beyond the consultant's expertise. Not wanting to appear ignorant or stupid, the expert witness experiences a strong temptation to try to answer these questions. The expert should avoid this temptation by responding to such questions with "I don't know" or "That's outside my area of expertise." Providing poor answers to questions beyond one's expertise reduces the expert's credibility and raises doubts about the validity of other parts of his/her testimony; it may also contradict the testimony of other expert witnesses working for the same client.

Finally, it is important for the expert to maintain his/her composure on the witness stand. If they are skillful, the opponent's attorneys will zero in on any weak or questionable parts of the consultant's testimony. They may also attempt to rattle the witness with a hostile manner and/or trick questions, obscure references, or quotations taken out of context. Try not to take these attempts personally or to react emotionally; remember, they are simply part of the "game." Think through each question carefully before giving an answer. Take plenty of time; there is no need to rush. If the opponent's attorney refers to certain materials, ask to see those materials. Respond to all questions, but feel free to answer "I don't know" or to elaborate if a short, direct answer might be inadequate or misleading. Hearing officers and judges typically grant experts a good deal of latitude in responding to questions. Remaining cool, calm, and collected makes a witness much more effective.

Conclusion

This case study illustrates how an applied demographic analysis can be carried out and presented in adversarial legal proceedings.[7] Although it focuses specifically on automobile dealerships in Florida, the demographic issues involved are applicable to many types of small-area analysis. I have worked on research projects involving hospitals, nursing homes, banks, electric utilities, telephone companies, cable television companies, department stores, school boards, water management districts, environmental advocacy groups, and civil rights groups. Some of these projects required that I take part in a legal proceeding; others simply called for assisting a company or government agency in planning for future development. In some projects, the demographic analyses were similar to those reported here. Others dealt with age, sex, or race characteristics; eligible voters; or seasonal residents. As my experience indicates, demographers have many opportunities to work as consultants and to testify at administrative hearings and in courts of law.

Testifying at an administrative or judicial hearing can be a valuable experience—and not only because of the consulting fee one receives! Presenting and defending an analysis in the crucible of adversarial legal proceedings leads to better demographic analyses. Poor or unsupported decisions are quickly exposed, challenged, and sometimes even attacked. This intense scrutiny forces the researcher to evaluate every data source and technique and to examine every assumption. I believe the lessons learned through experiencing the adversarial process carry over to other areas, improving one's skills for a variety of research projects.

In addition, working as an expert witness can help the demographer identify topics that need further research. A number of my academic research projects have grown out of questions raised in adversarial legal proceedings. I believe the involvement of demographers in such proceedings will induce research that makes major contributions in the field of applied demography.

Finally, I believe the participation of professional demographers in adversarial legal proceedings can be beneficial to society as a whole. Better demographic analyses lead to better judicial and administrative decisions. By improving the quality of the data and analyses upon which legal decisions are based, demographers enhance the fairness and economic efficiency of our nation's legal and regulatory systems.

Discussion Questions

1. Identify some industries in your state that have regulatory agencies. Is there a demographic component in any of the application processes? If so, discuss the implications for applied demography.

2. Consider the challenges of making estimates and projections for this market.

3. Keeping the background of this case in mind, evaluate other methods (besides "housing unit") of estimating subcounty level population.

4. Why did the consultant use four techniques to calculate projections?

5. What did the consultant do to strengthen his conclusions?

6. Outline the most useful information presented in the author's section on "Testifying in Adversarial Legal Proceedings."

Notes

The author would like to thank Peter Morrison, Dean Bunch, Bill O'Hare, Sherrilyn Ifill, Bill Serow and Roger Blair for helpful comments and suggestions at various stages in the preparation of this manuscript. The excellent typing and secretarial support of Janet Fletcher and Pam Middleton is also gratefully acknowledged.

1. An administrative hearing is one that takes place before a hearing officer or panel appointed by the executive branch of government, whereas a judicial hearing is one that takes place before a judge in federal or state court.

2. "Line-make" refers to a specific brand of motor vehicle (e.g., Ford, Mercury, Chevrolet, Pontiac, Toyota, BMW).

3. I will use "consultant" to identify the person performing the demographic analysis and "client" to identify the party requesting the analysis. In some instances, the consultant may be an employee of the client. This may create tension between the demographer's desire to conduct an objective, scientific analysis and the employer's desire for a favorable outcome.

4. Demographers often distinguish between the terms "projection" and "forecast" (e.g., Smith 1984). In this discussion I use these terms interchangeably to mean estimates of future population.

5. This section is based on Smith (1993).

6. A third perspective could be mentioned as well: a willingness to use inaccurate data and improper techniques, falsify results, lie under oath, and do anything else necessary to support the client's case. I am assuming that no readers of this discussion would consider engaging in such tactics.

7. This case study focused on a situation in which the expert presented his/her own analysis of a demographic issue. There are also situations in which an expert is asked to provide rebuttal testimony (i.e., critique someone else's analysis). Most of the discussion regarding the preparation and presentation of expert testimony is applicable in both types of situation. For rebuttal testimony, however, the scope of the analysis is relatively narrow: the expert's analysis must focus on the analysis to which he/she is responding. In addition, the time available for preparation of rebuttal testimony may be relatively short.

References

Ahlburg, Dennis. 1987. "Population Forecasting." In *The Handbook of Forecasting.* S. Makridakis and S. Wheelwright, eds. New York: John Wiley.

Brodsky, Stanley L. 1991. *Testifying in Court: Guidelines and Maxims for the Expert Witness.* Washington D.C.: American Psychological Association.

Dorram, Peter B. 1982. *The Expert Witness.* Planners Press. American Planning Association.

Eckard, E.W., Jr. 1985. "The Effects of State Automobile Dealer Entry Regulation on New Car Prices." *Economic Inquiry.* XXIV:223–242.

Florida Legislature. 1989. *Florida Statutes.* Tallahassee: State of Florida.

Hamilton, C. Horace and Josef Perry. 1962. "A Short Method for Projecting Population by Age from One Decennial Census to Another." *Social Forces.* 41:163–170.

Haskins, Mary E., and Walter E. Forehand. 1988. "New Regulations for Motor Vehicle Manufacturers and New Protections for Their Franchisees." *Florida State University Law Review.* 16:763–788.

Irwin, Richard. 1977. *Guide for Local Area Population Projections.* Technical Paper No. 39. Washington, D. C.: U. S. Bureau of the Census.

Kale, Balkrishna, Paul Voss, Charles Palit, and Henry Krebs. 1981. "On the Question of Errors in Population Projections." Unpublished paper presented at the annual meeting of the Population Association of America. Washington, D. C.

Kalmuss, Debra S. 1981. "Scholars in the Courtroom: Two Models of Applied Social Science." *The American Sociologist.* 16:212–223.

Larry Dimmitt Cadillac v. *Seacrest Cadillac*. 1990. 558 So. 2d 136, Florida 1st District Court of Appeal.

Loftus, Elizabeth S. 1986. "Experimental Psychologist as Advocate or Impartial Educator." *Law and Human Behavior.* 10:63–78.

MacHovec, Frank J. 1987. *The Expert Witness Survival Manual.* Springfield, Illinois: Charles C. Thomas Publishers.

Mahmoud, Essam. 1984. "Accuracy in Forecasting: A Survey." *Journal of Forecasting.* 3:139–159.

McCloskey, Michael, Howard Egeth, and Judith McKenna. 1986. "The Experimental Psychologist in Court: The Ethics of Expert Testimony." *Law and Human Behavior.* 10:1–13.

Metro Dade County Planning Department. 1990. Unpublished print-out.

Murdock, Steve H., F. Larry Leistritz, Rita R. Hamm, Sean-Shong Hwang, and Banoo Parpia. 1984. "An Assessment of the Accuracy of a Regional Economic-Demographic Projection Model." *Demography.* 21:383–404.

Murdock, Steve H. and David R. Ellis. 1991. *Applied Demography.* Boulder: Westview Press.

National Research Council. 1980. *Estimating Population and Income for Small Areas.* Washington, D. C.: National Academy Press.

Northwestern University School of Law. 1957. "The Automobile Dealer Franchise Act: A 'New Departure' in Federal Legislation?" *Northwestern University Law Review.* 52:253–283.

Pittenger, Donald B. 1976. *Projecting State and Local Populations.* Cambridge, Massachussetts: Ballinger.

Rogers, Robert P. 1986. *The Effect of State Entry Regulation on Retail Automobile Markets.* Washington, D. C.: Federal Trade Commission.

Siegel, Jacob S. 1953. "Forecasting the Population of Small Areas." *Land Economics.* 29:72–88.

Smith, Richard L. 1982. "Franchise Regulation: An Economic Analysis of State Restrictions on Automobile Distribution." *Journal of Law and Economics.* XXV:125–157.

Smith, Stanley K. 1984. "Population Projections: What Do We Really Know?" *Monograph No. 1.* Gainesville: Bureau of Economic and Business Research, University of Florida.

_____. 1986. "A Review and Evaluation of the Housing Unit Method of Population Estimation." *Journal of the American Statistical Association.* 81:287–296.

_____. 1993. "Expert Testimony in Adversarial Legal Proceedings: Some Tips for Demographers." *Population Research and Policy Review* 12:43–52.

Smith, Stanley K., and Ravi Bayya. 1990. "Projections of Florida Population by County 1989–2020." *Population Studies, No. 92.* Gainesville: Bureau of Economic and Business Research, University of Florida.

Smith, Stanley K. and Scott Cody. 1990. "Number of Households and Average Household Size in Florida: April 1, 1989." *Population Studies, No. 91.* Gainesville: Bureau of Economic and Business Research, University of Florida.

Smith, Stanley K., and Mohammed Shahidullah. 1993. "Evaluating Population Projection Errors for Census Tracts." Unpublished paper presented at the annual meeting of the Population Association of America. Cincinnati.

Smith, Stanley K., and Terry Sincich. 1990. "The Relationship Between the Length of the Base Period and Population Forecast Errors." *Journal of the American Statistical Association.* 85:367–375.

———. 1992. "Evaluating the Forecast Accuracy and Bias of Alternative Population Projections for States." *International Journal of Forecasting.* 8:495–508.

U.S. Bureau of the Census. 1989. "Projections of the Population of the United States, by Age, Sex, and Race: 1988 to 2020." *Current Population Reports.* Series P-25, No. 1018.

Voss, Paul, and Balkrishna Kale. 1985. "Refinements of Small-Area Population Projection Models: Results of a Test Based on 128 Wisconsin Communities." Unpublished paper presented at the annual meeting of the Population Association of America. Boston.

Weiss, Roger J. 1963. "The Automobile Dealer Franchise Act of 1956—An Evaluation." *Cornell Law Quarterly.* 48:711–742.

Wolfgang, Marvin E. 1974. "The Social Scientist in Court." *Journal of Criminal Law and Criminology.* 65:239–247.

13

Locating Fire Station Sites:
The Response Time Component

Jeff Tayman, Bob Parrott, and Sue Carnevale

One of the primary responsibilities of a government is to provide for the health and safety of its residents. People and businesses expect water to flow from faucets, garbage to be collected, and streets to be safe. They also demand prompt service from police, fire, and health agencies during emergencies. Providing adequate public services, however, is one of the most difficult problems with which elected officials must deal. Faced with revenues that fail to keep pace with the increasing demand for more and better services, decision makers are constantly searching for ways to finance public facility projects (Frank and Downing 1988, Chapter 1). And economic constraints are not the only impediments to the timely development of public facilities. One well-known impediment is the NIMBY ("Not in My Back Yard") attitude often expressed by residents who want and need a facility but prefer that it be placed elsewhere.

This case study shows how small-area forecasts were developed and applied to a site location problem, namely the location of fire stations. Rather than focusing on present levels of service and response time, our analysis addressed likely future needs. Many site location decisions require a long-range perspective, allowing for the fact that user demand and travel patterns can change depending on the area's dynamics and growth potential. Yet, even when a fire station will not be needed until some time in the future, decisions concerning its location often must be made long in advance. Making location decisions in advance not only gives officials time to address financial issues, but it also helps insure that the site is not developed for other uses or that nearby land is planned for activities incompatible with a fire station.

Institutional Context

Encinitas, located in the north coastal area of San Diego County, is a city of 55,386 according to the 1990 Census. In 1989 the San Diego Association of Governments (SANDAG) conducted a study at the request of the Fire Protection District of Encinitas (FPD). The FPD wanted to know how different configurations of fire station locations would—in light of future demand and travel conditions—meet the district's goals for fire protection service and affect fire equipment travel times to places where people live and work. The FPD wanted this information to help determine the optimum number and location of fire stations to best serve future demand. SANDAG conducted a study through its Local Technical Assistance (LTA) program. A brief discussion of this program will serve to illustrate the client relationship between SANDAG and the FPD.

SANDAG is a voluntary organization whose voting members consist of one elected official from each incorporated municipality and from the county. Each member pays an annual fee based on population size; payment of this fee entitles members to use the LTA program and to participate in other SANDAG functions. The LTA program provides members with access to SANDAG's information system and with expertise that would cost more if obtained from a private-sector firm. Projects costing less than $1,000 are done free, with members paying only for SANDAG's costs over $1,000. SANDAG works for its members on a sole source basis exclusively and does not compete for projects with private-sector firms.

But saving money is just one advantage of the LTA program. In addition, members are entitled to use the most comprehensive data base for San Diego County. SANDAG maintains information on small-area demographic, economic, land use, and transportation activities. Census information along with current estimates and forecasts are available for virtually any geographic area in the county. Our members demand accurate information and want a quick turnaround at a reasonable price. SANDAG's data bases, custom software, and geographic information system (GIS) enable requests from members to be handled in an efficient and cost effective manner. Without these resources, SANDAG could not have completed this study within the FPD's two-month time frame and $12,000 budget.

Applied demographers rarely work in a vacuum. Identifying the key players and their relationship to a project is vital to insuring its success. Applied demographers often must interact with people having different backgrounds and motivations, from technically oriented persons to key decision makers. Being technically competent and well versed in a particular subject matter constitutes a necessary but not a sufficient condition for producing a successful, accepted project. It is equally important that all key players have, to the extent possible, a clear understanding of the project's objectives and that they support the approach used to reach those objectives. Everyone's responsibilities must be clearly specified to minimize misunderstandings and prevent "turf battles" that could affect the project schedule or hinder acceptance of the project's findings.

It was the chief of the FPD who made the request for the fire station site location study, and it was he who served as project manager. Although the chief was the administrative point of contact, his assistant worked on the project's day-to-day details. Because travel time analysis and future land uses were central to this study, SANDAG recommended that persons from the Encinitas traffic engineering and planning departments also be assigned to the project. SANDAG was responsible for the bulk of the technical work, report preparation, and development of presentation materials. The FPD and city staffs served primarily as reviewers of the inputs, assumptions, and results. This client involvement was important. It helped the FPD and Encinitas officials understand the methods and data and, hence, have confidence in the study's conclusions.

Demographic Perspective

To address public safety concerns, the FPD needed to determine the optimum number and location of fire stations required to meet future demands for fire protection. One important criterion governing these decisions was the response time to a call for fire protection service. The FPD board, consisting of elected officials, adopted three response time goals: (1) a first unit responds within five minutes, (2) a second unit responds within seven minutes, and (3) a ladder company responds within ten minutes. All three goals were to be met 80 percent of the time or, in other words, cover 80 percent of the activity in Encinitas. The FPD wanted an evaluation of these three goals in light of the anticipated growth and the changes in both travel patterns and times within the city.

While small-area population, housing, and place-of-work employment forecasts are in SANDAG's data base, calls for fire station service are not. One option was to produce a calls-for-service forecast specifically for this project, but SANDAG advised the FPD that neither the time nor the cost to prepare such a forecast was warranted. Since calls for service are related to population, housing, and employment densities, these variables would serve as excellent surrogates. Discussions between SANDAG and the FPD also led to the study's inclusion of response times to such high-priority sites as schools, hospitals, child care centers, recreation areas, and major commercial and agricultural sites. Agricultural sites were considered high priority due to the chemicals and other hazardous materials stored on them.

Another issue centered around whether the FPD wanted to simulate the maximum amount of future jobs and population (build-out) in Encinitas or fix the analysis to a specific time point. SANDAG told the FPD that its forecasts extended to the year 2010, and did not necessarily represent the city's ultimate capacity in either population or employment activities. The FPD opted for the 2010 time point because it (1) provided a definite time referent for planning and budgeting purposes, (2) avoided the potential ambiguity and disagreement about the definition of build-out and how it should be calculated, and (3) was based on a forecast that has been accepted for use in planning studies by every jurisdiction and by the SANDAG board of directors.

It was important that the response time concept be correctly defined and measured. Response time and travel time are not the same. Travel time is a subset of response time and does not include either dispatch time or the time required to prepare fire equipment and personnel to respond to a call for fire protection service. The FPD estimates the additional dispatch/preparation time to be around 1.5 minutes. Since SANDAG's models use travel time, we used the lower travel time increments in our analysis to match district goals.

Our analysis measured the achievement of the district's goals in terms of the percent of the 2010 population, housing, employment, and high-risk land uses within 3.5, 5.5, and 8.5 minutes of travel time from fire stations. Adding 1.5 minutes for dispatch and preparation time to these travel times approximates the district's response time goals of five, seven, and ten minutes for first unit, second unit, and first ladder company responses to a call for fire protection service.

The FPD provided six scenarios to SANDAG for travel time evaluation. Five of the six combined existing and potential new sites, while the base case involved only existing sites. As indicated in Figure 13.1, there are four existing stations— numbered 1 through 4—within the FPD boundaries (represented by the bold line). The four potential new sites are designated A, B, C, and D on Figure 13.1.

Here are the six scenarios provided by the FPD for the SANDAG evaluation:

1. BASE: Existing stations 1–4
2. SCEN1: Existing stations 1–4 and proposed station A
3. SCEN2: Existing stations 1–4 and proposed stations A and B
4. SCEN3: Existing stations 1–4 and proposed stations A, C, and D
5. SCEN4: Existing stations 2, 3, and 4, proposed station A, and existing station 1 relocated to the proposed location of B
6. SCEN5: Existing stations 2, 3, and 4, the closure of station 1, and proposed stations A, C, and D

The FPD has automatic aid agreements with neighboring fire districts wherein the engine company closest to the incident is automatically dispatched as part of the normal alarm assignment. There are 11 automatic aid stations assisting the Encinitas FPD, and each scenario included the six closest ones (numbered 5 through 10 on Figure 13.1). The other five automatic aid stations were not included in the study because a travel time analysis revealed that they were too far away to meet FPD response time goals.

Data, Methods, and Assumptions

We used SANDAG's Public Facilities Management Model to analyze the response times for the six scenarios. This model combines the methods and data from three disciplines: demography, urban planning, and geography. Its major components comprise the ARC/INFO ALLOCATE subprogram (Environmental Systems Research Institute 1989), SANDAG's DIME file—computerized street network, and SANDAG's Regional Growth Forecast (San Diego Association of

Governments 1989a). A discussion of each of these components and how they interrelate follows.

Regional Growth Forecasts

SANDAG has been producing long-range forecasts of population, housing, and employment since the early 1970s. The latest effort, known as the Series 7 Regional Growth Forecast, covers the years from 1986 to 2010. SANDAG produces these forecasts in two stages. In stage one, SANDAG develops a forecast for the entire region (San Diego County). In stage two, SANDAG uses land-use based allocation models to distribute the regionwide forecast to various geographic areas within the county.

The regionwide forecast is based on the Demographic and Economic Forecasting Model, or DEFM (San Diego Association of Governments 1989b, 1989c, 1989d). The demographic portion of DEFM uses a cohort-component methodology to forecast the population by age and sex. It determines in and out migration levels from a set of econometric equations that relate migration to job creation, home prices, unemployment rates, and shifts in the U.S. and San Diego age structures. The economic portion of DEFM consists of five sectors: (1) construction, (2) prices, (3) employment, (4) local revenues and expenditures, and (5) income. DEFM links all five sectors directly to each other and to the demographic module through a series of econometric equations.

Regardless of the form and complexity of the forecasting technique, any forecast is based on one or more underlying assumption(s). The key assumptions in DEFM are:

1. No major wars or natural disasters will befall the nation, state, or San Diego region.
2. The region's economy is inextricably linked to the U.S. economy which acts as a driver to the economic forecast. The U.S. forecast used in DEFM comes from Data Resources Inc.
3. The econometric equations are correctly specified (i.e., proper variables and functional form) and have acceptable statistical properties. This assumption was verified during the DEFM calibration which was based on a 35-year historical data series.
4. The statistical coefficients for the equations do not change over the forecast period.
5. The region's 1980 age specific fertility and survival rates will merge towards the projected U.S. rates. Full convergence takes 100 years to reflect differences between San Diego and the U.S. in race and ethnic structure. The U.S. rates come from the Census Bureau's middle projection series. Tests of DEFM's accuracy have shown that trending off the middle series yields the most accurate forecasts.

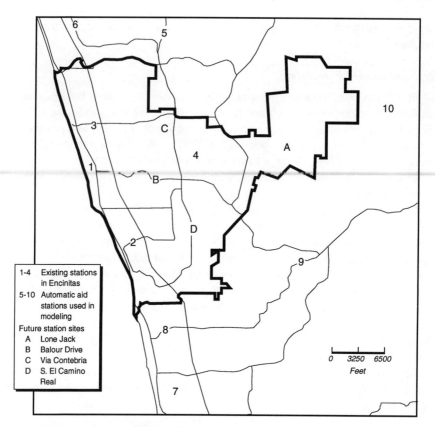

SOURCE: San Diego Association of Governments, August 22, 1989.

Figure 13.1—Encinitas Fire Protection District study area—existing and future fire station sites

DEFM's forecasts are distributed to cities, census tracts, transportation planning zones, and various other geographic entities within the county. The principal variables forecast are population, housing, employment, household income, and land use. Particularly relevant to this project were SANDAG's forecasts for microgeographic areas. The region is divided into 25,000 geographic pieces, each of which is called a Master Geographic Reference Area, or MGRA. MGRAs range in size from 2 to 92 acres.

MGRA forecasts are derived with spatial allocation land-use models. Lowry (1964) is generally credited as the pioneer in developing urban location models. Two hypotheses guided Lowry's work. First, place of work is a primary determinant of place of residence. Second, the greater the length (in distance, time, or cost) of a trip, the lower the likelihood a person will make that trip. Over the years other spatial allocation models have been developed with names like EMPIRIC (Putman 1979, Chapter 3), PLUM (Gouldner et al. 1962) and DRAM/EMPAL

(Putman 1983). All three models are in use today. While they represent important elaborations and improvements on Lowry's initial effort, the two hypotheses that guided his work are common to all three models.

Two models, PLUM and SOAP, are used to produce the MGRA forecasts (San Diego Association of Governments 1988, 1989e). SOAP was developed by SANDAG and is unique to our modeling system. These models are based on two assumptions regarding change in an area's residential and nonresidential activity: (1) Such change is directly related to the area's capacity to handle additional development, and (2) the change is inversely related to the area's distance from other activities. The two factors are combined into a probability that measures the area's potential for change, either up or down. Development capacity is based on the amount of vacant land by type of use (e.g., single family, commercial) and its development density as well as the quantity of land likely to redevelop (e.g., single family houses replaced by condominiums). These land-use assumptions come from the General and Community Plan land-use elements developed by the region's local jurisdictions. Transportation accessibility is measured as the travel time between areas, with travel times based on the speeds and connectivity patterns of the region's street network.

DIME File

A key component of the Public Facilities Management Model is the availability of a computerized street network. The basis for SANDAG's network is the DIME file, developed in large part as a result of the Census Bureau's decision to conduct the 1980 census largely by mail. The main purpose of the DIME file was to code individual addresses to specific geographic areas for tabulation of census data. Because of its importance to SANDAG's regional information system, the DIME file (which evolved into the TIGER system used in the 1990 census) is continuously updated with new streets and subdivisions.

The DIME file is actually a computerized map that contains both street and nonstreet features. Node points occur where a street or special feature (e.g., a stream bed that represents a census tract boundary) intersects another street or special feature, ends, or changes direction. A line drawn between two nodes is called a segment. Each segment contains address ranges and geographic boundary codes for both of its sides, an X-Y coordinate value at each node point, and a street type indicator (e.g., freeway, highway, or local road). Not a standard DIME file characteristic, the street type indicator was added for use in transportation analyses.

SANDAG—in cooperation with and with full review by both FPD and city staffs—updated the street network to reflect future street patterns in the year 2010. Future streets are identified in the circulation element of the city's General Plan. Potential delays or blockages to fire equipment travel (such as signalized intersections, left turns, and railroad crossings) were also added to the network.

Demographic and economic information—e.g., the 2010 population, housing and employment counts, and the number of high-priority sites—were added to the street network as well. A simple scheme was used to allocate the Series 7 MGRA forecasts to each street segment. The activity assigned to a street segment was based on the length of the segment relative to the lengths of all other segments in the MGRA. High-priority sites were added to the network using a GIS procedure known as ADMATCH or address matching. ADMATCH matched the high-priority site addresses to the street names and address numbers in the DIME file. When it found a match, the computer assigned a street segment identifier to each high-priority site.

ARC/INFO ALLOCATE Subprogram

ARC/INFO, a widely used GIS software package, contains virtually all GIS operations from creating, displaying, and manipulating geographic boundary files to ADMATCH and street network analysis. ALLOCATE, which is part of the network module, builds a path along a street network from a given location and then assigns a travel time or distance to each street segment. Our study used travel time calculations because our focus was on fire station response time. Once the computer assigns travel times, the attributes for each segment (e.g., population) are summarized into user-defined travel time bands (e.g., within 3.5 minutes of a fire station).

For this study we ran ALLOCATE from the four existing, four proposed, and six automatic aid fire station locations. For each scenario we compared the travel times to a street segment from the various fire stations involved and used the smallest value in the time band summaries. The following example illustrates the rationale for this procedure. With a single station ten minutes away from a house, the response time to that house would be ten minutes. If another station just three minutes away from the house were added to the scenario, however, the response time to that house would be reduced from ten minutes to three minutes.

In summary, applied demographers often must synthesize a wide variety of information to solve problems or answer questions, usually within unreasonable time frames and skimpy budgets. We pulled together many specialized data sets, methodologies, and assumptions to answer questions regarding fire station response time. While demographic methods and ideas are applicable to many problems, it is important to recognize that other disciplines have resources that should not be overlooked. The Public Facilities Management Model is a system that integrates ideas, data, and methods from a variety of disciplines—including demography.

Spatial allocation models, for example, offer a way to prepare reasonable and defensible population, housing, and employment forecasts for small areas. GIS techniques, which play a key role in SANDAG's Public Facilities Management System and represent valuable tools for the demographic practitioner, provide yet another example. GIS and mapping software are available for microcomputers and are accessible to those with limited training and experience. The proliferation of GIS software and the development of (and, hopefully, the maintenance of) TIGER files are important keys to information systems development and applications in the 1990s.

Results

No matter how complicated their methods or analysis, applied demographers must present their results in a manner their intended audience can understand. In many instances, applied demographers have to convey technical information to nontechnical audiences. This study, for example, was prepared for FPD administrators and elected officials having minimal, if any, experience in technical matters. While we had to make this audience believe that our analysis and approach were reasonable and defensible (i.e., have confidence in our findings), we also had to keep in mind that the primary interest of these administrators and officials was learning about future fire protection response times.

One effective way to convey information to a nontechnical audience is to use graphics. A well-designed graphic—i.e., one that minimizes complexity—provides an excellent way to summarize a key point. Nontechnical audiences find it cumbersome to sift through complicated tables and reams of tabular information. Like any technique, however, graphics can be overdone and misused. A poorly constructed graphic or a graphic that makes too many points is not very useful for conveying information (Schmid 1983; Zelazny 1985).

Our report to the FPD contained (1) a section summary, (2) a brief description of our methods and data, (3) a concise statement of our results, using bar charts and a single table, and (4) several appendices with definitions, a list of high-risk sites, and travel time impediments. The district staff received poster-size computer-generated maps that showed individual station service areas and the travel times within them. For presentation to the FPD board, we had the bar charts contained in the report made into posters.

Figure 13.2 shows the percent of population, employment, and high-risk sites within a 3.5-minute travel time of the first responding unit for all of the scenarios. Model results reveal that less than 60 percent of the future population, employment, and high-risk sites are within 3.5 minutes of the first responding units for the base (or "do nothing") scenario. All of the scenarios except for number 5 capture more activity than the existing configuration of four stations. None of the scenarios, however, meet the FPD's goal of having 80 percent of the activity within five minutes of the first responding units.

In terms of first responding units, scenarios 2 and 3 come closest to meeting the FPD's goal. At more than 70 percent they both access a significantly higher percentage of activity than do either the existing configuration or future scenarios 4 and 5. Although both scenarios serve a similar amount of population within a 3.5-minute travel time, scenario 2 serves a higher percentage of employment and

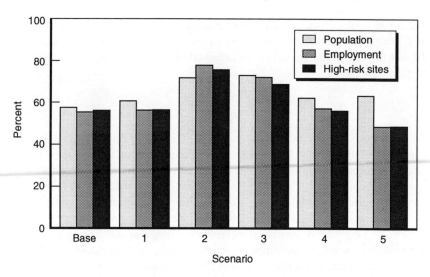

**Figure 13.2—Comparison of modeled scenarios first responding units
percent of activity within 3.5-min. travel time**

high-priority sites than does scenario 3. Scenario 2, moreover, accomplishes these results with one less station than scenario 3.

Figure 13.3 shows the modeling results for a 5.5-minute travel time for second responding units. Again, the base scenario falls well short of the FPD's response time goal, with just over 40 percent of the city's employment and high-priority sites and only 22 percent of its population within 5.5 minutes of a second responding unit. All of the future scenarios capture more activity than the base run, and once again scenarios 2 and 3 provide a significantly higher percent of activity within a 5.5-minute travel time. These two scenarios have almost 80 percent of the employment and high-risk sites within 5.5 minutes of a second responding unit, but they capture only around 60 percent of the population—well short of the FPD's goal.

The final district goal involved response time for ladder equipment. Although not shown, the results of that analysis indicated that approximately 50 percent of the city's activities can be served within a ten-minute response time of the ladder company's existing location—far short of the FPD's response time goal in 2010. But a shift of the ladder company to the proposed Balour Drive site (labeled B on Figure 13.1) accomplishes the goal. From that location the ladder company can serve 90 percent of employment and high-priority sites and 81 percent of the population within ten minutes.

In summary, none of the proposed fire station configurations meets the FPD's two main response time goals, but scenarios 2 and 3 come the closest. In terms of travel times to population, employment, and high-risk sites, scenario 2 is slightly

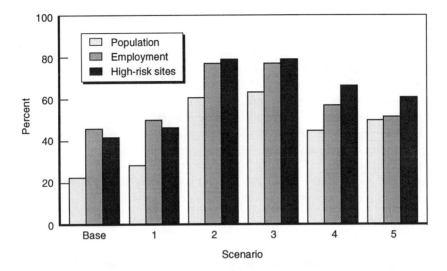

Figure 13.3—Comparison of modeled scenarios second responding units percent of activity within 5.5-min. travel time

better than scenario 3. Scenario 2 is also more cost effective because it uses six stations compared to seven stations for scenario 3. On the other hand, scenario 2 is more controversial than scenario 3 because proposed future site B has been designated for use as a park.

This study was well received by the FPD administrators and elected officials not because they liked the implications of every finding but because they understood and had confidence in the results. The findings pointed out the difficulties involved in achieving the district's future response time goals, and it provided some direction for overcoming those difficulties. The study made clear that the current fire station configuration would not be adequate to serve future demand. To the decision makers this was an important finding because they all recognized that some changes—and additional expenditures—would be required to achieve the FPD's goals. In addition, the study identified a new ladder company site that would achieve the response time goal.

This study looked at one aspect of fire station site selection: the percent of activities that could be reached within certain critical time limits. While important, this is not the only consideration affecting site selection. Other variables—such as available funding, land ownership and acquisition, zoning, public opinion, and politics—affect the final decisions. For example, to implement scenario 2 (which came closest to meeting the FPD's response time goals) would require rezoning of land currently designated as a park. A rezoning effort would likely face opposition from area residents and from the councilperson who represents them.

As it happened, FPD officials decided that none of the configurations shown in this study was suitable for inclusion in the district's Master Plan. They eliminated scenario 2 because of the controversy surrounding conversion of the park site. Cost considerations precluded the implementation of scenario 3 which required seven stations. The two five-station scenarios (1 and 4) were more realistic alternatives from a fiscal standpoint. Although scenario 4 provided much better response time performance than either scenario 1 or the existing configuration, it was disqualified because it, too, included the site on park land. FPD officials disliked scenario 1 because its response time performance was similar to the existing configuration and yet would require the expense of building and maintaining an additional station.

The FPD requested that SANDAG evaluate another five-station scenario. This scenario—which involved the relocation of two existing stations, the addition of one new site, and keeping an existing site in its present location—failed to meet the district's response time goals. It did, however, come closer to these goals than scenario 1, and it represented a significant improvement over the existing four-station configuration. Moreover, this scenario enjoyed broad political and local support. Not surprisingly, therefore, FPD officials selected this five-station scenario for analysis and later included it in the district's Master Plan.

Conclusion

This case study typifies many of the situations that applied demographers encounter, involving a problem that was broad in scope and requiring more than demographic expertise. As such, this study illustrates the interdisciplinary aspect of applied work and the need for broader training of persons interested in this area of demography. Applied demographers can benefit from many areas of formal education, such as market research (Dillon et al. 1990) and methods from other disciplines (Wheelwright and Makridakis 1980; Tayman and Kunkel 1986). In addition, they will likely find skills in GIS and cartography as important as skills in statistical methods.

The Public Facilities Management Model shows the advantage of bringing together multiple resources to solve a problem. Used separately, none of the techniques likely would have addressed future fire station response time as adequately. In addition, the model's structure is general and can be used to answer travel time and distance questions in other applications (e.g., market studies). It also is flexible enough to model alternative simulations such as the effect of a new road on response time, a change in land use on the distribution of future population and employment, or the impact of road blockage during a disaster. Finally, and perhaps most importantly, this model can be implemented within "real world" data and budget constraints. Models and methods that are not workable within these constraints are of very limited use to the applied demographer.

This case study also makes clear that technical expertise is a necessary but not a sufficient condition for a successful project and acceptance of one's work. Doing applied demography means working with people who, in many instances, differ in background and motivation—from each other as well as from the demographer. Being sensitive to these personal differences and minimizing misunderstandings is just as important to achieving the project's objectives as is a proper and defensible analysis.

Related to this last point is the need to communicate effectively to an audience. One of the applied demographer's most difficult tasks is conveying technical information to nontechnical people. Although clients usually have neither the skills nor the inclination to understand in detail the technical aspects of the study, they must be made to feel confident that the results are accurate and defensible. For example, we did not present the mathematics of spatial allocation models (e.g., calibration, nonlinear travel time function, and allocation probabilities) and how they generated the forecast. Instead, we explained to the FPD administrators and elected officials that future activity in an area is a function of two things: (1) the land uses and densities found in the Encinitas General Plan, and (2) the travel time to the area from other activity centers inside and outside the city. Our explanation used concepts and terms that this audience could understand and relate to the pattern of activity shown in the forecast.

Effective communication also involves a clear and concise presentation of the findings. The results and the implications of those results are the bottom line for most clients. Presentations should focus on the key findings and describe them in nontechnical terms—e.g., "None of the scenarios meet FPD response time goals." Communication of results often can be enhanced by using graphics and simple tabulations rather than complicated and extensive tables. One common approach to dealing with detailed output is to place it in a report appendix, where it is available to interested readers as well as serving as documentation (San Diego Association of Governments 1989f).

Clients depend on the ability of applied demographers to provide them with the information they need to make decisions. To provide this information, we often must make small-area estimates and forecasts that bend, if not break, traditional thresholds for accepted accuracy and reliability. This study and other research (Fonseca and Tayman 1989; Tayman 1991) have shown that reasonable estimates and forecasts of detailed demographic and economic characteristics can be developed for small areas. By synthesizing a wide variety of material—much of which may be quite unfamiliar—we not only can give administrators and elected officials the information they need to make decisions but also prepare ourselves to answer the many questions posed to applied demographers.

Discussion Questions

1. Evaluate the five assumptions in the DEFM. Are they appropriate for this city, region, and state?

2. What decisions did the authors ask the clients to make to simplify the task?

3. How important was the use of data and methods from a variety of disciplines?

4. Do you think that SANDAG was correct in advising the fire department that population, housing, and employment densities could serve as excellent surrogates for calls-for-service?

5. How did SANDAG produce its population forecast and assign population counts to street segments? Why did they assign projected population counts to updated street segments?

6. What factors strengthened the confidence of the clients to accept the results of both studies?

7. The SANDAG organization had a unique database. How would you perform this analysis without the database? What new assumptions would be needed? Would it be necessary to use other ways to measure achievement of the Fire Protection District goals?

8. Discuss the author's words in the last paragraph of this case. " ... we often must make small-area estimates and forecasts that bend, if not break, traditional thresholds for accepted accuracy and reliability."

Notes

This chapter was prepared especially for this casebook and is not to be quoted, cited, or used in any manner without permission of the authors.

References

Dillon, W., T. Madden, and N. Firtle. 1990. *Marketing Research in a Marketing Environment.* 2nd Edition. Boston: Irwin.

Environmental Systems Research Institute. 1989. *ARC INFO Users Guide, Vol I.* Redlands, California.

Fonseca, L., and J. Tayman. 1989. "Postcensal Estimates of Household Income Distributions." *Demography.* 26(1):149–159.

Frank, J., and P. Downing. 1988. *Patterns of Impact Fee Use, in Development Impact Fees: Policy Rationale, Practice, Theory and Issues.* A. Nelson, ed. Chicago: Planner Press.

Gouldner, W., S. Rosenthal, and J. Meredith. 1972. *Projective Land Use Model—PLUM: Theory and Application.* Berkeley, Calif.: Institute of Transportation and Traffic Engineering, University of California.

Lowry, I. 1964. *A Model of Metropolis.* Report RM 4125-RC. Santa Monica, Calif: The Rand Corporation.

Putman, S. 1979. *Urban Residential Location Models.* Boston: Martinus Nijhoff.

_____. 1983. *Integrated Urban Models.* London: Pion Limited.

San Diego Association of Governments. 1988. *Series 7 Regional Growth Forecasts. Vol II: Technical Users Manual for PLUM and SOAP.* San Diego, California.

_____. 1989a. *Series 7 Regional Growth Forecasts.* Vol I, *Overview of the Regional Growth Forecasting System.* San Diego, California.

_____. 1989b. *Demographic and Economic Forecasting Model.* Vol I, *DEFM86 Forecasting Manual.* San Diego, California.

_____. 1989c. *Demographic and Economic Forecasting Model.* Vol II, *Technical Manual and Users Guide.* San Diego, California.

_____. 1989d. *Demographic and Economic Forecasting Model.* Vol III, *Data Base Documentation and Update Manual.* San Diego, California.

_____. 1989e. *Series 7 Regional Growth Forecasts.* Vol III, *Data Bases and Exogenous Forecasts.* San Diego, California.

_____. 1989f. Encinitas Fire Protection District Travel Time Study. San Diego, California.

Schmid, C. 1983. *Statistical Graphics: Design Principals and Practices.* New York: John Wiley and Sons.

Tayman, J. 1991. "Population and Housing Estimates for Micro-Geographic Areas: A Blend of Demographic and GIS Techniques." Paper presented at the Population Association of America Conference, Washington, D.C.

Tayman, J. and S. Kunkel. 1989. "Improvements to the Projective Land Use Model for Producing Small Area Forecasts." Paper presented at the Population Association of America Conference, Baltimore, Maryland.

Wheelwright, S., and S. Makridakis. 1980. *Forecasting Methods for Management.* 3rd Edition. New York: John Wiley and Sons.

Zelazny, G. 1985. *Say It with Charts.* Homewood, Illinois: Dow Jones-Irwin.

14

A Demographic Analysis of the Market for a Long-Term Care Facility: A Case Study in Applied Demography

Steven H. Murdock and Rita R. Hamm

Long-term care represents a growth market in most parts of the United States. The number of people 65 years or older is projected to reach nearly 35 million by the year 2000 and 60 million by 2025 (Spencer 1989), a dramatic increase from the 25.5 million in 1980. Since about 5 percent of the elderly population reside in nursing homes at any given time, 9 percent use such homes at some point in any given calendar year, and more than 25 percent spend at least some time in a nursing home before death (Liu and Palesch 1981; Palmore 1976; Manton et al. 1984), the market for long-term care is clearly one with long-term growth potential (Bishop 1988).

This growth potential is just one of the factors that places nursing home care among the most promising investment opportunities for entrepreneurs (Scanlon 1980; Jerboe and McDaniel 1985). Even though Medicaid increasingly finances nursing home care, it is among the highest components of the entire health care industry in terms of private-sector involvement. Private for-profit firms own and operate almost 75 percent of all nursing homes (Bishop 1988), and of all the revenues spent on nursing home care, nearly half comes from private resources rather than from either the government or insurance companies.

The Problem: Verifying the Size of a Market

This case study describes the use of demographic analysis to support a prospectus presented by a private-sector concern to a bank in order to obtain financing for the purchase of a nursing home. The concern—a general partnership of individuals having only limited experience in managing long-term care facilities—identified a nursing home for sale in a rural (agriculturally dominated) area of Texas. The nursing home, which we will call Legacy House,[1] had a good record for profitability under its former owner, and it was available for purchase with a low-interest loan guaranteed by an agency of the Federal Government.

A problem arose, however, with the financial institution chosen by the federal agency to manage its loan program in the Southwest. Citing Legacy House's "poor" demographics as their rationale, the officers of the financial institution denied the loan to the partnership. The institution's demographic report for Legacy House's market area estimated that there had been a rapid decline in the elderly population through outmigration from 1980 to 1988, and it projected a further decline in the elderly population in the future. Moreover, the sole hospital in the site-area city had recently closed, thereby decreasing the likelihood of hospital referrals to Legacy House.

Based on this demographic analysis, the officers of the financial institution concluded that the market was insufficient to make Legacy House profitable and not a good risk for either their institution or the federal agency guaranteeing the loan. At the same time, the officers informed the partnership that they would reconsider their decision if presented with evidence to show that their analysis was somehow "incomplete."

The managing partner for the concern was surprised at the denial, but he was particularly taken aback by the assertion of unpromising demographics for Legacy House. His layman's analysis of the site area suggested a stable population, especially in regard to its elderly component. He sought confirmation of his analysis with state agencies, and they, in turn, referred him to the authors of this study. We were then retained by the partnership to review the financial institution's demographic analysis and to provide an independent assessment of the likely change in the area's elderly population—i.e., the market.

Because (1) our analysis was supplementary to existing data, (2) the partnership had already borrowed funds from and was paying interest to another source for its down payment on Legacy House, and (3) the application period (before all processes had to be reinitiated) with the federal agency guaranteeing the loan was about to expire, the partnership required that we perform our analysis and provide our report within two weeks of the initial contact. We informed the partnership that we could complete only a limited analysis under such time constraints and that it would be impossible to know before completion whether the results would help or hinder its attempt to win a reconsideration of its loan denial. While recognizing the limitations and uncertainties inherent in the situation, the partnership nonetheless authorized us to undertake the analysis.

The Demographic Perspective and Analysis

Our task involved evaluating a set of estimates and projections for an area and the likely effects of population change on a health-related market. It thus required knowledge of population estimation and projection techniques, knowledge of methods for evaluating estimates and projections, knowledge of data sources for small areas, and knowledge of market analyses as applied to long-term care facilities.

We completed the work in three phases. First, we made an attempt to review the financial institution's analysis in terms of its demographic content, including the population estimation and projection methodologies and its actual population estimates and projections. Second, we examined the historical demographic trends and characteristics of counties and subcounties in the vicinity of Legacy House; we examined several alternative (to those used by the financial institution) estimate and projection series for the area; and we compared the results of the financial institution's analysis to the historical data and to the estimates and projections from the other sources. Finally, we performed an alternative analysis of the likely market for Legacy House through the year 2000.

Reviewing the Financial Institution's Analysis

The financial institution, we discovered, had purchased its demographic and other analyses to assess the likely market for Legacy House from a consulting firm. This consulting firm, operating under a blanket agreement with the federal agency guaranteeing the loans, conducted analyses of all the long-term health care facilities in the United States that were being considered for financing by the agency. The consulting firm, in turn, purchased its demographic information from a national data vendor.

The consultant's report clearly was a standardized form, used for many types of marketing studies rather than specifically for analysis of a health-care facility. For example, it contained detailed estimates of housing additions based on the Census Bureau's C-40 Housing Construction Reports, along with detailed data on changes in employment and income—by sector—from the Bureau of Economic Analysis. Still other data included households by type, families by type, and households and families by level and source of income. Although such information may be useful for evaluating the likely ability of Legacy House clients to pay for services, much of it was largely peripheral to the marketing questions at issue and appeared to have been intended for other kinds of analyses.

The crux of the consulting firm's evaluation as it related to the market for Legacy House appears in the data shown in Tables 14.1–14.6. Table 14.1 data estimated that the site-area city had experienced some population decline from 1980 to 1988 and projected it to decline further between 1988 and 1993. Table 14.2 data estimated that even more dramatic patterns of decline had occurred in the site-area county from 1980 to 1988 and were projected to continue into the future. Table 14.3 data estimated that population in the adjacent county closest to the site area had increased from 1980 to 1988 but was projected to decline from 1988 to 1993. More importantly, data contained in Tables 14.4, 14.5, and 14.6 estimated relatively large percentage declines among elderly age groups—the key market segments for nursing-home care.

Table 14.1 Distribution of the Population by Age in the Site-Area City in 1980, 1988 (estimated), and 1993 (projected)

Age Group	1980 Population		1988 Population		1993 Population	
	Number	Percent	Number	Percent	Number	Percent
0–4	136	6.6	159	7.8	157	8.1
5–9	118	5.7	153	7.5	154	8.0
10–14	148	7.2	131	6.5	146	7.6
15–17	116	5.6	79	3.9	73	3.8
18–20	91	4.4	76	3.8	62	3.2
21–24	95	4.6	94	4.6	83	4.3
25–29	126	6.1	175	8.6	145	7.5
30–34	93	4.5	153	7.5	153	7.9
35–39	83	4.1	133	6.6	136	7.1
40–44	96	4.7	93	4.6	120	6.2
45–49	92	4.5	87	4.3	87	4.5
50–54	88	4.3	92	4.5	83	4.3
55–59	109	5.3	93	4.6	84	4.4
60–64	117	5.7	96	4.7	79	4.1
65–69	130	6.3	96	4.7	82	4.3
70–74	155	7.5	90	4.4	74	3.8
75–79	110	5.3	87	4.3	70	3.6
80–84	75	3.7	75	3.7	66	3.4
85 +	79	3.9	70	3.4	76	3.9
Total city population	2,057	100.0	2,032	100.0	1,930	100.0

Sources: 1980 Census of Population and a national data provision firm

In order to evaluate the reasonableness of the data in Tables 14.1–14.6, we needed to know the detailed assumptions used in the estimation and projection methodologies. Unfortunately, such information was not forthcoming. The consulting firm claimed that it did not do original demographic analysis, readily admitting that it relied on the national data vendor for such information. The vendor, in turn, claimed that it produced estimates based on several original data sets and statistical procedures that—although founded on census and other data—were proprietary. The data vendor further noted that the consulting firm had used a software program from yet another vendor. This program allocated estimates of the total population of the county and subcounty areas to produce age-specific estimates from the estimates of total population. As a result, the data vendor could not vouch for the integrity and reasonableness of the age-specific estimates. For its

Table 14.2   Distribution of the Population by Age in the Site-Area County in
1980, 1988 (estimated), and 1993 (projected)

Age Group	1980 Population		1988 Population		1993 Population	
	Number	Percent	Number	Percent	Number	Percent
0–4	1,183	6.6	1,356	7.9	1,314	8.2
5–9	1,170	6.5	1,239	7.2	1,288	8.0
10–14	1,308	7.3	1,116	6.5	1,163	7.2
15–17	991	5.5	739	4.3	615	3.8
18–20	813	4.6	642	3.8	514	3.2
21–24	932	5.2	861	5.0	747	4.7
25–29	1,081	6.0	1,458	8.5	1,217	7.6
30–34	906	5.1	1,309	7.7	1,300	8.1
35–39	729	4.1	1,119	6.5	1,134	7.1
40–44	732	4.1	817	4.8	999	6.2
45–49	841	4.7	676	4.0	765	4.8
50–54	961	5.4	717	4.2	644	4.0
55–59	1,045	5.8	876	5.1	665	4.1
60–64	1,100	6.1	916	5.4	721	4.5
65–69	1,210	6.8	834	4.9	760	4.7
70–74	1,135	6.3	791	4.6	635	3.9
75–79	854	4.8	688	4.0	595	3.7
80–84	500	2.8	521	3.0	504	3.1
85+	417	2.3	445	2.6	496	3.1
Total city population	17,908	100.0	17,120	100.0	16,076	100.0

Sources: 1980 Census of Population and a national data provision firm

part, the software firm claimed to use standard ratioing techniques to perform al-
locations, but it also insisted that the exact computational procedures for these allocation techniques were proprietary.

In sum, it was impossible for us to obtain the detailed information needed to reproduce either the estimates or the projections shown in Tables 14.1–14.6.

We encountered another difficulty in attempting to obtain the information we
needed to evaluate the data in Tables 14.1–14.6, a difficulty that illuminates the
difference between working in an applied rather than in an academic setting. Our
inquiries regarding the detailed procedures used in the estimates and projections
became threatening to the individuals at the consulting firm and other organizations who were responsible for the analysis. Although lacking the information we
needed to evaluate how the values shown in Tables 14.1–14.6 had been ob-

Table 14.3 Distribution of the Population by Age in the County Adjacent to the Site-Area County in 1980, 1988 (estimated), and 1993 (projected)

Age Group	1980 Population		1988 Population		1993 Population	
	Number	Percent	Number	Percent	Number	Percent
0–4	1,778	7.8	2,101	9.0	2,133	9.3
5–9	1,736	7.7	1,883	8.1	2,070	9.0
10–14	1,889	8.3	1,704	7.3	1,855	8.1
15–17	1,262	5.6	1,114	4.8	973	4.2
18–20	999	4.4	783	3.4	645	2.8
21–24	1,226	5.4	1,135	4.9	1,027	4.5
25–29	1,435	6.3	1,883	8.0	1,371	6.0
30–34	1,371	6.0	1,739	7.4	1,850	8.1
35–39	1,201	5.3	1,574	6.7	1,705	7.4
40–44	986	4.3	1,288	5.5	1,458	6.3
45–49	1,082	4.8	1,039	4.4	1,252	5.4
50–54	1,179	5.2	948	4.1	1,014	4.4
55–59	1,210	5.3	1,079	4.6	881	3.8
60–64	1,192	5.3	1,105	4.7	933	4.1
65–69	1,304	5.7	1,084	4.6	941	4.1
70–74	1,068	4.7	1,008	4.3	883	3.8
75–79	832	3.7	830	3.5	787	3.4
80–84	523	2.3	578	2.5	635	2.8
85+	421	1.9	520	2.2	584	2.5
Total city population	22,694	100.0	23,395	100.0	22,997	100.0

Sources: 1980 Census of Population and a national data provision firm

tained—information essential to evaluating the consulting firm's results—we had to drop our inquiries so as not to alienate a hierarchy of officials with whom our client needed to retain a positive working relationship. The experience made clear that such standard aspects of our academic heritage as the norm that results should be reproducible from the data available—as well as answers to questions about the details of a study—may not be readily attainable in a real-world setting.

Given these limitations, we had to evaluate the findings in Tables 14.1–14.6 by using data from other sources for past (in particular, 1970–80) and for recent (e.g., 1980–87) periods and by making an analysis relative to the general base of knowledge regarding demographic processes as they tend to operate in rural areas. An examination of our comparative evaluation using data from other sources appears in the next section.

Table 14.4 The Site-Area City Elderly Population Growth Patterns 1980, 1988 (Estimated), and 1993 (Projected)

Age Group	Population 1980	Estimated 1988	Projected 1993	Change		Percent Change	
				1980–88	1988–93	1980–88	1988–93
60/+	666	514	447	–152	–67	–22.8	–13.0
70/+	419	322	286	–97	–36	–23.2	–11.2
Total	2,057	2,032	1,930	–25	–102	–1.2	–5.0
% of Total:							
60+	32.4	25.3	23.2				
70+	20.4	15.8	14.8				

Sources: 1980 Census of Population and a national data provision firm

Table 14.5 The Site-Area County's Elderly Population Growth Patterns 1970–1980, 1988 (estimated), and 1993 (projected)

Age Group	Population		Estimated 1988	Projected 1993	Numerical Change			Percent Change		
	1970	1980			1970–80	1980–88	1988–93	1970–80	1980–88	1988–93
60+	4,762	5,216	4,195	3,711	454	−1,021	−484	9.5	−19.6	−11.5
70+	2,412	2,906	2,445	2,230	494	−461	−215	20.5	−15.9	−8.8
Total	17,300	17,908	17,120	16,076	608	−788	−1,044	3.5	−4.4	−6.1
% of Total:										
60+	27.5	29.1	24.5	23.1						
70+	13.9	16.2	14.3	13.9						

Sources: 1970 and 1980 Census of Population and a national data provision firm

Table 14.6 The Adjacent County's Elderly Population Growth Patterns 1970–1980, 1988 (estimated), and 1993 (projected)

Age Group	Population		Estimated	Projected	Numerical Change			Percent Change		
	1970	1990	1988	1993	1970–80	1980–88	1988–93	1970–80	1980–88	1988–93
60+	4,921	5,340	5,125	4,763	419	–215	–362	8.5	–4.0	–7.1
70+	2,566	2,844	2,936	2,889	278	92	–47	10.8	3.2	–1.6
Total Population	20,028	22,694	23,395	22,997	2,666	701	–398	13.3	3.1	–1.7
% of Total:										
60+	24.6	23.5	21.9	20.7						
70+	12.8	12.5	12.5	12.6						

Sources: 1970 and 1980 Census of Population and a national data provision firm

Drawing on the general base of demographic knowledge, we concluded that several aspects of the data shown in Tables 14.1–14.6—along with the conclusions in the text of the consulting firm's report—appeared contrary to expectations obtained from the migration and population literature. For example, the elderly are usually among the least likely to migrate, and the rural elderly are especially unlikely to leave areas of lifetime residence (Ritchey 1976; Fuguitt 1985). Yet the values in Tables 14.1–14.3 suggest outmigration for all age groups over 50 years of age with net inmigration for all age groups under 40 years of age from 1980 to 1988. Although net migration is more likely among young adults than among other groups, we did not expect net inmigration for young adults and net outmigration among the elderly.

In addition, we questioned some of the explanations in the consulting firm's report. The report's authors concluded that "elderly outmigration has likely occurred because of the lack of a hospital and other service facilities in the area." All expectations regarding migration patterns show rural elderly as unlikely to move from their home counties, even though service facilities are more readily available in urban locations. Indigenous rural persons seldom migrate in order to be nearer such facilities (Ritchey 1976; Greenwood 1985), and most rural areas (in Texas as well as in other states) contain a disproportionate number of elderly living with poor access to a hospital and other health care facilities (Saenz 1987; Wilson and Heckler 1989). We could only conclude, therefore, that the general literature on rural migration offered little to suggest that the patterns shown in Tables 14.1–14.6 were the commonly expected ones. Clearly, a more detailed analysis would be required in order to draw further conclusions about the likely patterns in the site area.

Review of Historical and Current Conditions in the Site Area

Tables 14.7 and 14.8 present information from several federal and state agency sources on net migration and population change in the two counties containing the market area for the periods 1970–1980 and 1980–87. We examined total counties because the consulting firm's report had emphasized county patterns, and we used data for 1987 because data for 1988 were not available.

Despite what was suggested in the consulting firm's report, the data in Table 14.7 show historical patterns of net outmigration in the site-area county among *young adults* rather than among the *elderly*. In fact, with its heavy outmigration among young adults the pattern shown in the table is typical of rural, agriculturally based counties. According to net migration estimates for 1970–80 from Hwang et al. (1985), such counties experienced net outmigration among young adults and net immigration among elderly age groups. Even during the 1960s, when the area was losing a large number of residents through outmigration, the loss was primarily due to the outmigration of young adults (Bowles et al. 1975).

Table 14.7   Net Migration and Net Migration Rates by Age for the Site-Area
County and Adjacent County, 1960-80

Age Group	Bowles et al. 1960–70		U.S. Census Bureau 1975–80	Hwang et al. 1970–80	
	Number	Rate	Number	Number	Rate
Site-Area County					
0–4	44	7.7	—	209	21.4
5–9	−49	−5.7	38	159	15.7
10–14	−157	−14.1	15	47	3.7
15–19	−295	−22.6	−77	54	3.5
20–24	−851	−61.5	−354	−497	−30.1
25–29	−640	−59.5	−125	−552	−33.8
30–34	−92	−18.0	43	121	15.4
35–39	−56	−10.3		124	20.5
40–44	−40	−6.3	32	127	21.0
45–49	−55	−7.4		169	25.0
50–54	−33	−4.1	212	126	15.1
55–59	−28	−3.0		184	21.3
60–64	31	3.5	166	196	21.6
65–69	35	4.4		163	15.5
70–74	32	4.7	−60	177	18.4
75+	35	3.2		66	3.9
Total	−2,119	−15.2	−110	873	5.1

On the other hand, migration data for 1975–1980 from the U.S. Census of 1980 were more supportive of the consulting firm's estimated patterns for post-1980 periods. These data showed some elderly outmigration (about 60 persons, aged 60 years or older) from the site-area county from 1975 to 1980. It occurred to us that the results in the consulting firm's report may have been obtained by using rates based on 1975 to 1980 migration patterns.

To test this idea, we computed a migration rate for persons 60 years of age or older using the average population in the cohort 60+ years of age (that is, the population in this cohort in 1970 and that in 1980 divided by 2) as the denominator. This computation resulted in a net outmigration rate of 1.6 percent for five years (or 0.32 per year). By applying this rate to the population aged 51.75 years or older in 1980 (because those persons 60 years of age as of July 1, 1988 would have been at least 51.75 years old as of April 1, 1980), we determined a net outmigration of only 163 persons from 1980 to 1988. Clearly, the technique used

Table 14.7 (continued)

Age Group	Bowles et al. 1960–70		U.S. Census Bureau 1975–80	Hwang et al. 1970–80	
	Number	Rate	Number	Number	Rate
County Adjacent to Site-Area County					
0–4	101	7.3	—	248	16.2
5–9	−80	−1.7	−28	257	17.4
10–14	−177	−8.1	163	−327	20.9
15–19	−594	−24.9	−80	154	8.5
20–24	−1309	−56.6	−634	−517	−25.2
25–29	−742	−45.9	−31	−346	−19.4
30–34	−45	−5.3	69	438	46.8
35–39	−58	−5.8		321	36.4
40–44	−75	−5.6	20	179	22.2
45–49	−74	−6.2		159	17.1
50–54	−27	−2.3	120	163	16.0
55–59	−24	−1.9		151	14.2
60–64	33	−2.7	107	169	16.5
65–69	99	9.8		196	17.7
70–74	75	8.3	−40	86	8.7
75+	79	5.3		20	1.1
Total	−2,818	−12.1	−334	1351	9.7

Sources: Bowles, G.K., C. Beale, and E.S. Lee, 1975; Net Migration of the Population, 1960–70, by Age, Sex and Color, Part 5—West South Central States, Athens: University of Georgia; U.S. Bureau of the Census, 1984; Gross Migration for Counties: 1975–80, Supplementary Report, PC 80-S1-17, Washington, D.C.: U.S. Government Printing Office.

in the consulting firm's report was not based on the assumption that the 1975–1980 patterns continued into the 1980s.

The data in Table 14.7 also raised doubt as to whether the consulting firm's reported decline of more than 1,000 elderly persons in the site-area county from 1980 to 1988 could be correct. Historical patterns showed that outmigration in the site area had occurred primarily among young adults. The consulting firm's report had estimated, however, that a decline of 788 in the total population had occurred from 1980 to 1988, and that figure—in conjunction with a decline of more than 1,000 in the elderly population—would suggest that net inmigration must have occurred among younger age groups in order to offset the decline in the elderly population. Obviously, the estimate patterns in the consulting firm's report were at odds with the historical record.

The data in Table 14.8 show recent estimates (from the U.S. Bureau of the Census and the State of Texas Population Estimates Program in the Texas Depart-

Table 14.8 Population and Population Change for the Site-Area County, Adjacent County, and Places Within the Site-Area County, Total and by Age, 1970–87

County	Total Population					Percent Change			
	1970	1980	1985a	1987b	1987c	1970–80	1980–85a	1980–87b	1980–87c
Site Area	17,300	17,908	17,619	17,126	17,500	3.5	-1.6	-4.4	-2.3
Adjacent	20,028	22,694	23,675	23,232	23,600	13.3	4.3	2.4	4.0

Site-Area City

	Total Population 1980	Population Estimates					
		U.S. Census Bureau			Texas Department of Commerce		
		1982	1984	1986	1986	1987	
Site City	2,057	2,097	2,102	1,960	1,924	1,895	

Age Group	Site-Area County			Adjacent County		
	1980	Estimated 1985a	1987b	1980	Estimated 1985a	1987b
0–4	1,183	1,568	1,345	1,778	2,329	2,042
5–9	1,170	1,168	1,197	1,736	1,747	1,782
10–14	1,308	1,151	1,046	1,889	2,027	1,686
15–19	1,583	1,254	1,205	1,958	1,775	1,822
20–24	1,153	819	1,395	1,529	1,001	1,916
25–29	1,081	904	1,194	1,435	1,476	1,557
30–34	906	1,077	1,001	1,371	1,616	1,402
35–39	729	850	939	1,201	1,507	1,422
40–44	732	722	750	986	1,156	1,352
45–49	841	890	690	1,082	1,076	1,030
50–54	961	1,015	789	1,179	1,210	996
55–59	1,045	1,073	858	1,210	1,229	1,107
60–64	1,100	1,137	909	1,192	1,268	1,087
65–69	1,210	996	904	1,304	1,227	1,036
70–74	1,135	1,103	970	1,068	1,116	1,046
75+	1,771	1,892	1,934	1,780	1,915	1,949
Total	17,908	17,619	17,126	22,698	23,675	23,232

a = U.S. Bureau of the Census, Experimental County Estimates by Age, Sex, Race and Year
b = Texas Department of Commerce, Population Estimates Program's Estimates
c = U.S. Bureau of the Census, County Population Estimates: July 1, 1987 and 1986. Current Population Reports, P-26, No. 87-A. 1988.

ment of Commerce) of the total population of the site-area county, the adjacent county, and the site-area community for post-1980 time periods. Population estimates by age for counties are also shown. A comparison of these estimates to the data in Tables 14.1–14.6 (from the consulting firm's report) reveals some similarities and some differences.

The estimates from the Texas Department of Commerce, for example, suggest that the population of the site-area county declined from 17,908 in 1980 to 17,126 by 1987. The estimate from the Census Bureau for 1987 was 17,500, while the estimate from the consulting firm for 1988 was 17,120. The overall pattern of decline in the total population from 1980 to 1987–1988 suggested by the consulting firm's estimates thus appears reasonable.

Similarly, the firm's estimate for the adjacent county's population of 23,395 and its estimate of the site-area community's population of 2,032 for 1988 were both quite close to the Texas Department of Commerce's 1987 estimates of 23,232 and 1,895 as well as the Census Bureau's 1987 estimates of 23,600 and 1,960, respectively.

There were major differences, however. These differences appear in the population estimates by age from the consulting firm's report and those from the Texas Department of Commerce for 1987 and the U.S. Bureau of the Census estimates for 1985, particularly for the site-area county; no data on age for places were available from either the Texas Department of Commerce or the U.S. Bureau of the Census. A comparison between the data in Table 14.2 and Table 14.5 from the consulting firm's report and the data in the bottom panel of Table 14.8 from the Texas Department of Commerce and the U.S. Census for the elderly age groups shows much larger estimated declines among such groups—particularly among the oldest age groups—in the firm's data. Whereas the firm estimated a decline of 1,021 in the population 60 years of age or older, 461 for persons 70 or older, and 117 for persons 75 or older from 1980 to 1988 in the site-area county (see Tables 14.2 and 14.5), the comparable figures from the Texas Department of Commerce for the years 1980–1987 were declines of just 499 in the population 60 years of age or older and 2 for persons 70 or older, and an *increase* of 163 for persons 75 or older. The Census Bureau's 1985 estimates for 1980 to 1985 showed a decline of only 88 persons 60 years of age or older and *increases* of 89 and 121 for the two older groups, respectively. Although estimates for 1988 were not available from the Texas Department of Commerce and the Census Bureau, the direction of change shown in the data from these sources (and the fact that the estimates from the Texas Department of Commerce are almost identical to those from the consulting firm for total population) clearly suggests that the consulting firm's estimates show too large a part of the population decline in the site-area county from 1980–1988 occurring among the elderly. Without detailed information on the methodology used to prepare the consulting firm's report, however, we cannot know whether migration or mortality assumptions might account for the firm's estimated large decline in the elderly population.

Table 14.9   Total 1980 Population and Projected Total Population (1990–2000)
for the Site-Area County and Adjacent County by Projection Agency

Total Population 1980 and Projected Population, 1990–2000

Agency/Year	Site-Area County			Adjacent County		
U.S. Census Bureau						
1980	17,908			22,694		
Texas Department of Health						
1990	18,671			24,325		
1995	18,207			24,927		
2000	17,728			25,522		
Texas Water Development Board	Low Series	High Series		Low Series	High Series	
1990	18,412	19,080		25,185	26,310	
2000	18,498	20,416		27,698	30,534	
Texas Department of Commerce	Scenario			Scenario		
	0.0	0.5	1.0	0.0	0.5	1.0
1990	17,186	17,576	17,795	24,072	24,879	25,480
1995	17,448	18,300	18,756	25,066	26,977	28,494
2000	17,894	19,211	19,792	26,248	29,421	32,030

We also considered how the projections in the consulting firm's report compared to those from other sources. Tables 14.9 and 14.10 provide information on projections of the total population and of the population in elderly age groups for the site-area and adjacent counties from several state sources. We compared these projections to those in Tables 14.2, 14.3, 14.5, and 14.6 from the consulting firm's report.

As shown in Tables 14.2 and 14.3, the consulting firm report projected that by 1993 the total population in the site-area county would decline to 16,076 (from 17,120 in 1988) and the population of the adjacent country would decline to 22,997 (from 23,395 in 1988). According to three sets of projections by state agencies (Table 14.9), however, the total population of the site-area county would be between 17,186 and 19,080, and the population of the adjacent county would be between 24,072 and 26,310 in 1990. By 1995, according to the state agencies' projections, the population of the site-area county would be between 17,448 and 20,416 and that of the adjacent county would be between 24,927 and 28,494. The significance of these projections is that they all show either a population increase from 1987 levels or population stability (in the Texas Department of Commerce 0.0 scenario).

The data in Table 14.10 indicate that the state agencies project a much smaller decline in the elderly population than the consulting firm's report projected. Whereas the firm projected a 1988–1993 decline of 484 persons in the population 60 years of age or older in the site-area county, the largest decline projected by any state agency was 476; the average decline for the state agencies' projections was just 246. Similarly, the firm projected a decline of 362 among this age group in the adjacent county, while the largest decline in the state agencies' projections was 273, with the average change being an *increase* of 93.

Even more significant—given that the primary age group needing nursing home care is the population 75 years or older—projections from the state agencies for the site-area county all showed increases in this age group by 1995. The increases varied from 60 to 217 for the years 1987–1995, depending on the agency projection. By contrast, the consulting firm's report projected a decline of 59 for this age group in the site-area county. For the adjacent county, the consulting firm's report projected an increase of 78, while the state agencies' projected increases ranged from 76 to 265 for the years 1987–1995.

What could we conclude about the likely validity of the demographic portions of the consulting firm's report? Although estimates and projections may be problematic, especially for relatively small areas (National Academy of Sciences 1980), and future patterns may depart from historic ones, it is unlikely that the estimated and projected patterns in the firm's report are correct. Although it is possible that the estimates and projections from the other sources are incorrect and those of the consulting firm are correct, the weight of the evidence suggests that the firm's data were overly pessimistic about patterns for the area's elderly population. This conclusion is reinforced by the presence of data from several sources that differ from the data supplied by the consulting firm and by the fact that the firm's data are contrary to both the past record in the area and to the patterns generally found among elderly populations in rural areas. We concluded, therefore, that the firm's overall conclusions regarding population change in the area were not supported by the preponderance of evidence and that an alternative analysis was necessary.

Determining the Market for a Nursing Home

With the analysis of the demographic data casting doubt on the consulting firm's report about the market for long-term care services in the area, we had to determine whether alternative demographic expectations would show a population base of sufficient size to support the client's facility. A complete market analysis would obviously include an examination of the financial characteristics of the persons in the market area as well as other financial information about the form of client payment (e.g., Medicaid versus self-payment) and other financial character-

Table 14.10 Total (1980) and Projected (1990–2000) Total Population and Elderly Population for the Site-Area County and Adjacent County by Projection Agency

Site-Area County	1980 U.S. Census	Texas Department of Health	Texas Water Development Board Series		Texas Department of Commerce Scenarios		
			Low	High	0.0	0.5	1.0
Projections of the Total Population							
1980	17,908	—					—
1990	—	18,671	25,185	19,080	17,186	17,576	17,795
1995	—	18,207	—	—	17,448	18,300	18,756
2000	—	17,728	27,698	20,416	17,894	19,211	19,792
Age Group			*1990: Projections of the Elderly Population*				
60–64	1,100	1,079			840	876	891
65–69	1,210	1,067			856	892	912
70–74	1,135	967			832	865	869
75+	1,771	2,154			2,049	2,071	2,095
60–75+	5,216	5,267			4,577	4,704	4,767
			1995: Projections of the Elderly Population				
60–64	—	968			750	818	860
65–69	—	949			759	834	880
70–74	—	934			738	809	845
75+	—	2,151			1,994	2,069	2,097
60–75+	—	5,002			4,241	4,530	4,682
			2000: Projections of the Elderly Population				
60–64	—	853			666	741	798
65–69	—	827			703	811	863
70–74	—	901			670	785	856
75+	—	2,151			2,013	2,164	2,230
60–75+	—	4,732			4,052	4,051	4,747

Site-Area County	1980 U.S. Census	Texas Department of Health	Texas Water Development Board Series — Low	High	Texas Department of Commerce Scenarios — 0.0	0.5	1.0
Projections of the Total Population							
1980	22,694	—					—
1990	—	24,325	25,185	26,310	24,072	24,879	25,480
1995	—	24,927	—	—	25,066	26,977	28,494
2000	—	25,522	27,698	30,534	26,248	29,421	32,030
1990: Projections of the Elderly Population							
Age Group							
60–64	1,192	1,076	—	—	1,069	1,102	1,117
65–69	1,304	1,164	—	—	1,044	1,080	1,098
70–74	1,068	842	—	—	946	978	981
75+	1,776	2,054	—	—	2,158	2,166	2,172
60–75+	5,340	5,136			5,217	5,326	5,368
1995: Projections of the Elderly Population							
60–64	—	990	—	—	961	1,032	1,053
65–69	—	1,059	—	—	993	1,066	1,100
70–74	—	771	—	—	919	991	1,014
75+	—	2,025	—	—	2,171	2,214	2,206
60–75+	—	4,845			5,044	5,303	5,373
2000: Projections of the Elderly Population							
60–64	—	902	—	—	872	971	978
65–69	—	951	—	—	899	1,005	1,039
70–74	—	698	—	—	900	1,001	1,044
75+	—	1,996	—	—	2,280	2,382	2,382
60–75+	—	4,547			4,951	5,359	5,443

istics about the facility and its financial structure. Our role was limited to completing the demographic part of a market analysis for Legacy House—that is, determining the number of clients for the nursing home likely to result from the demographic changes in the area.

The demographic market analysis for Legacy House involved the following steps:

1. Determine the market area for the nursing home.
2. Identify competing nursing homes in the market area.
3. Determine the market share for Legacy House within the market area.
4. Project the size of the future population within the market area.
5. Project the demand for long-term care services in the market area and the number of clients for Legacy House.

Determination of Market Area

We determined the market area for Legacy House by examining the areas of residence for past and present clients of the nursing home. Our analysis showed that most Legacy House clients had lived in close proximity to the home prior to admission. In fact, about 50 percent of the total admissions came from the site-area community and that about 80 percent had lived within 20 miles of the facility. We designated his area—the site-area community and its adjacent areas—as the primary market area for Legacy House.

The balance of the home's admissions (about 20 percent of the total) came from residences located within the site county or the adjacent county. We designated the two-county area outside the primary area as the secondary market area for Legacy House.

Identification of Competing Nursing Homes in the Market Area

Four other facilities, besides Legacy House, served the long-term care needs of the two-county market area. Although the four facilities were not in Legacy House's site area, they were close enough to compete with it.

Legacy House enjoyed some advantages over the other four facilities. Among these advantages were its provision of skilled nursing beds (those for persons with severe physical limitations), its relatively high occupancy rate, and its staff physician. Its one major disadvantage was the absence of a hospital in the site area, but it had compensated for this by negotiating a referral agreement with three hospitals to refer cases requiring skilled bed care to Legacy House. In addition, the Legacy House staff physician was also the area's major physician and had staff privileges at all the hospitals in adjoining areas. As a result, it seemed safe to assume that Legacy House would remain as competitive in the future as it had been in the past. Selected characteristics of the five facilities are shown in Table 14.11.

Table 14.11   Characteristics of the Site-Area Legacy House Nursing Home and Competing Nursing Homes in the Site-Area and Adjacent Counties (December 1987)

Facility[1]	Number of beds	Occupancy Rate %	Number of Skilled Nursing Beds	Hospital in Community	Physician in County	Referral Arrangement with Hospital	Medicaid Approved
Legacy House (Site Facility)	104	93.3	52	No	Yes	Yes	Yes
Quality Nursing Home	84	92.9	0	Yes	Yes	Yes	Yes
Pleasant Acres Nursing Home	41	100.0	0	Yes	Yes	Yes	Yes
Green Valley Rest Home	96	86.9	0	No	No	No	Yes
Oakwood Nursing Home	111	92.8	0	Yes	Yes	Yes	Yes

[1] All names are fictional, although other data are actual data for the nursing home in the actual study.

Determination of the Market Share for Legacy House
Within the Market Area

To complete our analysis of the market share for the five facilities for a base year of 1987, we assumed that the national average of nursing home admissions per population unit—5 percent of the population 65 years of age or older—had prevailed in the primary and secondary areas. Based on this assumption and the 1987 population estimates from the Texas Department of Commerce, we estimated that the total demand for nursing home services was 84 beds in the primary market and 308 beds in the secondary market (see the first row of data in Table 14.13).

By placing these data in conjunction with the Legacy House occupancy rate (shown in Table 14.11) and Legacy House client-origin data, we noted that 78 of the estimated 84 residents from the primary market area—or 93 percent—in 1987 were Legacy House residents. The other 19 Legacy House residents came from the secondary market area, which we assumed was equal to 6 percent of the demand (19 is 6 percent of 308). Based on these data, one could expect Legacy House to obtain 93 percent of all nursing home admissions from the primary market area but only 6 percent of the admissions from the secondary market area. All available evidence suggested that these proportions were reasonable and likely had maintained themselves over time. For the remainder of the analysis, therefore, we assumed these percentages to be Legacy House's market shares for its primary and secondary markets.

Projection of the Size of the Future Population
Within the Market Area

To project the future population in the market areas, we had to make several relatively simplistic assumptions. In order to obtain projections for the subcounty areas which form the primary and secondary markets, we assumed that those market areas would have the same proportions of the total county populations that they had in the 1980 census. We used these proportions because an analysis suggested that they had remained relatively stable from 1970 to 1987. To take into account variations in future populations that form the clientele base for the nursing home, we used all three of the alternative projections from the Texas Department of Commerce. These projections allowed us to take into account the possible variability in the size of future populations while utilizing values that had a common methodological base.

We then obtained the market area population by simply multiplying the assumed proportions of the site-area and adjacent counties' populations in each part of the market area by the projected population values for the counties. We thus used these proportions and projections for the total population, for the population 65 years of age or older, and for the population 75 years of age or older to obtain projections of the total and elderly population (including both 65 and 75 years of age or older) in the primary, secondary, and total market areas for the years 1990, 1995, and 2000. The results of this analysis appear in Table 14.12.

Table 14.12 Characteristics of the Population in the Primary and Secondary Market Areas for the Legacy House Nursing Home for 1980 and Projected for 1990, 1995, and 2000

	Primary Market Area									Secondary Market Area			Total Market Area (Primary & Secondary)		
	Site-Area Community			Remaining Primary			Total Primary								
1980 Population															
Total		3,459			3,231			6,690			33,988			40,678	
65+ years of age		923			863			1,786			6,498			8,284	
75+ years of age		445			415			860			2,699			3,559	
Projections by Scenario															
	0.0	0.5	1.0	0.0	0.5	1.0	0.0	0.5	1.0	0.0	0.5	1.0	0.0	0.5	1.0
1990 Population															
Total	3,317	3,392	3,434	2,788	2,861	2,908	6,105	6,253	6,342	35,153	36,202	36,933	41,258	42,455	43,275
65+ years of age	837	857	868	819	836	845	1,656	1,693	1,713	6,229	6,349	6,414	7,885	8,042	8,127
75+ years of age	512	518	524	488	491	495	1,000	1,009	1,019	3,207	3,228	3,248	4,207	4,237	4,267
1995 Population															
Total	3,367	3,532	3,620	2,855	3,020	3,127	6,222	6,552	6,747	36,292	38,725	40,503	42,514	45,277	47,250
65+ years of age	782	831	856	782	825	844	1,564	1,656	1,700	6,010	6,327	6,442	7,574	7,983	8,142
75+ years of age	499	518	524	481	496	499	980	1,014	1,023	3,185	3,269	3,280	4,165	4,283	4,303
2000 Population															
Total	3,454	3,708	3,820	2,947	3,212	3,374	6,401	6,920	7,194	37,741	41,712	44,628	44,142	48,632	51,822
65+ years of age	758	842	885	769	842	873	1,527	1,684	1,758	5,938	6,464	6,656	7,465	8,148	8,414
75+ years of age	503	541	558	494	524	533	997	1,065	1,091	3,296	3,481	3,521	4,293	4,546	4,612

Projection of the Demand for Long-Term Care Services in the Market Area and the Number of Clients for Legacy House

The final part of our market analysis involved projecting the specific market and the actual number of clients for Legacy House. We started by determining the number of nursing home clients likely to be found among the market area's elderly population. This number represented the total demand for nursing home services in the market area. To obtain the total size of the market, we used the standard figure of 5 percent of persons 65 years of age or older as the rate of demand in the elderly population for nursing home care. Our projections of demand in the market area for each time period appear in Table 14.13.

We obtained our projections of the Legacy House client population by multiplying the values of total demand (shown in Table 14.13) by the Legacy House market shares: 93 percent for the primary market area and 6 percent for the secondary market area. These projections, as shown in Table 14.14, suggested relative stability in the facility's client population. With a client population of 97 in 1987, for example, Legacy House could be projected to have a client population ranging from 88 to 102 during the years from 1990 to 2000. The occupancy rate, which was 93.3 percent in 1987, would be between 85 (88 divided by 104) and 98 (102 divided by 104) percent. Since Legacy House could remain profitable at an 85 percent level of occupancy, our analysis suggested that even at the lowest population growth rate the facility would have enough clients to remain profitable.

Our analysis also suggested, however, that there was almost no margin for slippage in either the projected population or Legacy House's market share. If the actual rate of population change fell below the projection or if Legacy House lost market share in either its primary or secondary market area, the facility could find itself with occupancy levels too low to remain profitable. While our projections did not suggest much future erosion of the market, neither did they suggest much growth or expansion. As a consequence, Legacy House would require careful management in order to remain profitable in a highly competitive market.

Several aspects of our market study were unusual and require some clarification. Due to time and resource limitations, we had to make more than the normally expected number of simplifying assumptions. For example, our use of constant proportions to project the market area population from county-level projections—rather than using trends in shares or completing direct projections for the market area itself—was somewhat unusual. So was our assumption of a simple 5 percent demand rate among the elderly population base. Given sufficient time, analysts should use figures derived from historical records and from surveys of service providers in the market area.

It was also unusual to have a market area characterized by county boundaries. It was possible in this case only because these Texas counties are relatively large, Legacy House is situated in a unique location relative to the boundaries of the two counties, and the clients of Legacy House have widely dispersed points of origin.

Table 14.13 Demand for Long-Term Care (in beds) in the Primary and Secondary Market Areas for the Legacy House Nursing Home for 1987, and Projected for 1990, 1995 and 2000

Year	Primary Market Area									Secondary Market Area			Total Market Area (Primary & Secondary)		
	Site-Area Community			Remaining Primary			Total Primary								
1987	43			41			84			308			392		
	Projections of Market-Area Nursing-Home Demand by Scenario														
	0.0	0.5	1.0	0.0	0.5	1.0	0.0	0.5	1.0	0.0	0.5	1.0	0.0	0.5	1.0
1990	42	43	43	41	42	42	83	85	85	311	317	321	394	402	406
1995	39	42	43	39	41	42	78	83	85	301	316	322	379	399	407
2000	38	42	44	38	42	44	76	84	88	297	323	333	373	407	421

Table 14.14 Projected Client Population (Market) for the Legacy House Nursing Home for 1990, 1995, and 2000 by Population Projection Scenario (0.0, 0.5, 1.0) for Primary and Secondary Market Areas

| | Primary Market Area | | | | | | | | | Secondary Market Area | | | Total Market Area (Primary & Secondary) | | |
| | Site-Area Community | | | Remaining Primary | | | Total Primary | | | | | | | | |
Year	0.0	0.5	1.0	0.0	0.5	1.0	0.0	0.5	1.0	0.0	0.5	1.0	0.0	0.5	1.0
1990	39	40	40	38	39	39	77	79	79	19	19	19	96	98	98
1995	36	39	40	36	38	39	72	77	79	18	19	19	90	96	98
2000	35	39	41	35	39	41	70	78	82	18	19	20	88	97	102

Finally, it should be noted that our analysis was unusual in that it lacked projections of income and other financial factors found in more complete market analyses.

The Final Outcome

We presented the partnership with all of the tables in this document along with about 25 pages of text and references. A financial analyst provided some additional information which the managing partner delivered with our analysis to representatives from the federal agency and the financial institution. These representatives then decided that the consulting firm's analysis had been incomplete. The federal agency demanded that the consulting firm supply a new market analysis using our demographic data.

Not surprisingly, the demographic portions of the new market analysis produced results that were virtually identical to our own, suggesting stability rather than decline in Legacy House's market-area population and in the likely level of total demand for Legacy House services. The consulting firm concluded, however, that while demand was sufficient, the area's loss of the hospital and the partnership's lack of experience in nursing home management would make it difficult to retain Legacy House's market share. As a result, it again recommended against financing the enterprise, and the federal agency and the financial institution once again concurred. The loan to the partnership was denied for a second time. Despite our success in providing our client both with the information needed to refute the consulting firm's demographic analysis and with data that projected a stable rather than a declining market for nursing home care in the area, the result insofar as the client was concerned remained unchanged.

Conclusion

What does this case study reveal about the applied demographic research process in general and its use in the analysis of long-term care facilities in particular? And what does it suggest about the demographic enterprise in both academic and applied settings? Each of these issues is addressed briefly below.

The Applied Demographic Process

This study was similar, in several respects, to many other applied analyses. The client sought the assistance of demographers only after an analysis completed by persons not trained in demography produced results contrary to what the client expected. It was more than a simple demographic analysis, requiring knowledge in addition to the demographic. What the client wanted was, in fact, a market analysis (although admittedly not a complete one) that required knowledge of market-area analysis techniques in addition to demographic techniques. It required not only methodological knowledge but also substantive knowledge of migration, rural demographic patterns, migration patterns among the elderly, and other demographic phenomena. Clearly, this case demonstrated that demographic expertise is substantive as well as methodological and that knowledge of demographic methods alone is often not enough to prepare an applied demographic analysis.

The study also involved social and organizational factors. Our need to avoid confrontations with other players in the process and our cautioning the client that the results of our study could prove more negative than the consulting firm's demonstrate that applied research involves interacting with people who may not share the norms of an academic researcher.

Finally, the short time frame for the study compelled the use of numerous assumptions and resulted in an analysis that was less complete than we—or most other demographers—would have wanted. As a matter of fact, the client allowed no time even for the preparation of a final draft. In terms of the depth of analysis and the refinement of presentation, therefore, this study suggested some of the limitations one is likely to experience in an applied setting.

Analysis of Long-Term Care Facilities

The results also have clear implications for demographic analysis of markets for long-term care facilities. The nation's aging population will increase the demand for long-term care, but the distribution of that demand will vary with the characteristics of the population. Local demographic information and expertise are essential, therefore, to identify the most advantageous markets.

The elderly, like other segments of the population, are not demographically homogeneous. Those who are involved in determining markets for long-term care facilities should become knowledgeable of demographic differences among the elderly in local areas. Although it is quicker and easier to rely on a single source for information about several locations, the careful demographic researcher learns to verify that information by turning to sources familiar with the demographic characteristics of each location. To rely on a single source for information about multiple locations is to invite erroneous decisions and market analyses.

The Demographic Enterprise

This case study also provides several general lessons for all demographers, academic and applied. One of its lessons is that many people take the results of our analyses more seriously than we do. Demographers are well aware of the potential errors in small-area estimates and projections (Murdock et al. 1984), and many would advise that age estimates or projections for areas as small as the market areas in this study should simply not be completed or used (National Academy of Sciences 1980). When a real-world decision must be made, however, such estimates and projections often guide the decision making.

Another lesson this case provides is that our knowledge base can make a difference. The broader our base of knowledge about demographic processes, characteristics, and methods, the more readily we will recognize an error in our estimates or projections. Knowledge is no guarantee that our estimates or projections will be more accurate, but the results are less likely to be in error if our demographic expertise is more complete.

This study also suggests that demographic training needs to be broadened if demographers are to be involved in applied work. The applied demographer needs training in methods of market research, in microeconomics and firm management, in organizational sociology, and in many other areas. Applied work almost always involves interdisciplinary analysis, and those demographers who are interested in such work should be encouraged to pursue training in as many disciplines as possible. In fact, academic departments of demography should consider multidisciplinary requirements for students interested in applied work.

This case, then, illustrates how applied analysis can extend the expertise and stretch the skills of the demographer. It demonstrates that his or her knowledge is needed and affects the decision-making process. It also suggests, however, that demographers must combine their academic expertise with skills in other areas and that they must be prepared to recognize the limits of their expertise. In applied settings, demographers must work in contexts that require them to consider organizational and interpersonal factors as well as methodological rigor and the norms of science.

Discussion Questions

1. What liabilities did the authors face at the onset of the study?

2. Do you agree with the authors' assumptions regarding rural elderly migration?

3. Prepare a projection of your own, using different assumptions and methodologies. Match your results with those in the study.

4. Evaluate the assumptions about the percentage of future Legacy House clients from primary and secondary markets.

5. What characteristics of the population's age structure provide insight for the future of long-term care?

Notes

This chapter was prepared especially for this casebook and is not to be quoted, cited, or used in any manner without the permission of the authors.

1. The names of the areas and total population value, as well as the name of the national vendor providing the data to the consulting firm, have been altered to avoid disclosing the area and the names of the parties at interest.

References

Bishop, Christine E. 1988. "Competition in the Market for Nursing Home Care." *Journal of Health Politics, Policy and Law.* 13(2):341–360.

Bowles, Gladys K., Calvin L. Beale, and Everett S. Lee. 1975. *Net Migration of the Population, 1960–70 by Age, Sex, and Color.* Athens, Georgia: The University of Georgia.

Fuguitt, Glen V. 1985. "The Nonmetropolitan Population Turnaround." *The Annual Review of Sociology.* Palo Alto, California: Annual Reviews, Inc.

Greenwood, Michael J. 1985. "Human migration: theories, models, empirical studies." *Journal of Regional Science.* 24:520–544.

Hwang, Sean-Shong, Steve H. Murdock, Edli Colberg, and Banoo Parpia. 1985. *Net migration in Texas: 1970–1980 by age and sex for whites and nonwhites.* Austin, Texas: Texas Data Management Program.

Jarboe, Glen R., and Carl D. McDaniel. 1985. "Influence Patterns and Determinant Attributes in Nursing Home Choice Situations." *Journal of Health Care Marketing.* 5(3):19–30.

Liu, K., and Y. Palesch. 1981. "The Nursing Home Population: Different Perspectives and Implications for Policy." *Health Care Financing Review.* 3:1815–1823.

Manton, Kenneth G., Max A. Woodbury, and Korbin Liu. l984. "Life Table Methods for Assessing the Dynamics of U.S. Nursing Home Utilization: 1976–1977." *Journal of Gerontology.* 30(1):79–87.

Murdock, S.H., F.L. Leistritz, R.R. Hamm, S. Hwang, and B. Parpia. 1984. "An Assessment of the Accuracy of a Regional Economic-Demographic Projection Model." *Demography.* 21:383–404.

National Academy of Sciences. 1980. *Estimating Population and Income of Small Areas.* Washington, D.C.: National Academy Press.

Palmore, Erdman. 1976. "Total Chance of Institutionalization Among the Aged." *The Gerontologist.* 16(6):504–507.

Ritchey, P.N. 1976. "Explanations of Migration." *The Annual Review of Sociology.* Palo Alto, California: Annual Review Inc.

Saenz, Rogelio. 1987. *A Portrait of Elderly Texans.* College Station, Texas: Department of Rural Sociology, Texas Agricultural Experiment Station.

Scanlon, William J. 1980. "A Theory of the Nursing Home Market." *Inquiry.* 17:25–41.

Spencer, G. 1989. "Projections of the Population of the United States, by Age, Sex, and Race: 1988 to 2080." *U.S. Bureau of the Census—Current Population Reports, Population Estimates and Projections.* Series P-25, No. 1018. Washington, D.C.: U.S. Government Printing Office.

Wilson, Susan L., and Jeffrey Heckler. 1989. *The Special Task Force on Rural Health Care Delivery in Texas.* Austin, Texas: The State of Texas.

Discussion Questions
for Part Four

1. Consider the different methods used for making projections in these cases. Discuss the forecast horizons, characteristics, and geographic areas involved.

2. What similarities and differences are there in the roles played by the local health planning committee (in Chapter 11) and the Department of Highway Safety and Motor Vehicles (in Chapter 12)?

3. Compare the demographer's role in Chapter 11 and 12.

4. Did any of the demographers testify as impartial observers? How would the testimony of an impartial observer differ from that of a client witness?

5. How did the analysis and techniques in the fire station study differ from the analytical techniques used in the other three cases? Could any of the others have applied similar projection techniques?

PART FIVE

Planning and Policy

15

Strategic Financial Planning for Hospitals: Demographic Considerations

Bill Rives

This chapter examines the demographic content of strategic financial planning for community hospitals, using the case method made popular during the last several decades by many American business schools. The case study involves Broadway Medical Center, a hypothetical community hospital located in Texas. The hospital is a "composite"—i.e., constructed from information I collected during several recent consulting engagements.

To comprehend and appreciate the contribution of demographic analysis to the Broadway case (and to hospital management in general), one must understand the analytical framework behind the process of strategic financial planning that hospitals use to evaluate market performance. This framework identifies the particular sources of information and analysis that hospital managers consider important to making key planning decisions.

One must also understand the contemporary economic climate within the hospital industry that has led many community hospitals to develop strategic financial planning procedures.

Strategic Financial Planning and the Hospital Industry

Once the health care centers for communities across the country, hospitals must now compete with a growing number of other service providers—including the hospitals' own physicians—in a world of rising dissatisfaction with medical costs, where cost-sensitive employers and insurance companies increasingly "call the shots" on treatment setting and method of care. Prior to 1983, hospital reimbursement was based simply on the cost of providing care. With reimbursement at cost, a hospital operated basically like a public utility—and rarely lost money. But then Medicare introduced the Prospective Payment System (PPS), which reimburses hospitals at predetermined prices according to diagnosis. Since the advent of PPS, hospitals must operate more like businesses, if only to survive. Responding to these changes in the market environment, many hospital managers have developed formal institutional planning procedures to guide their organizations through the more difficult financial climate.

The phrase "strategic financial planning" actually reveals a good deal about the contemporary organizational character of community hospitals. The word "strategic" reflects a growing concern on the part of many hospital managers about the position of their institutions in the marketplace further down the road, perhaps three to five years from now rather than just next month or next year. An unfortunate, although hardly unpredictable, preoccupation with the annual "bottom line" has left many hospitals largely unprepared to cope with rapidly changing market structure. Greater emphasis on strategic planning should broaden the role demographic methods (especially population projections) can play because strategic analysis usually involves more distant planning horizons and almost inevitably more change and uncertainty.

The word "financial" reflects the major thrust of hospital planning in the late 1980s. While still acknowledging its traditional mission of patient care, the community hospital has become a visible business enterprise driven almost exclusively by financial considerations. The conflict between patient care and financial survival is a sensitive issue at present for both the hospital industry and its critics.

Finally, the word "planning" underscores the emphasis that hospital managers place on the use of systematic procedures to solve problems. The whole field of health care management is very process-oriented, more so than many lines of business. Working with good information and analysis, most hospital managers actually believe that they can achieve the goals and objectives set forth in strategic plans. This emphasis on "process" favors the use of more advanced and more refined analytical methods in hospital planning research, and that clearly works to the advantage of demographic analysis.

The following section introduces the analytical framework behind the process of strategic financial planning at Broadway Medical Center. This framework varies somewhat among hospitals, primarily to accommodate different planning objectives and resources. The framework presented in this case is, therefore, a composite of approaches taken by several different institutions. The next section of the paper addresses the particular steps in the Broadway planning model that involve demographic issues. Apart from simply identifying these issues and describing them in greater detail, I will examine the perceptions held by Broadway managers regarding the relative importance of demographic information and analysis to the planning process. The final section of the paper reviews some practical lessons that emerge from the Broadway case study about the use of demographic analysis in hospital planning research.

Strategic Financial Planning at Broadway Medical Center

Broadway Medical Center is a 385-bed general acute-care hospital that opened in 1967. The hospital has enjoyed good financial performance over the years, although recently operating margins have slipped in the wake of Medicare Prospective Payment. The hospital presently operates 310 of the 385 licensed beds; roughly 235 beds support the large medical-surgical service while the rest are split almost evenly between obstetrics and pediatrics. The average daily occupancy rate for beds currently in operation is 67 percent, somewhat under the more profitable levels of earlier years but still well within range of the target occupancy rate of 75 percent.

Two other hospitals—Oak Park Memorial and Southwest General—are in the same market Broadway serves. Both are smaller than Broadway, and only Oak Park offers roughly the same range of services. Southwest General recently was bought by a Tennessee hospital management company, and the new managers have begun an aggressive campaign to recruit primary-care physicians to their medical staff. The Broadway medical staff numbers almost 700, but fewer than 100 physicians carry the hospital, collectively accounting for more than 75 percent of total patient-days. If the new Southwest General initiative were to cut deeply into Broadway staff loyalties, drawing valuable physicians and their patients to another hospital, Broadway Medical Center might find itself facing even more difficult financial problems. To counter the anticipated impact of the Southwest challenge, Broadway managers began a reassessment of the hospital's position in the local market.

Strategic financial planning at Broadway Medical Center addresses the effect of local market forces and hospital operating characteristics on financial performance. The ability to forecast these linkages into the future allows Broadway managers to examine a wide range of operating scenarios, along with their attendant financial consequences.

Table 15.1 outlines the Broadway strategic financial planning model. This model is designed to move logically from one end of the financial planning spectrum (the population the hospital serves) to the other (hospital cash flow). Broadway managers like this approach because it clearly articulates the path to follow and the particular information needs at each consecutive step.

Steps 1–9 in Table 15.1 address the market environment. What geographic segment of the local market does Broadway effectively serve? How many persons reside in this area? What characteristics do they have that affect the use of health care services? How do residents of the service area become Broadway patients? Does the hospital draw patients from outside the service area? These are just some of the questions that Broadway managers ask when analyzing the market environment.

Steps 10–12 in Table 15.1 address facility utilization. Once patients enter the hospital, where do they go? How long do they stay? How many patient-days do groups of patients generate? Broadway classifies patients according to their Diagnosis-Related Group (DRG), a case mix system developed primarily for the hospitals on Medicare PPS. Each DRG is associated with certain standards of treatment, and the extent of the treatment generally determines the length of stay. The

Table 15.1   General Strategic Financial Planning Model for Broadway Medical
Center Case Study

Step	Task
1	Define subject hospital (Broadway Medical Center) service area and determine service-area population
2	Compute admission rate to all hospitals combined for service-area population—ratio of total (annualized) admissions to population
3	Compute total admissions to all hospitals combined from service-area population—call these "total resident admissions"
4	Compute retention rate for total resident admissions—proportion of total resident admissions that go to service-area hospitals
5	Compute total resident admissions that go to service-area hospitals— call these "retained resident admissions"
6	Compute market share for retained resident admissions—percent of retained resident admissions that go to each service-area hospital
7	Compute retained resident admissions to subject hospital
8	Compute admissions to subject hospital from outside the service area— call these "nonresident admissions"; determine as a percent of total admissions to subject hospital
9	Compute total admissions to subject hospital—add retained resident and nonresident admissions
10	Allocate total admissions to subject hospital by service category—use Diagnosis-Related Groups (DRGs) or similar classification system
11	Determine average length of stay (in days) for each service category
12	Compute patient-days for each service category—multiply number of admissions by corresponding average length of stay
13	Determine gross patient-service charges for each service category— charges are "retail" prices for routine/special/ancillary care
14	Compute gross patient-service revenues for each service category—call this amount "total patient-service revenues at billed charges"
15	Determine deductions from revenues (allowances for contractual and courtesy discounts and uncollectible accounts) by payment source
16	Compute net patient-service revenues for subject hospital
17	Determine nonoperating revenues—income from contributions, joint ventures, and lines of business other than inpatient care

Table 15.1   (continued)

18	Compute total net revenues for subject hospital—add net patient-service revenues and nonoperating revenues
19	Compute total operating expenses per patient-day—include interest expense and (funded) depreciation; use audited financial statements for historical estimates and trend extrapolation for projections.
20	Compute total operating expenses for subject hospital—multiply the patient-days total by operating expenses per patient-day
21	Compute net income for subject hospital
22	Compute cash flow for subject hospital

treatment standards are protocols assembled by clinical staff to help the hospital managers understand patterns of resource consumption and how to price services generally in line with expected costs.

Steps 13–18 in Table 15.1 address hospital revenues. These revenues fall into two broad groups: (1) revenues from patient services (operating revenues), and (2) revenues from other sources (nonoperating revenues). According to the most recent management accounting, Broadway derives most of its revenues from patient operations. This figure, however, has been falling recently as a percent of total revenues due primarily to changes in reimbursement payments from Medicare and other insurers as well as a sharp increase in allowances that the hospital takes for charity care and bad debt. Nonoperating revenues represent income primarily from contributions to the hospital and from rent on the Broadway Professional Building, which the hospital owns and leases to physicians for their offices. The hospital also has a small long-term investment portfolio which generates nonoperating income. Since the hospital is nonprofit, the managers must be careful not to let nonoperating income become too large in relation to total revenues—especially if more and more of the nonoperating total comes from sources that do not involve direct patient care. Hospitals that derive too much of their revenue from activities not directly related to their principal line of business, patient care, may find themselves owing taxes on what the IRS calls "unrelated business income." If the violation is found to be more serious, the IRS may cancel the hospital's nonprofit certification.

The operating-revenue calculations in Steps 13–16 bring together charges for services provided for routine care (medical-surgical, obstetric, pediatric), special care (primarily medical and surgical intensive care), and ancillary care (notably radiology, pathology, and pharmacy). The gross revenue figure from Step 14 must be reduced by charges billed but not collected (allowances for contractual discounts, charity care, and bad debt). Adding net patient-service revenues (Step 16) to nonoperating revenues (Step 17) yields total net revenues (Step 18). The

Broadway managers are anxious to determine this final figure, for it provides an important measure of hospital earning power.

Steps 19 and 20 in Table 15.1 address hospital operating expenses. These expenses were drawn from audited financial statements (the only reliable source) and expressed on a cost-per-patient-day basis to facilitate projection of total expenses at a later date. Most hospitals are comfortable with this somewhat more expedient method of handling the expense component, and Broadway was no exception.

Step 21 in Table 15.1 addresses hospital net income (the excess of revenues over expenses). Subtracting interest expense and (funded) depreciation (Step 22) from net income yields hospital cash flow (Step 23), the amount of money that actually "flows" through the institution during an operating cycle. Cash flow is one of the most popular indicators of an organization's financial health.

The Broadway Medical Center strategic financial planning model described in Table 15.1 enables hospital managers and trustees to understand systematically the interplay among factors that shape hospital market performance. Every factor, from service-area population growth to the salaries paid nurses, can be examined within a deterministic simulation framework. Broadway managers prefer this approach because it fits well with their "process" orientation.

Demographic Components of Strategic Financial Planning

Demographic analysis dominates the market environment segment (Steps 1–9) of the Broadway strategic financial planning model. The key demographic issues in this segment are:

- the identification of patient migration patterns and the designation of the effective hospital service area
- the determination of service-area retention rates and hospital market share
- the estimation and projection of service-area population by sex and age group (minimum characteristic requirements)

Patient migration patterns are critically important to the delineation of the hospital service area and, more generally, to an understanding of perceptions of time and distance associated with care-seeking behavior. Basically, there are two sources of information on patient migration patterns: (1) patient-origin studies, and (2) household surveys. Both are designed to generate data on people who use hospitals—who they are (demographic characteristics) and where they live (typically residence ZIP code). The hospitals they use are also identified. Household surveys can be designed to provide a more complete picture of patient migration patterns, but the more detailed surveys can be expensive for hospitals with limited planning and research budgets. The more efficient source of information (at least from the standpoint of cost and time required to obtain results) is the patient-origin study, but this source is not always available. The Texas Hospital Association conducts a statewide patient-origin study annually and provides information on patient migration patterns at relatively low cost to those who request it.

A patient-origin study involves a systematic survey of hospital administrative records. A participating hospital in the Texas study is randomly assigned one "reporting" week during each quarter. The hospital agrees to provide copies of *all* its patient admission records for that week to the state hospital association. The association then codes the key information on each record for computer entry:

- hospital ID number
- resident ZIP code of the patient
- patient demographic characteristics (age, sex, race/ethnicity)
- inpatient service to which the patient was admitted (medical-surgical, obstetric, pediatric, psychiatric, long-term care, rehabilitation, personal care, or other hospital service)
- admission source (emergency room, outpatient clinic, physician referral, or other admission source)

Two important demographic tabulations result from patient-origin studies. One is the patient-origin profile, which shows the estimated ZIP-code distribution of admissions for a particular hospital. The other demographic tabulation is the patient-destination profile, which shows the hospital distribution of admissions for patients residing in each ZIP code (or group of ZIPs). For this tabulation to be useful to hospital managers, all the hospitals in a particular market must participate in the patient-origin study. If even only one hospital declines (the Texas study is voluntary), then the picture of patient migration for the market as a whole will be incomplete.

Table 15.2 shows the patient-origin and patient-destination profiles for Broadway Medical Center. The patient-origin profile identifies annualized flows for total admissions to the hospital from each ZIP code. Additional results from the Broadway profile (not presented in this case) show numbers of patients by inpatient service (medical-surgical, obstetric, and pediatric). The patient-destination profile presents annualized flows for total admissions from the Broadway service area (all 13 ZIP codes combined) to each hospital. Further results (not presented in this case) show numbers of patients by resident ZIP code. Most patient-destination profiles are reported for the entire medical service area in question rather than for individual ZIPs because the patient data are based upon samples and involve relatively high margins of error for smaller geographic units.

Managers can use the patient-origin profile in Table 15.2 to determine the effective service area of the Broadway Medical Center—the area surrounding the hospital from which it will draw most of its patients. Community hospitals have service areas in the same way that public schools have attendance areas and states have regional labor markets. A hospital service area commonly is defined by a

Table 15.2   Patient Origin and Destination Profiles for Broadway Medical
              Center Case Study

Panel A—Patient Origin Profile

Resident ZIP Code	Annual Total Number	Admissions Percent
76501	810	7.8
76502	1,070	10.3
76503	603	5.8
76504	405	3.9
76505	706	6.8
76506	727	7.0
76507	1,008	9.7
76508	1,196	11.5
76509	436	4.2
76510	800	7.7
76511	1,018	9.8
76512	665	6.4
76513	945	9.1
All ZIPs	10,389	100.0

Panel B—Patient Destination Profile

Annual Total Admissions From Service Area To:	Value
Service-Area Hospitals	16,462
Broadway Medical Center	9,548
Southwest General Hospital	6,914
Other Local Hospitals	7,290
Oak Park Memorial Hospital	7,290
All Hospitals	23,752
Service-Area Retention Rate (= 16,462/23,752)	69%
Broadway Medical Center Market Share (= 9,548/16,462)	58%
Southwest General Hospital Market Share (= 6,914/16,462)	42%

group of contiguous ZIP codes; the ZIPs included are those that contribute the largest number of admissions to the hospital.

Defining the Broadway service area first required sorting the patient-origin profile in Table 15.2 by total admissions to produce a ranking in descending order. The next step was to proceed down the column from the top of the ranking and select ZIPs until those representing a predetermined percent of all the admissions had been chosen (this can be done fairly quickly with a cumulative frequency distribution for admissions by ZIP). Since the threshold for the Broadway service area was 90 percent, ZIP codes were added "to the pot" until ZIPs representing the top 90 percent of all the admissions had been selected. Some community hospitals use a more conservative threshold level, possibly as low as 70 to 75 percent. Others use no threshold at all, moving out from the hospital in all directions and adding ZIPs to the pot as long as they are contiguous to ones previously chosen. Eleven of the 13 ZIPs in the patient-origin profile in Table 15.2 were selected for the Broadway Medical Center service area.

Once the effective hospital service area is defined, area retention rates and hospital market shares can be estimated. Since both reflect patient migration patterns, they are basically demographic measures. The service-area retention rate measures the extent to which service-area residents who require inpatient care use service-area hospitals. In principle, retention rates should be high for service areas containing at least one or two hospitals. Other factors, however—notably hospital reputation and physician practice locations—can intervene to cause many service-area residents to seek care farther from home.

The retention rate for the Broadway Medical Center service area is about 69 percent, which the hospital managers considered low on the strength of more subjective estimates of patient migration from physician referral patterns. The managers blamed the apparent drop in service-area retention on competition from Oak Park Memorial Hospital, which is outside the Broadway service area to the north and which recently opened a new imaging center. The Broadway managers wanted to believe the estimated retention rate if only because it seemed more solid than piecemeal reports from medical staff on patient referral. They finally decided, however, that all the information should be considered, and they chose a larger value (75 percent) as the "official" service-area retention rate.

The rate used in the final version of the strategic financial planning projections (80 percent) was even higher, having been arbitrarily increased yet a second time by one of the hospital managers. No explanation was given for this adjustment, but two of the hospital board members commented at the end of the briefing on the strategic planning analysis that the service area really seemed to be able to "hold its patients!"

Hospital market share measures the relative competition for patients among the hospitals located in the service area. In a nutshell, market share reveals how the hospitals in the service area have managed to slice the local "patient pie"— i.e., service-area residents who use service-area hospitals. Because it bluntly reveals the degree of success each hospital has had competing against all the other providers in its "own backyard," market share is an emotional issue for many hospital managers. Managers know that market share values reflect such fundamental factors as hospital reputation, quality of care, and the like, but they tend to see market share as a form of combat. As one Broadway manager commented, "all the battles are forgotten when we have a report on the progress of the war."

Southwest General Hospital is the only other facility in the Broadway service area, and Broadway seems to be doing reasonably well against this competitor. According to the patient-destination profile in Table 15.2, Broadway has 58 percent of the service-area market and Southwest General has the rest. Of course, Broadway managers have been concerned that Southwest General's new marketing initiative could change the balance of power, and they undertook the whole strategic financial planning study to explore this particular issue.

The final demographic component mentioned at the beginning of this section is the set of estimates and projections for service-area population that Broadway requires for planning analysis. These figures are very important to the whole planning effort. The Broadway managers indicated on several occasions during the planning analysis project that the major thrust of their capital planning turns on demographic change—how much? where? what type? The programs at Broadway Medical Center cater to a broad population base, and "all demographic groups were to be estimated and projected" for the strategic planning study—at least that was the initial instruction from the Broadway managers.

Defining these groups proved to be a real challenge. Every characteristic on the 1980 Census schedule appeared on the first list of items to be forecasted, and the list seemed to get longer with each meeting. Widows aged 80 and over. Single parents with preschool children. Business executives with back pain. Teenagers with drug problems. The Broadway managers wanted to know everything about the future, at least everything likely to affect the hospital business. Demographers can produce such data—can't they?

No problem! But what will the managers do with the mountain of results? Do they really *need* all this information to run Broadway Medical Center five or six years down the road? Can they make plausible assumptions about the future for all the factors (population subgroups) they have in mind? Do we really know anything at all about business executives with back pain—in the state of Texas? In ZIP 76508? Rather than start by estimating and projecting everything, why not begin with a few basic demographic characteristics and see how far these will carry the analysis?

The demographic characteristics most commonly used in health care planning and research are age, sex, race/ethnicity, and income. These characteristics provide a great deal of useful information about a population—aging, cultural diversity, social and economic status. The first two characteristics—age and sex—have a distinct advantage; they are easily measured (even for smaller geographic areas), and analytical models exist for their projection over time. The other two characteristics—race/ethnicity and income—present problems from the standpoint of estimation and projection despite the tremendous value of the information they provide. These problems are reasonably well known, at least in the demographic literature.

Demographers are comfortable forecasting age and sex, and these two characteristics play a major role in shaping care-seeking behavior. The National Center for Health Statistics reports almost all of the data it collects on household health status and the use of health services by sex and age group, an indication of the importance it places on these two characteristics. Quite a few hospitals use NCHS reports for planning activities.

This sort of information finally convinced the Broadway managers to revise their initial instruction about estimating and projecting "all demographic groups." As a result, the first round of population estimates and projections was prepared for the Broadway service area as a whole using sex and seven age groups—0–4, 5–14, 15–24, 25–44, 45–64, 65–74, and 75+. The age breaks were selected mainly for their correspondence to different hospital services; women aged 25–44, for example, were selected for their obstetric needs. The Broadway managers would have liked to have had more age detail at the older ages (especially age 75 and beyond) because older people consume more health care resources during the year—infrequently by choice—than younger people. But detailed demographic information is always a problem for smaller geographic areas, even in the census. Given the growing national fascination with aging, however, the 1990 Census can be expected to devote more attention to older population groups.

Table 15.3 presents 1988 estimates and annual projections to the year 2000 for the resident population of the Broadway Medical Center service area, arrayed by sex and age group. The 1988 estimates for total population were prepared using a variant of the housing-unit method, probably the most commonly used procedure for small-area population estimation in the United States (Smith 1988; Shryock and Siegel 1976, 427–428). Annual population projections to 2000 were developed from separate projections for total households, average household size, and population in group quarters. The household projections were based upon trends established for the benchmark period 1980–1988.

Household projections really should be screened against available vacant land for residential development, but in this case using household projections to build projections of total resident population for the Broadway service area was an advisable strategy because the service area is geographically small. One of the most common flaws of small-area population projection procedures is the tendency to ignore the "carrying capacity" of land to accommodate projected growth.

The age-sex projections for the Broadway service area were produced using a "synthetic" aging technique described in Shryock and Siegel (1976, 454). A population projection for the metropolitan area in which the service area is located forms the basis for this procedure. The metropolitan projection had to have the

Table 15.3 Population Estimates and Projections for Broadway Medical Center Service Area: 1988–2000

Age-Sex Group	1988	1989	1990	1991	1992	1993	1994	1995	1996	1997	1998	1999	2000
Female													
0–4	10,028	10,352	10,696	10,907	11,134	11,374	11,637	11,921	12,237	12,587	12,968	13,409	13,865
5–14	19,205	19,464	19,747	20,293	20,867	21,476	22,128	22,830	23,584	24,411	25,312	26,173	27,062
15–24	18,318	18,319	18,338	18,667	19,018	19,416	19,854	20,338	20,873	21,456	22,125	22,877	23,655
25–44	48,259	49,572	50,922	51,285	51,708	52,188	52,739	53,371	54,092	54,915	55,873	57,773	59,737
45–64	23,484	23,634	23,815	24,742	25,719	26,747	27,838	29,012	30,273	31,638	33,128	34,254	35,419
65–74	6,802	7,040	7,298	7,548	7,824	8,120	8,447	8,799	9,192	9,627	10,104	10,448	10,803
75+	4,925	5,098	5,285	5,466	5,665	5,880	6,116	6,372	6,656	6,972	7,317	7,566	7,823
Total	131,021	133,479	136,101	138,908	141,935	145,201	148,759	152,643	156,907	161,606	166,827	172,499	178,364
Male													
0–4	10,750	11,132	11,527	11,789	12,069	12,376	12,705	13,067	13,449	13,885	14,372	14,861	15,366
5–14	20,549	20,897	21,282	21,932	22,626	23,361	24,160	25,009	25,947	26,967	28,094	29,049	30,037
15–24	19,426	19,495	19,602	20,023	20,503	21,020	21,578	22,203	22,901	23,683	24,551	25,386	26,249
25–44	44,501	45,678	46,900	47,140	47,427	47,778	48,196	48,696	49,298	50,022	50,867	52,596	54,385
45–64	21,107	21,342	21,615	22,645	23,727	24,874	26,095	27,399	28,815	30,355	32,040	33,129	34,256
65–74	4,937	5,141	5,355	5,553	5,765	6,003	6,262	6,550	6,864	7,212	7,610	7,868	8,136
75+	2,580	2,690	2,805	2,910	3,023	3,150	3,287	3,442	3,609	3,794	4,008	4,145	4,286
Total	123,850	126,375	129,086	131,992	135,140	138,562	142,283	146,366	150,883	155,916	161,542	167,034	172,714
All Groups	254,871	259,854	265,187	270,900	277,075	283,763	291,042	299,009	307,790	317,522	328,369	339,534	351,078

Sources: 1980 Census of Population and a national demographic data firm

same age-sex detail as the service area. The synthetic aging technique actually is a variant of the ratio method for projection. The key assumption behind the procedure is that the age-sex structure of the service area will converge to the metropolitan age-sex structure at some more distant point in the future, perhaps 30 to 40 years down the road. Behavioral arguments can be made to support this assumption.

The results of the synthetic aging projections for the service area looked quite plausible, especially in light of trends running from the early 1970s for the metropolitan area (the market as a whole) and projected age-sex composition for the United States. Broadway managers seemed to accept the synthetic aging results because a demographer had recommended the methodology and the service area seemed to be moving in a demographic direction that fit their perceptions of social change at the moment. No attempt was made to explain why conventional cohort-component projection was not used to produce internally consistent age-sex detail for the Broadway service area; technical problems surrounding the calibration of more refined analytical procedures for small-area populations would not have drawn a very large audience among hospital managers and board members.

The Case in Retrospect: Practical Lessons

Every consulting assignment seems to bring new insights into the application of technology, and the use of demographic analysis in hospital planning is no exception. Several practical lessons emerged from the Broadway project on strategic financial planning.

The first lesson is that demography matters—at least in hospital planning and research. While financial considerations inevitably dominate a field like hospital management (especially in the late 1980s), demographic information and analysis do contribute to the planning enterprise, particularly as "strategic" concerns become more and more important.

The second lesson is that demographers who work on projects that involve other areas of expertise, such as hospital planning and financial management, really do need to acquire a working knowledge of these other areas if they are to be effective contributors to the research effort. Not understanding the process of strategic financial planning, at least the underlying analytical framework, can effectively blunt the demographer's sensitivity to the application of demographic analysis, possibly causing some of the analysis to be off target.

The third lesson is that demographers have a great deal to offer business planning and research efforts that value custom analysis. When planning decisions involve large amounts of money (and risk), hospital managers understandably are reluctant to use canned demographic information from commercial firms that sell numbers without supporting analysis and interpretation. Broadway managers wanted the kind of personal interaction with their consultants that gives custom analysis its special appeal—and reduces the chance for bad decisions.

The Broadway strategic financial planning exercise has become an annual activity for hospital managers and trustees. The hospital renewed the demographic consultant contract for two years at the end of the initial study and substantially expanded the scope of work.

Discussion Questions

1. What questions would you ask the Broadway managers to help them focus the scope of their inquiry? How would you explain (prior to the number-crunching stage) the problems and limitations for making estimates and projections?

2. Why did a housing-unit method seem appropriate? What are the pitfalls to avoid when using this method?

3. Suppose you were asked to explain why another method (such as cohort-component) was not chosen. Give your rationale.

4. In the conclusion, the author states that one of the lessons learned is that "demography matters." Develop a strategy to convince hospital management of this lesson.

Notes

This chapter was prepared for presentation at the 1989 Annual Meeting of the Population Association of America, Baltimore, Maryland.

References

Berman, H.J., L.E. Weeks, and S.F. Kukla. 1986. *The Financial Management of Hospitals.* 6th edition. Health Administration Press.

Coile, R.C. 1986. *The New Hospital.* Aspen Publications.

Dever, G.E.A. 1980. *Community Health Analysis.* Aspen Publications.

Levey, S., and N.P. Loomba. 1984. *Health Care Administration.* 2nd edition. J.B. Lippincott Company.

Pegels, C.C., and K.A. Rogers. 1988. *Strategic Management of Hospitals and Health Care Facilities.* Aspen Publications.

Shryock, H.S., J.S. Siegel, and Associates. 1976. *The Methods and Materials of Demography.* Condensed edition edited by E.G. Stockwell. Academic Press.

Smith, S.K. 1989. Review and evaluation of the housing unit method of population estimation. In *Small-Area Estimation Methods for Total Population.* H. Goldsmith, B. Rives, and W. Serow., eds. Washington, D.C.: National Institute of Mental Health.

16

Estimating Vital Rates from Corporate Databases: How Long Will GM's Salaried Retirees Live?

Hallie J. Kintner and David A. Swanson

The Problem: How Long Will GM's Salaried Retirees Live?

Employers sponsor health benefits for more than three-fourths of Americans with health care coverage (Employee Benefits Research Institute 1986). Providing health care benefits represents a major cost for many employers. For instance, one of General Motors' greatest costs is health care benefits for its employees and retirees and their dependents. In 1988, the corporation spent $3.034 billion on health care (Lippert 1988).

Employers are particularly concerned about the cost of health care benefits for retirees. Retiree health care costs are important because they are large. At General Motors they accounted for at least 30 percent of the corporation's health care costs during 1984–88 (General Motors Annual Report 1984–1988).

Retiree health care costs are also important because the Financial Accounting Standards Board (FASB) has proposed that they be listed as liabilities on corporate balance sheets (Financial Accounting Standards Board 1989). If this were done, it would potentially influence corporate earnings and borrowing ability—as well as the prices of stocks and bonds (Henriques 1989). Although not currently expected to take effect for several years (Loomis 1989; Freudenheim 1989; Keller 1989; and Bacon 1988), this proposal had begun to receive considerable attention in the press. In general terms,"Corporations will first have to estimate future spending on health benefits for current and future retirees and all covered dependents. They must then discount these obligations to present value and begin charging them gradually to earning" (Loomis 1989, p. 61).

This case study describes the development of demographic information about the longevity of General Motors salaried retirees. The Health Care Cost Analysis Activity of GM's financial staff needed this information to forecast retiree health care costs for both long-term planning (like FASB) and short-term accounting purposes. The impetus for this work came from an ongoing collaboration between the Operating Sciences Department in the General Motors Research Laboratories and the Health Care Cost Analysis Activity. It was not prompted by a particular request but rather arose in the course of applying a demographic perspective to the activity's mission. Previous work had demonstrated that General Motors' health benefits population differed from the U.S. population in both its age-sex composition and growth rate (Kintner and Smith 1987; Kintner 1989).

The project we describe is just part of the work being done with regard to forecasting retirees, work which will take several years to complete. But at this point we can address one of the policy questions posed by the health care needs of retirees: How long will everyone currently retired be eligible for health benefits? To answer this question we developed a method for projecting the size and composition (by age and gender) of the retiree population. Information about population composition is necessary because health status and health care utilization— and hence *costs*—differ by age and gender. This population projection will provide some of the information required to forecast total health care utilization by all retirees and their dependents.

The Demographic Perspective

Our task involved identifying a life table suitable for projecting GM's surviving retirees and then showing how this information could be used to anticipate retiree health care utilization. The task thus required us to know potentially appropriate life tables for this group, techniques to evaluate alternative projections, and data about health care utilization.

We did the work described below in several stages. First, we obtained alternative survivorship schedules from life tables we thought to be appropriate. Second, we evaluated the alternative survivorship schedules using statistical tests and tests of projection accuracy. Finally, we identified a single "best" schedule and used it to project surviving current retirees.

After we describe this work we present two examples to show how this information was used to address business issues. The first example demonstrates how retiree utilization of health care was forecast by tying the population projection to national data about hospitalization. The second example compares the costs of auditing the corporate databases for retiree deaths to the benefits of having this improved information.

This case study describes how we obtained a life table from corporate databases. We had two reasons for constructing a life table specifically for GM salaried retirees. First, we suspected in advance that it would be inappropriate to apply life tables representing the general population because the GM salaried retirees are a special group. Not only were they carefully selected to work for GM, but also they chose to stay with the firm until retirement. These salaried workers include many engineers and managers who have lower mortality rates by virtue of their occupation. In addition, GM retirees probably are, on average, better off financially than their counterparts in the U.S. population. Finally, as we mentioned earlier, we knew that GM's health benefits population differed from the U.S. population in terms of growth rate and age-sex composition. We suspected that mortality risks for GM salaried retirees differed from those for U.S. whites, and that suspicion was subsequently validated.

The second reason why we constructed a life table specific to GM salaried retirees was to gauge the reliability of the information available from the corporate administrative databases about employee transitions. If the mortality risks estimated here were substantially lower than those derived from other sources, then the databases underreported deaths.

General Motors does not maintain a vital records system. Rather, the corporation relies on informal reporting of deaths. For instance, if an employee fails to report to work, then his/her supervisor calls to find out why. Since retirees do not have supervisors, the corporation depends upon the next of kin or other parties (even neighbors) to report such deaths. There are no incentives to report deaths nor disincentives if deaths are not reported. In contrast, federal and state governments require completion of a death certificate before burial.

We also examined the possibility that employee records indicating deaths were deleted. We found that documentation for the corporate databases showed that such deletion had not occurred to any large extent. We estimated the extent of underreporting and used these estimates to evaluate the cost effectiveness of performing a death audit of the corporate databases.

We describe our methods in some detail because applied demographers frequently need to obtain demographic information from nonstandard sources. Demographers typically deal with data from censuses, surveys, and vital registration. In addition, applied demographers may have access to proprietary data sets that describe employees, customers, members, donors, or some other set of individuals of interest—individuals who cannot be examined from typical sources because they have a unique relationship with an organization. Since these databases have received little attention in the demographic literature, we discuss our experience in detail, including some things to watch for.

Probabilities estimated from corporate databases provided the basis for GM salaried retiree life tables, which show the duration an individual is at risk of incurring postretirement health care costs. We used survival ratios from the life tables to survive forward persons who were retired by year-end 1983. We evaluated the quality of these projections by comparing them to the actual number of retirees in an age-gender category by year-end 1987. This exercise also demonstrated the importance of using mortality probabilities for GM salaried retirees instead of those for the general U.S. population or those for group annuitants.

We used this information to estimate the number of years that will pass before all individuals who were retired by year-end 1988 will die—time to extinction for the closed group. This projection also forecast the future composition of this group.

Obtaining Alternative Life Tables

We projected surviving retirees using life tables based on U.S. whites 1984/86 (U.S.), group annuitants 1983 (GAM83), and GM salaried retirees 1983/87. We chose the first because it is a general population life table with mortality rates comparable to those for the financially well-off GM salaried retirees. It is the average of the 1984 and 1986 life tables for U.S. whites (National Center for Health Statistics 1986a, 1988a). We chose the GAM83 because from it actuaries usually obtain mortality probabilities for retirees (Employee Benefits Research Institute 1987, p. 13). Actuaries prefer to use life tables based on annuitants rather than those based on general populations because employed persons are generally thought to be healthier (i.e., to have lower mortality rates) than all persons in the general population. Actuarial data differ from those usually used by demographers in that they are not collected, calculated, or disseminated by a government statistical agency. The GAM83 also differs from U.S. life tables in that it is not based directly on survivorship data for insured group annuitants but rather was devised by applying mortality projection rates to a 1966 life table (Committee on Annuities 1983).

Estimating Life Tables from Payroll and Insurance Data

We describe in detail how we estimated the GM life tables because, although specific steps might be different in another setting, we believe it is important to describe the level of attention one should pay to proprietary databases if one is considering using them for a purpose other than that for which they were intended.

The Data

Our first steps in estimating a life table for GM retirees involved gaining access to and documentation for the corporate databases. We were fortunate in that key individuals in the personnel staff and in Electronic Data Systems (the GM subsidiary responsible for GM's computer databases) had already given the Operating Sciences Department access to the payroll and insurance databases. This access included shipping yearly snapshots of the databases to the department as well as allowing us to view the database on-line. At the time we began the study the department had accumulated tapes for 1983–88.

Permission to use the databases included the ability to obtain documentation for and technical assistance in using them. We required documentation about the fields on the databases as well as the codes used for each field. Since we were using tapes from different time periods, we requested documentation about any changes in the system during these years. Note that this permission to use the databases did not mean we had access to every field (variable) contained in them. Since we did not need information about individual salaries—information which is private—this field was filled in with blank characters in the tapes prepared for us.

We were able to estimate mortality probabilities (deaths per person-year exposed) directly rather than indirectly by first deriving mortality rates (deaths divided by the midyear population) and then converting rates to probabilities. First, we constructed a longitudinal data set to track a cohort from December 31, 1983 to December 31, 1987. We constructed this data set from the databases used for payroll processing and insurance administration. Both databases have a record for each person receiving salary or benefits from the corporation. Both are "live" databases that are continually updated. We used "snapshots" of these databases on December 31st (referred to as year-end tapes) because the Operating Sciences Department had a unique collection of them. We took the data from the year-end tapes for 1983–88. We included data from 1988 tapes to allow for the possibility that some deaths occurring in 1987 may not have been reported by the end of the year. Table 16.1 defines variables for each record in a year-end tape.

We selected only those records concerning retirees. A *retiree* is an employee with health benefits in force and with an employment code indicating retirement. This definition does not include every individual receiving a pension from General Motors. Some individuals—such as those who were vested in the pension system but who left GM employment prior to retirement—receive pension benefits without being eligible for health benefits. We excluded those individuals from our analysis.

Note further that the individuals in this study may not be retired in the sense of being out of the U.S. labor force. We define health benefits according to the Hospital-Surgical-Medical (HSM) Plan Code, HSM Suffix, and Hospital Rate Indicator. We considered those individuals who were eligible for health benefits but who waived coverage as not having coverage in force.

We were able to restrict the study in this (and in another) fashion because GM has a very large number of retirees. For this pilot study we further restricted the sample to retirees from GM's salaried workforce and excluded retired hourly workers who compose most of GM's retirees. We decided to focus on the salaried group because it is large enough (over 50,000) to obtain vital rates but small enough (compared to hourly retirees) to facilitate data analysis and minimize data processing costs. We do not recommend estimating vital rates from proprietary data unless sufficient data on exposure can be obtained either by following a large group for a few years (as we did here) or by tracking a smaller group over a longer time span. It is also important to have many vital events. After we completed our analysis, we found that the mortality probabilities were based on roughly 6,000 deaths.

We selected a cohort of individuals living and retired as of December 31, 1983 in the following manner. First, we eliminated (as described later) duplicate re-

Table 16.1   Variables from Payroll and Insurance Administration Databases

Variable	Definition
Social Security number	Social Security number
Service date	Date joined corporation
Birthdate	Day, month, and year of birth
Gender	Male or female
Cisco	Division number on master record
Hospital surgical medical plan code	Carrier providing HSM coverage
Hospital surgical medical suffix	Shows HSM coverage before 1987
Hospital rate indicator	Shows HSM coverage after 1987
Status of employment code	Describes status (e.g., regular active)
Status change code (three last)	How obtained status (e.g., new hire)
Status change date (three last)	Date status change code changed

cords in the 1983 file. Then we used the 1983 data to identify individuals who were retired and had in-force coverage. Next, we used data from the 1984 tape to identify additional individuals who, though they retired before 1984, for some reason had not been chosen for the cohort from the 1983 tape. Most of these individuals had not been selected from the 1983 data because their retirement had not been processed when the year-end tape was created.

We followed the 53,314 cohort members over time by matching their social security numbers to data from the 1984–88 year-end tapes. Before doing the matching, we removed duplicate social security numbers in each year-end tape to prevent mismatching records across years. The corporate databases contain duplicate records because they keep track of transactions like pay raises and transfers between plants. It is standard to have two records for employees who change plants—one for the transfer from plant A and another for the transfer to plant B. We regarded records with identical social security numbers that disagreed on two of three crucial items—sex code, birth date, and service date—as referring to different persons and we retained them. Otherwise, we put duplicate records through a series of edit checks to determine which single record we would retain for matching to the cohort member's social security number.

For more efficient data processing, we did no further matching on cohort members after their death. We identified deaths by the status change code, by replacement of an employee record with a surviving spouse record, or by cancellation of coverage.

As a result of this matching process, we lost only 69 retirees (0.13 percent of the cohort) in the sense of lacking records after a particular date. We obtained death dates for all 69 individuals from the current on-line insurance administration database and the pension administration database which performs a yearly death audit using the Social Security Administration's Death Master file. Since this database is entirely separate from the other systems, we had to obtain permission from a different staff. Access was strictly limited to on-line queries seeking death dates for the individuals lost to follow-up. Consequently, the database came to include information about all 53,314 cohort members from December 31, 1983 to either December 31, 1987 or their deathdate, which was earlier.

We relied on technical assistance to help us decide about purging and to answer questions about duplicate social security numbers because these matters were not fully covered in the documentation. We also had help from programmers in merging the yearly data files in an efficient manner.

Constructing the Life Tables

From the cohort data set we estimated the probability by retiree age and sex that an individual would die in a year. We estimated mortality risks for women between the ages of 60 and 85 and men between 50 and 85 because these age groups have a sufficiently large number of individuals and deaths. We chose 85 rather than an older age because national statistics end at age 85.

We based our calculations on deaths and person-years of exposure pooled over the entire 1983–87 time period. We decided to pool the data rather than average yearly risks because pooling results in smaller standard errors when few deaths occur each year—as was the case here.

The longitudinal data set contains three status change codes from each year-end tape 1984–88. To identify deaths we examined the most recent status change code and worked backwards in time. When we found a code indicating a death, we used the status change date as the deathdate. We believed this date accurate to within 60 days of the date when the death actually occurred. Our analysis was based only on deaths occurring between January 1, 1984 and December 31, 1987.

We used actuarial, moment, and maximum likelihood estimators to calculate mortality risks (London 1988; Batten 1978). The actuarial estimator relates the number of deaths to the number of person-years of exposure assuming that (1) deaths count in a particular age group only if they occur after exact age i is attained (it assumes that everyone is alive at exact age i), (2) survivors contribute to person-years of exposure only between January 1st and their birthdate, (3) individuals dying between exact age i and age i + 1 contribute a full year of exposure to that age group. In contrast, the moment estimator assumes that an individual contributes to exposure only between January 1st and his/her birthdate, regardless of survival. In this calculation, deaths do not contribute a full year of exposure. This "scheduled" exposure is based on the dates when an individual is scheduled to enter and exit an age group based on his/her birthdate. The third estimator, the maximum likelihood estimator (also commonly used by actuaries), is based on exact exposure. Survivors therefore contribute to exposure in a single year age group only between January 1st and their birthdates. Individuals who die contribute to exposure only until their deathdates.

Since the resulting probabilities of dying between ages i and i + 1 (called raw q_i) displayed some variability due to the relatively small number of persons at each age, we smoothed them by an analytic procedure. We smoothed each estimator in a series of two regression equations. First, the raw q_i (transformed as logarithms) were regressed on age. We estimated separate equations for each sex using ordinary least squares regression. We examined various functional forms for this relationship and chose the form which accounted for the most variance that had the fewest number of terms. Second, we obtained the predicted values for the q_i from these equations, transformed them as logarithms, and regressed them on 1984/86 U.S. mortality risks (also transformed as logarithms). The predicted values from this last regression are the smoothed q_i found in the remainder of this paper.

We constructed life tables for male and female GM salaried retirees from the smoothed q_i using a LOTUS spreadsheet to apply the q_i to a hypothetical cohort of 100,000 births. We calculated life expectancies at birth for the GM and GAM83 tables by assuming that the q_i values for men ages 50 and under or women ages 60 and under were those for the U.S. whites 1984/86. In addition, we did not compare life expectancies at age 85 and above because in order to close out the life table we assumed that person-years lived for survivors to age 85 in the GM and GAM83 life tables equaled that for the U.S. life table. Tables 16.2 and 16.3 compare life expectancies at various ages for the United States whites 1984/86, the group annuity mortality table 1983 (GAM83), and for General Motors salaried retirees as estimated by the three procedures described earlier (Tables 16.4 and 16.5).

GM salaried retirees have a longer life expectancy than do whites in the general U.S. population. For men, the difference between GM salaried retirees and U.S. whites declines with age from 1.81 years at age 60 to 0.5 years at age 80. For women, the difference in life expectancy between GM salaried retirees and U.S. whites is not as great. GM salaried retirees have about 1.3 years greater life expectancy than do U.S. whites until age 80, when this difference halves. Life expectancy for group annuitants is greater than that for either U.S. whites or GM salaried retirees at all but the oldest ages. For men, this difference falls from 0.5 years at age 60 to 0 at age 75. For women, it declines from 1.1 years at age 60 to rough parity at age 70.

We decided to use only the q_x values based on the maximum likelihood estimator because it is based on exact exposure and does not depend on the unrealistic assumptions inherent in the other methods. It implies the lowest life expectancy of the three GM estimates, but the estimated life expectancy still exceeds U.S. fig-

Table 16.2   Life Expectancies at Various Ages, Men, U. S. Whites 1984/86, GM
Salaried Retirees 1983–87, and Group Annuitants, 1983

| Age | U.S. Whites 1984/86 | GM Salaried Retirees | | | GAM 83 |
		Actuarial	Moment	MLE	
0	71.93	72.64	72.63	72.50	74.71
50	25.94	26.72	26.72	26.57	28.99
55	21.85	23.63	23.63	23.48	24.63
60	18.09	20.04	20.04	19.90	20.44
65	14.69	16.44	16.44	16.29	16.48
70	11.64	13.01	13.01	12.87	12.94
75	9.04	10.01	10.01	9.87	9.87
80	6.86	7.45	7.46	7.36	7.26

Table 16.3   Life Expectancies at Various Ages, Women, U. S. Whites 1984/6,
GM Salaried Retirees 1983–87, and Group Annuitants, 1983

| Age | U.S. Whites 1984/86 | GM Salaried Retirees | | | GAM 83 |
		Actuarial	Moment	MLE	
0	78.79	80.01	80.01	79.94	81.73
60	22.63	23.98	23.98	23.90	25.03
65	18.72	20.01	20.10	20.10	20.63
70	15.07	16.36	16.36	16.28	16.44
75	11.77	12.82	12.82	12.76	12.62
80	8.83	9.50	9.50	9.46	9.32

ures. Note that this decision was conservative in the sense of choosing the best estimate of GM life expectancy. It was not conservative in the sense of protecting
the utilization forecast by using the highest survivorship probabilities, a tactic
commonly used by actuaries. These life tables are presented next.

Evaluating the Alternative Life Tables

Now that we had obtained three alternative life tables the next step was to identify
which life table was the best one to use for surviving current retirees. This section
describes how we evaluated the life tables by statistical tests and tests for forecast

Table 16.4 Life Table, GM Salaried Retirees, Males, 1983/87

Age (x)	q_x	d_x	l_x	L_x	T_x	e_x
50	0.0174678	1591	91104	90308.5	2420539.0	26.568
51	0.0159062	1423	89513	88801.5	2330230.0	26.032
52	0.0147318	1297	88090	87441.5	2241429.0	25.444
53	0.0138790	1204	86793	86191.0	2153987.0	24.817
54	0.0132996	1138	85589	85020.0	2067796.0	24.159
55	0.0129564	1094	84451	83904.0	1982776.0	23.478
56	0.0128077	1067	83357	82823.5	1898872.0	22.780
57	0.0128310	1055	82290	81762.5	1816049.0	22.068
58	0.0130149	1057	81235	80706.5	1734286.0	21.349
59	0.0133549	1070	80178	79643.0	1653580.0	20.623
60	0.0138480	1095	79108	78560.5	1573937.0	19.896
61	0.0144857	1130	78013	77448.0	1495376.0	19.168
62	0.0152475	1172	76883	76297.0	1417928.0	18.442
63	0.0161269	1220	75711	75101.0	1341631.0	17.720
64	0.0171405	1276	74491	73853.0	1266530.0	17.002
65	0.0182711	1337	73215	72546.5	1192677.0	16.290
66	0.0195916	1408	71878	71174.0	1120131.0	15.583
67	0.0212107	1494	70470	69723.0	1048957.0	14.885
68	0.0232302	1602	68976	68175.0	979234.0	14.196
69	0.0256691	1729	67374	66509.5	911059.0	13.522
70	0.0284451	1867	65645	64711.5	844549.5	12.865
71	0.0315290	2010	63778	62773.0	779838.0	12.227
72	0.0349121	2156	61768	60690.0	717065.0	11.609
73	0.0385610	2298	59612	58463.0	656375.0	11.010
74	0.0424996	2435	57314	56096.5	597912.0	10.432
75	0.0467806	2567	54879	53595.5	541815.5	9.8729
76	0.0514343	2690	52312	50967.0	488220.0	9.3328
77	0.0564859	2802	49622	48221.0	437253.0	8.8116
78	0.0619474	2900	46820	45370.0	389032.0	8.3090
79	0.0677251	2974	43920	42433.0	343662.0	7.8247
80	0.0737912	3021	40946	39435.5	301229.0	7.3567
81	0.0799539	3032	37925	36409.0	261793.5	6.9029
82	0.0860498	3002	34893	33392.0	225384.5	6.4593
83	0.0918432	2928	31891	30427.0	191992.5	6.0202
84	0.0965182	2795	28963	27565.5	161565.5	5.5783
85+	1.0000000	26168	26168	134000.0	134000.0	5.1208

NOTE: Life table is based on a radix of 100,000 males alive at age zero. Prior to age 50, q_x and other life table values were obtained from the 1984/86 U. S. life table for white males.

Table 16.5   Life Table, GM Salaried Retirees, Females, 1983/87

Age (x)	q_x	d_x	l_x	L_x	T_x	e_x
50	0.003425	95312	326	95149	3089230.0	32.411
51	0.003800	94986	361	94806	2994081.0	31.521
52	0.004190	94625	397	94427	2899275.0	30.639
53	0.004584	94228	432	94012	2804848.0	29.766
54	0.005016	93796	471	93561	2710836.0	28.901
55	0.005470	93325	511	93070	2617275.0	28.044
56	0.005968	92814	554	92537	2524205.0	27.196
57	0.006541	92260	604	91958	2431668.0	26.356
58	0.007206	91656	660	91326	2339710.0	25.527
59	0.007945	90996	723	90635	2248384.0	24.708
60	0.008885	90273	802	89872	2157749.0	23.902
61	0.009482	89471	848	89047	2067877.0	23.112
62	0.010107	88623	896	88175	1978830.0	22.328
63	0.010746	87727	943	87256	1890655.0	21.551
64	0.011422	86784	991	86289	1803399.0	20.780
65	0.012141	85793	1042	85272	1717110.0	20.014
66	0.012939	84751	1097	84203	1631838.0	19.254
67	0.013838	83654	1158	83075	1547635.0	18.500
68	0.014865	82496	1226	81883	1464560.0	17.753
69	0.016028	81270	1303	80619	1382677.0	17.013
70	0.017292	79967	1383	79276	1302058.0	16.282
71	0.018669	78584	1467	77851	1222782.0	15.560
72	0.020165	77117	1555	76340	1144931.0	14.846
73	0.021790	75562	1647	74739	1068591.0	14.141
74	0.023563	73915	1742	73044	993852.2	13.445
75	0.025496	72173	1840	71253	920808.2	12.758
76	0.027711	70333	1949	69359	849555.2	12.079
77	0.030161	68384	2063	67353	780196.2	11.409
78	0.032924	66321	2184	65229	712843.2	10.748
79	0.036058	64137	2313	62981	647614.2	10.097
80	0.039640	61824	2451	60599	584633.2	9.456
81	0.043777	59373	2599	58074	524034.2	8.826
82	0.048563	56774	2757	55396	465960.2	8.207
83	0.054214	54017	2928	52553	410564.2	7.600
84	0.060954	51089	3114	49532	358011.2	7.007
85+	1.000000	47975	47975	308479.2	308479.2	6.430

NOTE: Life table is based on a radix of 100,000 females alive at age zero. Prior to age 50, q_x and other life table values were obtained from the 1984/86 U. S. life table for white females.

accuracy. We also tried to evaluate the life tables by comparing the costs and benefits of obtaining and using the information.

Statistical Tests

The preceding tables suggest that the probability of dying is greater among U.S. whites 1984/86 than it is for GM salaried retirees 1984–87. To determine whether this difference was statistically significant we performed a z-test (Chiang 1984). We performed the test separately for each age-sex category, using for each test the null hypothesis that the q_i values were equal and the alternative hypothesis that the q_i values for the U.S. were greater than those for GM. The test statistic for each age-sex category was the standardized normal random variable:

$$Z = \hat{q}^{U.S.} - \hat{q}^{G.M.} \ / \ S.E. \ (\hat{q}^{U.S.} - \hat{q}^{G.M.}).$$

We rejected the null hypothesis if the z-test statistic exceeded 1.65.

The data necessary to perform the calculations for men are shown in Table 16.6. In order to calculate standard errors for

$$\hat{q}^{U.S.}$$

we obtained the number of deaths among U.S. whites 1984/86 from National Center for Health Statistics, 1986b, 1988b. This data led us to reject the null hypothesis that the mortality probabilities were equal for men ages 60 to 84 and for women ages 78–81 and 84. The results for women differed from those for men because there were fewer deaths, thereby inflating the standard errors of the q_i.

It was not possible to perform statistical tests involving GAM83 because no data concerning standard errors, exposure, or deaths were available; we needed such data to calculate the z-test statistic.

Surviving 1983 Salaried Retirees to 1987: Accuracy Tests

We examined the relative accuracy of the three life tables by tracking the survivors of the 1983 retiree cohort to year-end 1987. This evaluation was possible only because we knew the actual number and composition of salaried retirees at year-end 1987. We compared how accurately mortality schedules from GM, GAM83, and U.S. survive the 1983 retirees to 1987 by projecting them in particular ages at year-end 1983 forward four years to year-end 1987. We did separate projections for males ages 50 to 79 and 80+ and for females ages 60 to 79 and 80+.

Formally, for males, this exercise projected

$$S^{m.} \ M^{83} = M^{87}$$

where S^m is a matrix of survivorship ratios for males, M^{83} is a column vector where each element is the number of males in a particular age group in 1983, and M^{87} is a column vector where each element is the number of males in a particular age group in 1987.

For instance,

$$M^{83} = \begin{matrix} M^{83}_{50} \\ \vdots \\ M^{83}_{80+} \end{matrix} \quad \text{and } M^{87} = \begin{matrix} M^{87}_{54} \\ \vdots \\ M^{87}_{84+} \end{matrix}$$

Similarly, for females,

$$S^{f\cdot} F^{83} = F^{87}$$

where S^f is a matrix of survivorship ratios for females,

$$F^{83} = \begin{matrix} F^{83}_{60} \\ \vdots \\ F^{83}_{80+} \end{matrix} \quad \text{and } F^{87} = \begin{matrix} F^{87}_{64} \\ \vdots \\ F^{87}_{84+} \end{matrix}$$

Each survivorship matrix S^m and S^f is a diagonal matrix containing survivorship ratios along the diagonal and zeroes elsewhere. As shown below, S^m has 31 rows and 31 columns while S^f has 21 rows and columns.

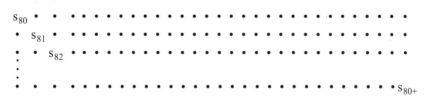

Each element of the two S matrices is a survivorship ratio based on life table parameters. The survivorship ratio is (L_{i+4}/L_i) for each age i up to the last age group and (T_{84}/T_{80}) for age 80+. For instance,

$$S^m_{50} = L^m_{54} / L^m_{50}$$

Note that projections were based on survivorship probabilities for the stationary population (which measures survival from the midpoint of the single year age group) rather than on the probability of surviving p_i ($p_i = 1-q_i$) which refers to survival between *exact ages*. This difference is important because in population pro-

Table 16.6 Z-Test Results for Statistically Significant Differences Between Mortality Probabilities for U.S. White Males 1984/86 and GM Male Salaried Retirees 1983/87, Ages 50–84

Age	U.S. 1984/86			GM Salaried Retirees			Z-Test Statistic
	q_i	Std. Error	Deaths	Death	q_i	Std.	
50	0.00612	0.000056	11614	6	0.01746	0.007068	-1.60
51	0.00678	0.000059	12779	8	0.01590	0.005578	-1.63
52	0.00751	0.000063	14071	8	0.01473	0.005169	-1.39
53	0.00833	0.000066	15486	14	0.01387	0.003683	-1.50
54	0.00923	0.000070	17005	19	0.01329	0.003030	-1.34
55	0.01019	0.000071	20027	18	0.01295	0.003034	-0.91
56	0.01122	0.000075	21843	31	0.01280	0.002285	-0.69
57	0.01235	0.000079	23759	37	0.01283	0.002095	-0.22
58	0.01358	0.000083	25810	61	0.01301	0.001655	0.34
59	0.01492	0.000088	27972	69	0.01335	0.001596	0.98
60	0.01637	0.000092	31076	99	0.01384	0.001382	1.82
61	0.01791	0.000097	33450	107	0.01448	0.001390	2.46
62	0.01952	0.000102	35800	136	0.01524	0.001297	3.28
63	0.02119	0.000107	38094	126	0.01612	0.001425	3.54
64	0.02294	0.000112	40376	164	0.01714	0.001326	4.36
65	0.02477	0.000121	40634	160	0.01827	0.001431	4.52
66	0.02677	0.000127	42819	186	0.01959	0.001422	5.02
67	0.02908	0.000134	45270	162	0.02121	0.001648	4.75
68	0.03180	0.000142	48063	194	0.02323	0.001648	5.18
69	0.03491	0.000151	51089	203	0.02566	0.001778	5.17
70	0.03828	0.000169	49190	209	0.02844	0.001939	5.05
71	0.04187	0.000180	51743	233	0.03152	0.002032	5.06

Table 16.6 *(continued)*

72	0.04568	0.000191	54083	234	0.03491	0.002242	4.78
73	0.04967	0.000204	56124	215	0.03856	0.002578	4.29
74	0.05390	0.000217	57873	222	0.04249	0.002791	4.07
75	0.05844	0.000246	52733	238	0.04678	0.002960	3.92
76	0.06337	0.000264	53833	214	0.05143	0.003424	3.47
77	0.06875	0.000283	54702	227	0.05648	0.003641	3.35
78	0.07467	0.000305	55323	241	0.06194	0.003864	3.28
79	0.08113	0.000329	55623	230	0.06772	0.004311	3.10
80	0.08824	0.000387	47252	228	0.07379	0.004703	3.06
81	0.09596	0.000421	46851	195	0.07995	0.005491	2.90
82	0.10431	0.000460	46043	172	0.08604	0.006272	2.90
83	0.11322	0.000503	44769	172	0.09184	0.006673	3.19
84	0.12257	0.000553	42981	162	0.09651	0.007207	3.60

jections the jump-off population (the population at the beginning of the projection) cannot all be assumed to be at exact ages. That is, we assumed that the population aged 50 to 51 is, on average, 50.5 years old at the beginning of the projection rather than 50.0 years (as is commonly done in actuarial calculations). We also assumed a constant mortality schedule for the projections here.

We evaluated how well the three survivorship functions projected 1983 retirees to 1987 according to eight standard measures of forecast error (Smith 1987), a standard measure of population growth (Stoto 1983), and a t-test for mean age. Comparative measures are defined below. We indexed ages from 54 to 84 (31 age categories), but refer to ages 64 to 84 for women (21 ages). We chose these ages because they were the only ones for which it was possible to estimate survivorship ratios for GM salaried retirees.

We defined the following measures using the number of ages for males.

1. Total Error $(\sum_{i=54}^{84} \hat{N}_i) - (\sum_{i=54}^{84} N_i)$

2. Total Percentage Error. $(\sum_{i=54}^{84} \hat{N}_i - \sum_{i=54}^{84} N_i) / \sum_{i=54}^{84} N_i) * 100$

3. delta r $= (100/4) * \ln (\sum_{i=54}^{84} \hat{N}_i / \sum_{i=54}^{84} N_i)$

4. Mean Absolute Error $(\sum_{i=54}^{84} |\hat{N}_i - N_i|) / 31$

5. Mean Absolute Percentage Error $100 * ((\sum_{i=54}^{84} |\hat{N}_i - N_i| / N_i) / 31)$

6. Root Mean Square Error (RMSE) $\sqrt{(\sum_{i=54}^{84}(N_i - N_i)^2 / 31)}$.

7. Index of Dissimilarity $(.5 * (\sum_{i=54}^{84} | (\hat{N}_i / \sum_{i=54}^{84} \hat{N}_i) - (N_i / \sum_{i=54}^{84} N_i) |)) \cdot 100$

8. Number of Ages with Extreme Errors (absolute percent error that is greater than one standard deviation unit above or below the mean absolute percentage error).

9. Percentage of Age Groups with Extreme Errors.

10. T-test for Mean Age.

We chose the various measures because they evaluated different aspects of the projection. Total error and total percentage error evaluated total size. Delta r compared growth rates of the total population averaged over the time period. Mean absolute error, mean percentage error, root mean square error (RMSE), and the index of dissimilarity compared the number of persons in an age-gender category. The index of dissimilarity provided the minimum percentage of the population that would have to be shifted from each age group in the actual population to the age groups in the projected population in order for the forecast and actual populations to be identically distributed in each of the age-gender categories.

Table 16.7 compares results from different measures. For both men and

Table 16.7 Errors in Projections of Surviving Retirees 12/31/83 to 12/31/87, Based on U.S., GM, and GAM83 Mortality Rates by Gender

Measure	Men			Women		
	U.S.	GM	GAM83	U.S.	GM	GAM83
Total Error	-915	170	570	-92	18	153
Total Percentage Error	-2.49%	0.46%	1.55%	-1.49%	0.29%	2.48%
Delta r	-0.516%	0.113%	0.384%	-0.376%	0.073%	0.613%
Mean Absolute Error	31.84	9.55	19.03	5.05	4.66	7.57
Mean Absolute Percentage Error	2.96%	1.22%	2.19%	2.08%	2.03%	2.95%
RMSE	37.77	12.48	21.91	6.57	5.64	9.17
Index of Dissimilarity	0.625%	0.394%	0.345%	0.729%	0.788%	0.735%
Ages with Extreme Errors	10	2	9	1	6	8
Percent with Extreme Errors	32.3%	6.5%	29.0%	4.8%	28.6%	38.1%
T-test for Mean Age	-1.85*	0.70	0.25	-0.38	0.50	0.29

*Statistically significant at the 0.05 level

women the projection based on survivorship ratios from the GM salaried retiree life tables was more accurate than those based on the U.S. or GAM83 life tables. The GM survivorship schedule predicted that there would be 188 more persons than there actually were at year-end 1987. This finding indicated that the estimated mortality probabilities were underestimated and suggested that deaths had been underreported in the corporate databases. We discuss this issue further in the section about the cost benefit analysis of death audits.

The GAM83 mortality schedule predicted that there would be more survivors than there actually were, although the total error (73) was much greater than that for the GM schedule. In contrast, the U.S. mortality schedule (which has much higher mortality rates than the other two) predicted that there would be 915 fewer men and 92 fewer women than there actually were. Total percentage errors for all three projections were small, however—under 3 percent. The GM projection also had the lowest values of delta r for both men and women.

We next considered how well the projections correctly forecast the age-gender composition. This was important for one application of the information—forecasting health care utilization, which relates the number of persons in an age-gender group number to utilization measures indexed by age and gender. As indicated by mean absolute error, mean absolute percentage error, and root mean square error, the GM projection forecast the number of persons in an age category most accurately for both men and women. Its values for the index of dissimilarity were also among the lowest.

The eighth and ninth rows of Table 16.7 show the number and percentage of ages with extreme errors. For men, the GM survivorship schedule had the fewest extreme errors. For women, the U.S. survivorship schedule had the fewest extreme errors, followed by the GM schedule.

The GM projection accurately predicted the gender composition of the population, although differences among the projections were not statistically significant. The actual year-end 1987 population was 14.34 percent female. In contrast, the gender composition implied by both the U.S. and GAM83 projections had slightly higher percentage female (14.47 and 14.46 percent, respectively).

Nearly all projections accurately forecast the average age for each gender. All projections accurately forecast the average age of women at 71.6 years, but there were differences for men. The actual average age for men was 68.949. Only the U.S. projection (at 68.858) had an average age significantly lower than this figure (according to a one-sided difference of means test at $p < .05$). The U.S. projection also significantly underestimated the percentage of the male population ages 65 and older (and therefore eligible for Medicare). The actual percentage was 71.43, higher than the 70.89 predicted by the U.S. projection.

It is generally not possible to minimize all error criteria simultaneously within a single forecast system (National Research Council 1980 for a discussion of this issue in relation to population estimates for geographic areas). For example, the GM projections provided the lowest values for all measures of error except the index of dissimilarity and extreme errors (for women). Taken together, however, the various accuracy tests strongly supported using the GM life table as a basis for surviving GM salaried retirees.

We also concluded that it was feasible to use corporate databases to estimate mortality rates. The records not only provided adequate information about deaths among retirees, but they also offered a relatively low-cost way of obtaining mortality rates.

Examples of How This Information Has Been Used to Date

Forecasting Hospitalization for a Retiree Cohort

The preceding analyses indicated that the GM survivorship values differed from those available from other sources and that these differences had important consequences for projections based on them. This section demonstrates how a tool for forecasting health care utilization can be developed from this demographic information. The forecasting methodology involved the following stages:

1. Project the cohort of current retirees by age and gender until extinction.
2. Obtain estimates of per capita hospital utilization by age and gender.
3. Forecast annual utilization for the cohort.

Each stage is briefly described below.

Projecting the Cohort of Current Retirees. We obtained the future number of current retirees and their demographic characteristics by simply "surviving" the cohort of current salaried retirees at December 31, 1988 until nearly all of them had died ("extinction"). We used the GM survivorship values for this projection because they had the lowest forecast errors in our earlier analyses. We projected survivors from this cohort using the same procedure that we had used for the 1983–87 projection. Table 16.8 shows the data needed to perform the projection.

Obtaining Estimates of Per Capita Utilization. We then obtained national estimates of hospital utilization per person by age and gender from the most recent (1987) National Hospital Discharge Survey (Glenn 1989). We decided to measure hospitalization by the hospital discharge rate (discharges per 1,000 persons) and the days of care rate (days of care per 1,000 persons). We chose these measures because they are so commonly used that the statistics are printed in reports and because they can be combined to obtain the average length of stay—a figure of interest to the corporation.

Before we could combine these two sets of data, we had to modify them to make the age groups consistent. The utilization data were only available for the following ages: under 1, 1–4, 5–14, 15–19, 20–24, 25–34, 35–44, 45–54, 55–64, 65–74, 75–84, and 85 years and over. The population projection produced the number of retirees by single years of age from 30 to 84 and over, allowing us to

Table 16.8   Sample Calculations for Projecting 1988 Salaried Retiree Cohort
Using GM Life Tables

Age	Retirees 12/31/88		GM Survivorship Ratios		Projected Survivors 12/31/89	
	Men	Women	Men	Women	Men	Women
31	1	0	0.99831	0.99936	0	0
32	0	0	0.99827	0.99932	1	0
33	0	0	0.99823	0.99926	0	0
34	0	0	0.99819	0.99922	0	0
35	0	0	0.99813	0.99916	0	0
36	1	2	0.99804	0.99909	0	0
37	0	2	0.99793	0.99899	1	2
38	6	4	0.99779	0.99890	0	2
39	6	5	0.99762	0.99879	6	4
40	8	8	0.99742	0.99866	6	5
41	13	7	0.99721	0.99851	8	8
42	9	10	0.99698	0.99836	13	7
43	13	4	0.99672	0.99820	9	10
44	30	10	0.99643	0.99803	13	4
45	30	5	0.99610	0.99784	30	10
46	41	16	0.99573	0.99762	30	5
47	44	12	0.99528	0.99735	41	16
48	54	16	0.99476	0.99708	44	12
49	80	20	0.98853	0.98674	54	16
50	100	27	0.98467	0.98640	79	20
51	151	35	0.98577	0.99600	98	27
52	174	56	0.98654	0.99561	149	35
53	425	93	0.98705	0.99520	172	56
54	1280	177	0.98734	0.99475	419	93
55	1413	248	0.98743	0.99427	1264	176
56	1673	288	0.98736	0.99374	1395	247
57	1827	307	0.98714	0.99313	1652	286
58	2121	309	0.98677	0.99243	1804	305
59	2172	357	0.98627	0.99158	2093	307
60	2458	385	0.98562	0.99082	2142	354
61	2715	420	0.98485	0.99021	2423	381
62	2625	415	0.98397	0.98958	2674	416
63	2768	501	0.98298	0.98892	2583	411
64	2844	573	0.98188	0.98821	2721	495
65	2719	511	0.98064	0.98746	2792	566
66	2612	538	0.97917	0.98660	2666	505
67	2569	551	0.97738	0.98565	2558	531
68	2320	552	0.97520	0.98456	2511	543
69	1857	461	0.97267	0.98334	2262	543
70	1938	441	0.96986	0.98202	1806	453
71	1828	361	0.96678	0.98059	1880	433

Table 16.8 (continued)

72	1704	404	0.96342	0.97903	1767	354
73	1682	362	0.95981	0.97732	1642	396
74	1514	311	0.95589	0.97548	1614	354
75	1311	299	0.95160	0.97342	1447	303
76	1203	270	0.94689	0.97108	1248	291
77	1079	225	0.94172	0.96846	1139	262
78	928	218	0.93608	0.96554	1016	218
79	891	213	0.92994	0.96218	869	210
80	812	210	0.92335	0.95833	829	205
81	698	139	0.91641	0.95389	750	201
82	546	153	0.90920	0.94868	640	133
83	467	137	0.90229	0.94252	496	145
84+	1886	482	0.82900	0.87200	1985	549
Total	55646	11150			53841	10905

combine the population numbers into the appropriate age groups—except for the oldest one. The oldest age group from the population projection was 84 and over. The oldest age group from the utilization data was 85 and over, resulting in a one-year mismatch.

Since there was no way to change either data set, we merely applied the utilization data to the oldest age group from the projection. This solution to the one-year mismatch resulted in a very slight overestimate of total utilization. We felt comfortable with this solution because our clients had previously indicated a preference for slight overestimates rather than underestimates, believing that the latter are more difficult to explain.

Forecasting Annual Utilization for the Cohort. Finally, we forecast annual hospital utilization for the retiree cohort by tying the population projection to the national hospital utilization rates.

$$C_t = \sum_{i=30}^{i=85+} \sum_{j=1}^{j=2} (N_{ijt} \cdot U_{ijt})$$

Cohort utilization in year t (C_t) is the weighted sum (over all ages and both genders) of the utilization rates (U_{ijt}), where the weights are the number of surviving retirees in that age-gender group in year t (N_{ijt}). Table 16.9 shows sample calculations for one year.

We forecast utilization from 1989 to 2000 for the 1988 cohort of salaried retirees. Since the members are subject to mortality and no replacements are possible, we projected cohort size to diminish over time. As the number of survivors declines over time, the number of hospital discharges declines also (Figure 16.1). The average length of stay, however, increases over time (Figure 16.2). This in-

Table 16.9 Sample Calculations for Forecasting Hospital Discharges and Average Length of Stay (ALOS) from U. S. Utilization Rates and Projection of 1988 Retiree Cohort Using GM Life Tables

Age	Projected Retirees 12/31/89	U.S. Hospitalization Rates		Forecast 1990 Hospitalization		
		Discharges	Days of Care	Discharges	Days of Care	ALOS
Men						
30–34	1	67.1	441.8	0.07	0.44	6.29
35–39	7	84.9	541.6	0.59	3.79	6.42
40–44	49	84.9	541.6	4.16	26.54	6.38
45–49	199	128.7	828.0	25.61	164.77	6.43
50–54	917	128.7	828.0	118.02	759.28	6.43
55–59	8,208	200.4	1,394.1	1,644.88	11,442.77	6.96
60–64	12,543	200.4	1,394.1	2,513.62	17,486.20	6.96
65–69	12,789	308.7	2,445.2	3,947.96	31,271.66	7.92
70–74	8,709	308.7	2,445.2	2,688.47	21,295.25	7.92
75–79	5,719	491.2	4,263.7	2,809.17	24,384.10	8.68
80–83	2,715	491.2	4,263.7	1,333.61	11,575.95	8.68
84+	1,985	619.1	5,371.4	1,228.91	10,662.23	8.68
Total Men	53,841			16,315.07	129,072.98	7.91
Women						
30–34	0	193.1	782.6	0.00	0.00	0.00
35–39	8	118.1	610.6	0.94	4.88	5.19
40–44	34	118.1	610.6	4.01	20.76	5.18
45–49	59	133.6	853.7	7.88	50.37	6.39
50–54	231	133.6	853.7	30.86	197.20	6.39

287

Table 16.9 (continued)

55–59	1,321	169.2	1,232.4	223.51	1,628.00	7.28
60–64	2,057	169.2	1,232.4	348.04	2,535.05	7.28
65–69	2,688	258.8	2,174.3	695.65	5,844.52	8.40
70–74	1,990	258.8	2,174.3	515.01	4,326.86	8.40
75–79	1,284	387.8	3,531.8	497.93	4,534.83	9.11
80–83	684	287.8	3,531.8	196.85	2,415.75	9.11
84+	549	499.2	4,915.1	274.06	2,698.39	9.85
Total Women	10,905			2,794.75	24,256.61	8.47
Combined Total				19,109.82	153,326.59	8.02

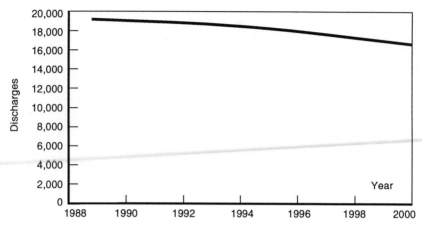

Figure 16.1—Projected hospital discharges by year, 1989–2000, G.M. salaried retirees alive 12-31-88, G.M. life tables

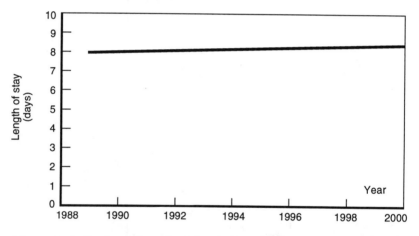

Figure 16.2—Projected length of stay, by year, 1989–2000, G.M. salaried retirees alive 12-31-88, G.M. life tables

crease occurs because the average age of the cohort is increasing, and the utilization data show that length of stay increases with increasing age.

This information proved useful in anticipating health care costs for retirees. It can also help in prioritizing cost containment strategies. There are two approaches to controlling hospitalization costs: (1) reduce admissions by requiring a second opinion before hospitalization is authorized, and (2) influence length of stay through reimbursement procedures. Our forecast demonstrated that to control the costs of providing health benefits to this retiree cohort, it was more important to influence length of stay than to reduce admissions.

Cost Benefit Analysis of Death Audits

The long time line permitted us to address a peripheral issue: How well are retiree deaths reported in corporate databases and how cost effective are corrective measures? We estimated the extent of underreporting in two ways. First, we compared the actual number of reported deaths to the number of deaths expected from the U.S. mortality probabilities and the GM exposure. We found that the number of expected deaths exceeded the reported number by 25.4 percent for men and 19.9 percent for women. Second, we estimated the least amount of underreporting by comparing the number of cohort members who survived December 31, 1983–December 31, 1987 to the number predicted from the GM mortality rates (Table 16.10). If survival in the cohort actually matched that implied by the life table, then the projected number of retirees at year-end 1987 would match the actual number. Instead, GM rates overestimated the number of survivors by 3.4 percent more deaths for men and 3.1 percent more deaths for women.

We estimated that the underreporting of deaths cost the corporation between $332,000 (using the lowest underreporting rate estimate) and $2,800,000 (using the highest underreporting rate estimate). We based these costs on internal data about health care costs for age-gender groups. We assumed that all retirees who were actually dead but who nevertheless were reported alive were incurring the same costs as others in their age-gender group. This assumption is reasonable for employers who pay insurance premiums or other nonrefundable fees. We compared these potential cost savings to the cost of matching the insurance administration data base to the Social Security master beneficiary file which reports all deaths. The cost would be $1,336 for the roughly 66,800 salaried retirees at year-end 1988. Therefore, the cost of verifying whether each salaried retiree was alive by matching with Social Security records could potentially return between 248 and 2,129 times the cost.

Conclusion

How does this case study compare and contrast with other cases in applied demography? It is similar in that the generic problem involves planning and in that it was done for a specific client (the Health Care Cost Analysis Activity).

In several respects, however, this study differs from usual demographic case studies. First, since the FASB proposal was not due to take effect for two to three years, the time frame was relatively lengthy. This time frame permitted us to perform a very complete analysis, including the estimation of a life table from payroll and insurance databases. It also allowed us sufficient time to track down the actuarial literature and to perform a cost benefit analysis of death audits.

Second, the client's request was very open-ended—more along the line of "here's a problem you might be able to contribute to" than a request for specific information. We were brought in sufficiently early to be able to tailor both the request and the response. For instance, we decided to focus on salaried retirees even

Table 16.10 Sample Calculations for Projecting 1983 Salaried Retirees Ages 50–80 to 1987 and Comparing to Actual 1987 Population Using GM Life Tables

Ages	Retirees 12/31/83		GM Survivorship Ratios		Projected Survivors 12/31/87		Actual Survivors 12/31/87	
	Men	Women	Men	Women	Men	Women	Men	Women
50	156		0.98467	0.98640				
51	243		0.98577	0.99600				
52	252		0.98577	0.99600				
53	336		0.98654	0.99561				
54	369		0.98705	0.99520	147		144	
55	786		0.98734	0.99475	230		227	
56	1,297		0.98743	0.99427	239		233	
57	1,580		0.98736	0.99374	319		313	
58	1,911		0.98714	0.99313	349		351	
59	2,052		0.98677	0.99243	746		754	
60	2,145	410	0.98627	0.99158	1,229		1,231	
61	2,182	449	0.98562	0.99082	1,497		1,502	
62	2,339	478	0.98485	0.99021	1,807		1,812	
63	2,256	509	0.98397	0.98958	1,934		1,949	
64	1,881	431	0.98298	0.98892	2,017	394	1,998	396
65	2,122	439	0.98188	0.98821	2,044	430	2,044	432
66	2,071	370	0.98064	0.98746	2,182	456	2,188	455
67	1,956	421	0.97917	0.98660	2,095	484	2,082	494
68	1,963	407	0.97738	0.98565	1,737	409	1,739	419
69	1,805	336	0.97520	0.98456	1,946	415	1,932	413
70	1,585	343	0.97267	0.98334	1,884	348	1,882	347
71	1,489	299	0.96986	0.98202	1,762	395	1,737	391

Table 16.10 *(continued)*

72	1,379	260	0.96678	0.98059	1,747	379	1,733	367
73	1,206	248	0.96342	0.97903	1,586	311	1,590	313
74	1,173	255	0.95981	0.97732	1,374	316	1,364	311
75	1,105	245	0.95589	0.97548	1,272	273	1,265	279
76	1,011	180	0.95160	0.97342	1,157	237	1,135	232
77	853	188	0.94689	0.97108	994	223	991	225
78	723	179	0.94172	0.96846	949	228	939	225
79	653	120	0.93608	0.96554	874	216	888	218
80	615	118	0.92994	0.96218	783	157	775	150
81			0.92335	0.95833	644	162	619	157
82			0.91641	0.95389	532	152	524	143
83			0.90920	0.94868	468	100	466	96
84			0.90229	0.94252	430	96	397	100
Total	41,494	6,683			36,974	6,181	36,804	6163

though this group is much smaller than all retirees. The long time line meant that we could explore various alternative assumptions. For example, we were able to evaluate three different methods for estimating mortality probabilities from the longitudinal data set.

Third, this case was unusual in that it involved no exchange of funds between the demographers and the clients. General Motors Research Laboratories supported the demographers and provided the support personnel. This arrangement considerably reduced pressure on the demographers to provide quick results and particular outputs ("deliverables").

Fourth, the nature of the information needed, the extent of support from management, and the long time frame allowed us to explore the feasibility of deriving demographic information from a proprietary database not originally intended to be used for life table construction. Part of the reason we did this was to inform ourselves both about the database and about the longevity of GM's retirees. We suspected that mortality rates would be different because this group was "selected" from the general population on the basis of education and occupation and because other aspects of GM's health benefits population differed from the U.S. population. Furthermore, the group we were interested in was large.

We do not recommend deriving demographic information from proprietary databases unless:

1. There is good reason for doing so—e.g., the costs of data production can be justified by improving the accuracy of the projection.
2. You believe that the resulting information will be of high quality.
3. You have the backing of the groups from whom permission must be obtained to access the data.

Access is particularly important in corporations, where information is usually disseminated on a "need to know" basis.

If you have considered both the size of the group and the likelihood that it exhibits demographic behavior different from national databases and you are still interested in obtaining demographic information from proprietary databases, here are some guidelines to follow:

1. Identify the key people to contact for obtaining information about the database and those from whom you need to receive permission for gaining access to it.
2. Find out if the database has written documentation that describes the fields (variables), the values for the fields, the source(s) of the information, and whether the information is continuously updated ("live") or produced at regular time intervals.

3. Ask whether the records are composed of "individuals" or "transactions."
4. Inquire as to what field(s) uniquely identify individuals.
5. Discover whether the database has a reputation for accurate or inaccurate information. Do not proceed with any database known to be inaccurate.
6. Evaluate the amount of technical assistance and computer resources you will need to devise the analytical database from the operating database.
7. Prepare edit checks to detect logical inconsistencies in the data.
8. Form the analytical database and obtain estimates.
9. Compare estimates to national data for smoothing and for examining the extent of any differences.

Finally, we reported the project in a very refined manner. We documented the details of the projection and forecast in a lengthy (roughly 80-page) Research Laboratories report. On this report—intended for a very small audience (20–25 people) within the corporation—we recommended that:

1. Forecasts of GM's possible liability under the proposed FASB rule be estimated using the GM life table.
2. The reporting of retiree deaths in the corporate databases be improved.
3. Retirement planning seminars incorporate information about the life expectancy of GM salaried retirees.
4. Corporate population projections use mortality schedules specifically for the corporation rather than those based on the U.S. national population or on group annuitants.

In addition, we highlighted the life tables for GM salaried retirees in a two-page Research Brief (Exhibit 16.1) targeted for wide dissemination within the corporation. We wrote the brief in lay terms and presented a table that showed a key finding from the study. Notice how the brief is worded. It attracts reader attention by immediately revealing the benefits of the "demographic perspective." We also reported the project in a series of oral presentations.

Discussion Questions

1. What is the most important information this case revealed?
2. Why is the life table the appropriate technique for projecting retirees?
3. What fundamental factors should be considered when constructing a life table? How do they apply to this case?
4. Outline some of the challenges an analyst using the GM Database would face.
5. Give an example of how another corporation might use the information about organizational databases, utilization, and forecasting benefits.

Notes

Lisa DeLisle, Debbie Pruent, and Kathy Kay (Operating Sciences) copied the SEIS and OLIVIA databases from tape to disk. Ernie Smith (Operating Sciences) and Janet Zarko (EDS) clarified questions about SEIS and OLIVIA databases. Mary Beth Palmer (EDS) and Jean Rose (Pension) assisted in looking up lost records on OLIVIA and PARS, respectively. Tim Bogar (EDS) provided information about SEIS purge criteria. Debbie Pruent and Ernie Smith carefully reviewed earlier drafts of the cohort data analysis. Jim Licholat entered life table programs and assisted with LOTUS spreadsheets.

References

Bacon, Donald C. 1988. "Benefits-Rule Migraine." *The Nation's Business,* October: pp. 22, 24, 25.

Batten, R.W. 1978. *Mortality Table Construction.* Englewood Cliffs: Prentice-Hall, Inc.

Chiang, Chin Long. 1984. *The Life Table and Its Applications.* Malabar, FL: Robert E. Krieger Publishing Company.

Committee on Annuities. 1983. "Development of the 1983 Group Annuity Mortality Table." *Society of Actuaries Transactions.* 35:859–900.

Employee Benefit Research Institute. 1986. "Employer-Sponsored Health Insurance Coverage." *EBRI Issue Brief.* p. 58.

———. 1987. "Measuring and Funding Corporate Liabilities for Retiree Health Benefits." *Employee Benefit Research Institute.*

Financial Accounting Standards Board. 1989. "Employers' Accounting for Postretirement Benefits Other than Pensions." Exposure Draft. Proposed Statement of Financial Accounting Standards No. 78. Norwalk, CT.

Freudenheim, Milt. 1989. *A Health-Care Taboo Is Broken. The New York Times,* May 8. p. 29.

General Motors Corporation. 1984–1988. *Annual Report.* Detroit: General Motors Corporation.

Graves, E.J. 1989. "National Hospital Discharge Survey: Annual Summary, 1987." National Center for Health Statistics. *Vital and Health Statistics.* series 13, number 99.

Henriques, Diana. 1989. "Double Whammy. FASB Readies a Blow to Corporate Earnings and Balance Sheets." *Barron's.* April 17. pp. 8–9, 28–29.

Keller, Maryann. 1989. "The Health Care Cost Crisis." *Automotive Industries.* May: p. 11.

Kintner, Hallie J., and Smith, Ernest B. 1987. "General Motors Provides Health Care Benefits to Millions." *American Demographics.* May: 44–45.

Kintner, Hallie J. 1989. "Demographic Change in a Corporate Health Benefits Population." *American Journal of Public Health.* 79:1655–1656.

Lippert, J. 1988. "GM Wants Its Pay System to Follow Market Goals." *Detroit Free Press.* January 29. p. 6b.

London, Dick. 1988. *Survival models and their estimation.* Second Edition. Winsted and New Britain, CT: ACTEX Publications.

Loomis, Carol J. 1989. "The Killer Cost Stalking Business." *Forbes.* February 27. pp. 58–68.

National Center for Health Statistics. 1986a. "Vital Statistics of the U.S., 1984. 2, sec. 6,

Life Tables." DHHS Pub. No. (PHS)-87-1104. Washington: U.S. Government Printing Office.

———. 1986b. Advance report of final mortality statistics, 1984. *Monthly Vital Statistics Report.* 35, n. 6, Supp. (2). DHHS Pub. No. (PHS) 86–1120. Public Health Service, Hyattsville, Maryland.

———. 1988a. "Vital Statistics of the U.S., 1986. 2, sec. 6, Life Tables." DHHS Pub. No. (PHS)-88-1147. Washington: U.S. Government Printing Office.

———. 1988b. "Advance Report of Final Mortality Statistics, 1986." *Monthly Vital Statistics Report.* 37, n. 6, Supp. DHHS Pub. No. (PHS) 88-1120. Public Health Service, Hyattsville, Maryland.

National Research Council. 1980. *Estimating Population and Income of Small Areas.* Washington, DC: National Academy of Science Press.

Smith, Stanley K. 1987. "Tests of Forecast Accuracy and Bias for County Population Projections." *Journal of the American Statistical Association.* 82:991–1003.

Stoto, Michael. 1983. "The Accuracy of Population Projections." *Journal of the American Statistical Association.* 78:13–20.

Exhibit 16. 1

Research Brief: GM Salaried Retirees Live Longer Than U.S. Population

Information about how long current GM salaried retirees are going to live may be useful to GM's salaried retirees and employees. GM's personnel administration and development staff and its financial staff also need this information to forecast what health benefits will cost when engaging in expense projections and benefits negotiations.

This information appears in the form of a "life table." A life table shows the long-term implications of current mortality rates. Using corporate payroll and insurance administration databases, we have developed the first life tables to deal specifically with GM's salaried retirees. We calculated these life tables by tracking the life histories of all salaried retirees from December 31, 1983 to December 31, 1987. These life tables cover all retirees regardless of the nature of their retirement.

Our research revealed that GM salaried retirees can expect, on average, to live longer than the general U.S. population. Table A compares life expectancies by gender for ages 50–85+ for the U.S. population during 1986 with General Motors salaried retirees during 1983–87. The columns labeled "U.S." show how long an individual will live if the mortality risks for the United States in 1986 continue indefinitely. Similarly, the columns labeled "GM" show how long an individual will live if the mortality risks for GM salaried retirees during 1983–87 continue indefinitely.

For instance, a male GM salaried retiree at age 50 can expect to live an average of 26.6 more years—or 0.8 years longer than a male of the same age in the general U.S. population. Women generally live longer than men. A 50-year-old female GM salaried retiree can expect to live, on average, another 32.4 years—or 5.8 years longer than her male counterpart.

For men, the difference between life expectancy for GM salaried retirees and that for people in the U.S. population generally declines with age from 1.9 years at age 60 to 0.50 years at age 80. The difference between U.S. life expectancy and that for GM salaried retirees is not as great for women. Life expectancy for female GM salaried retirees is about 1.3 years greater than women in the general U.S. population until age 80, when the difference is cut in half.

The final row of the table refers to people age 85 and over. It shows that male retirees reaching 85 will live, on average, 5.1 additional years. When we calculated the life tables, we assumed that there was no difference between the GM and U.S. figures at this age.

Exhibit 16.1 [Table A] Average Remaining Lifetime by Age and Gender for U.S. 1986 and GM Salaried Retirees 1983–87

	Men		Women	
Age	U.S.	GM	U.S.	GM
50	25.8	26.6	31.0	32.4
51	25.0	26.0	30.1	31.5
52	24.1	25.4	29.2	30.6
53	23.3	24.8	28.3	29.8
54	22.5	24.2	27.5	28.9
55	21.8	23.5	26.6	28.0
56	21.0	22.8	25.8	27.2
57	20.2	22.1	24.9	26.4
58	19.5	21.4	24.1	25.5
59	18.8	20.6	23.3	24.7
60	18.0	19.9	22.5	23.9
61	17.3	19.2	21.7	23.1
62	16.7	18.4	20.9	22.3
63	16.0	17.7	20.1	21.5
64	15.3	17.0	19.4	20.8
65	14.7	16.3	18.6	20.0
66	14.1	15.6	17.9	19.2
67	13.4	14.9	17.1	18.5
68	12.8	14.2	16.4	17.7
69	12.2	13.5	15.7	17.0
70	11.7	12.9	15.0	16.3
71	11.1	12.2	14.3	15.6
72	10.6	11.6	13.7	14.8
73	10.1	11.0	13.0	14.1
74	9.6	10.4	12.4	13.4
75	9.1	9.9	11.7	12.8
76	8.6	9.3	11.1	12.1
77	8.2	8.8	10.5	11.4
78	7.7	8.3	9.9	10.7
79	7.3	7.8	9.4	10.1
80	6.9	7.4	8.8	9.5
81	6.5	6.9	8.3	8.8
82	6.1	6.5	7.8	8.2
83	5.8	6.0	7.3	7.6
84	5.5	5.6	6.8	7.0
85+	5.1	5.1	6.4	6.4

17

Enrollment Projection in a Multicampus University System

Harriet Fishlow

In late 1979, I was asked to develop an undergraduate enrollment projection model for the central administration of the University of California. The level of future enrollments is at the heart of planning at the University of California, as it is at other institutions of higher education. Although technical knowledge is essential in preparing such a crucial planning instrument, creation of an undergraduate enrollment projection model requires much more than demographic training.

The model's assumptions must be acceptable to all parties having important stakes in university planning. These assumptions—and the structure of the model itself—must reflect an understanding of important institutional goals. If the results show that the university may find it difficult to achieve desired goals or, worse, even to maintain its current position, those results must be based on unassailable evidence. In addition, the important audiences for the model must be carefully prepared to receive those results.

The assignment in 1979 was, therefore, both technical and—in the broadest sense of the term—political. It is my belief that most exercises in applied demography involve this dual function.

My experience in developing the undergraduate enrollment projection model makes clear that the best and surest way to gain acceptance for such a project is to involve, right from the model's inception, those audiences important to its development. Not only does early involvement enhance the audiences' comprehension of sometimes esoteric concepts, but it also alerts the demographer to important issues that he or she must consider if the model (or any other demographic planning effort) is to be useful. I perceived three major audiences for this project: (1) the central office administration (which had commissioned it), (2) the campus administrations, and (3) state personnel involved in determining the university's budget. This paper describes how I went about securing the involvement of these critical audiences.

The Institutional Setting

The setting in which I developed the model can perhaps best be described as the home office of a large, quasi-public bureaucracy. Called the Office of the President, this "home office" of the University of California system has as its principal function negotiation with the outside world, primarily for resources. Like any large bureaucracy, the University of California has its own particular culture. An important element of this culture is the tension, or balancing of interests, between highly prestigious "branches" that enjoy substantial independent reputations and the "home office" which is charged with looking after the interests of the institution as a whole. Although the university administration is substantially centralized, it must manage—not command—its constituent parts.

The outside world with which the central administration negotiates is an essentially political one. As a state institution, the University of California is heavily dependent on both the legislature and the governor for its support. Under the state constitution, however, it is guaranteed considerable freedom from state control, and in many important ways the university has been managing its own affairs since its founding in the middle of the nineteenth century. It must answer to the state government in terms of results, but it plots its own course.

The Model's Audiences—A Description

The First Audience: The University's Central Administration

Although the University of California consists of several campuses, by law and tradition it is regarded as one university with a considerable degree of centralization. The central administration (i.e., the Office of the President) negotiates the annual budget for the entire university with the State of California and allocates the funds to the individual campuses. Planned levels of enrollment play a central role in the budget negotiations with the state, both for the annual operating budget and for capital planning. As part of the budget process, the university president must approve enrollment plans for the campuses.

The Second Audience: The Campus Administrations

Despite the centralized nature of the University of California, individual campuses enjoy a good deal of autonomy. The central administration allocates funds to the campuses in large blocks, to be used at the discretion of the chief campus officers—the chancellors. The faculty senate on each campus has primary responsibility for determining the academic program, within the guidelines laid down by the Statewide Academic Senate to which each campus sends representatives. Each campus has its own distinct character, its own traditions, its own loyal alumni, and its own fund-raising programs.

The autonomy of the campuses is due in part to their historical development and in part to faculty insistence on academic freedom. But it is also the product of deliberate planning. The University of California system is so large and diverse that it would be extremely inefficient to try to manage it closely from the center. The central administration delegates a good deal of authority, and much that lies within the prerogatives of the Office of the President is in fact accomplished by an iterative procedure of campus proposals and subsequent negotiation rather than through orders from above.

Enrollments are negotiated by this process, particularly at the undergraduate level. The system of central authority and de facto semiautonomous units, in which both must be party to the planning process, is a familiar arrangement in large bureaucracies. The university, however, has its own flavor as a result of the independent prestige of its constituent parts.

The Third Audience: State Agencies—The Demographic Research Unit

The State of California provides the university's operating and capital budgets, both of which depend in large measure on enrollment projections approved by the president and agreed to by the state. The Office of the President and the State Department of Finance negotiate agreements on levels of enrollment. One critical measure that Department of Finance staff use for reaching agreement on enrollment levels, especially long-range enrollment levels, are projections produced by the demographers in the department's Demographic Research Unit. These demographers thus perform a crucial function in the process of state acceptance of the university's long-range enrollment projections.

The Concerns of the Three Audiences

The Office of the President—Realistic and Campus-Specific Projections

Obviously, the Office of the President has a very considerable interest in producing accurate enrollment projections. While the administration typically hopes for growth—the source of additional funding and facilities—its projections must be as realistic as possible. In order to achieve the most realistic projections, the university tries to include as many crucial factors amenable to quantitative modeling as feasible. In California, one of the most important of these factors (aside from change in the size of the student population) is ethnic distribution. Ethnic diversity in enrollments is also a topic of considerable political interest.

In addition to providing a realistic projection of total undergraduate enrollments for the university, the projection had to be campus-specific. The campuses, each of which has a somewhat different enrollment pool and attractiveness, submit individual enrollment proposals to the Office of the President for approval. Although each campus must conform to assessment guidelines, campus autonomy—considerable and jealously guarded—makes central office enrollment forecasting a matter of some delicacy.

The Campus Administrations—Campus Autonomy

In practice, campuses plan enrollments according to a mix of reasons and then negotiate for approval with the Office of the President. In the late 1970s, most short-term (i.e., for the upcoming budget year) campus enrollment proposals were, at least at the undergraduate level, accepted with little discussion. If a proposed enrollment appeared ill-advised, it was the task of central administration to convince the campus to change. Due to the strong ethos of campus autonomy, however, the Office of the President rarely requested changes—even if there were doubts about the proposed enrollment.

The Demographic Research Unit—Validity

The final audience for the model was the State Department of Finance's Demographic Research Unit. Because the State of California has a profound fiscal interest in the University of California's enrollment plans, the model had to be defensible to the state. Highly competent state demographers, whose principal interest was accuracy, would examine the model's methodology, assumptions, and results. Any substantial divergence from well-known procedures would have to be explained and defended.

Development of the Model

Exploration of the Field

I had learned the principles of demographic projections during graduate training; now I had to apply those principles to an actual problem. The first order of business was to discover what went into the construction of an undergraduate enrollment model. I reviewed a number of enrollment projections that had been produced for individual states and the nation, as well as two done earlier for the University of California. The first university model had been produced seven years earlier with much effort and fanfare but had soon been abandoned. The more recent model, done just prior to my assignment, had been quietly rejected.

My examination of the state and national projections and of the history of the earlier of the two university models provided a warning against complex models, particularly those that require large quantities of data from different sources in an attempt to model reality. I did not then, and do not now, believe that trying to duplicate reality with multitudinous variables yields results worth the trouble and expense. In addition, the more complicated the data requirements, the harder the model is to maintain. In fact, as far as I could determine, what accounted for the fate of the first of the two university models I reviewed was the inability to maintain it.

On the other hand, what happened to the more recent university enrollment model (whose unsatisfactory results appeared to have inspired my assignment) served as a warning that too simple a model would fail to show the mediating effect of university admission and enrollment practices on the enrollment pool. This rejected model simply had applied observed participation rates to projected populations by age and consequently had projected overall declines—including especially sharp declines at the Berkeley campus. Nobody had believed that Berkeley would decline at all because it clearly had surplus demand which the overly simplistic projection had failed to take into account.

Communication with the Audiences

My task, clearly, was to balance simplicity and accuracy. But I needed to do something more: I had to communicate with the audiences. The rejection of the overly simplistic projection revealed the importance of such communication.

As a matter of fact, the ill-fated projection accomplished precisely what it had set out to do—model the effect of demographic changes on the size of the enrollment pool. It had not been intended as a comprehensive enrollment projection model. Although the text accompanying the projection suggested some mitigating influences that would keep Berkeley enrollments above those projected, this crucial material had never been adequately conveyed to the model's audiences. The most dissatisfied of these audiences, and the one most instrumental in rejecting the model, consisted of the campus administrations. They were inherently hostile to projections of decline and needed persuasive evidence in order to accept even the suggestion of such a possibility. They were not about to be convinced by a model, even one of simple demographic effect, that ignored "unmet demand."

Contacting the Audiences

The nature of the task suggested that I begin the process of contacting audiences with the demographers in the State Department of Finance. The originator of the assignment, the administrators in the Office of the President, wanted results; the campus administrators would be interested in a proposed methodology as well as projection results. Before I could propose either a methodology or results, however, I needed to discuss my ideas with people who had experience in such matters. The demographers in the State Department of Finance, producers of the official state population and enrollment projections for both K–12 and higher education, were the ideal consultants.

The State Department of Finance

On the basis that a very large portion of the university's newly enrolling undergraduate students were recent California high school graduates, I had tentatively decided to use high school graduates as a base rather than population by age. The college-age population in California contains many migrants who come seeking work and are not in the university's enrollment pool, and changes in the size of this group—actual or projected—might have little to do with changes in university enrollments. Moreover, the State Department of Education takes an annual census of K–12 students by grade and, at the same time, counts the number of high school graduates for the previous year. Since population figures between censuses are only estimated, school enrollment figures are likely to be more accurate, especially in periods of substantial migration.

The Department of Finance demographers agreed that school enrollments provided a better base for a University of California model, although at that time they used population by age for their projections. Similarly, they agreed with the use of a flow model even though they employed an annual participation rate method. They further suggested that I talk to the enrollment planner at the California State University, who was experimenting with using tenth graders rather than high school graduates as a base. This turned out to be valuable advice because projected tenth graders proved more demographically stable than projected high school graduates. Since most students who are going to drop out do so after the first part of tenth grade (when the annual school census is taken), projecting tenth graders required one less layer of assumption. By following up on the Finance Department's suggestion, I was able to use a better measure for the model.

Campus Administrators

Once I had chosen my demographic base, I could proceed to construct a model. I obtained counts of actual and projected tenth graders from the Department of Finance, and I collected data on new students—by level, campus, and county and year of high school graduation—from university data sources. With Department of Finance concurrence, I developed a method (utilizing projected students in the lower grades) to extend the tenth grade projections beyond the department's ten-year projection period. This extension was important. Projections to the early 1990s showed steady demographic decline in California, but births began to rise sharply in 1974, and it was the 1974 cohort that formed the freshman class of 1992. The extension enabled us to project enrollments to 1998 and thereby pick up future growth.

During this time I held lengthy conversations with campus enrollment planners, describing my methodology and collecting suggestions. Finally, I secured a set of results and sent the figures out to the campus planners for a response. The first run showed potential undergraduate enrollment declines in the 1980s, including steep declines at Berkeley and UCLA. Through subsequent conversations with the planners and inspection of internal data we were able to agree on a decision rule and assumed magnitudes for calculating surplus demand, thereby removing the projected decline at Berkeley and rendering the overall decline much less steep. Although no one was happy with any projected decline, even a temporary one, everyone was aware of the current demographic projections. Everyone understood, moreover, that forecasting no decline in a demographically based projection would be regarded by the public as lacking credibility.

We consistently designated the results as demographic resource documents, thus enabling each campus to produce enrollment plans that described how they intended to maintain steady enrollments. Any departure from pure demographics required a rationale, but it was possible—as long as the argument was a good one. Our attention to the concerns of the campus planners and our incorporation of their suggestions gained their acceptance of what was, in essence, a central office model. I must admit, however, that the demographic fact of future growth (which was totally beyond any demographer's control) probably aided in securing the support of the campus planners.

The University's Central Administration

Aside from wanting enrollment projections by campus for fifteen or so years into the future, the administrators in the Office of the President never specified any concerns they wished to see addressed by the model. I had to deduce their concerns—four in all—from the context in which we were working; subsequent experience has shown me that this is frequently the case when dealing with upper management.

First, I knew the administrators would need to have some reasonably objective standard against which to compare campus long-range enrollment plans. Second, they would want to know which campuses were potentially more vulnerable to demographic change, particularly declines in the college-age population. Third, the administrators would like the model to examine the effect of demographic change in the context of actual university enrollment patterns; these patterns could potentially mediate changes in the enrollment pool in unpredictable ways. Fourth and finally, I deduced an increasing concern among the administrators about the effect on enrollments of the state's changing ethnic distribution.

The shift in ethnic distribution among California's youthful population presented significant potential consequences for the university's undergraduate enrollments because the state's major ethnic groups differed substantially in terms of preparation for college and, therefore, in rates of application and admission. University administrators had been aware of these differences since the late 1970s.

The Master Plan for Higher Education in California gives the University of California the mandate to select students from the top 12.5 percent of the state's public high school graduates and to set entrance requirements for all other California applicants accordingly. In practice, this has meant that a California resident must have at least a B or B+ average in the traditional high school academic subjects in order to gain admission to the University of California. Every several years, the state's higher education coordinating agency samples transcripts to ascertain if the University of California's entrance requirements target the top 12.5 percent (top 33.3 percent for the state university system).

A university-sponsored follow-up to the 1975 sample of transcripts was the first to examine eligibility by ethnicity. The follow-up study to the 1975 examination showed that Black and Hispanic students were only one third as likely as whites to qualify for university admission, while Asian students were twice as eligible as whites. Subsequent eligibility studies included ethnicity from the start and produced essentially the same results through the 1980s. The projected rapid increase in the proportion of Black and Hispanic high school graduates would clearly affect future enrollments since a larger proportion of high school graduates would come from lower-achieving groups.

After consulting with the campus enrollment administrators and the Department of Finance demographers, I added variables that would show the considerable downward effect on future enrollments, even with surplus demand at Berkeley, unless the eligibility figures for Blacks and Hispanics improved.

Acceptance of the Model and Last-Minute Changes

Apparently the concerns I deduced among the administrators in the Office of the President were correct because my model was accepted and used internally for several years. In the fall of 1983, however—just before the first public distribution of the model as part of the January 1984 presentation of an updated undergraduate enrollment plan to the Regents—the administration changed. The new president directed that a fourth run be included, one that showed the effect of improvements in eligibility for Blacks and Hispanics. This presentation marked the beginning of the next stage in the model's development, a stage in which the Office of the President displayed an active interest in the model and its assumptions.

Flexibility in the use of variables became important. The model was converted into menu-driven software for the personal computer I had just been issued, and over time a multitude of optional variables were added. As a consequence, one can now—in addition to many other possibilities—vary eligibility assumptions, explore the effects of regional participation shifts, and store alternative data files. Yet my model still uses just three major data files: (1) projected tenth grade students by county from the State Department of Finance, (2) new students by level from university data files, and (3) public school students by grade and ethnicity.

Conclusion

The University of California's undergraduate enrollment model (it is called the demographic potential model in most public presentations) is the longest running model in the state. Its results are generally accepted by all audiences, and it remains the backbone of long-range undergraduate enrollment planning. In 1988 it was used to justify the need for three new campuses of the University of California, and it will soon be updated again for a new round of projections. I attribute this success to my careful attention to the needs and perceptions of the model's various audiences and to its basic simplicity of design, especially with respect to data requirements.

Discussion Questions

1. If you could question the author, what would you ask to clarify the procedures in this case?

2. Given the stakeholders and their levels of interest, discuss the challenges of working with each particular group.

3. What other groups would you contact to provide insight into school enrollment projection methodologies?

4. Compare and contrast the flow model and annual participation rate method.

5. Evaluate the author's decision to use: a) California high school graduates as a base; b) the annual census of K-12 students as a base; and c) tenth graders as a base.

6. What circumstances beyond the scope of the original projection might lead to change in enrollment demand in California State Universities?

7. What other steps need to be taken in evaluating the base data used for the K-12 projections?

8. How did the author move beyond the demographic data to create a workable model?

9. How could the author have moved from "deducing" the administrators' concerns to encouraging them to state their concerns (beyond the enrollment projections)?

10. Consider the challenges of producing campus-specific projections.

18

Predicting College Enrollment
Results from a Variant of the Life Table

Philip Garcia

The results of population projections by public agencies become political entities whenever they must be sanctioned by governing bodies. Forecasters who find themselves in this political situation usually must decide whether to engage in complex model building or to pursue elementary models that lay audiences are more likely to understand. Not surprisingly—given the widespread perception that policy makers prefer uncomplicated models—most forecasters choose simplicity over complexity.

Public sector projection models tend to employ the following principles:

1. *parsimony*—partition the total population under study into the fewest number of subgroups and keep the arithmetic simple.
2. *naivete*—deem last year's growth rate the best best predictor of next year's growth rate.
3. *moderation*—regardless of observed population trends, presuppose that any demographic changes will stabilize in the very near future.

In most instances, utilizing these principles—i.e., seeking approval for projections by employing easily intelligible assumptions and methods—is an effective strategy. But how persuasive is this strategy in the face of organized opposition or when rival projections are part of the approval process?

This case study examines two sets of rival projections regarding the future demand for college enrollment in California. The first set of projections, mandated by the state legislature, was developed by the California State University (CSU) in the Office of the Chancellor. The alternative set, which would serve as a touchstone, was developed by the State of California's Central Planning Office (CPO, a pseudonym). Although both forecasts were based on modest statistical models that used similar data, they produced markedly different results.

The debate over the rival projections was vigorous. Each side fiercely contested the assumptions and methods of the other. The story of how this dispute was ultimately resolved highlights the benefits of constructing a multifaceted model and the hazards of clinging to the principles of parsimony, naivete, and moderation. The California State Legislature ultimately accepted enrollment projections derived from a model that was far more intricate than either of its predecessors.

Prior to 1991, projections of CSU enrollments were based entirely on the ratio of observed college enrollments to estimates of the college-age population in California. CSU's new projection model, labeled the "student flow model," employed actuarial techniques associated with the demographic life table. It deviated from the previous projection efforts by (1) predicting the influx into state universities of high school graduates and community college students, and (2) simulating the reenrollment behavior of these university students as they made their way toward a baccalaureate degree. The latter innovation made it possible to assess how changes in continuation and graduation rates affected enrollment size.

The following sections relate the development of the student flow model and its output. We begin with a brief synopsis of the political setting from which the mandated projections emerged. Next, we outline the development of the original sets of estimates (CSU's and CPO's) and discuss the reasons for the differences between the two forecasts. It was the evaluation of those differences that served as the impetus for developing the student flow model. We then describe the life table approach and present an illustration using CSU data.

Background

In July 1988, the California legislature included supplementary language in its annual budget requiring each of the three segments of the state's public higher education system—the University of California (UC), the CSU, and the California Community Colleges (CCC)—to develop enrollment projections for fall 1989 through the academic year 2005/06. At this time, postsecondary enrollments were at an all-time high. More than 1.8 million students were enrolled in California's public higher education system in 1987/88: 150,000 at UC's nine sites, 361,000 at CSU's 19 sites, and 1.3 million at CCC's 107 campuses.

Given the political climate of the time, the legislature's requirement implied three issues of public interest. The first issue involved the impending growth of college enrollments. Available projections suggested that the number of new high school graduates would grow from 230,000 to more than 400,000 per year by the end of the 1990s (California Department of Labor 1988). The second issue concerned the lack of educational equity. Afro-Americans, Latinos, and American Indians continued to be underrepresented among the recipients of bachelor's degrees from public colleges and universities in California—despite a statewide commitment to increase the presence of these populations in all areas of higher education. The third and final issue focused on the relationship between degree recipients and the work force. The proportion of occupations requiring a college education was rising, leading to little doubt that the state's higher education system would be challenged to accommodate growing numbers of students.

The First Response

The Population-Participation Model

The CSU's first long-range enrollment plan assumed that it would continue to admit freshmen applicants from the top one-third of their high school graduating classes in California and undergraduate transfer students who had successfully completed an approved lower division curriculum at community colleges. CSU's primary role of conferring bachelor's and master's degrees would remain intact.

Because its basic pool for its new students would stay the same, the CSU's future enrollments would be founded on the observed relationship between enrollments and the age-specific populations of the state's major ethnic groups—whites, Asians, Latinos, and Afro-Americans. For example, in the fall term of 1988, 3,445 Latinos aged 22 were enrolled at the CSU, and the state's population of 22-year-old Latinos was estimated to be 117,574. These figures yield a population-participation rate of 293 per 10,000. By applying this rate to future Latino population estimates, the CSU could produce projected Latino enrollments. At hand were census enumerations, intercensal estimates, and population projections for the period 1970–2020 (California Department of Finance 1988).

To execute its first series of enrollment projections, the CSU took the following steps:

1. Adopted California's gender and age-specific population projections for selected ethnic categories.
2. Calculated ethnic-specific population-participation rates across corresponding gender and age categories for the extant CSU enrollment data.
3. From observed trends, derived future levels of population-participation for each age-specific ethnic subgroup. Specifically, the CSU applied one-half of the average change over the three most recent observations (1986–1988) to projected populations for the next two years, then held each rate constant thereafter. In homage to the principles of naivete and moderation, the CSU assumed college-entry rates would grow for two years and then stabilize.
4. For each age-specific ethnic subgroup having a lower than average population-participation rate, the CSU adjusted the expected rate upward so that by the academic year 2005/06 the rate would equal the expected average.

Figure 18.1 presents a diagram of these steps, with X_{ijk} representing the estimates of each subpopulation , P_{ijk} representing population-participation rates, and

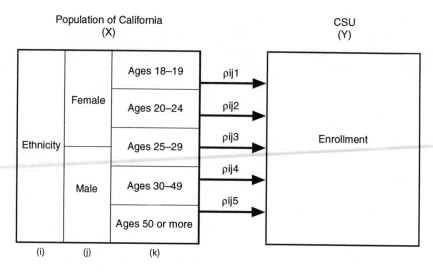

Population of California   CSU
          (X)   (Y)

Figure 18.1—Population-participation model

Y representing the projected enrollment. By all accounts, the model's output was relatively easy to describe and reproduce. In fact, the first three steps were common procedures, practiced (more or less) by other state agencies. The CSU's rationale for the final step (4) was that it reflected the legislature's equity goals.In October 1989, the CSU officially adopted the projection and promptly submitted it to the legislature (CSU 1989). To assess the plan, the legislature obtained an alternative projection from the state's central planning office (CPO). The CPO projection yielded an enrollment figure of 465,700. Close examination of the CSU-CPO projections revealed that the disparity in enrollment figures centered entirely on undergraduates. The reaction from the legislature was swift and concise. How could there be such a sizable difference between the two projections? After all, the difference of 75,600 students was the equivalent of three large campuses.

Procedural Differences

The first step in trying to answer the legislature's question was to compare methodologies. One obvious difference was the way each projection handled ethnicity. The CSU enrollment projection relied on age-specific ethnic participation rates while the CPO projection was based solely on age-specific rates. In other words, the CPO's method assumed that enrollment rates remained the same across all ethnic subgroups and that population growth rates were also equivalent. Historical data indicated, however, that ethnic differences clearly affected trends in both enrollment and population growth.

Despite this important difference, the two rival projections shared important similarities. The CPO projection was based on the assumption that recent trends in population-participation rates would continue for the next several years, begin to moderate, and finally reach a plateau by the end of the century. Those rates were then applied to the same set of expected gender and age-specific population estimates used by the CSU. Both projections, therefore, employed somewhat improved population-participation rates. In addition, both relied heavily on common estimates of California's future population size. In fact, when based on the assumption of constant 1987–1988 population-participation rates, both projections produced essentially the same future enrollments: 435,900 (CSU) VERSUS 426,000 (CPO).

Nonetheless, representatives of the CSU and CPO could not arrive at a compromise projection. At issue: How to incorporate change in participation rates. The CPO argued that the assumption about improved rates should emerge from historical trends. The CSU argued that past experiences alone do not necessarily reflect future direction. Supporting the CSU in this regard were the current enrollment levels which exceeded all prior predictions.

After a thorough briefing regarding the rival procedures, the legislature found itself at an impasse. On the one hand, the projections from the CSU model seemed overly optimistic. On the other hand, the CPO projection model could not answer important questions about the status of the ethnically diverse constituencies in California's higher education system. Moreover, neither projection model could show how improved reenrollment rates affect growth in the total undergraduate population.

The Second Response

The Student Flow Model

In July 1990, the CSU received a second legislative request. The legislature wanted a new set of enrollment projections which would include: (1) an analysis of the trend in college-entry rates for new students from the major ethnic groups within California; and (2) a range of enrollment projections through the academic year 2005/06, utilizing alternative assumptions about whether current upward trends in college-entry rates would continue.

The CSU's projection model could be amended to address both of these issues, but what if the debate turned to another issue—e.g., the impact of changing graduation or attrition rates? It had become clear during the comparison of the CSU and CPO methods that the participation-population model could never yield more than crude results regarding such rates. And changing graduation and attrition rates were expected to be the focus of many future policy discussions.

Data organized around age categories for continuing students mask important differences related to the probability of students reenrolling for a subsequent term and how long it will take to earn a bachelor's degree. Entering freshmen, for example, are more likely to leave the university without a degree than are undergraduate transfer students who come to the university with some college credits. On the other hand, the undergraduate transfer students will spend less time at the university than will the entering freshmen. Both of these situations affect the size of continuing enrollments. Each situation's individual effects, however, are lost within the participation-population model because it does not disaggregate such observations by class level at matriculation.

The Chancellor's staff decided to scrap the population-participation model and proceed on a path that would yield a more realistic representation of how college enrollments emerge. The new model would employ not only the conceptual categories of college-entry rates for new students but also the reenrollment rates and graduation rates for continuing students. In addition, the new model would separate enrollments by the admission track that governs each of the two rates—i.e., entering freshmen and undergraduate transfer students. The CSU was particularly interested in having an accurate portrayal of the incoming community college students because undergraduate transfers account for 60 percent of all new undergraduates.

Figure 18.2 diagrams the conceptual framework for the new forecasting model.

The Chancellor's staff could estimate the student flow model despite its more extensive data requirements. First, historical and projected numbers of high school graduates (X_1) and community college enrollments (X_2) were already part of the statewide educational database. In addition, the CSU (like other institutions of higher education) routinely enumerated entering freshmen (Y_{1a}) and new transfers (Y_{1b}). Therefore, ethnic-specific college-entry rates for first-time freshmen (α_1) could be calculated by dividing the number of new entrants by the number of high school graduates recorded in the previous year. Similarly, ethnic and age-specific transfer rates could equal the ratio of new entrants to community college enrollments (α_2) in the previous year.

Second, a tracking system that monitored continuation (Y_2), withdrawals (W_1), and graduates (W_2) was in place in the CSU. Developed in 1973, it generated the rates at which students left the university (ω_1, ω_2).

With the new student flow model, the CSU was able to complete an expanded version of the information requested by the state legislature. This information included: (1) an analysis of the trend in both college-entry *and continuation* rates for the CSU's first-time freshmen and undergraduate transfers; and (2) a range of enrollment projections through the 2005/06 academic year based on alternative assumptions about whether current upward trends in college-entry *and continuation* rates will persist for the CSU's first-time freshmen and undergraduate transfers.

The staff agreed that the range of enrollment projections would consist of four alternative forecasts. The first would be a baseline projection in which enrollment

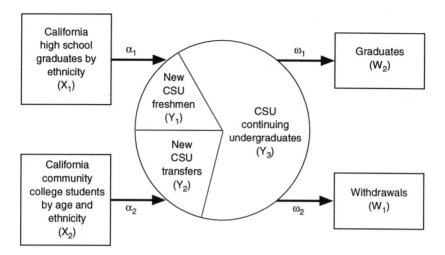

Figure 18.2—The student flow model

growth would be the sole function of the expected growth in the number of high school graduates and community college transfer students. In this first forecast, the CSU continuation rates and college-entry rates would be held constant at levels observed during the 1989/90 college year.

The second alternative forecast would add expected improvements in continuation rates. The third alternative forecast would add expected improvements in freshmen college-entry rates. The fourth alternative forecast would add expected improvements in undergraduate transfer rates.

One major concession would be made to critics of the initial enrollment plan: All assumptions about change would be extrapolated from historical trends. Rising rates, however, would not be halted by arbitrary time constraints; instead, reenrollment rates for continuing students would be limited (if necessary) by national norms for comparable institutions. College-entry rates for new freshmen and transfers would be confined (if necessary) by the experience of CSU subgroups whose rates appeared to have reached a common plateau.

Trends in Continuation Rates

Research studies at the national level have documented the relationship between admissions selectivity and how persistent freshmen are in obtaining a degree. For example, at the lowest end of the selectivity spectrum, senior institutions of higher education that have open-door admissions policies can expect first-year continuation rates in the range of 60 to 65 percent. At the middle of the spectrum, senior institutions that take students only from the top half of their high school classes

Table 18.1   One-Year Continuation Rates for Successive Groups of Entering
CSU First-Time Freshmen from California Schools and CSU
Transfers from California Community Colleges

Fall Term	First-Time Freshmen	CCC Transfers
1979	0.739	0.716
1980	0.748	0.729
1981	0.760	0.737
1982	0.762	0.750
1983	0.767	0.752
1984	0.773	0.758
1985	0.772	0.762
1986	0.775	0.770
1987	0.772	0.772
1988	0.779	0.786

can expect a first-year continuation rate of 75 percent. Senior institutions taking
only from the top 25 percent can expect a first-year continuation rate of 80 to 85
percent. Finally, at the highest end of the spectrum, senior institutions that restrict
admissions to the top 10 percent of a high school graduating class can expect a
first-year continuation rate near 90 percent (Noel et al. 1985, Chapter 1).

The CSU's most recent reenrollment history suggested that its first-year continuation rate had moved steadily upward (see Table 18.1). The observed changes
suggested that first-year continuation rates for both entering freshmen and undergraduate transfers would continue to improve, and the trend lines for each rate indicated that these rates could reach 82 percent by the year 2000. Thus, the staff assumed that first-year continuation rates would increase by approximately four
percentage points over the following twelve years and then remain more or less
stable. As long as the CSU's policy of selecting students from the top third of their
classes remained in effect, this level of improvement—when contrasted with national norms—appeared reasonable.

As a consequence of improved first-year continuation rates, the CSU's eventual graduation rate would be expected to rise from 50 to 60 percent for new
freshmen, and from 60 to 70 percent for new transfer students. The patterns of improvement denoted by these changes served as the basis for the second alternative
projection: growth in enrollment due to improved persistence rates.

Trends in College Entry

Throughout the 1980s, the CSU annual college-entry rates for new freshmen hov-
ered between 9 and 10 percent of the pool of recent high school graduates in California. During the same decade, the CSU college-entry rates for undergraduate
transfers fluctuated between 3.5 and 4.5 percentage points of the state's commu-

nity college student population. If these rates remained constant, the annual enrollment of new freshmen at the CSU would rise from 32,000 to 55,000 by fall 2005; new transfers would grow from 56,000 to about 68,000.

Masked within these apparently stable growth rates, however, were wide variations by ethnicity. For example, in 1984, college-entry rates among Afro-Americans and Latinos were less than 30 percent of the observed norm. By decade's end they were nearly 60 percent. Thus, these two significant subgroups were making considerable progress toward parity in admissions.

In fact, if the current upward trend in college-entry rates among Afro-Americans and Hispanics were to persist for another decade, the annual numbers of new freshmen and transfer students would rise to 60,000 and 75,000, respectively. The staff adopted the college-entry rates associated with these changing figures as the basis for the third and fourth alternative projections: growth in enrollment due to improved freshmen college-entry rates and improved transfer rates.

The Enrollment Life Table: Technical Overview

One problem remained following the establishment of alternative forecasts for college-entry and continuation rates (i.e., change or no change): How to transform those forecasts into a range of enrollment projections? The solution was to call upon a standard tool of actuarial analysis, the so-called "life table."

Used as a demographic tool, the life table traces the lifetimes of a cohort of individuals all born in the same year. The life table serves as the basis for studying population characteristics (e.g., natural increase, the difference between births and deaths). In a student flow study, the life table treats a new student (freshman or transfer) as a birth, the years enrolled as an individual's age, and graduation as death.

Implementing the life table model required a complete enumeration of incoming students by admission basis (i.e., first-time freshmen or undergraduate transfers). It also necessitated longitudinal data documenting student survival from first attendance to final departure from campus.

Once the life table was able to summarize the flow of students through the system, it became possible to describe the enrollment status of students at different stages of their respective careers. The model also could be adapted to portray changes in response to the influx of new entrants and the changes in survival rates.

Functions of the Enrollment Life Table

The CSU life tables summarize enrollment survival over a twelve-year span, with each year representing fall-to-fall intervals. In appearance, the life table is a matrix consisting of rows identified by college year and columns designating enrollment functions. The first college year of attendance has an assigned value of zero, and the last year of attendance has an assigned value of eleven. As a result, each row indicates the number of years since the first year of college attendance. The last row is a collapsed category representing observations of events that took eleven years or more. The loss of precision from aggregating observations is nominal; historical data suggest that 98.8 percent of all CSU baccalaureate recipients earn their degrees within twelve years.

Values for the college year also may represent dates of enrollment (e.g., the 1978/79 college year). This is a useful practice when life table functions represent future enrollment outcomes. In the enrollment life table, the subscript x' represents dates.

The enrollment life table, with two decrements, begins with six primary functions for each observed year (x): (l_x), (d'_x), and (d''_x) are the numbers who enrolled, graduated, or withdrew, respectively. (P_x), (Q'_x), and (Q''_x) are the corresponding proportions. The summary expression for the observed data is

$$l_{x+1} = l_x - d'_x - d''_x$$

And the summary expression for all three proportions is

$$P_x = 1 - Q'_x - Q''_x$$

Table 18.2 defines the functions of the enrollment life table.

A complete explanation of the basic life table functions and their applications can be found in *The Methods and Materials of Demography* (Shryock and Siegel 1973). An alternative example of the life table with two decrements can be found in *Demographic Techniques* (Pollard et al. 1974).

An Illustration of the Enrollment Life Table

Table 18.3 summarizes survival for first-time freshmen who entered the CSU in 1978/79. This partial view of the life table reveals how the multiple-decrement model can describe the enrollment history of an incoming group of new students.

Starting with the l_x, 25,311 first-time freshmen entered the CSU during the 1978/79 college year. Naturally, enrollments for the 1978 cohort declined each year. For the next three years, attrition successively reduced the size of the continuing student population to 18,755 (l_1) by fall 1979, 15,698 (l_2) by fall 1980, and 14,426 (l_3) by fall 1981.

During the 1981/82 academic year, the original 1978 enrollments were reduced by both attrition and graduation. Those leaving the CSU without a degree numbered 1,399 (d'_3) while 2,265 left the undergraduate ranks (d''_3) by earning their bachelor's degree. The cohort's fifth year, 1982/83, was the modal year for degrees conferred, with 5,058 graduates (d''_4). Except for the exit year, the fifth year was also the interval with the lowest "conditional probability" for reenrollment in the subsequent fall term $(P_x = 0.448)$.

In fall 1983, a net number of 285 former withdrawals (stopouts) reentered the CSU to continue their pursuit of an undergraduate degree. This net gain is ex-

Table 18.2. The Six Basic Functions of the Enrollment Life Table

---

l_x At year 0, this is the number of students who enroll as a new cohort of students. Thereafter, it is the number of survivors at the start of the year x.

d'_x This is the number of students who did not survive to the subsequent college year.

For example, values for $d'x_{+1}$ represent the number of students who left the university after completing year x but before the commencement of the year $x+2$. Withdrawing from college, however, is not a terminal event. Students who have withdrawn may reenter the university at a later date. For some x-values, therefore, d'_x may represent the net number of withdrawals (i.e., withdrawal plus reentry students).

d''_x Entries for d''_x represent numbers of students who earned their undergraduate degree within each college year.

For example, d''_{x+3} equals the number of students who attain their degree during the fourth year of enrollment. Like the values for d'_x, the values for d''_x represent numbers of students who are no longer enrolled as undergraduates.

P_x This enrollment ratio between two adjacent college years.

$$P_x = l_{x+1} + l_x$$

If the analogy between enrollment-or-graduation and life-or-death were perfect, the proportions P_x would be a conditional probability specifying the odds of being enrolled in year $x+1$, given prior enrollment in the previous year x.

Q'_x This is the proportion of l_x who did not survive to the next year.

$$Q'_x = d'_x + l_x$$

Q''_x This is the proportion l_x who earned a bachelor's degree in year x.

$$Q''_x = d''_x + l_x$$

---

pressed as a minus value in the d'_x column and a minus proportion in the Q'_x column.

Finally, by fall 1989, only 280 of the original cohort were still enrolled, and by the end of the academic year all had either earned a degree or left the university without a degree (as postulated by the model).

Table 18.3 Continuation and Graduation for CSU First-Time Freshmen: 1978–79 Cohort

| Student Year | Proportion | | | For 25,311 Students Enrolled | | | College Year |
| | Continued as undergraduate | Did not continue as undergraduate | Earned a CSU bachelor's degree | At year x still enrolled at CSU without earning a bachelor's degree | Left CSU at year x without earning a bachelor's degree | Earned a CSU bachelor's degree at year x | |
x	P_x	Q'_x	Q''_x	l_x	d'_x	d''_x	x'
0	0.741	0.259	0.000	25,311	5,652	0	1978–79
1	0.837	0.163	0.000	18,755	3,057	0	1979–80
2	0.919	0.081	0.000	15,698	1,272	0	1980–81
3	0.746	0.096	0.157	14,426	1,399	2,265	1981–82
4	0.448	0.082	0.470	10,762	883	5,058	1882–83
5	0.494	−0.059	0.565	4,821	−285	2,724	1983–84
6	0.596	−0.090	0.493	2,382	−212	1,174	1984–85
7	0.709	−0.127	0.418	1,420	−181	594	1985–86
8	0.741	−0.109	0.368	1,007	−110	371	1986–87
9	0.775	−0.151	0.376	746	−112	280	1987–88
10	0.485	0.054	0.461	578	32	266	1988–89
11		0.050	0.950	280	14	266	1989–90

Source: Garcia (1991).

Functions of the Stationary Population

In the standard life table, estimates of the average population size during the entire year are derived from three additional functions associated with stationary populations—i.e., those populations in which total persons are determined by a constant number of equal births and equal deaths. In the case of enrollments, the stationary population implies no growth in the number of new entries (either freshmen or transfer students) and invariable exit rates (either graduation or withdrawal).

The three additional functions that complete the enrollment life table are L_x, T_x, e_x. Table 18.4 defines these functions.

Table 18.5 provides estimates of the stationary population of enrollees implicit in the life table displayed in Table 18.3.

Table 18.3 reveals that fully 25,311 (l_0) first-time freshmen enrolled at the start of fall 1978, year o. In fall 1979, the number who reenrolled amounted to 18,755 (l_1). If the 6,556 who left the CSU did so uniformly throughout the year, then the likely number of new students enrolled at anytime during the year o is equal to:

$$L_0 = (l_0 + l_1) \div 2 = 22,033$$

This calculation (specified in Table 18.4), however, is incorrect for CSU undergraduate enrollments. Two-thirds of the entering freshmen who eventually leave CSU, with or without having received a bachelor's degree, leave between spring and fall terms. To compensate for the uneven distribution of exits (and entries), the equality for L_x was modified to reflect actual term-to-term student flow. The adjusted expression for CSU first-time freshmen is:

$$L_x = .55\, l_x + .45\, l_{x+1}$$

For most applications we expect values of L_x to fall between

$$L_x = .5\, l_x + .5\, l_{x+1}$$

and

$$L_x = .7\, l_x + .3\, l_{x+1}$$

In the CSU example, L_0 is equal to 22,361, the first figure of the L_x column in Table 18.5.

How many students are still enrolled eleven years after their first year of attendance? The T_x column of the life table answers that question. In this example, the answer would be either T_{11} or L_{11}. Both represent the 154 students still enrolled during the year as undergraduates eleven years or more after first entering the university.

T_{10} is equal to the 598 students still enrolled who have completed *at least* ten years of attendance. T_9 is equal to the 1,268 students still enrolled who have completed *at least* nine years of attendance. T_0 is equal to the *total* enrollment implied from an annual influx of l_0 new students and a given set of survivor rates. In our

Table 18.4   The Functions of a Stationary Population

L_x This is the average number of students enrolled during the x and $x+1$ time frame. Therefore, L_x is not equal to l_x. It is, however, dependent on values of l_x.

[See 4a]

T_x This is the number of students who are still enrolled after x years have elapsed since they first entered college.

$$T_{11} = L_{11}$$
$$T_{10} = T_{11} + L_{10}$$
$$T_9 = T_{10} + L_9$$

and

$$T_0 = (L_x) + (L_x+1) + (L_x+2) + (L_x+3) + \dots (L_x+_{11})$$

Values of T_x also indicate the number of person-years of attendance experienced by a cohort of l_x students.

e_x This is the average number of future years of school attendance that a student who has already completed x years can anticipate.

Table 18.5   Stationary Population for CSU First-Time Freshmen: 1978–79 Cohort

	Stationary population for 25,311 students enrolled			
Student Year	Year x	Year x and over	Average before graduation or leaving without earning a bachelor's degree	College Year
x	L_x	T_x	e_x	x'
0	22,361	84,796	3.35	1978–79
1	17,379	62,435	3.33	1979–80
2	15,126	45,056	2.87	1980–81
3	12,777	29,930	2.08	1981–82
4	8,089	17,153	1.59	1982–83
5	3,723	9,064	1.88	1983–84
6	1,949	5,341	2.24	1984–85
7	1,234	3,392	2.39	1986–87
8	890	2,158	2.14	1987–88
9	670	1,268	1.70	1988–89
10	444	598	1.03	1989–90
11	154	154	0.55	1990–91

Source: Garcia (1991).

example of the complete life table (Tables 18.3 and 18.5), therefore, an annual influx of 25,311 first-time freshmen (regular admits) supports a stationary, or *average annual,* population of 84,796 students.

As Table 18.4 indicates, values of T_x indicate not only the number of enrolled students who have completed exactly x years and over but also the total number of person-years of attendance experienced by a cohort of l_x students. Again, from the complete life table example, one expects that 25,311 new students will produce 84,796 years of attendance during their academic careers. It follows, therefore, that the equality for the average number of future years of attendance is equal to

$$e_x = T_x \div l_x$$

To illustrate, e_0 in our example is equal to

$$3.35 = 84,796 \div 25,311$$

In other words, the average new freshman could expect to have 3.35 years of attendance before leaving the university. Likewise, students who survived their first year at the CSU could expect future years of attendance equal to

$$e_1 = T_1 \div l_1$$

or

$$3.33 = 62,435 \div 17,379$$

These students are expected to attend an *additional* 3.33 years. Altogether, therefore, these first-year survivors are expected to attend 4.33 years at the CSU before leaving with or without a bachelor's degree.

Consequently, another advantage of the life table model over the population-participation model is that the life table model can inform us about the expected life span of students at the university. If one manipulates columns d''_x and x, one can make the life table yield both a graduation rate—

$$\sum_{0}^{11} d''_x \div l_0$$

—and an estimate for average-time-to-degree:

$$\left[\sum_{0}^{11} (d''_x)(x + .55) \right] \div \sum_{0}^{11} d''_x$$

Projecting Enrollments from Values of T_x and L_x

Under a restrictive set of assumptions, the functions of the stationary population can be used to answer some questions about future enrollments. For instance, what would be the projection of future undergraduates at the CSU in the academic year 2005/06 if new enrollments were confined to first-time freshmen and the admission goal was a stationary population? As implied above, it would be the value for T_0, or 84,796 students. In this instance, administrators would strive each year to admit new students equal in number to the count of actual leavers

$$[i.e., \; l_0 = \sum (d'_x + d''_x) \,].$$

Under this scenario, therefore, only one complete life table is necessary to generate an informed forecast.

Naturally, when the numbers of new students and the rates of continuing students are not expected to remain constant, the process for generating projections will have more steps. First, individual life tables must be constructed for each interim year between the last observation date and the final projection date. In order to incorporate expected growth, new values for l_0 must be inserted sequentially into the subsequent life tables. Next, new proportions for (P_x), (Q'_x), and (Q''_x) must be inserted sequentially into the life tables to reflect expected changes in continuation. Then new values for the remaining six functions must be recalculated. Finally, L_x values must be appropriately summed across life tables to obtain the desired projection.

For example, the sum of the following values from their corresponding life tables would yield the expected number of continuing enrollments for the academic year 2005/06:

L_1 for x'= 2004/05
L_2 for x' = 2003/04
L_3 for x' = 2002/03
L_4 for x' = 2001/02
L_5 for x' = 2000/01
L_6 for x' = 1999/00
L_7 for x' = 1998/99
L_8 for x' = 1997/98
L_9 for x' = 1996/97
L_{10} for x' = 1995/96
L_{11} for x' = 1994/95

Adding the expected number of new entrants for 2005/06 to the sum of the L_x values above would complete the college-year projection. This entire process mirrors the "component method," a procedure demographers use. In the component method, demographers use annual registration of births and deaths along with future estimates of these components to adjust census populations in order to obtain postcensal projections.

The Final Estimates

The new range of CSU enrollment projections were completed and resubmitted to the legislature in August 1990. The four alternative projections, presented in Table 18.6, reveal the following changes. First, enrollment is expected to grow by 116,600 students due to growth in California's population. Second, the university's ability to retain and graduate more students from all ethnic groups is expected to contribute 19,600 more students. Third, higher college-going rates among high school graduates as new first-time freshmen are expected to increase the enrollment rolls by 19,200 students. Fourth and finally, improved transfer rates among community college enrollments is expected to result in 10,600 more students.

In other words, current CSU enrollment is expected to grow by 32.3 percent over the next fifteen years, primarily due to population growth. In addition, the CSU enrollment is expected to grow by another 13.6 percent if improvements continue in the educational pipeline leading to the CSU and in the student persistence to graduation.

For us, these results confirmed our view about how ineffectual the population-participation model was for projecting enrollments more than a few years into the future. In contrast to the life table model, the population-participation model is prone to underestimate the impact of both population growth and prolonged changes in participation rates.

In retrospect, two of the most positive outcomes resulting from enumerating the life table were (1) the ability to show all concerned how changes in continuation patterns can significantly affect enrollment growth; and (2) the revelation that changes in the freshmen/transfers mix among new students can alter enrollment forecasts because the average CSU freshman stays on campus one more year than the average CSU transfer student (see appendices).

The initial reaction to the revised projections outside the university was articulated by the California Postsecondary Education Commission (1991), a review arm of the legislature: "The (California) State University has done excellent work in revising its undergraduate enrollment projections. The new enrollment projection model ... should be commended."

Thus, the move away from a simple arithmetic model (whose steps produced goodness-of-fit for recent historical data) to a model conceptually linked to the phenomenon under study produced a decisive victory in at least one political battle.

Table 18.6   Components of Increased Enrollment Demand CSU Projections for
2005–06

Component	Enrollment Demand	Net Increase	Percent Increase
1987–88 enrollment	361,300		
Population growth	477,900	116,600	32.3
Growth in persistence rates	497,500	19,600	5.4
Improved freshman participation rates	516,700	19,200	5.3
Improved transfer rates	527,300	10,600	2.9
Total		166,000	45.9

Source: Adapted from Garcia (1991).

Discussion Questions

1. What difficulties might there be in communicating the results of life table analysis to the stakeholder audience?

2. Describe the assumptions made in the population-participation rates used in the execution of the projections.

3. What was the rationale for the second legislative request for new enrollment projections?

4. Explain how the second set of projections incorporates the change in ethnic distribution of college students.

References

California State University. 1989. *The 1989 CSU Growth Plan for 1990–2005 Growth and Diversity: Meeting the Challenge.* Long Beach: The California State University, Office of the Chancellor.

California Department of Finance. *California Public K–12 Enrollment Projections by Ethnicity, 1988 Series.* Sacramento: Demographic Research Unit.

Garcia, Philip. 1991. *Projections of Enrollment Demand: 1990 to 2005.* Long Beach: The California State University, Office of the Chancellor.

Noel, Lee R., Randi Levitz, and Diane Saluri. 1985. *Increasing Student Retention.* San Francisco: Jossey-Bass Publisher.

Pollard, A.H., Frahat Yusuf, and G.N. Pollard. 1974. *Demographic Techniques.* Sydney: Pergamon Press.

Shryock, H.S., and J.S. Siegel. 1973. *The Methods and Materials of Demography.* Washington, D.C.: U.S. Government Printing Office.

Update on Long-Range Planning Activities: Report of the Executive Director. 1991. Commission Report 91-16. Sacramento: California Postsecondary Education Commission .

Appendix 18.1 Enrollment Life Table CSU First-Time Freshmen: 1978–79 Cohort

	Proportion			For 25,311 Students enrolled			Stationary Population of Enrolled Students			
Student Year	Reenrolled as under-graduate	Did not reenroll as under-graduate	Earned a CSU bachelor's degree	At year x still enrolled at CSU without earning a bachelor's degree	Left CSU at year x without earning a bachelor's degree	Earned a CSU bachelor's degree at year x	Year x	Year x and over	Average years left before graduation or leaving without earning a bachelor's degree	College Year
x	P_x	Q_x	Q''_x	l_x	d'_x	d''_x	L_x	T_x	e_x	x'
0	0.741	0.259	0.000	25,311	5,652	0	22,361	84,796	3.35	1978–79
1	0.837	0.163	0.000	18,755	3,057	0	17,379	62,435	3.33	1979–80
2	0.919	0.081	0.000	15,698	1,272	0	15,126	45,056	2.87	1980–81
3	0.746	0.096	0.157	14,426	1,399	2,265	12,777	29,930	2.08	1981–82
4	0.448	0.082	0.470	10,762	883	5,058	8,089	17,153	1.59	1982–83
5	0.494	−0.059	0.565	4,821	−285	2,724	3,723	9,064	1.88	1983–84
6	0.596	−0.090	0.493	2,382	−212	1,174	1,949	5,341	2.24	1984–85
7	0.709	−0.127	0.418	1,420	−181	594	1,234	3,392	2.39	1985–86
8	0.741	−0.109	0.368	1,007	−110	371	890	2,158	2.14	1986–87
9	0.775	−0.151	0.376	746	−112	280	670	1,268	1.70	1987–88
10	0.485	0.054	0.461	578	32	266	444	598	1.03	1988–89
11		0.050	.950	280	14	266	154	154	0.55	1989–90

Source: Garcia (1991).

NOTES: (1) Eventual graduation rate = 514 per 1,000. (2) Average time to degree = 5.49 years.

Appendix 18.2 Enrollment Life Table CSU Undergraduate Transfers: 1978–79 Cohort

Student Year	Proportion			For 50,113 Students Enrolled			Stationary Population of Enrolled Students			
	Reenrolled as undergraduate	Did not reenroll as undergraduate	Earned a CSU bachelor's degree	At year x still enrolled at CSU without earning a bachelor's degree	Left CSU at year x without earning a bachelor's degree	Earned a CSU bachelor's degree at year x	Year x	Year x and over	Average years left before graduation or leaving without earning a bachelor's degree	College Year
x	P_x	Q'_x	Q''_x	l_x	d'_x	d''_x	L_x	T_x	e_x	x'
0	0.717	0.270	0.013	50,113	13,531	651	45,149	113,652	2.27	1978–79
1	0.620	0.170	0.210	35,931	6,108	7,546	31,152	68,503	1.91	1979–80
2	0.438	0.085	0.477	22,277	1,894	10,626	17,895	37,351	1.68	1980–81
3	0.485	-0.017	0.532	9,757	-166	5,191	7,998	19,456	1.99	1981–82
4	0.558	-0.112	0.554	4,732	-530	2,622	4,000	11,458	2.42	1982–83
5	0.695	-0.516	0.821	2,640	-1,362	2,167	2,358	7,458	2.83	1983–84
6	0.706	0.108	0.186	1,835	198	341	1,646	5,100	2.78	1984–85
7	0.749	-0.311	0.562	1,296	-403	728	1,182	3,454	2.67	1985–86
8	0.844	-0.418	0.574	971	-406	557	918	2,272	2.34	1986–87
9	0.852	-0.403	0.551	820	-331	452	778	1,354	1.65	1987–88
10	0.173	0.038	0.789	699	26	552	497	576	1.82	1988–89
11	0.000	0.000	1.000	121	0	121	79	79	0.65	1989–90

Source: Garcia (1992).

NOTES: (1) Eventual graduation rate = 630 per 1,000. (2) Average time to degree = 3.45 years.

19

Planning for Children's
Residential Care

Nancy Dunton

Applied demographers who work for state and local governments collaborate with policy and program specialists in a variety of ways. One common assignment involves producing specialty projections for use in program planning. This case study, which describes the production and use of a set of projections for residential care, illustrates (1) the need for collaborating with specialists who are not demographers, (2) a typical set of difficulties demographers encounter when using administrative data, and (3) the politics of integrating demographic information into decision-making processes.

The Problem

The residential care system for children in New York State is one of the largest and most highly differentiated of all such systems in the United States. In 1985, the system was serving approximately 40,000 children through eight separate agencies—each offering a variety of residential programs to meet the diverse needs of these children.[1]

Although each of the eight agencies has a distinct formal mission to guide the development of its programs, in practice the boundaries among programs of different agencies are not always well defined. Particularly at the local level the distinction between one program and another may not be clear, either in terms of the services offered or the characteristics of the children served (New York State Council on Children and Families 1984). Even at the state level the eight agencies do not operate independently, with changes in one agency's programs sure to affect those of other agencies. For example, changes in one agency's funding streams, intake procedures, or program closings will invariably create a change in demand for another agency's programs.

Despite these commonalties and connections, agencies providing residential care traditionally conducted program planning independently of each other. As a result, the individual budget examiners for the eight agencies had no way of knowing whether requests for new programs were warranted or whether existing programs provided by another agency were sufficient. In this era of scarce resources, it had become increasingly important that future policy development and program planning for the children's residential care system proceed from a comprehensive statewide perspective.

In 1983, the State Division of the Budget expressed its interest in finding a way to consolidate agency assessment of the need for children's residential care. The governor responded by assigning the New York State Council on Children and Families (Council) the task of developing a comprehensive statewide plan for children's residential care. This plan—the core of which was to consist of a set of comprehensive statewide projections—was to be used as a guide in developing children's residential care programs. The plan's projections, in conjunction with its goals and objectives, were intended to provide a rational data-based mechanism for decision-making.

Institutional Context

The Council, an agency within the executive department of the government of New York State, has the responsibility for interagency coordination of children and family issues. The commissioners and directors of the fourteen state agencies that provide services to children, youth, and their families make up the Council's constituent members.

Within the Council two bureaus shared joint responsibility for developing the comprehensive plan. The Research Bureau had the lead responsibility for developing interagency projections of the need for children's residential care. The Policy Bureau had the lead responsibility for developing comprehensive interagency goals and objectives. The production of a plan in which the goals were consistent with the projections depended, therefore, on these two bureaus collaborating successfully. Since this project represented the Council's first interbureau effort, it required the invention of project management procedures designed to maximize consistency.

Early in the project, the Council established an Interagency Steering Committee. Committee members—representatives from the eight agencies that provide residential care and from the Division of the Budget—possessed high levels of authority and expertise within their respective agencies, each being at the associate commissioner or division director level. Formally, the Committee's role was to provide advice and guidance on all activities relating to the development and use of the plan. Informally, Committee members were instrumental in fulfilling two essential functions: (1) identifying policy and program specialists for interviews, and (2) facilitating access to each agency's data system on residential care.

Project Strategy

Changing the way in which residential care planning is conducted must be an incremental process. Agencies are invested in the programs, many of which have taken the agencies years to develop and which embody staff members' professional opinions concerning design and operation. In addition, the programs typically involve substantial budgets and frequently entail a web of contracts with local providers. The Interagency Steering Committee provided the agencies with an opportunity to commit themselves to—and influence—changes in the planning process that would affect these programs.

The residential care projections would be put to use by (1) the Interagency Steering Committee in developing system goals and objectives, (2) individual agencies as guidelines in preparing annual budget requests and in developing their own program models, and (3) the Division of the Budget in making funding decisions consistent with the comprehensive plan. The interagency plan would provide the Division of the Budget with a framework within which it would be possible to assess the need for new projects and to reconcile competing requests for apparently similar projects.

Demographic Perspective

Prior to the development of these interagency projections, each agency had used a different method of forecasting the need for services. The agencies typically included their projections in five-year plans and used them in making their annual budget requests. Although the agencies utilized a variety of methods in making these forecasts of future need, many based their projections on admissions data.

Use of admissions data as an indicator, however, had at least two serious drawbacks. First, it did not—in the absence of information on length of stay—indicate load on the system. And second, plans and budget requests were usually based on numbers of admissions rather than on admission rates. The failure to account for changes in population size had led to some costly errors. In at least one case, for example, the Division of the Budget had granted approval for capital construction of a new facility for juvenile delinquents on the basis of numbers of admissions just as the baby boom was aging out of the teenage years. As a result, the Division for Youth constructed an unneeded facility.

Such practical lessons convinced many planners—as well as the Division of the Budget—that they needed demographically-based projections. When the comprehensive planning project was established, therefore, a demographer was included among the principal staffing items.

An interagency, demographically-based set of projections of residential care utilization would provide a common framework for decision-making by the individual agencies and by the Division of the Budget. Each agency would continue to prepare its own specific plan while the interagency plan would establish the overall system's direction for development or retrenchment.

Analytic Design: Defining "Need"

Although the projections of residential care utilization were clearly fundamental to the plan's development, the "need" for care turned out to be a very difficult concept to measure. Children in residential care in New York State suffer from a wide variety of problems: mental illness, developmental disabilities, health problems, as well as abuse, neglect, and abandonment. Estimates were available regarding the prevalence of some of these problems but not all of them.

Furthermore, the available prevalence estimates were of limited value for the following reasons:

1. They were frequently based only on the noninstitutionalized population. In almost all cases, moreover, they lacked information as to whether the severity of the condition indicated a need for residential services.
2. They were, in many instances, not specific to the children and youth population.
3. They were usually based on national surveys and, therefore, provided no reliable data on the population in New York State.
4. Most importantly, previous research into the reasons for children being placed in residential care (New York State Council on Children and Families 1985) revealed that while a child's problem contributes to the probability of placement, it is the family's inability to care for the child that actually determines whether a residential placement will occur. Such a finding, of course, presents a huge obstacle to assessing the "need" for residential care on the basis of prevalence estimates.

Unlike some prevalence estimates, utilization data were readily available. Although it is commonly believed that such data represent only the demand for services, they actually reflect the intersection of supply and demand. Basing projections on the historical trend in the rate of residential care assumes that the previous pattern of supply and demand will continue. This methodology has been shown to result in relatively accurate projections for the near future (i.e., three years) when supply and demand are relatively stable. In situations where children's residential care is in a state of transition, where there is a turnaround in trend, or where the pace of change is relatively rapid, however, using historical trends to project the future use of residential care may result in inaccurate projections (Shryock and Siegel 1975).

Because (1) there had been a rather gradual decline in New York State's use of residential care over the past eight years, and (2) there were few alternative sources of data, we obviously decided to use historical utilization as the basis for our projections. We found it continuously necessary, however, to reiterate to the Steering Committee that the projections were of the "utilization" of residential care and not of the "need" for such care.

Analytic Design: Data Acquisition

In many ways, the applied research lesson that emerged from this project revolved less around the selection of a projection technique than around such data issues as the appropriate use of administrative data sets and establishing data comparability among a variety of sources. Before they can develop any applied projections, demographers must make a series of decisions regarding the projection characteristics. The characteristics that typically require decisions include such details as age categories, geographic units, date of data collection, and number of years on which to base the historical trend. In this project, most of the decisions were relatively straightforward, although the implementation of decisions was complicated by the need for using eight different data systems. What were not straightforward at all, however, were several decisions that arose while learning enough about the eight agencies' data systems to achieve comparability. These unanticipated, rather thorny issues included the definitions of "child" and "in care," the creation of program categories, and the establishment of problem types.

All of the decisions regarding projection characteristics were subject to review and approval by the Interagency Steering Committee. As it turned out, obtaining such approval proved to be one of the most difficult parts of this project. Although the Steering Committee's advice was not only valuable but necessary—given that the projections were for their use and therefore had to be programmatically relevant—it fell to the researchers to educate the Steering Committee in the art of making projections so that their recommendations would fall within the framework of the possible and the desirable. It also became the task of the researchers to arbitrate among Committee members whose real and perceived differences reflected the stakes they and their agencies had in the outcomes of these decisions.

Standard Decisions

Council staff had decided that it was necessary to construct historical age-specific utilization rates in order to enhance the accuracy of the projections. The Steering Committee, however, displayed very little interest in what age categories were selected. We chose categories that corresponded roughly to children's life-cycle stages and to policy guidelines regarding age-appropriate placement of children into specific types of care. The four categories we selected were birth to 5, 6 to 13,

14 to 17, and 18 to 20.[2] Although we used these age categories in computing our projections, we did not publish age-specific results, thereby reducing the amount of detail that policy makers needed to digest.

We found that obtaining consistent age information from the agencies was not a straightforward task. Some agencies could provide only very broad age categories while others had single years of age. We distributed the data from agencies lacking sufficient detail for our categories according to the most relevant standard available. In most cases, we obtained age detail either from a special study or from a year prior to our period of interest. When this was not possible, we distributed the program-specific population according to the total residential-care population's age distribution.

The Steering Committee was much more interested in having projections produced for various areas of the state. Initially, Committee members thought that it would be best to have projections for each county, but we were able to convince them that such projections were impractical given the small number of children in care in the majority of counties. Therefore, the Committee chose to have projections for regions of the state. Unfortunately, however, only two agencies had matching regional boundaries. Council staff thereupon developed interagency regions that maximized the overlap among all eight sets of agency regions. With little further discussion, the Steering Committee accepted these regions for interagency planning purposes.

Since the agencies' data systems did not recognize these interagency regions, we collected data by county and then aggregated it into the regional definitions. We requested data by the child's county of origin—which, while an apparently simple concept, proved different in each agency. Some agencies retained an identifier for the county where the child entered care, other agencies identified the county paying for the care, and still other agencies had the county where the parents were currently living. One agency, in fact, did not maintain an indicator of the child's county of origin at all; it simply had the county of placement. Since we had no way to reconcile these different definitions, we had no choice but to use whatever data were available.

We decided to collect data for a single date each year: March 31. We chose this as the facility census date (with little discussion or input from the Steering Committee) because it is a relatively average day. It occurs during the school year (the modal situation for residential care), it corresponds with the end of the state's fiscal year, and it coincides with the date of the State Data Center's population projections (used as estimates for rate construction).

Only one of the eight agencies—the State Education Department (SED)—could not provide census counts for March 31. SED, which operates a variety of special schools for the developmentally disabled and for the blind and deaf, did have data in the form of fall enrollments. Fortunately, from a data collection point of view, the average length of stay in a SED school is several years. Therefore, fall enrollments (usually finalized sometime during November) are probably very representative of a March 31 census count.

The Steering Committee showed little concern regarding the length of the historical period used to set the trend for projections. It seemed appropriate to us to look at trends since 1978 because in that year the Department of Social Services (DSS) implemented a law creating new regulations promoting prevention of foster care placement and short lengths of stay. This was a turning point because DSS foster care accounted for 75 percent of all residential placements. Conveniently, most agencies' data systems went back to 1978, and we were able to make estimates for occasional lapses in data series by interpolating between adjacent years.

Unanticipated Decisions

The Steering Committee discussed three issues related to the question: "Who is a 'child'?" (i.e., Who should be included in the utilization counts?). The first issue concerned the fact that most of the agencies have different maximum ages—16 for some, 18 for others—at which they will accept a child into care. Once they admit a child, however, some agencies will retain that young person through his or her early twenties. Thus, the maximum age for care can be quite variable.

The second issue involved the policy of one agency, the Office of Mental Retardation and Development Disabilities, not to recognize the concept of "child" or to plan services specifically for children but rather to provide developmentally-appropriate services for all its clients. The third issue, finally, dealt with the fact that some agencies maintain children's wards or facilities while others mix children in with the general population. In some instances, children's facilities contain adults.

The Steering Committee eventually answered the question of who should be included in the utilization counts by including anyone present in a children's ward or facility as well as all those persons in care who had not yet reached the age of 22.

Although utilization of residential services was intended to cover children who were in care as of the census date, nearly every agency defined "in care" differently. In a formal sense, this term refers to a reimbursement criterion: Children who meet certain residency requirements are regarded as "in care" and thus will have their per diem costs paid. Agencies allow a child to be absent for a certain length of time without being "out of care." For example, a child may be out of residence on a home visit or trial discharge for up to a week or on a medical leave for up to two weeks without agencies taking him or her off the rolls. Since it frequently takes another week for the local provider to process the paperwork on an absence of unusual length, the Steering Committee decided to count as "in care" all children who were absent less than two weeks for general reasons and less than three weeks for medical reasons.

All of the participants in this project saw clearly that projections of residential care would be more valuable if they were made for specific types of care rather than merely for total usage. This was an important distinction because the use of family care, for example, would not be interchangeable with the use of institutional care, but family care managed by foster care agencies could be more easily interchanged with family care managed by a mental hygiene agency. With the eight agencies operating or licensing nearly three dozen different residential care program types for children and youth, however, Committee members found little agreement on how these program types should be allocated among categories of care. While they agreed that family care was distinct from congregate care, they debated at length whether there should be one, two, or three categories of congregate care. They eventually resolved their differences by identifying the dimensions along which programs could be assessed—i.e., the intensity of services provided and the degree of integration with the community. As a consequence of this strategy, the Steering Committee decided that there would be three levels of care: family care, community-based group care, and noncommunity-based group care.

Within each of these levels of care, the Steering Committee also requested projections for utilization by children with different types of problems. While such projections seemed intuitively desirable, we urged the Steering Committee to exercise restraint in creating problem categories for two reasons.

First, only one of the data systems among the eight agencies maintained information on problem type. Although the Department of Social Services—the agency responsible for the majority of children in residential care—had recently completed a one-time survey with information on a related concept, its information was not clearly comparable with that from the agency having data on problem type. We might assume that an agency's mission (e.g., mental illness, developmental disabilities, substance abuse) would identify the problem that children in its care had, but this assumption might well be invalid given the lack of a formal process determining how children entered the residential care system. Previous unpublished research cast further doubt on the validity of such an assumption by showing that many children were inappropriately placed.

The second reason for our urging restraint in developing problem categories had to do with maintaining the philosophy of the plan. The Steering Committee's initial intention had been to provide a framework within which interagency planning could occur, thereby reducing or eliminating artificial distinctions between agencies. Identifying problem types, especially as restricted by the available data, clearly represented a move back toward planning for individual agencies. Furthermore, this idea reinforced the mistaken tendency of Steering Committee members to view the projections as if they showed the "need" for specific kinds of services instead of projected utilization.

As a result of our urging, the Steering Committee agreed to present problem-type projections only as an elaboration upon the baseline set. Not only did the plan discuss the severe limitations of the data, but it also included the caveat that the projections did not indicate a level of need for a problem-related service. The Committee decided upon four kinds of problems: mental illness, developmental disabilities, health, and behavior. While there was some argument for making abuse/neglect a separate problem category and for creating a category for "multiple problems," the Committee eventually concluded that to avoid an endless list of problems it would simply identify a fifth, and final, residual category labeled "other."

These negotiations concluded, we collected data from the agencies and adjusted it for missing values and for enhanced comparability. We were confident that our estimation was reasonable and that the resulting trends provided a reliable representation of trends in the children's residential care system.

Analytic Design: Projection Models

The methodology for producing the projections was relatively straightforward. We assumed future utilization to be a function of the projected population and projected utilization rates.[3] The projection interval was five years, although the policy discussions focused on the first three years. We computed these rates for combinations of age categories, regions, and levels (types) of care.

We obtained the projected population data from the State Data Center's population projections for New York. These projections, however, were in five-year age groups which did not correspond to our interagency groups. Therefore, we separated the five-year age groups into single years of age through a nonlinear interpolation, and then we regrouped the results into the interagency age categories (Shryock and Siegel 1975).

Although one may legitimately have a great deal of confidence in the population projections, it is more difficult to have confidence in the projections of future trends in utilization rates. Therefore, we produced two sets of projections, modeling two different scenarios for the future.

We produced the first series of projections, Method A, by multiplying the projected population for each year by the utilization rate obtained from the last year of observed data. This procedure—equivalent to assuming that the factors producing the supply of and demand for service would remain constant at their most recent level—coincided with the opinion of many Steering Committee members that the historical decline in the use of residential care had bottomed out.

We produced the second series of projections, Method B, by estimating the trend in utilization rates from the historical data and then extrapolating that trend into the future. Underlying Method B was the assumption that the factors producing the demand for and supply of services would continue to change in the future as they had in the past. We investigated several techniques for projecting the utilization rates, eliminating time series analysis due to an insufficient number of observations (seven to eight years).

Of the two statewide comprehensive plans produced during the course of this project, the first (released in 1985) had Method B projections based on the following regression:

$$(UR_y = a + bUR + b_iA_i + b_jL_j + b_{ij}A_iL_j).[4]$$

We tested the equation to see if we could improve results by including a set of social indicators related to service utilization (single-parent families, unemployment rates). These indicators, however, did not improve the predictive power of the equation.

When we examined the ability of the equation to produce accurate projections, the results were quite encouraging. We used the first five years of data to project two years forward, and then we compared the projections for these two years with the actual utilization data for those years. The errors ranged around 5 percent.

In the second plan (released in 1987), we changed the method of projecting utilization rates to a series of curve-fitting procedures that fit the rate of change in the rates. The change in method enabled us to model more accurately any evidence of a trend toward a bottoming out of the decline in rates.

The development of both Method A and Method B projections produced a range within which we could assume with some degree of confidence that future utilization would occur. We prepared both series of projections for six age groups, three levels of care, and seven regions. As a final step, we distributed the projected utilization by our estimates of problem type.

Results of Analysis

Tables 19.1 and 19.2 present the baseline projections (from the second plan) of the number of children in residential care. Table 19.1 contains projections based on the assumption that utilization rates would remain constant at their 1985 levels through 1991. Table 19.2 contains projections based on the assumption that utilization rates would continue to change according to the pattern between 1978 and 1985. The range in results between these projections was smaller earlier in the projection period than in later years.

We projected the number of children in residential care to decline during the ensuing six years, albeit at a slower rate than during the recent past. Between 1978 and 1985, the number of children in care declined by an average of 5 percent each

Table 19.1   Projections of Children in Residential Facilities,[a] Method A

| Year[b] | Family Care | Level of Care | | Total[c] |
		Community Integrated Group Living	Noncommunity Integrated	
1986	20,540	4,860	11,100	37,270
1987	20,480	4,750	10,910	36,910
1988	20,380	4,640	10,710	36,490
1989	20,270	4,530	10,510	36,080
1990	20,160	4,420	10,320	35,670
1991	20,180	4,400	10,280	35,610
Percent Change:[d]				
1986–1991	−2	−10	−7	−4

[a]Rounded to the nearest 10. Regional figures by level of care may not sum to state totals due to rounding.
[b]As of March 31 of each year.
[c]Includes some placements that could not be assigned to a level of care.
[d]Based on unrounded projections.

Table 19.2   Projections of Children in Residential Facilities,[a] Method B

| Year[b] | Family Care | Level of Care | | Total[c] |
		Community Integrated Group Living	Noncommunity Integrated	
1986	19,480	4,950	11,000	36,180
1987	18,400	4,970	10,690	34,830
1988	17,350	4,980	10,400	33,490
1989	16,360	4,990	10,120	32,230
1990	15,420	5,000	9,870	31,050
1991	14,640	5,040	9,700	30,140
Percent Change:[d]				
1986–1991	−25	+2	−12	−17

[a]Rounded to the nearest 10. Regional figures by level of care may not sum to state totals due to rounding.
[b]As of March 31 of each year.
[c]Includes some placements that could not be assigned to a level of care.
[d]Based on unrounded projections.

year. The projections for the years 1986 to 1991 indicated a yearly decline of between 1 percent (Method A) and 3 percent (Method B).

In the past, some types of care had been used more extensively than others. For
example, the number of children in family care had declined regularly during the
historical period, and we projected it to decline throughout the projection period.
Use of family care underwent a 35 percent decline between 1978 and 1985, and
we projected such use to decline between 1986 and 1991 by a much slower pace
under Method A (2 percent by 1991) than under Method B (25 percent).

Although the use of community-based group care increased by 12 percent between 1978 and 1985, the increase in such use ceased after 1983. Our projections
of the number of children using this type of care were quite different under
Method A than under Method B. The assumption of constant rates under Method
A—coupled with a declining children's population—resulted in a projected decline of 10 percent in the number of children in community-based group care by
1991. The assumption under Method B of a continued increase in utilization rates
(although much more slowly than in the past) resulted in a projected increase of 2
percent in the number of children in this type of care by 1991.

Our projections regarding the number of children in noncommunity-based
group living indicated a continuation of the historical decline in the use of this
type of care. We assumed, based on the fact that the rate of decline had slowed in
recent years, that the rate of decline would continue to moderate until 1991. There
had been a 36 percent reduction in the number of children in this type of facility
between 1978 and 1985. We projected a further decline of 7 percent under Method
A and 12 percent under Method B.

We apportioned the baseline projections of community-based and
noncommunity-based group living according to the problem area of the child. Table 19.3 presents the distribution of children by problem area and level of care.
These distributions apply to projections under both Method A and Method B.

As Table 19.3 indicates, behavioral problems were the most common and
health problems were the least common for children in both types of residential
care. But in community-based care "Other" problems ranked second while in
noncommunity-based care "Mental Illness" held that ranking.

Lessons for the Future

The statewide residential care planning project described here began in 1983 and
produced two plans, one in 1985 and the other in 1987. At the end of this four-year
period of development, the project ceased to include comprehensive projections
of utilization. The following two or three years were a period in which we assessed the programmatic needs of very specific populations (e.g., technology-de-
pendent children, chemically-dependent youth, specialized family care) and made
recommendations for the development of service models. Finally, in 1990, the Division of the Budget ceased to fund this project altogether. Of the various recommendations for residential care that we had developed during the six years of the

Table 19.3 Percentage Distribution of Children with Each Problem Area by Level of Care

Problem Area	Community Integrated Group Living[a]	Noncommunity Integrated[a]
Total[b]	100.0	100.0
Developmental disabilities	17.4	21.8
Health	2.0	5.7
Mental illness	15.2	24.3
Behavior	42.0	34.7
Other	23.4	13.6

[a]Applies to both Method A and Method B.
[b]Problem areas may not sum to 100 percent due to rounding.

project, the ones dealing with specialized family care were, for the most part, the only ones implemented.

This experience provided three types of lessons about applied demography: (1) lessons about accuracy, (2) lessons dealing with potential elaborations of the methodology, and (3) lessons concerning working relationships with policy makers and program planners.

Regarding the limits and functions of accuracy, this project produced projections of the use of children's residential care that were—in the short term—quite accurate. They certainly were as accurate as they needed to be for planning purposes. The degree of accuracy was assessed by comparing the projections released in 1985 (based on 1984 data) and in 1987 (based on 1985 data) with an actual count of the residential care population in 1987. The projections from the first (1985) plan were 5 percent too high according to Method A and 4 percent too low according to Method B. The projections from the second (1987) plan were off by a similar magnitude but in the opposite direction; they were too low by 2 percent according to Method A and too low by 8 percent according to Method B. After 1987, however, there was a dramatic turnaround in the previous decline in the use of care, invalidating the assumptions upon which our projections had been based, as the children's residential care system was overrun by childhood victims of the crack cocaine epidemic and, to a more limited extent, of AIDS. By 1990, the number of children in care was twice the number that had been projected in 1985.

If better data had been available, we could have taken a number of steps to improve the accuracy and utility of our projections. Under ideal circumstances, we could have incorporated race and ethnicity into the model. Not only are the nonwhite and Hispanic populations growing more rapidly than non-Hispanic whites, but also nonwhite and Hispanic children are more likely to be in residential care.

Regarding a potential elaboration of the model, it would be worth investigating the replacement of the one-day census with the product of admissions times length of stay as a measure of utilization. Several agencies contended that, given a fixed number of beds, program staff must reduce lengths of stay in order to handle rising admission rates. Since many agency staff members believe that shorter stays are inappropriate, a simulation of the number of beds that would be needed under various assumptions about appropriate lengths of stay would be a powerful planning tool.

It would also be helpful for planning purposes to have an indication of the amount of unmet demand for residential care relative to existing capacity. While there is little evidence to show that an epidemiological approach would be helpful in estimating the *need* for residential care, it may be possible to measure met and unmet demand for care. For example, existing waiting lists and records of out-of-state placements could be the basis for constructing an estimate of unmet demand. Although those data may be incomplete, they would provide an indication of the demand not currently being met within the New York State system. Capacity, on the other hand, is probably more difficult to determine. While agencies that serve populations composed primarily of children can provide the number of beds designated for use by children, other agencies may not set aside a distinct number of beds for children. Agencies differ, moreover, in that some maintain information on "designed" capacity, others on "budgeted" capacity, and still others on "operating" capacity.

The final lessons to be learned from this project concern the attempts by the Council's Research Bureau staff to integrate the projections into the planning process, which was orchestrated by Policy Bureau staff. As difficult as it was to combine the data from the eight agencies into a comprehensive set of projections, it was much harder to change the way in which planning for children's residential care occurred. In fact, after we developed the two comprehensive statewide plans, it became apparent that the Committee was willing or able to develop interagency recommendations only for specific populations. These recommendations, moreover, were frequently in opposition to the utilization patterns outlined in the projections. For example, the Committee made a series of recommendations regarding the further development of residential beds despite our projections of declining utilization.

Several factors seemed to be involved in the poor integration of projections and policy recommendations. The Committee was engaged initially in plan development through the methodological decision-making processes surrounding the construction of the projections. This was followed by a brief period in which the Committee developed its recommendations.

It is now clear that the Committee should have spent more time at the beginning of the project discussing the kinds of recommendations it could eventually make, how a set of projections could contribute to the development of recommendations, and how the recommendations would be used. Such a discussion could have focused the agencies' positions in two ways.

First, one must understand that each agency saw itself at risk of losing autonomy through the coordinated planning process. The Division of the Budget's goal for this project was to create an interagency plan for children's residential care, but the eight separate agencies knew it would continue to be their task to offer services. Coming to an early consensus on the level of specificity desired in the recommendations and identifying more clearly how the recommendations would fit into the annual planning and budgetary processes would have clarified the agencies' "stakes" and, accordingly, could have contributed to a more useful specification of the projections. Such early discussions also could have produced a synthesis of the agencies' actual intentions in participating in this project and the project goals as set out by the Division of the Budget.

Second, an early emphasis on the use of the projections vis-à-vis the Committee's recommendations would have highlighted the tendency of Committee members to think in terms of very specific projects and very narrow problem areas. Our projections were comparatively, and intentionally, general. Earlier attention to the relationship between the recommendations and the projections would have resulted in either the recommendations having a generalized interagency focus or the projections having an agency-specific focus.

Also contributing to the poor integration of the projections into the recommendations was the belief of many Committee members that the long-term decline in the use of children's residential care had ceased. They had heard stories from field staff about a supposed increased demand for services. As researchers, however, we saw no evidence in the data to support such stories, and we were convinced that the historical trend provided the best basis for projecting future utilization.

Despite our efforts to portray the projections as a reasonable set of scenarios about the future, Committee members were simply not convinced of the validity of the assumptions on which the projections were based. In retrospect, of course, the Committee members were right. Field staff had sensed a reversal of the long-term trend a year or two before it began to show up in the data. Yet, while the Committee members may have wanted a projections series showing that the long-term decline in the use of children's residential care had ceased, there were absolutely no data on which to base such a series.

In the long run, Committee members viewed the projections as not useful for two reasons: (1) The projections had not picked up on the increased demand for services, and (2) the projections could not be easily incorporated into planning for specific programs or specific populations. As a consequence, Committee members refocused the planning project on developing service models for more narrowly defined populations.

In summary, the project was a difficult but in many ways typical exercise in applied demography. It not only illustrated the range of skills that the applied demographer must use, but it also highlighted the need for integrating techniques learned in graduate school with the practical demands of working with government officials. Having to work with a large committee of nonresearchers presented abundant opportunities for education and negotiation, but the project's chief difficulty lay in overcoming the lack of quality and comparability in the administrative records. These liabilities also resulted in substantial restrictions on the projection methodology.

Discussion Questions

1. Outline the scheme for developing a comprehensive statewide plan for residential care, highlighting the projections within this scheme. Include the planned use of the projections of the State Division of the Budget, the Council, and the individual agencies. How would you have proceeded, given this breakdown?

2. The projections in this case were based on "residential care utilization." What other method could have been used?

3. This case exemplifies how standard methods (requiring "hard" demographic data) were not effective in making accurate projections. What would you have done in this case? Should one stick rigidly to standard demographic methodologies?

4. Discuss the conflicts between the researchers and the Steering Committee.

5. Would different projection techniques have yielded different results?

Notes

This case is based on research done while the author was affiliated with the New York State Council on Children and Families.

1. The providers of residential care are the Department of Social Services, the Office of Mental Health, the Office of Mental Retardation and Developmental Disabilities, the Division for Youth, the Department of Health, the State Education Department, the Division of Alcoholism and Alcohol Abuse, and the Division of Substance Abuse Services.

2. The 18 to 20 age category also included those few individuals over the age of 20 who were in children's residential care.

3. These rates were computed by dividing the number of children in care by the general population and then multiplying by 1,000.

4. Where UR_y = the projected utilization rate, a = the constant, b = regression coefficients, UR = the lagged utilization rates, A_j = a series of dummy variables for age groups, L_j = a series of dummy variables for levels of care, and A_iL_j = a set of interaction terms.

References

New York State Council on Children and Families. January 1984. *Characteristics of Children in Out of Home Care.* Albany, NY: Author.

———. February 1985. *Critical Factors Affecting Families' Decisions to Place Developmentally Disabled Family Members.* Albany, NY: Author.

Shryock, Henry S., Jacob S. Siegel, and Associates. September 1975. *The Methods and Materials of Demography.* Washington, D.C.: U.S. Department of Commerce, Bureau of the Census.

20

Documenting State Underemployment Patterns

Gordon F. De Jong

Promoting economic development has become a priority task for state executives, state legislatures, and state agencies. Human service needs have always been a focal point of state policy, but the economic recessions of the early 1980s and 1990s—along with the prospects for increased worldwide economic competition in the coming decade—have spotlighted regional economic development as a state and local, as opposed to a national, policy issue.

Labor force indicators, such as the unemployment rate, are important measures that policy makers use in launching and terminating both public and corporate economic development programs and policies. Unfortunately, measures such as the unemployment rate do not provide a complete picture of those workers who suffer from forms of job-related and economic hardships that are not defined as unemployment.

This case study describes how I used an applied demographic perspective to document state underemployment patterns for public policy decision makers. Specifically, it focuses on seven ways that demographic analysis can contribute to an understanding of state labor force patterns or other problems related to public policy—e.g., poverty, elderly services, child care, education priorities, income inequality, housing adequacy.

The seven ways for using demographic analysis in this context are:

1. Defining the concept (underemployment) that is important to public policy.
2. Providing a policy-relevant framework to measure underemployment.
3. Documenting the number, proportions, and demographic characteristics (i.e., age, gender, race) of underemployed workers, using information from a credible data source. This case study uses data for Pennsylvania to illustrate the applied demographic perspective for documenting underemployment patterns (De Jong, Cornwell, and Guidos 1990; De Jong, Casper, and Cornwell 1990).

4. Describing how the incidence of underemployment in the state has changed over time.
5. Comparing state underemployment with national patterns or with those of other states.
6. Illustrating the spatial pattern of underemployment in the state.
7. Developing a profile of the population characteristics of different types of underemployed workers.

The Changing Demographic
Context of State Labor Force Policy

The demographic context of state labor force policy has changed in several ways from what it was a decade ago. First, state population trends have focused more attention on the elderly and less on the youth population. Second, the participation of women in the labor force has increased at the same time that the participation of men (largely due to early retirement) has gradually diminished. Third, the higher birth rate among minority populations and the immigration of Hispanics and Asians have created a situation in which minorities make up a larger proportion of the work force than they have at any time in the past. Fourth and finally, there has been an increase in the proportion of families with two wage earners, an indication of the increasing impact of work on family life.

In a recent assessment of employment policy for the 1990s, Sawhill (1989) argues that there are four key objectives for state and national policy makers:

1. Provide jobs (reduce unemployment).
2. Create more good jobs (improve productivity and earnings).
3. Assist the disadvantaged (make the poor, including the working poor, self-sufficient).
4. Insure both fair treatment of workers and economic efficiency.

These four objectives are central not only to the long-term growth of a state's economy, but also to the well-being of each population group in the changing labor force.

Where will states get workers to fuel economic development during the 1990s? One source of productive full-time employees may be each state's population of currently unemployed and underemployed workers. Who are the underemployed workers? State executives and legislative officials must address that question in order to develop laws and policies that will enhance employment opportunities and economic development within their jurisdictions.

The clients for this report were members of the Pennsylvania General Assembly and executives of the state government. In cooperation with the Pennsylvania State Data Center (which has an office in the state capitol building), I along with other members of our applied demography group and State Data Center staff members met with legislators and state agency executive personnel to identify emerging population-related policy issues.

As political leaders discussed the limitations of unemployment statistics in adequately describing the employment realities of constituent groups in their local districts, underemployment emerged as a significant demographic issue. For some officials, the unemployment rate seemed to understate the labor distress and depressed employment conditions experienced by people who have given up looking for work or can find only part-time positions. To these leaders, not including such workers in the unemployment statistics made a travesty of public policy decision making. On the other hand, to officials from localities with labor shortages, the unemployment statistics seemed to provide a limited view of the pool of potential workers. Both groups of state leaders questioned whether demographers could better define, provide estimates of, and profile the labor force beyond the employed/unemployed distinction.

The Policy Context for Labor Force Analysis:
The Case of Pennsylvania

The policy context for labor force analysis in Pennsylvania had several dimensions. The first was that the governor not only had made economic development a priority for his administration, but also had sought to address several family policy issues—maternal leave and child care—under the rubric of enhancing economic productivity. Documenting this linkage between family policy and economic productivity required information on both the growing number of women in the state's labor force and the adequacy of female labor force utilization in the state. State agencies dealing with labor and industry strategic planning had the information and expertise that provided a basis for understanding projected patterns for women's labor force participation and labor utilization through the 1990s.

A second impetus for analyzing the state labor force was the emergence of labor shortages in the Philadelphia labor market during the late 1980s. After generations of labor surplus (a situation that continues in some areas of the state), both public and private sector planners in Philadelphia's labor market attempted to adjust to the changing economic and demographic factors that produced the earlier labor surpluses and more recent shortages. This planning context created an interest not only in the unemployed, but also in underemployed workers who perhaps could alleviate anticipated future shortages in the labor supply.

A third reason for an interest in labor force analysis stemmed from the legislature's consideration of maternal leave and child care bills. While the basic decision making on these bills largely evolved from ideological positions and the presumed costs and benefits to business, legislators sought to understand the impact that maternal leave and child care regulations might have on unemployed and underemployed women in the state.

In sum, policy makers clearly recognized the importance of unemployment information, knowing that government policies and programs—as well as business decisions—are often initiated or abandoned on the basis of monthly unemployment indicators. But it was equally clear that policy makers were not familiar with either the concept or the statistical indicators of underemployment.

Defining the Concept and a Demographic Framework

The concept "underemployment" refers to conditions of hardship related to the labor market. In 1976 Congress instructed the National Commission on Employment and Unemployment Statistics (NCEUS) to consider data relating to hardship and the underemployed (Pub. L. 94-144 1977), and two commissions have recommended the development and publication of underemployment indicators on "labor market-related hardship" (U.S. President's Commission 1962; NCEUS 1979, p. 60).

The demographic framework that seems most appropriate for addressing the underemployment issues raised by policy makers is the Labor Force Utilization Framework (LUF), developed and elaborated by Clogg and colleagues (Clogg 1979; Clogg and Sullivan 1983; Lichter 1988). This framework is based on the concepts underlying the widely used U.S. Bureau of the Census unemployment statistics—figures that are both readily accepted and understood by public officials.

As shown in Figure 20.1, the Labor Force Utilization Framework starts with the conventional distinction between (1) persons in the labor force, and (2) persons not in the labor force. Employed persons are those individuals in the labor force who are currently working; unemployed persons are those individuals in the labor force who are looking for work but are not currently working. The LUF also identifies workers—both in and out of the labor force—who are suffering economic distress. These groups include:

- Discouraged Workers—persons who are not working and have dropped out of the labor force because they are unable to find work. Conventional unemployment statistics ignore this group because they no longer are actively seeking work.
- Involuntary part-time workers—persons who are working fewer than 35 hours per week but want full-time work.
- Working poor—persons who work full time (35 hours or more per week) but earn less than 1.25 times the official individual poverty threshold (approximately $6,450 in 1989).

All other workers are defined as *adequately employed*—i.e., persons in the labor force, employed either full time or part time by choice, who do not fall into any of the above groups.

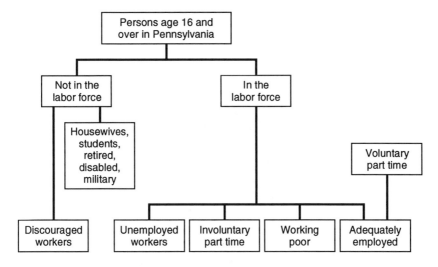

Figure 20.1—Labor utilization framework

Besides discouraged workers, involuntary part-time workers, and working poor, there are other forms of underemployment. Two examples are workers who have more education than required for their jobs and workers who have been involuntarily terminated and cannot find comparable positions that utilize their experience and skills. Unfortunately, these forms of underemployment cannot be adequately operationalized with current state-level data.

One benefit of the LUF for the applied demographer is that public officials readily understand LUF categories. That is, public officials can attach constituent names and faces to discouraged workers (persons who have stopped looking for work) and to the working poor (full-time workers who don't earn enough to put themselves much above the poverty threshold). As a result, applied demographers who can provide estimates of the number and percentage—as well as demographic profiles—of these workers may well see their findings have a meaningful impact on policy decision making.

An alternative framework to address labor force demographic questions consists of developing age and sex projections of labor supply for future years based on current and past census data, and then comparing these results with age and sex projections of labor demand during the same time period. While this approach has the advantage of providing a much more detailed age and geographic focus, it suffers from a lack of information about why many workers of labor force age are not gainfully employed. The validity of results is also affected by the length of time from the latest census on which population projections must be based.

Besides defining the major concepts and documenting how they interrelate to provide a composite picture of adequate and inadequate employment, the LUF authors have also provided a methodology to operationalize the concepts. This methodology utilizes data from the U.S. Bureau of the Census Current Population Survey (Clogg and Sullivan 1983), the monthly source of national labor force information. Each March the Current Population Survey includes a supplementary series of questions on individual and household demographic characteristics. From this data file of approximately 60,000 households we identify the approximately 6,000 respondents of labor force age living in the state of Pennsylvania. In order to improve the accuracy of yearly results, we combine the nonoverlapping households over a three-year time period. With this framework, methodology, and data, we can:

1. Provide annual data on the number of men and women in the Pennsylvania labor force.
2. Provide estimates (assuming that the Current Population Survey sampling frame for the state yields a random sample of the labor force population) of the number and percent of individuals in the labor force who are discouraged workers, working poor, and involuntary part-time workers as well as of those who are unemployed.
3. Compare state with national estimates on the proportion of workers in each underemployment category.
4. Describe labor utilization of both male and female workers as well as of other population subgroups.
5. Develop profiles of the demographic characteristics of workers who are most likely to fall into each of the underemployment categories.

In sum, the Labor Force Utilization Framework and Current Population Survey data make it possible for us to develop meaningful and timely underemployment information that describes the changing composition of adequately and inadequately employed workers in the state of Pennsylvania.

Documenting Underemployment by Gender: Pennsylvania and U.S. Comparisons

In this case study we presented the following illustrative data by means of graphics in order to provide policy makers with easy to comprehend frequencies and relationships rather than more difficult to interpret regression results. It has been my experience that relatively few policy makers are comfortable with the concept of "statistical control" as a basis for public policy decision making.

Population-based inquiry asks questions such as: How likely are workers of a given age, education, or gender to be underemployed? Figure 20.2 addresses these issues with data that we presented to policy makers in a "bullet" format. The results showed that:

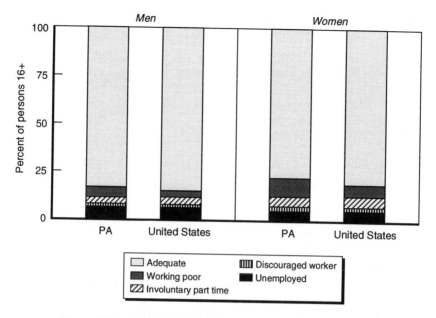

Figure 20.2—National and state underemployment for men and women, 1987

- The majority of men and women in the Pennsylvania labor force reported adequate employment in 1987. That is, they either worked full time and received a wage that provided an income at least 1.25 times the poverty level or they worked part time by choice.
- Of the women in the 1987 Pennsylvania labor force, however, 22 percent were either unemployed or underemployed. The largest percent (9.3) of this group were working poor. That is, they were earning just over the individual poverty threshold even though they were working full time. Five percent of the women in the Pennsylvania labor force were working part time because they could not find full-time work, and an additional 5.5 percent were unemployed. The remaining 2.2 percent were discouraged workers—women who had dropped out of the labor force and stopped looking for work.
- In all, approximately 375,000 women in the Pennsylvania labor force in 1987 were either unemployed or underemployed.
- By comparison, 16.6 percent of the men in the Pennsylvania labor force were either unemployed or underemployed. The largest percent (6.9) of this group were unemployed, while 5.1 percent were categorized as working poor, and 3.4 percent were working part time because they could not find a full-time job. Just over one percent (1.2) were discouraged workers.

- In sum, approximately 450,000 men in the 1987 Pennsylvania labor force were either unemployed or underemployed.
- On a percentage basis, Pennsylvania had more working poor men and women than did the United States as a whole: 5.1 percent versus 3.1 percent for men, and 9.3 percent versus 5.6 percent for women. For other types of underemployment and for unemployment, however, the state and national figures were quite similar.

Describing How Underemployment Has Changed over Time

Providing decision makers with evidence on changing patterns of underemployment helps identify emerging policy issues. The data in Figure 20.3 give evidence regarding underemployment patterns in Pennsylvania. Since I have already illustrated our "bullet" format of highlighting key findings for policy makers, I will only briefly summarize the results from this part of the analysis.

Between 1980 and 1987, state unemployment decreased while underemployment increased for both male and female workers. The increase in underemployment was largely attributable to the rising proportion of working poor, particularly among women in the labor force, and involuntary part-time workers. These opposite unemployment and underemployment trends provided a particularly significant finding for policy makers.

Illustrating Spatial Patterns of Underemployment

Legislators are particularly sensitive regarding the relative number of underemployed workers among their local constituents. As a consequence, we sought to disaggregate our analysis in order to identify underemployment patterns for metropolitan and nonmetropolitan areas of the state. Clearly, policy makers would like to have information about their home districts, which effectively means county-level analyses. Unfortunately, the Current Population Survey is designed to present labor force patterns for the nation and for the larger states. It does not have a sufficient sample size or an appropriate sampling design for county-level analyses. Thus we could accurately analyze underemployment only for (1) the Philadelphia and Pittsburgh metropolitan areas, (2) all other metropolitan areas combined, and (3) the nonmetropolitan areas of the state.

Figure 20.4 shows that employment patterns vary across the state, with the Philadelphia metropolitan area having a lower combined unemployment and underemployment rate than the Pittsburgh metropolitan area. The highest combined unemployment and underemployment rate, however, was for women workers in the nonmetropolitan areas of the state; their primary source of employment hardship was low income (the working poor category).

In general, policy makers from both economically depressed nonmetropolitan areas and metropolitan areas were surprised at the magnitude of total labor force

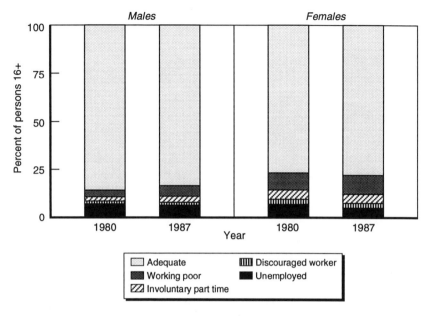

Figure 20.3—Underemployment for the PA labor force by sex,
1980 and 1987

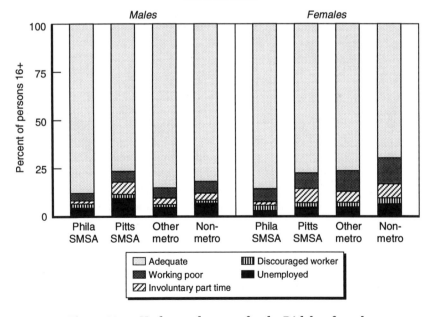

Figure 20.4—Underemployment for the PA labor force by
sex and metro status, 1987

hardship rates in their areas. These rates ranged from 25 to 33 percent, much higher than the official 1987 unemployment rates of 7 to 10 percent. On the other hand, policy makers from the Philadelphia metropolitan area—characterized in 1987 by low unemployment, even a labor shortage—saw the underemployment data as evidence of a supply of potentially underutilized workers in their locality.

Underemployed Worker Profiles

Applied demographic inquiry into labor force issues also seeks information about the social, demographic, and family characteristics of underemployed workers as compared to all workers in the state. Policy makers are interested in this type of analysis because it provides "people profiles" of labor hardship groups—i.e., the working poor, unemployed, discouraged workers, etc. Figure 20.5 illustrates this type of analysis by providing a social, demographic, and family profile of discouraged workers compared to all workers in the state.

The data show that blacks and female heads of households were, in comparison to all workers, between three and four times more likely to be discouraged workers—i.e., persons who are not working and have stopped actively seeking work. Young workers and those with less than a high school education were also overrepresented in this category. When compared to the state labor force as a whole, discouraged workers were more likely to reside in the state's two largest metropolitan areas.

In an era of limited resources for human service and worker retraining programs, the need to target carefully the most distressed population groups in the labor force becomes increasingly important. Policy makers see demographic profiles as one means to achieve this aspect of program goals.

Lessons for Public Sector Applied Demography

What does this case study illustrate about public sector applied demographic research and problem solving? As in many other applied demographic studies, client groups (in this case legislators and state executives) sought the assistance of a demographer to provide information about a population group: the underemployed in the state labor force. This important information was not available from economic data sources, including employment data obtained from firms. The analysis needed to be based on politically relevant employment policy categories and on timely information from a source of high credibility. Given these political requirements, the use of a federal data source that could be integrated with commonly accepted labor force concepts—such as the unemployment rate—was crucial to assuring acceptance of the study's results.

As noted earlier, the Current Population Survey is a unique source of demo-

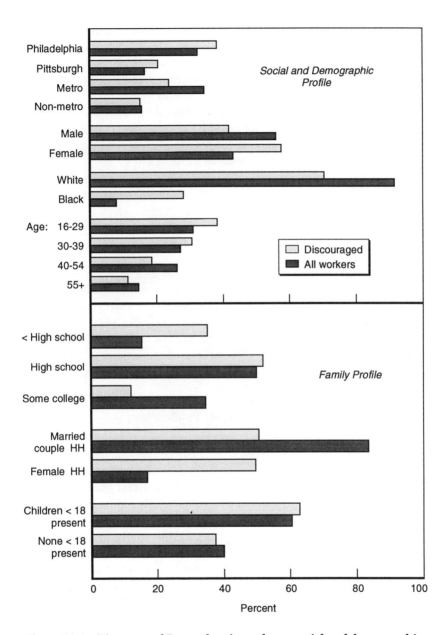

Figure 20.5—Discouraged Pennsylvania workers: social and demographic
profile and family profile

graphic data. Updated every year, the survey provides important information for applied demographic research into labor force issues. When dealing with one of the larger states, for example, the researcher can extract a data file with a sufficient sample size for statistically significant state-level analysis. Data from the Current Population Survey also allow a demographer to compare state results with both national parameters and results from earlier years.

In our analysis, however, data limitations restricted the range of alternative explanations that we could provide for the series of questions raised by state decision makers. For example, the data set was not of sufficient size to permit county-level analysis of underemployment patterns as requested by many state legislators. Furthermore, by restricting the analysis to a descriptive format, the data set made it impossible to present valid estimates for small populations, such as minority populations.

Despite the high quality of the data we used, our results must be interpreted with care since sampling error can account for some variation, particularly in small populations. Systematic checking of results against decennial census and independent employment data is very important. Another approach that we have used to improve the accuracy of our results is to combine the nonoverlapping households from the Current Population Surveys over a three-year period (i.e., 1986, 1987, and 1988). Because many clients are not familiar with sampling error and statistical deviation concepts, demographers must emphasize the need to examine the validity of their findings. Public officials sometimes take our results more seriously than we do.

Feedback: Impact on Public Policy

While our research results brought greater recognition to the issue of underemployment, state leaders neither proposed nor evaluated new programs to assist the underemployed workers in the state. The intent of the research was to document the trends and differentials in underemployment for different population groups. These target population groups are, in turn, differentially represented by legislative districts and policy agendas. As a consequence, the results have more of an indirect than a direct effect on specific policy initiatives. The most pointed evidence of an impact on public policy of our applied demographic research came not from written policy or program citations but from personal communications from legislative and state executive personnel who acknowledged the influence of our "politically neutral" analyses in galvanizing policy maker and public attention on important public policy issues.

Notwithstanding the limited impact of this study, my experience with public sector applied demographic analysis is that demographic knowledge can and does make a difference. The revolution in data availability over the last 20 years and the increased use of demographic indicators as criteria for the distribution of program funds have made public sector decision makers much more attuned to the demographic basis of public policy decisions. The political impact of a demographic analysis, however, probably depends on the analyst's ability to relate macro-level demographic facts and trends to state and local political and economic contexts—and ultimately to the well-being of the decision makers' constituents. Success in this regard demands not only scientific rigor, but also an appreciation of the normative context within which political officials function.

Discussion Questions

1. One dilemma is that policymakers were not familiar with the concept of unemployment or its statistical indicators. Explain how you would communicate this information to policymakers to persuade them that the study is necessary.

2. What are the inherent limitations of the CPS as applied to this case? Would you reveal these limitations to your client? How?

3. Help the policymaker bridge the gap between the data presented and the three dimensions of the labor force outlined early in the case: 1) family policy and economic productivity; 2) labor force shortages; and 3) consideration of maternal leave and childcare bills.

Notes

This chapter was prepared especially for this casebook and is not to be quoted, cited, or used in any manner without the permission of the author.

References

Clogg, Clifford C. 1979. *Measuring Underemployment.* New York: Academic Press.

Clogg, Clifford C., and Teresa A. Sullivan. 1983. "Labor Force Composition and Underemployment Trends, 1969–1980." *Social Indicators Research.* 12:117–152.A.

De Jong, Gordon F., Lynne M. Casper, and Gretchen T. Cornwell. 1990. *A Demographic Profile of Pennsylvania's Unemployed and Underemployed Workers.* Middletown, Pennsylvania: Pennsylvania State Data Center.

De Jong, Gordon F., Gretchen T. Cornwell, and Marianne E. Guidos. 1990. *Underemployment of Pennsylvania Workers.* Middletown, Pennsylvania: Pennsylvania State Data Center.

Lichter, Daniel T. 1988. "Racial Differences in Underemployment in American Cities." *American Journal of Sociology.* 93:771–792.

National Commission on Employment and Unemployment Statistics (NCEUS). 1979. *Counting the Labor Force.* Public Law No. 94-144:1977, 90 Stat. 1483, 29 U.S.C. 952. Washington D.C.: United States Government Printing Office.

Sawhill, Isabel V. 1989. Rethinking Employment Policy. D. Lee Bawden and Felicity

Skidmore (eds.). *Rethinking Employment Policy.* Washington, D.C.: The Urban Institute Press. pp. 9–29.

United States President's Committee to Appraise Employment and Unemployment Statistics. 1962. *Measuring Employment and Unemployment.* Washington, D.C.: United States Government Printing Office.

Discussion Questions
for Part Five

1. Compare the unique sources of origin of the demographic data used in these planning exercises. What were the original purposes of these databases? How did that affect the analysis outcome and process?

2. Compare these cases in terms of the length of the planning time horizons.

3. Explain the original intent of the life table. How were life tables used in the cases in this section? Consider the possibility of transferring these methods to other cases in the book.

4. Compare the satisfaction level of the clients in these cases. Examine the client's ability to utilize and interpret the results for planning. What factors seem to affect the levels of satisfaction and utilization?

5. Explain the commonalities among these cases. Consider: type of planning; budget; concerns; market served; and changing population trends.

About the Book

Understanding changing demographics is becoming critically important to a growing number of professionals and decisionmakers in business and government. Written in nontechnical language and presented in a classroom-tested format, this easy-to-use guidebook offers case studies of important applications of applied demography in government planning, long-term corporate strategy, forecasting, human resource management, and marketing. The authors show how to tie financial, political, and legal analysis into a consideration of demographic data and trends.

About the Editors and Contributors

David M. Ambrose is the Enron Professor of Business Administration and Director of the Executive MBA Program at the University of Nebraska at Omaha. Ambrose is active in hospital administration, economic development, and the area of entrepreneurship.

George H. Billings is a consultant, operating manager, and investor in the mobile communications industry. He has built and managed cellular telephone businesses and has assisted communications equipment manufacturers, cellular companies, paging businesses and satellite carriers in the areas of corporate strategy, marketing, operations and organization. He lectures occasionally to communications industry groups and teaches periodically at the university and graduate levels.

Nancy Bolton is a consulting demographer who focuses on the demographics of California and Los Angeles County. She writes a quarterly article on California demographics for the UCLA Business Forecast Project and provides demographic projections to users of the Business Forecast. She frequently serves as an expert for Los Angeles County agencies.

Sue Carnevale is a Senior Research Analyst with the San Diego Association of Governments. She is a specialist with the ARC/INFO Geographic Information System (GIS) software and has been using ARC/INFO in a wide variety of projects and applications since 1985. Her major interests are in environmental and natural resource applications.

W. A.V. Clark is Professor of Geography at the University of California at Los Angeles. His current research interests include tenure choice and residential mobility, and demographic change in major metropolitan areas and their impacts on neighborhoods, schools and electoral districts. He is the author of *Human Migration* and coeditor of *Residential Mobility and Public Policy.*

Gordon F. De Jong is Distinguished Professor of Sociology and Director of the Graduate Program in Demography at Penn State University. He is former editor of *Demography* (the official scientific journal of the Population Association of America) and has edited two books: *Social Demography* and *Migration Decision Making.*

Nancy Dunton is with the Strategic Planning Office of the New York State Department of Social Services where she is responsible for conducting policy research and providing other information to policy makers. Dunton is one of the principal investigators for Kids Count in New York State.

Harriet Fishlow is Coordinator for Universitywide Enrollment Planning in the University of California Office of the President. She has responsibility for coordinating campus enrollment planning and undergraduate enrollment projections, and providing demographic information to units within the Office of the President and to campus administrations.

Philip Garcia is a Senior Policy Analyst for the California State University in the Office of the Chancellor. He is responsible for directing studies on student outcomes, such as time-to-degree, transfer rates, and survival among high-risk students.

Rita R. Hamm is a Socioeconomic Research Specialist with the Institute for Business and Industry Development at North Dakota State University. Her research covers a broad range of topics including energy-related developments and health care issues. She has authored numerous economic and demographic reports.

Kenneth M. Johnson is an Associate Professor at Loyola University Chicago, where his research focus is population redistribution trends in nonmetropolitan America. Dr. Johnson has done extensive applied demographic research for large corporations.

Hallie J. Kintner is a Staff Research Scientist with General Motors Research Labs where she is responsible for conducting workforce and other studies. Kintner is the former chair of the Business Demography Interest Group of the Population Association of America.

Thomas W. Merrick is Senior Population Adviser with The World Bank. Prior to joining The Bank, he headed the Population Reference Bureau, the preeminent publisher of educational materials on U.S. and international demographic topics. Merrick is coauthor of *Demographics: People and Markets*.

Peter A. Morrison is on the senior staff of the RAND Corporation. His principal interests are applied demographic analysis and forecasting, population aging, the demography of families, school enrollment forecasting, and electoral redistricting. He teaches at The RAND Graduate School, lectures periodically at universities, and conducts executive briefings on demographics and business.

Steven H. Murdock is Professor and Head of the Department of Rural Sociology at Texas A&M University. He serves as Chief Demographer for the State of Texas and has authored *Applied Demography: An Introduction to Basic Concepts, Methods, and Data,* published by Westview Press.

Bob Parrott is the Director of Research and Information Systems for the San Diego Association of Governments. He is the chairperson for the Regional Agencies Special Interest Group of the Urban and Regional Information Systems Association (URISA).

Louis G. Pol is a Professor of Marketing at the University of Nebraska at Omaha. He is the author of *Business Demography* and coauthor of *The Demography of Health and Health Care.*

Bill Rives teaches planning and marketing in the Graduate School of Business at Franklin University in Columbus, Ohio. At the time his casebook chapter was prepared, Rives headed his own demographic consulting firm with offices in Houston and San Antonio. His teaching, research, and consulting activities are concentrated in health care and public education. Rives is coauthor of the book *Introduction to Applied Demography.*

William J. Serow is Professor of Economics and Director, Center for the Study of Population, at the Florida State University in Tallahassee. He has authored over seventy papers published in professional journals and books and has edited or authored ten books. Among his areas of interest are the economics and demography of aging, migration, and small-area analysis.

Stanley K. Smith is Professor of Economics and Director of the Bureau of Economic and Business Research at the University of Florida. He also directs the Bureau's Population Program, which produces the official state and local population estimates and projections for the State of Florida. He has published widely in the areas of population estimates and projections and has consulted on many projects involving demographic data and analysis.

David A. Swanson is a Senior Demographic Specialist at the Arkansas Institute for Economic Advancement, University of Arkansas at Little Rock. He holds a joint appointment with the Center for Rural Mental Health Care Research, University of Arkansas for Medical Sciences. He has practiced demography in a wide range of geographic and institutional settings.

Jeff Tayman is Senior Demographer with the San Diego Association of Governments, where he directs the preparation of small-area demographic and economic estimates and forecasts. Tayman also teaches in the MBA program at a local university in San Diego.

E. Walter Terrie is a Research Associate in Florida State University's Center for the Study of Population. He has served as a consultant to the Florida State Government for political redistricting and has done reapportionment for numerous local governments. Terrie has coauthored several articles and papers on redistricting and small-area intercensal population estimation.

Richard K. Thomas is a health care consultant with Medical Research Services Group in Memphis, Tennessee. He provides consultation to hospitals, physician groups, and other medical organizations in the areas of health services research, marketing, planning, and database development.

Paul R. Voss heads the University of Wisconsin's Applied Population Laboratory. He chairs the State and Local Demography Interest Group of the Population Association of America and is a frequent speaker before business and educational groups.

Bob Weller is the Scientific Review Administrator for the Social Sciences and Population Study Section in the Division of Research Grants at the National Institutes of Health. Formerly on the faculties at Brown University and Florida State University, he is the coauthor or coeditor of *Population: Demography and Policy; The Population of the South; Handbook on International Migration;* and *Florida in the 21st Century.*

Richard W. Wichmann received an M.S. degree in Demography from Florida State University in 1990.